New Riders' Reference Guide to AutoCAD® Release 12

Robert Knight

William Valaski

NRP
NEW RIDERS
PUBLISHING

New Riders Publishing, Carmel, Indiana

New Rider's Reference Guide to AutoCAD® Release 12

By Robert Knight and William Valaski

Published by:
New Riders Publishing
11711 N. College Ave., Suite 140
Carmel, IN 46032 USA

Printed in the United States of America 1 2 3 4 5 6 7 8 9 0

Library of Congress Cataloging-in-Publication Data

```
Knight, Robert L. (Robert Louis), 1964-
New Riders' Reference Guide to AutoCAD Release 12 / Robert
Knight, William Valaski.
      p. cm.
  ISBN 1-56205-058-3 : $19.95
1. Computer graphics.  2. AutoCAD (Computer program)
I. Valaski, William.  II. Title.
T385.K5645      1992
620'.0042'02855369—dc20        92-24224
        CIP
```

Publisher

David P. Ewing

Associate Publisher

Tim Huddleston

Acquisitions Editor

Brad Koch

Managing Editor

Cheri Robinson

Product Director

Ken Billing

Editors

Margaret Berson
Gail Burlakoff
Rob Lawson
Richard J. Limacher
Nancy Sixsmith

Technical Editor

Kenneth W. Billing

Book Design

Scott Cook

Book Production

Hartman Publishing

Proofreaders

Peter Kuhns
Nora Loechel
Rob Tidrow
Lisa D. Wagner

About the Authors

Robert L. Knight

Robert L. Knight graduated from the University of Cincinnati with a degree in Architectural Engineering. For six years, he was the CAD Operations Manager at LOM Corporation, Indianapolis. Mr. Knight now is a partner with Architectural Alliance in Indianapolis, IN. He is involved with the AutoCAD users' group in Indianapolis. Mr. Knight has co-authored several books about AutoCAD Releases 10 and 11.

William Valaski

William Valaski graduated from the University of Cincinnati with a degree in Architectural Engineering. He is CAD Operations Manager for CDS Associates in Cincinnati, OH, where he has worked for six years. A computer applications programmer, Mr. Valaski programs in several languages. He is active in the Cincinnati CAD Users' Group.

New Riders Publishing extends special thanks to the following contributors to this book:

Kenneth W. Billing

Kenneth W. Billing has consulted on AutoCAD networks, management, customization, AutoLISP programming, and presentation graphics since 1985. Mr. Billing is a frequent contributor to *CADENCE* magazine. He is the author of *Managing and Networking AutoCAD*, and a contributing author of *AutoCAD: The Professional Reference*, both published by New Riders Publishing.

Kevin Coleman

Kevin Coleman has been using AutoCAD and other computer graphics programs since 1985. He attended the University of Oregon. Mr. Coleman has contributed to many New Riders books as an author, developer, and technical reviewer.

Kurt Hampe

Kurt Hampe is a graduate of the Kentucky Polytechnic Institute. He has been using and teaching AutoCAD for a number of years. Mr. Hampe also is a professional programmer and creates custom programs in a variety of languages. He is a contributing author to *Inside AutoCAD Release 12*, published by New Riders Publishing.

Jeffrey Pike

Jeffrey Pike is an employee of Autodesk, Inc. and has worked with AutoCAD since 1985. Mr. Pike graduated from Oregon State University.

Acknowledgments

New Riders Publishing would like to thank the following people and companies for their contributions to this book:

The entire staff at Autodesk, Inc., for their continuing support and encouragement.

Tim Huddleston, for directing the editing and production of this book, and Nancy Sixsmith, for her assistance in the book's development.

The book's editors—Margaret Berson, Gail Burlakoff, Rob Lawson, Richard Limacher, and Nancy Sixsmith—for their many efforts.

The entire NRP staff, for pitching in during the last phase of this book's creation.

Bill Hartman, for doing the impossible, again.

NRP extends special thanks to the members of Prentice-Hall Computer Publishing's production and manufacturing staff. Their extraordinary efforts are deeply appreciated.

Table of Contents

Introduction

Autodesk unveiled AutoCAD Release 12, the twelfth version of the world's most popular CAD program, in the summer of 1992. AutoCAD Release 12 has widely been acknowledged by Autodesk as the "wishlist" version, featuring changes and enhancements in over 170 areas that have long been requested by users. This version of AutoCAD offers users dramatic improvements in speed in many commands, a wider use of dialog boxes for both new and existing commands, the addition of PostScript Type 1 font support, raster file support, and the inclusion of AutoShade functionality directly into AutoCAD. All these features make this version of the software one of the most significant updates for both new and experienced AutoCAD users alike.

New Riders' Reference Guide to AutoCAD Release 12 provides a condensed reference to both the new and old commands of the AutoCAD software. The Guide is designed to be a complementary resource to the *AutoCAD Reference Manual*, but much more approachable.

How this Book is Different from Most AutoCAD Books

New Riders' Reference Guide to AutoCAD Release 12 has been designed and written to accommodate the way you work. The authors and editors at New Riders Publishing know that you probably do not have a great deal of time to page through the *AutoCAD Reference Manual*, and that you need to quickly learn how the AutoCAD commands work.

This book, therefore, does not lead you through endless exercises for every AutoCAD command. Each command summary has complete descriptions of each command option, as well as relevant pointers to commands that perform similar or complementary functions. The examples focus on the ways in which the commands are most often used.

Who Should Read this Book?

New Riders' Reference Guide to AutoCAD Release 12 is written for two types of readers: experienced AutoCAD users who are interested in coming up to speed as quickly as possible with the new features of Release 12, and new AutoCAD users who are looking for a quicker reference to AutoCAD's abundance of commands.

The Benefits of Release 12 to New AutoCAD Users

AutoCAD Release 12 has been dramatically improved to increase its ease of use to new users through over 50 new dialog boxes. Most of the commands new to Release 12 incorporate the use of dialog boxes that comply with the Common User Access standard. The dialog boxes for many current AutoCAD commands also have been refitted to meet the new guidelines.

The more complex AutoCAD commands have been simplified through the use of dialog boxes. For example, all dimensioning variables can now be set through the descriptive dialog boxes. The PLOT command is now completely dialog-box driven, including plot preview, which makes the complex task of setting up plot parameters much easier. The task of editing an AutoCAD drawing also is much simpler through the use of entity grips for click-and-drag operations.

Each AutoCAD command now has context-sensitive help, which you can access by entering **?** at any prompt. AutoCAD help also has information for each option of the command, which can also be retrieved at an option's prompts.

The Benefits of Release 12 to Experienced AutoCAD Users

For the experienced user, AutoCAD's greatest benefit is speed. With Release 12, AutoCAD now utilizes a 32-bit virtual display, which means that you can zoom in to your drawing with approximately a million-to-one ratio before forcing a regeneration. A new HIDE algorithm accelerates hidden line removal by 5 to 100 times. Entity selection and object snap are improved through spatial organization of the drawing.

AutoCAD now supports PostScript Type 1 fonts, which widens the range of high-quality fonts available to AutoCAD users with or without access to a PostScript printer.

AutoCAD Release 12 also has the new AutoCAD SQL Extension, which enables you to connect to external databases directly from within AutoCAD. The Dialog Control Language enables you to create your own custom dialog boxes, without requiring third-party products. The new Region Modeler creates 2D solid objects with associative hatching that can be extruded into AME 3D solid models.

The Benefits of this Book to Both New and Experienced AutoCAD Users

In contrast to many books on AutoCAD Release 12, *New Riders' Reference Guide to AutoCAD Release 12* is designed to be a compact reference guide that quickly explains the functions of the AutoCAD commands and how they may be used most effectively. This book does not dwell on unnecessary examples or wordy explanations, but provides you with the information that is most pertinent to your use of the AutoCAD software.

Conventions Used in this Book

Throughout this book, certain conventions are used to help you distinguish the various elements of AutoCAD, DOS, and the data files that are used by AutoCAD. Before you look ahead, you should spend a moment examining these conventions.

- Key combinations appear in the following format:

  Key1-Key2: When you see a hyphen (-) between key names, you should hold down the first key while pressing the second key. Then release both keys. In most commands, for example, Ctrl-C is the shortcut key for the Cancel option.

  Key1,Key2: When a comma (,) appears between key names, you should press and release the first key and then press and release the second key.

- On-screen, AutoCAD underlines the letters of some buttons in the dialog boxes that can be used as hot keys. For example, the Size button in the Plot Configuration dialog box is displayed on-screen as <u>S</u>ize. The underlined letter is the letter you can type to choose that option. (In this book, however, such letters are displayed in bold, underlined type: **<u>S</u>ize**.)

- Text that is displayed by the AutoCAD program often appears in a `special typeface`.
- Information you type is in **boldface**. This applies to individual letters and numbers, as well as text strings. This convention, however, does not apply to special keys, such as Enter, Esc, or Ctrl.
- New terms appear in *italics*.
- In the examples, the ↵ symbol represents the Enter key.

Special Text Used in this Book

Throughout this book you will find examples of special text. These passages have been given special treatment so that you can instantly recognize their significance and so that you can easily find them for future reference.

Notes, Tips, and Warnings

New Riders' Reference Guide to AutoCAD Release 12 features many special "sidebars," which are set apart from the normal text by icons. The book includes three distinct types of sidebars: "Notes," "Tips," and "Warnings."

A *note* includes "extra" information that you should find useful, but which complements the discussion at hand instead of being a direct part of it. A note may describe special situations that can arise when you use certain AutoCAD commands, or the effects of one AutoCAD command on another.

A *tip* provides you with quick instructions for getting the most from AutoCAD Release 12 as you follow the general discussion. A tip might show you a quicker way to perform an action, or how to set a variable to get a quicker response from AutoCAD.

A *warning* tells you when a procedure may produce undesired results—that is, when you run the risk of losing data, or even damaging your hardware. Warnings generally tell you how to avoid such losses, or describe the steps you can take to remedy them.

The Command Reference

The command reference section of this book describes all the commands in AutoCAD Release 12 in alphabetical order. For each command, the sequence you follow to invoke the command from the screen or pull-down menu is shown. A short definition of the command or description of the command's effects gives you the most important points about each command.

The Icons

At the beginning of each command summary, you will find icons that group each of the AutoCAD commands into distinct categories. These icons give you a quick guide to the types of commands you are dealing with, as well as which commands are new to AutoCAD Release 12. Table I.1 describes the icons and the types of commands that they represent.

Table I.1
Icons Used in this Book

Icon	Description
R12	This icon indicates a command new to Release 12, or an existing command that has a new feature or option in Release 12.
	These commands create or edit two-dimensional objects, although the objects may be located anywhere in 3D space.
	These commands create or edit three-dimensional objects.
	These commands affect how AutoCAD is displayed on the screen, as well as how the drawing is shown on-screen.
	This icon indicates any type of command that creates an AutoCAD entity, such as a line or circle.
	These commands enable you to modify AutoCAD entities.
?	The Inquiry commands display information about the drawing, entities, or the operating system that you are using.
	These commands enable you to organize your drawing information into a more manageable drawing file.
	These commands affect the actions of other AutoCAD commands.
	These commands relate to the new Release 12 Region Modeler.
'	This group of commands can be executed from within other commands, without first having to cancel the active command.
	The Utility commands perform functions that are not necessarily related to the basic act of creating your drawing.

Each command has a Prompts and Options section, which describes the choices that the command presents to you. The prompts typically request information or present defaults needed to complete the command. This section also describes any dialog boxes and their contents.

Following the Prompts and Options section, there may be an example. Most examples are preceded or followed by one or more illustrations, which depict the results of the example. The numbers shown in circles refer to points in the illustrations. You will often see the symbol ⏎ in the examples. Your computer may have a key labeled Enter, or one labeled Return, or one with an arrow symbol. In any case, ⏎ or "press Enter" means to press the key that enters a return (generally using the little finger of your right hand).

If you re-create the examples, you often will enter commands from the keyboard. Similarly, you must often type point coordinates, distances, and option keywords. The example text generally indicates when typed input is required by showing it in bold text following a prompt, such as Command: **UNITS** ⏎ or To point: **3,5** ⏎. You should type the characters in bold as they appear, and then press Enter (⏎).

After the example are two sections that list any commands that are related to the current command, or which complement the command. Also listed are any AutoCAD variables that are used by the command. These variables are summarized in the appendixes following the command reference. Appendix A is a table of AutoCAD system variables, and Appendix B is a table of dimension variables.

New Riders Publishing

The staff of New Riders Publishing is committed to bringing you the very best in computer reference material. Each New Riders book is the result of months of work by authors and staff, who research and refine the information contained within its covers.

As part of this commitment to you, the New Riders' reader, New Riders invites your input. Please let us know if you enjoy this book, if you have trouble with the information and examples presented, or if you have a suggestion for the next edition.

Please note, however, that the New Riders staff cannot serve as a technical resource for AutoCAD or AutoCAD-related questions, including hardware- or software-related problems. Refer to the documentation that accompanies your AutoCAD software for help with specific problems.

If you have a question or comment about any New Riders book, please write to New Riders at the following address. We will respond to as many readers as we can. Your name, address, or phone number will never become part of a mailing list or be used for any other purpose than to help us continue to bring you the best books possible.

New Riders Publishing
Prentice-Hall Computer Publishing
Attn: Associate Publisher
11711 N. College Avenue
Carmel, IN 46032

If you prefer, you can FAX New Riders Publishing at the following number:

(317) 571-3484

Thank you for selecting *New Riders' Reference Guide to AutoCAD Release 12*!

AutoCAD Command Reference

ABOUT

Screen **[UTILITY] [next] [ABOUT:]**

Pull down **[File] [About AutoCAD]**

The ABOUT command displays the AutoCAD information banner and the ACAD.MSG file in the AUTOCAD dialog box shown in figure ABOUT.1. Because the ACAD.MSG file can be deleted or customized, the contents of the list box may vary from system to system. If the ACAD.MSG file is longer than the list box in which it is displayed, a slider bar is present on the right side of the list box. If the ACAD.MSG file has been deleted, the dialog box still displays, but the list box is empty. You can issue the ABOUT command transparently if you preface it with an apostophe.

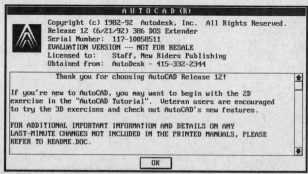

Figure ABOUT.1:
The AUTOCAD dialog box.

11

ALIGN

Pull down **[Modify] [Align]**

The ALIGN command moves and reorients selected objects to align with points you specify, regardless of the current UCS. You may enter two or three pairs of points for ALIGN to consider in calculating a transformation for the new location of the entities to align. Two pairs of points are required for 2D alignment; three pairs allow either a 2D or 3D alignment.

 ALIGN is especially useful when you need to both move and rotate objects in two or three axes. Repeated uses of the ALIGN command can replace several executions of MOVE and ROTATE.

Prompts and Options

- **Select objects:**

  Select the objects to align in a new location by any object selection method.

- **1st, 2nd, 3rd source point:**

  You enter a point relative to the selected objects to align with its corresponding destination point chosen in the following prompt. Enter first and second source points to perform 2D transformations. Enter a third source point in a different plane than the first two source points to perform 3D transformations.

- **1st, 2nd, 3rd destination point:**

  You enter a point at the destination location where you want the selected objects aligned by the corresponding source point. Enter first and second destination points to perform 2D transformations. Enter a third destination point in a different plane than the first two destination points to perform 3D transformations.

- **<2d> or 3d transformation:**

At this prompt, you specify either a 2D or 3D transformation. This prompt is issued only if you entered three source and destination points at the previous prompts. If you entered only two source and destination points, a 2D tranformation is performed by default because AutoCAD has insufficient information to perform a 3D transformation.

Example

The following example uses ALIGN to move and rotate an object selection set (see fig. ALIGN.1) in two dimensions so that it aligns with other objects.

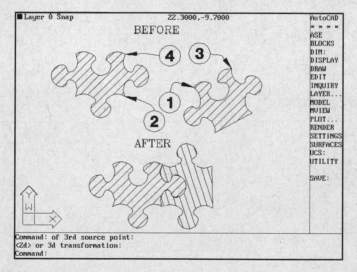

Figure ALIGN.1
Objects moved and rotated in one step with ALIGN.

```
Command: ALIGN ↵
Select objects: Select the objects to align
Select objects:
1st source point: Pick point ①
1st destination point: Pick point ②
2nd source point: Pick point ③
2nd destination point: Pick point ④
3rd source point: ↵
<2d> or 3d transformation: ↵
```

13

Related Commands

MOVE
ROTATE
ROTATE3D

APERTURE

Screen **[SETTINGS] [APERTUR:]**

The APERTURE command sets the size of the *object snap selection target*, which is the box-like target that appears at the intersection of the crosshairs while you use object snap selection. The aperture's size refers to its width and height in pixels (see fig. APERTURE.1). The value must be a whole number between 1 and 50 pixels, which is the distance from the center of the crosshairs to the edge of the aperture box.

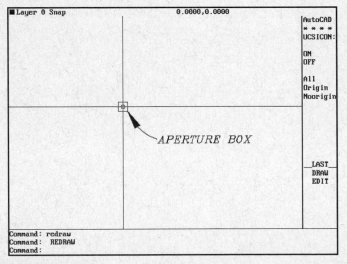

Figure APERTURE.1:
The object snap selection box.

The APERTURE command can be executed transparently by preceding the command name with an apostophe ('APERTURE).

Aperture size directly affects the number of possible points AutoCAD must check to find the best qualified match. A small setting speeds object snap selection. A large setting is easier to see and requires less pointing accuracy. Experiment with various settings to find the ones that work best for you.

Prompts and Options

- **`Object snap target height (1-50 pixels):`**

  You can specify a new target height at this prompt to assign a new value to the APERTURE system variable. This value, which is stored in the AutoCAD configuration file, is used in all subsequent editing sessions until you change it. The default value for APERTURE is 10.

- **`<current>:`**

  This option accepts the current value without change.

  The DDOSNAP dialog box contains a scroll bar and example graphic for dynamically adjusting the size of the APERTURE box.

Example

The following example shows how different values affect the size of the aperture box (see fig. APERTURE.1):

```
Command: APERTURE ↵
Object snap target height (1-50 pixels) <10>: 30 ↵
Command: LINE ↵
From point: NEA ↵
to Press Ctrl-C
```

Related Commands

DDOSNAP
OSNAP

Related System Variables

APERTURE
PICKBOX

APPLOAD

The APPLOAD command enables you to selectively list and load
AutoLISP and ADS applications. You also can unload ADS applications.
APPLOAD displays the Load AutoLISP and ADS Files dialog box. The
user-defined list of applications can be saved and redisplayed each time
the APPLOAD command is issued. By maintaining a list of commonly
used applications, you can save time loading them. APPLOAD saves
the default settings in APPLOAD.DFS. APPLOAD can be issued transparently if you preface it with an apostrophe.

Do not edit the APPLOAD.DFS file. Make your changes
through the APPLOAD command.

Prompts and Options

The Load AutoLISP and ADS Files dialog box has the following options.

- **Files to Load.** You select the application(s) you want to load,
  unload, or remove from the list. If the list of applications is longer
  than the list box, a slider bar is displayed on the right side of the
  list box. The MAXSORT system variable controls the order of the
  applications listed.

- **File.** The File option displays the Select LISP/ADS Routine dialog box, from which you can select an application to put in the Files to Load list box.

- **Remove.** The Remove option deletes all selected applications from the Files to Load list box.

- **Load.** The Load option lists all selected AutoLISP and ADS applications in the Files to Load dialog box. If all the listed files are loaded, AutoCAD disables the Load button.

- **Unload.** This option unloads all selected ADS applications. If all the selected applications cannot be unloaded, AutoCAD disables the Unload button. Unloading an ADS application frees memory.

 AutoLISP applications cannot be unloaded. Therefore, in order to save memory, you should avoid loading unnecessary applications.

- **Save List.** If this box is checked, the APPLOAD.DFS file is updated when you select Load, Unload, or Exit. To prevent updates to the APPLOAD.DFS file, be sure Save List is unchecked.

Example

The following example loads one AutoLISP and and ADS program and unloads the ADS program. See figure APPLOAD.1.

Command: **APPLOAD.**⏎
Click on File *and display the SAMPLE directory*
Double-click on ALIAS.LSP in the Files: *list box*
Click on File
Double-click on AMELINK.EXP in the Files: *list box*
Click on ALIAS.LSP and AMELINK.EXP in the Files to Load *list box to select them*
Click on Load
Command: ⏎
Select ALIAS.LSP from the Files to Load *list box and click on* Remove
Select AMELINK.EXP from the Files to Load *list box and click on* Unload

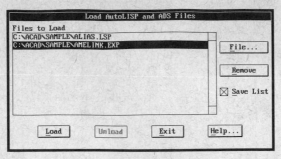

Figure APPLOAD.1:
The Load AutoLISP and ADS Files dialog box.

Related Command

LOAD

Related System Variable

MAXSORT

ARC

Screen **[DRAW] [ARC]**

Pull down **[Draw] [Arc >]**

The ARC creates arcs of any length or radius. By using this command, you can draw an arc with eight basic options. You can use different combinations to create the various arcs shown in figures ARC.1 and ARC.2. This command also includes an option for continuing an arc that is tangent to the preceding arc or line segment.

Prompts and Options

- **<Start point>:**
  At this prompt, pick the starting point of the arc. Press Enter to continue an arc that is tangent to the preceding arc or line segment.

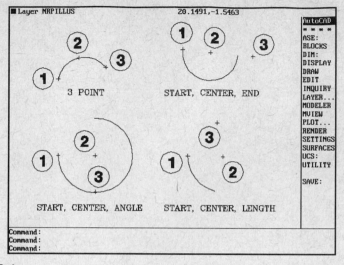

Figure ARC.1:
The basic arc-creation options.

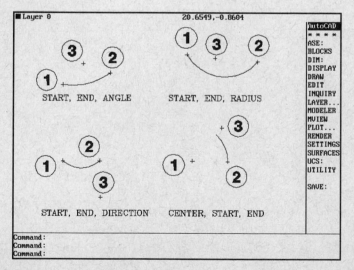

Figure ARC.2:
More arc-creation options.

- **Center:**

  At this prompt, pick the center of the arc.

- **<Second point>:**

  When you are creating an arc by specifying three points, pick the second point at this prompt. This point is a point through which the arc will pass.

- **End point:**

  This option prompts you to specify the end of the arc.

- **Angle:**

  The Angle option enables you to specify the interior angle of the arc. A negative value draws the arc clockwise; a positive value draws the arc counter-clockwise.

- **Length of chord:**

  The Length of chord option is used to specify a length for the arc's chord segment (the distance between the arc endpoints).

- **Radius:**

  The Radius option enables you to specify the radius for the arc you wish to create.

- **Direction:**

  The Direction option is used to define a direction from which the arc will be drawn tangent.

Preset Features

- **Start, Center, End**. Specify the starting point, center of the arc's radius, and end point.
- **Start, Center, Angle**. Specify the starting point, center of the arc's radius, and angle of the arc.
- **Start, Center, Length**. Specify the starting point, center of the arc's radius, and length of the arc's chord.
- **Start, End, Angle**. Specify the starting point, end point, and ending angle.

- **Start, End, Radius**. Specify the starting point, end point, and arc's radius.
- **Start, End, Direction**. Specify the starting point, end point, and arc's direction.
- **Center, Start, End**. Specify the center of the arc's radius, starting point, and end point. This option is the same as the Start, Center, End option, but the points are selected in a different order.
- **Center, Start, Arc**. Specify the center of the arc's radius, starting point, and arc's angle.
- **Center, Start, Length**. Specify the center of the arc's radius, starting point, and length of the arc's chord.

Example

This example illustrates how to create arcs by using different arc options (see fig. ARC.3):

```
Command: ARC↵
Center/<Start point>: Pick point ①
Center/End/<Second point>: Pick point ②
End point: Pick point ③
Command: ARC↵
Center/<Start point>: C↵
Center: Pick point ④
Start: Pick point ⑤
Angle/Length of chord/<End point>: A↵
Included angle: 90↵
```

Related Commands

PLINE
FILLET
VIEWRES

Related System Variable

LASTANGLE

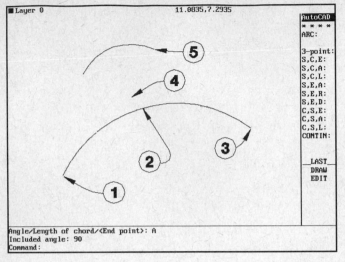

Figure ARC.3:
Arcs created by using the three-point and the center, start, end options.

AREA

?

Screen **[INQUIRY] [AREA:]**

Pull down **[Assist] [Area]**

The AREA command calculates the area of an entity (such as a 2D polyline or circle) or a group of points. AREA also can be used for calculating the perimeter, line length, or circumference of an object. The area of an open polyline is calculated as if a straight segment existed between the start and end points. You also can use AREA to create a running total area by adding and subtracting areas.

To define a boundary for measurement, you must pick three or more nonlinear, coplanar points. Use the same method when selecting polylines for measurement; the polyline must contain three or more nonlinear, coplanar points. Figure AREA.1 illustrates correct and incorrect selection sets.

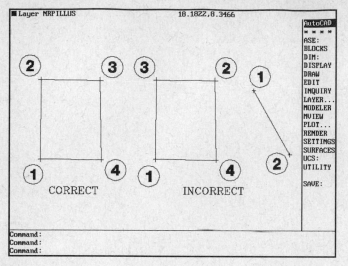

Figure AREA.1:
Correct and incorrect boundary selections.

Prompts and Options

- **`<First point>`:**

  Use this option to calculate the area defined by a group of points selected on the fly. At this prompt, enter or pick the first point of the group.

  After you enter the first point, the `Next point:` prompt appears. This prompt is repeated so you can enter any additional points to the group. After you enter all the points, press Enter to end the area-selection process.

- **`Entity`:**

  Use this option to select a polyline, polygon, or circle to define the boundary of the area to be calculated.

- **`Add`:**

  Use this option to keep a running total area by adding successive object areas or point set areas to previous ones.

- **Subtract:**

    Use this option to subtract the area of the selected polyline, polygon, circle, or defining points from the running total area.

 Many third-party applications create temporary polyline boundaries to simplify area calculation and ensure accurate results. You can do the same. By using ENDpoint and INTersection object snap modes, draw a polyline around the area you want to calculate. Use the AREA command's Entity option to select the temporary polyline. After you receive your calculations, you can erase the polyline or store it on a layer that is turned off. You can incorporate this technique into a menu macro.

Example

This example uses the AREA command's Add option to illustrate how this option performs. The entity shown in figure AREA.2 is a polyline. You will use the Entity option to calculate the polyline's area first, then pick a few points to define an additional area to calculate.

```
Command: AREA↵
<First point>/Entity/Add/Subtract: A↵
<First point>/Entity/Subtract: E↵
(ADD mode) Select circle or polyline: Pick point ①
   Area = 12.6287, Perimeter = 16.4473
   Total area = 12.6287
(ADD mode) Select circle or polyline: ↵
<First point>/Entity/Subtract: Pick point ②
(ADD mode) Next point: Pick point ③
(ADD mode) Next point: Pick point ④
(ADD mode) Next point: Pick point ⑤
(ADD mode) Next point: Pick point ↵
   Area = 9.4770, Perimeter = 12.5722
   Total area = 22.1058
<First point>/Entity/Subtract: ↵
```

 When you add or subtract areas, AutoCAD does not recognize overlapping boundaries. Make selections carefully to obtain accurate results.

24

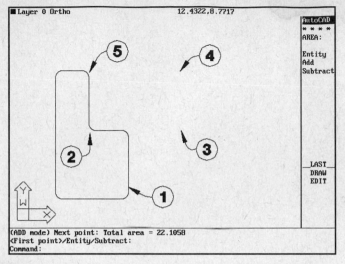

Figure AREA.2:
Using AREA's add option.

Related System Variables

> AREA
> PERIMETER

ARRAY

Screen **[EDIT] [ARRAY:]**

Pull down **[Construct] [Array]**

The ARRAY command creates multiple copies of objects that repeat at regularly spaced intervals. The ARRAY command can work in the X direction (columns), Y direction (rows), or both, each with its own spacing. ARRAY can also place multiple copies around an imaginary circle or arc.

You can array objects in a positive or negative direction in relation to the origin of the source object(s).

If you are creating a rectangular array, you can specify the X and Y spacing with just two screen picks. The X and Y difference between the two points determines the row and column spacing.

If the array you are creating is not parallel to the current X and Y axes (if it is rotated at 60 degrees, for example), you can use the Snap Angle option in the DDRMODES command dialog box. This option rotates the crosshairs and the direction for the X and Y axes, thus allowing you to create a rotated array.

ARRAY creates copies within the X and Y axes of the current User Coordinate System (UCS). If you need to create arrays within 3D space, use the 3DARRAY.LSP routine supplied in the SUPPORT directory when you installed AutoCAD Release 12. 3DARRAY can be found on the Construct pull-down menu as Array 3D.

Prompts and Options

- `Select objects:`

  This prompt asks you to select the objects to be arrayed. You can select any type or number of AutoCAD entities, including 3D surfaces and solids. After you select an object, the prompt repeats, so you can select additional objects. Press Enter to end the selection process.

- `Rectangular or Polar Array (R/P) <R>:`

  The default option is to create a rectangular array. If you wish to create a polar array instead, enter **P**.

- `Number of rows (—) <1>:`

  At this prompt, three hyphens remind you that rows are horizontal along the X axis of the current User Coordinate System (UCS). Enter the number of copies you wish to make along the X axis. You must make at least one row (the default).

- `Number of columns (||||) <1>:`

  The three vertical bars in this prompt remind you that columns are vertical along the Y axis of the current UCS. You enter the number of copies you wish to make along the Y axis. The default value, 1, is also the minimum value.

- **Distance between rows (—):**

  This prompt requests the vertical spacing between rows. A negative value creates an array in a negative direction from the origin of the source objects. This prompt appears only during rectangular arrays with two or more rows.

- **Distance between columns (||||):**

  This prompt requests the horizontal spacing between columns. Negative column spacing values are created in the same way as negative row spacing values. When creating bidirectional arrays, you can use a combination of negative and positive values for row and column spacing. This prompt appears only during rectangular arrays with two or more columns.

- **Center point of array:**

  You see this prompt when you create polar arrays. The center point refers to the polar reference point, about which the selected objects are arrayed.

- **Number of items:**

  This prompt refers to the number of copies of your selected objects.

- **Angle to fill (+=ccw, -=ccw) <360>:**

  The angle you supply at this prompt determines the portion of a circle to be "filled" during a polar array. The default value, 360, is for a full circle. You cannot enter values greater than 360.

- **Rotate objects as they are copied? <Y>**

  If you answer **Y** (the default), objects are rotated relative to the center point of the array. If you answer **N**, the objects maintain the orientation of the source objects.

Example

This example demonstrates both the rectangular and polar options of the ARRAY command. Figure ARRAY.1 and ARRAY.2 illustrate how the ARRAY command can be used to arrange seating within a room.

```
■ Layer 0                        163.4353,37.1304        AutoCAD
                                                         * * * *
                                                         ARRAY:

                                                         Select
                                                         Objects

                                                         Rectang
                                                         Polar

                                                         Yes
                                                         No


                                                         LAST
                                                         DRAW
                                                         EDIT

Unit cell or distance between rows (---): 36
Distance between columns (|||): 30
Command:
```

Figure ARRAY.1:
Creating a rectangular array.

Command: **ARRAY**↵
Select objects: *Select the objects to array at* ①
Select objects↵
Rectangular or Polar array (R/P) <R>: ↵
Number of rows (-) <1>: **3**↵
Number of columns (||||) <1>: **6**↵
Distance between rows (—): **36**↵
Distance between rows (—): **30**↵
Command: **ARRAY**↵
Select objects: *Select the objects to array at* ①
Select objects↵
Rectangular or Polar array (R/P) <R>: **P**↵
Center point of array: *Pick point* ②
Number of items: 15
Angle to fill (+=ccw, -=ccw) <360>: ↵
Rotate objects as they are copied? <Y>↵

Related Commands

COPY
MINSERT

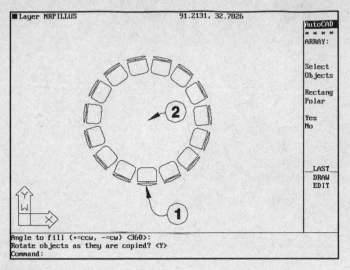

Figure ARRAY.2:
Creating a polar array.

Related System Variable

SNAPANG

ASCTEXT

Pull down [Draw] [Text] [Import Text]

The ASCTEXT command is an AutoLISP function that enables you to place text from an ASCII file into your drawing. ASCTEXT is useful when you want to insert large amounts of text into a drawing. You can use your word processing, database, or spreadsheet program to enter the text, perform spell checking and basic formatting, and then save the text as an ASCII file.

ASCTEXT provides you with a great deal of flexibility in determining how the text you are importing will look. You can set character height, justification, style, rotation, and line spacing. The ASCTEXT command also enables you to import text into columns to form data tables.

Prompts and Options

- **File to read (including extension) <*default*>:**

  At this prompt, you enter the full path and file name with extension to locate the ASCII text file you want to insert in your drawing. This prompt appears only if the FILEDIA system variable is set to 0. If FILEDIA is set to 1 (the default), use the File to Read dialog box to choose a file to import.

- **Start point or Center/Middle/Right/?:**

  At this prompt, you specify a starting point for the default (left) justification or enter an alignment option for inserting the text. As you can with the TEXT and DTEXT commands, you can specify any of AutoCAD's text alignments in addition to those shown in the prompt. AutoCAD's alignment types are shown in the following table. You can view this table by entering a question mark (**?**) at the prompt.

  ```
  Alignment Options
  TLeft     TCenter   TRight
  MLeft     MCenter   MRight
  BLeft     BCenter   BRight
  Left      Center    Right
  Aligned   Middle    Fit
  ```

- **Height <*default*>:**

  At this prompt, you specify the height for the text. This prompt does not appear if the current style has a fixed height.

- **Rotation Angle <0>:**

  You enter the angle at which the inserted text is rotated.

- **Change text options? <N>:**

  You specify the way the text is inserted in your drawing. If you enter **Y** at this prompt, you receive all of the following prompts. If you press Enter or enter **N** at the prompt, ASCTEXT uses its default parameters and draws the text.

- **Distance between lines/<Auto>:**

  You specify a distance that you want to maintain between the lines of imported text. If you do not specify a value here, the default (Auto) line spacing specified by the text style is used.

- **First line to read/<1>:**

  By default, ASCTEXT imports text starting with the first line of the file you specified. If you want to start importing text after a certain line, specify that line number here.

- **Number of lines to read <All>:**

  By default, ASCTEXT imports the full ASCII file into your drawing. If you want to insert only a certain portion of the lines in the ASCII file, specify the number of lines here.

- **Underscore each line? <N>:**

  You can underline each line of text as it is imported. The command does this by placing the %%U underline character code at the start of each line of text.

- **Overscore each line? <N>:**

  You can overscore each line of text as it is imported. The command does this by placing the %%O overscore character code at the start of each line of text.

- **Change text case? Upper/Lower/<N>:**

  You can import all of the characters in the text file in either upper- or lowercase. The default is to import all text exactly as it appears within the ASCII file. You can enter a **U** to force all characters to uppercase, or enter an **L** to force all to lowercase.

- **Set up columns? <N>**

  You can import the text in your ASCII file as a set of columns, which makes it easy to set up tables in AutoCAD. ASCTEXT formats columns by assigning a specified number of text lines to each column. (If you want characters within each column to align,

31

use a text style that specifies a monospace font, such as
MONOTXT.SHX.)

- **Distance between columns:**

  At this prompt, you specify the spacing between each column of
  text.

- **Number of lines per column:**

  At this prompt, you enter the number of lines you want placed in
  each column as the text is imported. The text file should be
  preformatted to match the number of lines per column. The first *n*
  lines are placed in the first column, the next *n* lines are in the
  second column, and so on.

 ASCTEXT does not enable you to set the style to use for the
imported text. You should use the TEXT, DTEXT, or STYLE
commands to ensure that the style is set correctly, then run
ASCTEXT and import your text.

Example

The following example uses the ASCTEXT command to import an
ASCII file. The file used is the ACAD.PGP file that comes with
AutoCAD and is automatically installed in the same directory with the
AutoCAD support files. This example assumes that ACAD.PGP is in the
\ACAD\SUPPORT directory.

```
Command: ASCTEXT↵
Choose the \ACAD\SUPPORT\ACAD.PGP file from the dialog box
Start point or Center/Middle/Right/?: 1,8↵
Height <0.2000>: .125↵
Rotation Angle <0>: ↵
Change text options? <N>: ↵
```

Related Commands

DTEXT
TEXT

Related System Variables

FILEDIA
TEXTSIZE
TEXTSTYLE

ATTDEF

Screen **[BLOCKS] [ATTDEF:]**

Screen **[DRAW] [ATTDEF:]**

The ATTDEF command, which stands for ATTribute DEFinition, creates attributes for inclusion in block definitions and insertion into drawings. ATTDEF is primarily a tool for building non-graphical intelligence into symbol libraries. During block insertion, the attribute definitions take on their final forms.

Attributes are alphanumeric data attached to a block. An unlimited number of attributes can be attached to any block definition. You can control the appearance of attributes individually through the use of text style, height, color, and layer. You also can control the visibility, default values, user prompts, and preset values of attributes. Attribute data can be extracted for further processing and is commonly used for schedule and bill-of-material generation.

  The ATTDEF command is designed to work from the AutoCAD Command: prompt. An easier method of creating attributes is to use the DDATTDEF command's dialog box.

Prompts and Options

- **Invisible:**

  This option controls attribute visibility. Invisible attributes can be combined with visible attributes within the same block, as can all other attribute modes.

- **Constant:**

  This option sets a fixed value for the attribute that cannot be changed. A constant value is used, rather than a variable, when it is important that the attribute value not change.

- **Verify:**

  This option ensures that you are asked to confirm all responses to attribute prompts.

- **Preset:**

  Use this option to establish editable, default values for attributes.

- **Attribute tag:**

  Use this option to define the name of the tag used to store attribute data that the user enters.

- **Attribute prompt:**

  This option sets the prompt AutoCAD uses to ask you for the attribute's value when the attribute is inserted.

- **Default attribute value:**

  Use this option so that each attribute can have a default value that is used if the user chooses not to enter another value.

After you set the preceding options, ATTDEF prompts you for text options: justification, insertion point, height, and rotation. Like the TEXT command, ATTDEF uses the current text style.

Example

This example creates a simple attribute definition using the default modes options (see fig. ATTDEF.1):

```
Command: ATTDEF↵
Enter (ICVP) to change, RETURN when done: ↵
Attribute tag: COST↵
Attribute prompt: Enter item cost↵
Default attribute value: $100↵
Justify/Style/<Start point>: Pickpoint ①
Height <0.2000>: .5↵
Rotation angle <0>: ↵
```

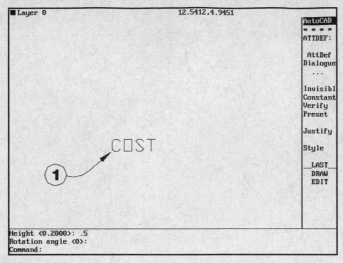

Figure ATTDEF.1:
A basic attribute created with ATTDEF.

Related Commands

ATTDISP
ATTEDIT
ATTEXT
BLOCK
DDATTDEF
DDATTE
DDATTEXT

Related System Variables

ATTDIA
ATTMODE

ATTDISP

Screen **[DISPLAY] [ATTDISP:]**

The ATTDISP command controls attribute visibility of inserted blocks. This command overrides the visibility mode used during attribute definition with the ATTDEF command. ATTDISP is useful for viewing attributes that normally are invisible and for turning off the visibility of all attributes.

 The ATTDISP command can be executed transparently by preceding the command name with an apostophe ('ATTDISP).

Prompts and Options

- **Normal:**

  This option is the default; it uses the attribute's defined visibility mode (visible or invisible).

- **ON:**

  This option turns on the visibility of all attributes, regardless of defined visibility mode. The defined visibility mode is retained and you can restore it by using the Normal option.

- **OFF:**

  This option turns off the visibility of all attributes, regardless of defined visibility mode. Use the Normal option to restore the defined visibility mode.

Example

This example displays a block with attributes in both viewports. When you use the ATTDISP command, the cost attribute is displayed (see fig. ATTDISP.1).

```
Command: ATTDISP↵
Normal/ON/OFF <Normal>: ↵
```
Once the ATTDISP command is used to force attribute display to ON, both attributes become visible.

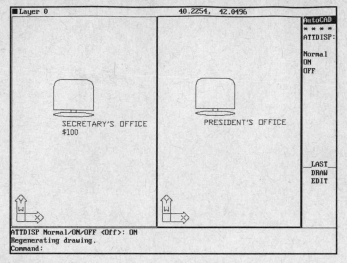

Figure ATTDISP.1:
Viewing attributes with ATTDISP.

Related Commands

    ATTDEF
    ATTEDIT
    ATTEXT
    DDATTDEF
    DDATTE
    DDATTEXT

Related System Variable

    ATTMODE

ATTEDIT

Screen **[EDIT] [ATTEDIT:]**

ATTEDIT, which stands for ATTribute EDIT, edits the characteristics of inserted attributes. You can edit an attribute's value, position, height, angle, style, layer, or color. You also can edit attributes individually or globally.

Note that AutoCAD does not highlight attributes when you select them. The attributes are highlighted during editing.

You also can edit attributes more easily from the DDATTE dialog box.

Prompts and Options

- **Edit attributes one at a time? <Y>**

  If you answer **Y**, you can edit each attribute individually. If you answer **N**, you can edit the attributes globally.

- **Block name specification <*> :**

  This prompt requests the block name to search for attributes. You can use wild cards at this prompt.

- **Attribute tag specification <*> :**

  This prompt requests the attribute tag name for editing. You can use wild cards at this prompt.

- **Attribute value specification <*> :**

  This prompt enables you to edit attributes with specific values only. This prompt often is used for globally updating one value to another across multiple blocks.

- **Select attributes:**

  You select attributes individually at this prompt. Attributes must be visible to be selected. If the attributes were not originally set to be visible, you must set ATTDISP to ON before selecting attributes at this prompt.

- **Value:**

  Use this option to change attribute values.

- **Position:**

  This option enables you to change the position of inserted attributes.

- **Height:**

  This option enables you to change the text height of inserted attributes.

- **Angle:**

  This option enables you to change the angle of inserted attributes' text.

- **Style:**

  This option enables you to change the text style of inserted attributes.

- **Layer:**

  This option enables you to change the layer assignment of inserted attributes.

- **Color:**

  This option enables you to change the color assignment of inserted attributes.

- **Next <N>:**

  This option enables you to edit the next attribute in the selection set.

Example

This example uses the attribute created and inserted with the ATTDISP command. It alters the value of the ITEM attribute to call the item a couch (see fig. ATTEDIT.1):

```
Command: ATTEDIT↵
Edit attributes one at a time? <Y>↵
Block name specification <*>:↵
Attribute tag specification <*>:↵
Attribute value specification <*>:↵
Select Attributes: Pick point ①
   1 attributes selected.
Value/Position/Height/Angle/Style/Layer/Color/Next <N>: V↵
```

```
Change or Replace? <R>: R↵
New attribute value: PERSONNEL OFFICE↵
Value/Position/Height/Angle/Style/Layer/Color/Next <N>: ↵
```

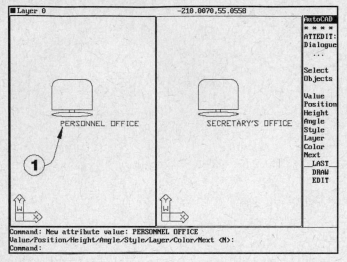

Figure ATTEDIT.1:
The new attribute value.

Related Commands

ATTDEF
ATTDISP
ATTEXT
DDATTDEF
DDATTE
DDATTEXT

ATTEXT

Screen **[UTILITY] [ATTEXT:]**

ATTEXT, which stands for ATTribute EXTraction, extracts attribute information contained in the block insertions of the current drawing. You can extract this information in several standard ASCII-file formats so the data can be placed in database or spreadsheet programs for further processing and analysis.

One example of an ATTEXT application is schedule building. With proper planning and setup, you can extract attributes to build material lists, door schedules, and for a variety of other purposes.

Prompts and Options

- **CDF:**

  CDF, which stands for Comma Delimited Format, requires a template file. This option enables you to extract the attribute information from the entire drawing.

- **SDF:**

  SDF, which stands for Space Delimited Format, requires a template file. This option enables you to extract the attribute information from the entire drawing.

- **DXF:**

  DXF, which stands for Drawing Interchange Format, enables you to extract the attribute information from the entire drawing.

- **Entities:**

  This option enables you to select specific entities for attribute extraction using one of the above formats.

Template Files

To extract attribute information to an external file, you need to create a template file first. This file provides the ATTEXT command with the types of information you want to extract (attribute values) and with the formatting to be used in the output file for storing the attribute information. Template files are only used during CDF or SDF information extractions.

41

For example, the block shown in figure ATTEDIT.1, has an attribute called Location, which is used to store the location of the chair in a furniture plan. To extract the information stored within the attribute, you can create a template file with the following line:

```
LOCATION     C040000
```

This tells the ATTEXT command the attribute to extract information from within the drawing and the type of information to be extracted (C for character data, or N for numeric). The six numbers after the data type are used to set the length of the field to extract the data to, as well as its decimal accuracy. The first three numbers indicate how large a value can be extracted from the attribute (in the above example, 40 characters). The last three digits relate to decimal accuracy. For character fields, this value defaults to 0. If you are extracting numeric data, you can tell how many decimal places of information will be placed in the extract file.

Related Commands

ATTDEF
ATTDISP
ATTEDIT
DDATTDEF
DDATTE
DDATTEXT

AUDIT

Screen **[UTILITY] [AUDIT:]**

The AUDIT command, available following Release 11, verifies the integrity of your drawings. When you invoke AUDIT from the drawing editor, AutoCAD can correct any errors in the drawing file automatically if the program detects them, or it can leave all errors uncorrected (the default)—but recommend specific corrective action.

Prompts and Options

- **Fix any errors detected? <N>**

  If you answer **No** (the default), AutoCAD creates a report that documents any errors found and recommends corrective action.

  If you answer **Yes**, AutoCAD creates a report and automatically performs the recommended corrective action.

 AUDIT works only on drawings saved with Release 11 or 12. AUDIT does not correct all damaged drawings. In cases where AUDIT is unable to recover damaged information, try using the RECOVER command also.

Related Command

RECOVER

BASE

Screen **[BLOCKS] [BASE:]**

The BASE command defines the insertion point of the current drawing. The results of this command are evident only when you insert the drawing or use the drawing as an external reference.

 You can execute the BASE command transparently by preceding the command name with an apostrophe ('BASE).

Prompts and Options

- **Base point <0.0000,0.0000,0.0000>:**

  This prompt requests a base point. You can define a point by picking a point on the screen or by entering the point's coordinates. (To specify a 3D point, you must enter the coordinates.) If you supply a 2D point, AutoCAD assumes that the Z value is equal to the current elevation.

The numbers shown in brackets, `<0.0000,0.0000,0.0000>`, show the current coordinate location of the base point. In this case, 0,0,0 is the default for a new drawing. The value shown may be different if you used the BASE command previously on the current drawing or if you initially created the drawing by using the WBLOCK command.

Related Commands

BLOCK
INSERT
XREF

Related System Variable

INSBASE

BHATCH

Screen **[DRAW] [BHATCH:]**

Pull down **[Draw] [Hatch...]**

BHATCH draws crosshatching within a boundary area that you select by picking a point inside the region to fill. Unlike the HATCH command, BHATCH creates a closed polyline boundary object automatically by intelligently tracing over existing intersecting objects surrounding the point you pick. You can elect to retain the boundary for later use or for creating additional drawing geometry.

A dialog box enables you to specify the hatch pattern name, angle, style, and scale. You can define your own simple hatch patterns, specify certain objects to consider for boundary calculations, experiment by selecting and viewing boundary selection sets, pre-explode the hatch block, and preview hatches before proceeding. Figure BHATCH.1 shows the main BHATCH dialog box.

```
┌─────────────────────────────────────────┐
│            Boundary Hatch                │
│ Pattern:     No hatch pattern selected.  │
│     ┌──────────────────┐                 │
│     │  Hatch Options...│                 │
│     └──────────────────┘                 │
│ Define Hatch Area                        │
│     ┌──────────────────┐                 │
│     │   Pick Points <  │                 │
│     └──────────────────┘                 │
│  ┌──────────────────┐ ┌──────────────────┐│
│  │  Select Objects <│ │ View selections <││
│  └──────────────────┘ └──────────────────┘│
│  ┌──────────────────┐ ┌──────────────────┐│
│  │  Preview Hatch < │ │ Advanced Options.││
│  └──────────────────┘ └──────────────────┘│
│  ┌──────┐ ┌──────┐ ┌───────┐ ┌───────┐    │
│  │ Apply│ │Cancel│ │Another│ │Help...│    │
│  └──────┘ └──────┘ └───────┘ └───────┘    │
└─────────────────────────────────────────┘
```

Figure BHATCH.1:
The primary BHATCH dialog box.

Prompts and Options

BHATCH displays no command-line prompts. Instead, you make selections from the following dialog boxes and options.

The Boundary Hatch dialog box (see fig. BHATCH.1) offers the following options:

- **Hatch Options.** Click on this button to display the Hatch Options dialog box (see fig. BHATCH.2).

- **Pick Points.** Click on this button to pick a point inside the area(s) you want to hatch. After you pick a point, AutoCAD analyzes the current object-selection set to create a hatch boundary. You can control the objects considered for boundary creation by selecting specific entities or by using the Advanced Options button.

- **Select Objects.** Click on this button to select the objects on-screen to be considered for the hatch boundary.

- **Preview Hatch.** Click on this button to see a temporary example of how the hatch would appear if created with the current settings.

45

- **View selections.** Click on this button to highlight the objects selected for boundary calculation.

- **Advanced Options.** Click on this button to display the Advanced Options dialog box (see fig. BHATCH.4).

- **Apply.** Click on this button to apply the hatch pattern to the selected area with the current settings.

- **Another.** Click on this button to apply the hatch pattern to another selected area. The Boundary Hatch dialog box reappears so that you can perform additional BHATCH operations.

The Hatch Options dialog box (see fig. BHATCH.2) offers the following options:

Figure BHATCH.2:
The Hatch Options dialog box.

- **Pattern Type.** The radio buttons in this group enable selection of either a hatch pattern definition stored on disk or specification of a user-defined pattern. If **U**ser-Defined Pattern is chosen, the following spacing and double hatch options are enabled.

- **Pattern.** Clicking on this button displays the Choose Hatch Pattern dialog box, which displays pages of names and graphic examples of hatch patterns stored in the specified disk file (see fig. BHATCH.3). Use the **P**revious and **N**ext buttons to browse through the various patterns. Click on the desired pattern icon to make your selection. Alternatively, you can enter a known pattern name in the edit box.

- **Scale.** You enter a hatch pattern scale factor. You may need to experiment to produce the desired results.
- **Angle.** You enter a hatch pattern angle.
- **Spacing.** You enter the inter-line spacing in drawing units for user-defined hatch patterns.
- **Hatching Style.** Click on one of the radio button options: <u>N</u>ormal, <u>O</u>uter, or <u>I</u>gnore. <u>N</u>ormal style hatches alternating interior areas within the current boundary. <u>O</u>uter style hatches only the outermost area. <u>I</u>gnore style hatches any inner boundaries indiscriminately.
- **Exploded Hatch.** If this box is checked, the resulting hatch pattern block is inserted exploded. Individual hatch entities may then be edited.

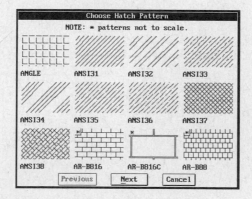

Figure BHATCH.3:
The Choose Hatch Pattern dialog box.

- **Double Hatch.** If this box is checked, the user-defined hatch pattern is mirrored perpendicularly to produce double hatching.
- **Copy Existing Hatch.** Click on this button to select an existing hatch for which you want to use the same settings.

The Advanced Options dialog box (see fig. BHATCH.4) offers the following options:

Figure BHATCH.4:
The Advanced Options dialog box.

- **Define Boundary Set.** You specify how boundary entities are calculated. Clicking on the Make **N**ew Boundary Set button enables you to pick entities on-screen. If a selection set is already active, the From E**x**isting Set radio button is enabled, and you may add or remove entities. The From E**v**erything on Screen radio button causes all visible entities to be considered.

- **Ray Casting.** This option specifies the direction in which AutoCAD first searches to find boundary entities. You can choose one direction from the positive and negative X and Y axes by selecting a method from the drop-down list box.

- **Retain Boundaries.** When this box is checked, it creates a new closed polyline object from the calculated boundary.

Example

The following example uses BHATCH to hatch an area bounded by various intersecting and non-intersecting objects (see fig. BHATCH.5). BHATCH performs this operation much faster than the HATCH command does.

Command: **BHATCH** ↵
Click on the Hatch Options *button*
Click on the **P**attern *button*
Click on the ANSI31 *icon*
Click on the OK *button in the* Define Hatch Pattern *dialog box*
Click on the **P**ick Points *button*
Select internal point *Pick* ①
Select internal point ↵
Click on the Apply *button to finish hatching (see fig. BHATCH.6)*

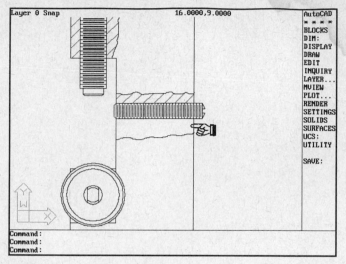

Figure BHATCH.5:
The area to hatch.

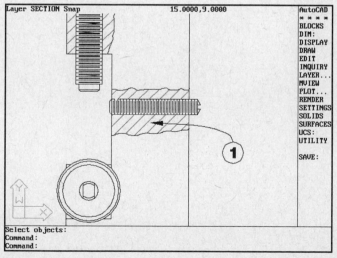

Figure BHATCH.6:
Completed hatch and boundary pick point.

Related Commands

BPOLY
HATCH

Related System Variables

HPANG
HPDOUBLE
HPNAME
HPSCALE

BLIPMODE

Screen **[SETTINGS] [BLIPS:]**

The BLIPMODE command controls the creation of blips when you pick points on-screen. A *blip* is a small plus sign (+) that appears at the exact pick point. Blips are not entities; you can clear them from the screen by using the REDRAW command. If you do not want to use blips, use BLIPMODE to turn off blip generation.

BLIPMODE can be toggled on and off from within other AutoCAD commands by issuing the transparent 'DDRMODES command.

Prompts and Options

* **ON/OFF <On>:**

    When BLIPMODE is on (the default), blips appear at pick points. When BLIPMODE is off, AutoCAD does not generate blips when you pick points.

Example

This example shows how AutoCAD draws entities with BLIPMODE turned on and off (see fig. BLIPMO.1):

```
Command: BLIPMODE↵
ON/OFF <On>: ↵
Command: LINE↵
From point: Pick point ①
To point: Pick point ②
Command: BLIPMODE↵
MODE ON/OFF <On>: OFF↵
Command: LINE↵
From point: Pick point ③
To point: Pick point ④
```

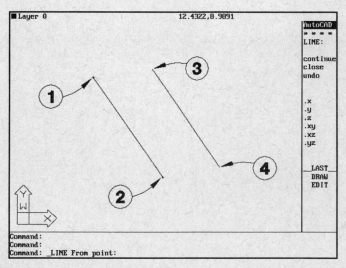

Figure BLIPMO.1:
Using BLIPMODE.

Related Command

'DDRMODES

Related System Variable

BLIPMODE

BLOCK

Screen **[BLOCKS] [BLOCK:]**

The BLOCK command groups entities together to form a single object called a block. Blocks aid in organizing and drawing repetitive entities, reduce the size of the drawing, reduce drawing time, and enable the use of attributes.

When you create a block, you give it a name. You can then insert the block by its name. A block can be inserted as many times as needed. Inserting a block, rather than duplicating entities, adds only one entity to the drawing—thus reducing the size of the drawing database. Blocks also can be inserted at any X, Y, and Z scale.

Blocks can be created with *hard-coded* or *soft-coded* layers. Hard-coded layers force a block's individual entities to remain upon the layers on which they were created. Soft-coded layers enable a block's individual entities to be placed on the layer on which the block is inserted and take on that layer's properties. You can create soft-coded layers by creating blocks that use entities on layer 0.

Prompts and Options

- **Block name (or ?):**

  At this prompt, you specify a block name that is not more than 31 characters in length. Letters, numbers, the dollar sign, the hyphen, and the underscore are valid characters for block names. The ? option lists the blocks currently defined within the drawing.

- **Block(s) to List <*>:**

  You can press Enter at this prompt to list all the blocks currently defined within the drawing. You can use wild-card combinations to create more specific lists. (Note that the lists are presented in alphanumeric order.)

- **Insertion base point:**

  This prompt requests the point, relative to the block itself, that will be used to insert the block. You can select this point from the screen by using an object snap mode. You also can type the point's coordinates or use XYZ point filters or a combination of screen and keyboard input. If you specify the point 0,0, the block will insert in the same relative position in other drawings as it appears in the current drawing.

- **Select objects:**

  This prompt is the standard prompt for selecting objects. The selected objects make up your block. You can use any standard object selection method.

  After you have selected objects and the block has been created, the original entities are erased from the screen. You can use the OOPS command to restore the entities back into the drawing.

Example

This example demonstrates both the creation of a block as well as its re-insertion into the drawing using the INSERT command. The objects shown in figure BLOCK.1 are both the original chair and the block after its insertion.

```
Command: BLOCK↵
Block name (or ?): CHAIR↵
Insertion base point: Pick point ①
Select objects: Select the objects to make up the block
Select objects: ↵
Command: OOPS↵
Command: INSERT↵
Block name (or ?) <>: CHAIR↵
Insertion point: Pick point ②
X scale factor <1>/Corner/XYZ: ↵
Y scale factor (default=X): ↵
Rotation angle <0>: 45↵
```

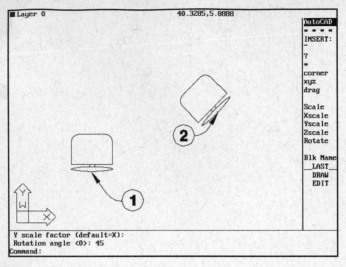

Figure BLOCK.1:
The entities that form the chair block.

Related Commands

> **ATTDEF**
> **DDATTDEF**
> **DDINSERT**
> **EXPLODE**
> **INSERT**
> **OOPS**
> **WBLOCK**
> **XREF**

BPOLY

The BPOLY command creates a new polyline object that outlines an area defined by existing entities. BPOLY performs a subset of the functions of the BHATCH command, but it does not hatch the enclosed area. Figure BPOLY.1 shows the BPOLY dialog box.

Figure BPOLY.1:
The BPOLY dialog box.

BPOLY is especially useful for creating irregular closed polylines from construction lines, arcs, circles, and other entities.

Prompts and Options

BPOLY displays no command-line prompts. Instead, you make selections from the following dialog box options.

The Polyline Creation dialog box (see fig. BPOLY.1) offers the following options:

- **Define Boundary Set.** Options in this group specify the way boundary entities are calculated. Clicking on the Make **N**ew Boundary Set button enables you to pick entities on-screen. If a selection set is already active, the From Existing Boundary Set radio button is enabled, and you can add or remove entities. The From **E**verything on Screen radio button causes all visible entities to be considered.
- **Ray Casting.** This option specifies the direction that AutoCAD first searches to find boundary entities. You can choose one direction from the positive and negative X and Y axes by selecting a method from the drop-down list box.
- **Pick Points.** Click on this button to pick a point on-screen to define the area from which you want a polyline to be made.

55

- **Retain Boundaries.** When this box is checked, it creates a new closed polyline object from the calculated boundary.

Example

The following example uses BPOLY to create a closed polyline boundary out of various construction objects (see fig. BPOLY.2).

```
Command: BPOLY↵
Click on the Pick Points button
Select internal point Pick point ①
Select internal point↵
```

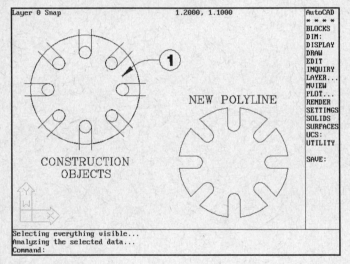

Figure BPOLY.2:
Boundary polyline created by BPOLY.

Related Command

BHATCH

BREAK

Screen **[EDIT] [BREAK:]**

Pull down **[Modify] [Break >]**

The BREAK command removes a portion of a line, arc, polyline, or circle. This command prompts you to select the target object and specify the first and second points of the break. You can break only one entity at a time. If the first and second break points are identical, the entity is divided into two pieces.

Prompts and Options

- **Select object:**

  Select the line, arc, circle, or polyline to break. By default, the point by which you pick the object is considered the first point of the segment to remove. Only one entity can be selected at one time.

- **Enter second point (or F for first point):**

  Select another point on the line, arc, circle, or polyline to break between. The original object-selection point becomes the opposite end of the break, and the portion of the entity between the two points will be removed.

- **Enter first point:**

  You specify a first point of the break that is different from the original object-selection point.

- **Enter second point:**

  The second point determines the portion of the entity to remove.

Example

This example demonstrates how you can use the BREAK command to remove a section of an entity. Figure BREAK.1 shows both the original entities and the result of using the command.

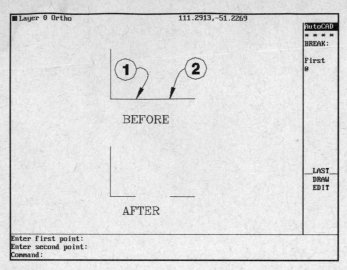

Figure BREAK.1:
The entities before and after using BREAK.

```
Command: BREAK↵
Select object: Pick point ①
Enter second point (or F for first point): F↵
Enter first point: Pick point ①
Enter second point: Pick point ②
```

Related Command

TRIM

CAL

Pull down **[Assist] [Calculator]**

The CAL command is an on-line calculator that evaluates points, vectors, or real and integer expressions. Calculations can use object snap modes to access existing geometry, and 'CAL can be issued transparently within another command to provide a point or number. CAL can also be used in AutoLISP functions.

If you use the AutoCAD object snap modes in your expressions, enter the three-character abbreviations of the object snap modes. You must pick entities—you cannot use the object selection methods.

CAL follows the standard mathematical order of precedence in evaluating expressions. Vectors and points are entered as a set of points or distance and angles. When you enter points in the WCS, use the * prefix, as in [*2,3,4]. Use the * for Scalar product of vectors and the & for Vector products of vectors. Numbers can be entered in scientific notation or a general number format. You can add ' and " for feet and inches on distances. Angles default to degrees; however, you can use the r suffix for radians or the g suffix for gradians. All angles will be converted to degrees. See the *AutoCAD Release 12 Extras Manual* for a complete list of the CAL functions and modes.

Example

The following examples use CAL and 'CAL to solve equations and to return points and vectors to other commands. See figure CAL.1.

```
Command: CAL ↵
>> Expression: A=(5.25+10.5)/1.5^2↵
7.0
Command: ↵
CAL >> Expression: B=3*(14-7) ↵
21
Command: ↵
CAL >> Expression: B/A ↵
3.0
Command: ↵
CAL >> Expression: CVUNIT(DIST(END,INT),INCH,CM) ↵
>> Select entity for END snap: Pick point ①
>> Select entity for INT snap: Pick point ②
5.08
Command: CIRCLE ↵
3P/2P/TTR/<Center point>: 'CAL ↵
>> Expression: MEE ↵
>> Select one endpoint for MEE: Pick point ③
>> Select another endpoint for MEE: Pick point ①
Diameter/<Radius>: 'CAL ↵
>> Expression: DIST(END,END)/3 ↵
>> Select entity for END snap: Pick point ③
>> Select entity for END snap: Pick point ①
```

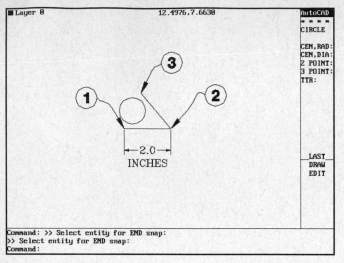

Figure CAL.1:
Entities and pick points for CAL.

Related Commands

DIST
ID
LIST
OSNAP
ROTATE
SOLMASSP

CHAMFER

Screen **[EDIT] [CHAMFER:]**

Pull down **[Construct] [Chamfer]**

The CHAMFER command creates a bevel, called a chamfer, between
two nonparallel lines or on continuous segments of 2D polylines.

CHAMFER extends or trims lines as necessary and adds a line to create the beveled edge. With 2D polylines, it adds vertices and a new segment representing the bevel.

You must supply the distance for the start of the bevel from the intersection of the two segments. You can set different distances for each side of the chamfer to create custom bevels. If you set the chamfer distance to 0, CHAMFER trims or extends the two lines to end neatly at their intersection. (This effect is also possible with the FILLET command.)

Prompts and Options

- **Polyline/Distances/<Select first line>:**

  If you press **P** at this prompt, you can select a 2D polyline for chamfering. The Distances option enables you to preset the chamfer distances applied to both sides of the entities' intersection. The default choice at this prompt is to select the first of two lines for chamfering. The first chamfer distance is applied to this line.

- **Select second line:**

  If you choose the default option, you are prompted for a second line. Your selection completes the CHAMFER command. The second chamfer distance is applied to this line.

- **Enter first chamfer distance <current>:**

  If you select the Distances option at the first prompt, you are prompted for the first chamfer distance. You can type a distance, or you can pick two points on the screen and let AutoCAD calculate the distance between them.

- **Enter second chamfer distance <current>:**

  After you enter the first chamfer distance, you are prompted for the second one. This value defaults to be the same distance as the value for the first chamfer distance.

- **Select 2D polyline:**

  The Polyline option requires you to choose a 2D polyline for modifying. The CHAMFER command attempts to bevel each vertex of the selected polyline using the current chamfer distances.

61

Example

This example demonstrates the differences between beveling two lines and a single polyline with the CHAMFER command. Figure CHAMFER.1 shows the results of using the CHAMFER command on both types of entities.

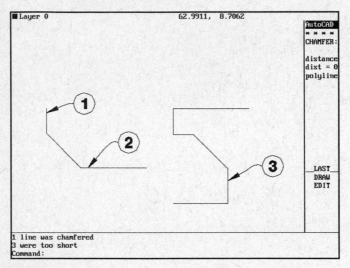

Figure CHAMFER.1:
Using the CHAMFER command.

```
Command: CHAMFER↵
Polyline/Distances/<Select first line>: D↵
Enter first chamfer distance <0.0000>: 24↵
Enter second chamfer distance <24.0000>: ↵
Command: CHAMFER↵
Polyline/Distances/<Select first line>: Pick point ①
Select second line: Pick point ②
Command: CHAMFER↵
Polyline/Distances/<Select first line>: P↵
Select polyline: Pick point ③
```

Related System Variables

CHAMFERA
CHAMFERB

Related Commands

FILLET
TRIM

CHANGE

Screen **[EDIT] [CHANGE:]**

Pull down **[Modify] [Change] [Points]**

The CHANGE command changes existing entities' properties, including color, linetype, layer, and text style. You can use CHANGE whenever you want to modify the properties of selected entities, edit text, or change a point's location.

Prompts and Options

- **Select objects:**

  At this prompt, you can choose objects individually or by using one of the other entity selection options. The prompt repeats until you press Enter to end the object-selection process.

Change Point Option

This option acts in different ways, depending on entity type, as shown in the following table:

Table CHANGE.1
Change Point Option Functions

Entity Type	Function of Change Point Option
Lines	Enables you to move the end points of selected lines. If Ortho mode is turned on, the selected lines are drawn horizontally or vertically, depending on the new point selected. If Ortho mode is turned off, the selected lines converge at the new point.
Text	Edits each text entity in your selection set. You can change the text style, height, rotation angle, or text string.
Circle	Resizes the circle's radius. The circle's center point remains stationary.
Block	Changes the insertion point or the rotation angle of selected blocks.
Attribute Definition	Edits attribute definitions just like text, with a few additional options. You also can change the attribute tag, prompt, and default value.

Change Properties Options

- **Change what property (Color/Elev/LAyer/LType/ Thickness) ?:**

  At this prompt, you can change various properties of the objects you have selected. The first option, Color, changes the color of selected objects. Entities with an explicit color assignment do not take on the color characteristics of the parent layer. To force entities to assume the parent layer's color, assign the special BYLAYER color property.

  The Elev option sets the base elevation of the entities selected.

  The LAyer option changes the layer on which the selected entities reside. The target layer must already exist.

If you specify a layer that does not exist, AutoCAD displays the message `Layer not found` and prompts you for another layer name. Use the transparent 'DDLMODES command, which enables you to create a new layer, and then return to the CHPROP command.

The LType option changes the linetype of selected objects. Entities with an explicit linetype assignment do not take on the linetype characteristics of the parent layer. To force entities to assume the parent layer's linetype, assign the special BYLAYER linetype property.

The Thickness option changes the thickness, or extrusion value, of selected objects.

Example

This example shows how to use CHANGE on various types of entities:

```
Command: CHANGE ↵
Select objects: Pick point ①
1 found
Select objects: Pick point ②
1 found
Select objects: ↵
Properties/<Change point>:
Pick point ③ (see fig. CHANGE.1)
```

Related Commands

CHPROP
COLOR
'DDEDIT
DDMODIFY

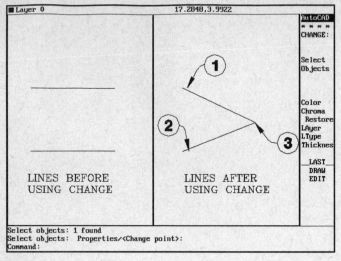

Figure CHANGE.1:
Two lines with changed end points.

Related System Variables

CECOLOR
CELTYPE
CLAYER
ELEV
ELEVATION
LINETYPE
ORTHO
THICKNESS

CHPROP

Screen **[EDIT] [CHPROP:]**

CHPROP, which stands for CHange PROPerties, offers a simple, direct method for modifying the properties of existing entities. It also modifies the properties of all the objects in a selection set at the same time. CHPROP performs a subset of the editing options available with the CHANGE command.

Prompts and Options

- **`Select objects:`**

  At this prompt, you can choose objects individually or by using one of the other entity-selection options. The prompt repeats until you press Enter to end the object-selection process.

- **`Change what property (Color/LAyer/LType/Thickness) ?:`**

  At this prompt, you can change various properties of the objects you select. The first option, Color, changes the color of selected objects. Entities with an explicit color assignment do not take on the color characteristics of the parent layer. To force entities to assume the parent layer's color, assign the special BYLAYER color property.

  The prompt's second option, LAyer, changes the layer on which the selected entities reside. The target layer must already exist.

If you specify a layer that does not exist, AutoCAD displays the message `Layer not found` and prompts you for another layer name. Use the transparent 'DDLMODES command, which enables you to create a new layer, and then return to the CHPROP command.

  The LType option changes the linetype of selected objects. Entities with an explicit linetype assignment do not take on the linetype characteristics of the parent layer. To force entities to assume the parent layer's linetype, assign the special BYLAYER linetype property.

  The Thickness option changes the thickness, or extrusion value, of selected objects.

Example

This example shows how the CHPROP options enable you to perfom most of the same types of entity editing as the CHANGE command. Figure CHPROP.1 shows both the original and new versions of the line entities modified with this command.

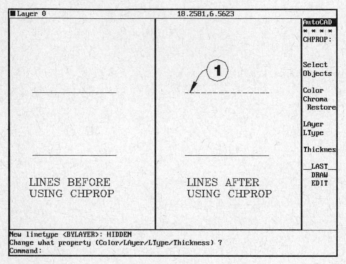

Figure CHPROP.1:
A line entity modified by the CHPROP command's LType option.

```
Command: CHPROP↵
Select objects: Pick point ①
1 found
Select objects: ↵
Change what property (Color/LAyer/LType/Thickness) ? LT↵
New linetype <BYLAYER>: HIDDEN↵
Change what property (Color/LAyer/LType/Thickness) ? ↵
```

Related Commands

CHANGE
COLOR
DDMODIFY
LINETYPE

Related System Variables

CECOLOR
CELTYPE
CLAYER
THICKNESS

CIRCLE

Screen **[DRAW] [CIRCLE]**

Pull down **[Draw] [Circle >]**

The CIRCLE command draws circles. Circles are created at the current elevation, parallel to the current UCS. By setting the ELEV command's THICKNESS option to a non-zero value, you also can create 3D cylinders. These cylinders are simply extruded circles, which do not actually have a top or bottom.

Prompts and Options

- **3P/2P/TTR/<Center point>:**

  The 3P option enables you to define a circle by specifying three points on the circle's circumference.

  The 2P option enables you to create a circle by selecting two points defining the diameter.

  The TTR option enables you to specify two points on an existing line, circle, or arc that will be tangent to the new circle, and then supply the new circle's radius.

  <Center point>, the default, enables you to specify the center point.

- **Diameter/<Radius>:**

  You specify the circle's radius (the default option) or enter **D** and specify the diameter. You can enter a value from the keyboard or pick two points on the screen to specify the distance.

- **Diameter:**

  At this prompt, you enter a value for the circle's diameter. You can enter a value from the keyboard or pick two points on the screen to specify the distance.

- **First point on diameter:**

  At this prompt, you enter the first point for creating a circle with the 2P method.

- **Second point on diameter:**

  At this prompt, you specify the second point for creating a circle with the 2P method.

- **First point:**

  At this prompt, you specify the first point for creating a circle with the 3P method.

- **Second point:**

  At this prompt, you enter the second point for creating a circle with the 3P method.

- **Third point:**

  At this prompt, you enter the third point for creating a circle with the 3P method.

- **Enter Tangent spec:**

  At this prompt, you enter the first tangency point used to draw the circle. The tangent object snap override enables you to choose your point.

- **Enter second Tangent spec:**

  At this prompt, you enter the second tangency point used to draw the circle. The tangent object snap override will be enabled to enable you to choose your point.

- **Radius <current>:**

  After choosing the two tangent points, you enter a value for the circle's radius.

Example

This example demonstrates two of the common methods for creating circles, as shown in figure CIRCLE.1.

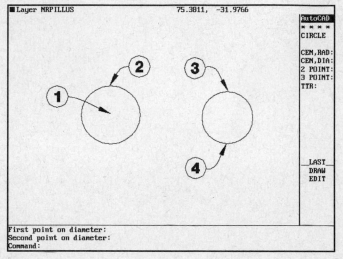

Figure CIRCLE.1:
Circles created using the Center/Radius and 2 point options.

```
Command: CIRCLE ↵
3P/2P/TTR/<Center point>: Pick point ①
Diameter/<Radius>: Pick point ②
Command: CIRCLE ↵
3P/2P/TTR/<Center point>: 2P ↵
First point on diameter: Pick point ③
Second point on diameter: Pick point ④
```

Related Commands

DONUT
ELLIPSE

Related System Variables

CIRCLERAD
VIEWRES

COLOR

Screen **[SETTINGS] [COLOR:]**

The COLOR command controls the color of new entities. If you explicitly set the color value instead of using the BYLAYER option, you can override the layer's default color assignment.

 You can use the COLOR command transparently by preceding the command name with an apostrophe ('COLOR).

Prompts and Options

- **New entity color <BYLAYER>:**

    If you enter **BYLAYER**, the most commonly used color setting, the entity color defaults to the color assigned to the layer of insertion.

    You also can enter **BYBLOCK** at the prompt. The BYBLOCK option creates new entities, in the color white, until they are saved and inserted as a block. When inserted, the entities take on the color value currently set with the COLOR command.

    You also can enter a color number or name at the prompt. By naming a color, you assign new entities a specific color value that overrides the color assigned to the current layer. The COLOR command accepts a number from 1 to 255, but what displays on your screen depends on the video board and monitor you are using. You can assign the first seven colors by number or name, as follows:

Color Number	Color
1	Red
2	Yellow
3	Green
4	Cyan
5	Blue
6	Magenta
7	White

 For best results, keep the color value specified by the COLOR command set to BYLAYER. Use the LAYER command's default color to control entity color, which helps to easily identify different layers in your drawing and to redefine colors.

Example

This example shows how the value of COLOR can affect any new entities that you create. In the example shown in figure COLOR.1, the color has been changed from its current default of BYLAYER to the color red (1).

```
Command: COLOR↵
New entity color <BYLAYER>: 1↵
Command: LINE↵
From point: Pick point ①
To point: Pick point ②
To point: ↵
```

 Plotter pen assignments usually are made by color. To achieve different line widths (or types), use a different color for each pen—even if you are using a monochrome monitor.

Related Commands

CHPROP
CHANGE
'DDEMODES
LAYER

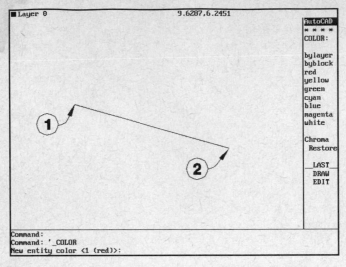

Figure COLOR.1:
A line entity drawn in the color red.

Related System Variable

CECOLOR

COMPILE

R12

Pull down **[File] [Compile...]**

The COMPILE command compiles shape and font definition files into SHP files before they can be used by AutoCAD. Shape files can contain definitions of symbols for use by the LOAD and SHAPE commands. The STYLE command uses shape files that contain text-character definitions to create styles for use by the dimensioning, TEXT, and DTEXT commands. Besides AutoCAD's native shape source-file format (SHX), COMPILE also compiles Adobe Type 1 font files (PFB) into SHP files.

When you execute the COMPILE command, AutoCAD displays a general file dialog box with SHP and PFB files listed for the current directory. Select the desired source file name; AutoCAD compiles it into a SHP file. If successful, COMPILE displays a notice message noting the size and name of the file produced. COMPILE responds with an error message if it encounters errors in the source file.

Related Commands

LOAD
TEXT
DTEXT
Dimensioning commands

CONFIG

Pull down **[File] [Configure]**

The CONFIG command enables you to configure the devices that AutoCAD uses and the various parameters that control the way AutoCAD works. You can configure AutoCAD any time the program is active, even with a drawing loaded. See your *AutoCAD Interface, Installation, and Performance Guide* for details on choices available on your particular computer platform.

Prompts and Options

When you first execute the CONFIG command, it displays your current hardware configuration. A configuration menu is then displayed. It offers the following choices:

- **Exit to drawing editor.** This option returns to the drawing—you are prompted to save any changes made.

- **Show current configuration.** This option displays a list of the current hardware configuration choices.

- **Allow detailed configuration.** This option enables prompting for advanced configuration information by the other configuration options.

75

- **Configure video display.** This option enables selection of a different video display.
- **Configure digitizer.** This option enables selection of a different pointing device.
- **Configure plotter.** This option enables selection of a different hard-copy output device.
- **Configure system console.** This option enables selection of platform-specific console options.
- **Configure operating parameters.** This option enables configuration of various directories, files, and data integrity, and networking features. This selection presents the following options:

```
Exit to configuration menu
Alarm on error
Initial drawing setup
Default plot file name
Plot spooler directory
Placement of temporary files
Network node name
Automatic-save feature
Full-time CRC validation
Automatic Audit after IGESIN, DXFIN, or DXBIN
Login name
Select Release 11 hidden line removal algorithm
Server authorization and file-locking
```

- **Enter selection <0>.** You enter the number corresponding to your choice and follow the prompts displayed.

Related Command

REINIT

Related System Variables

PLOTID
PLOTTER

POPUPS
SCREENBOXES
SCREENMODE
TABMODE

COPY

Screen **[EDIT] [COPY:]**

Pull down **[Construct] [Copy]**

The COPY command makes single or multiple copies of as many existing objects as you want. The original selection set remains unchanged after the copy is made.

Prompts and Options

- **Select objects:**

  At this prompt, you can choose objects individually or by using one of the other entity-selection options. The prompt repeats until you press Enter to end the object-selection process.

- **<Base point or displacement>/Multiple:**

  The Base point or displacement option, which is the default, specifies the point from which you are copying the entities. You can specify a 2D or 3D point. If you use a 2D point, the COPY command uses the current elevation setting for the Z value.

  The Multiple option enables you to make multiple copies of the selection set, repeating the following prompt until you press Enter or Ctrl-C.

- **Second point of displacement:**

  You specify the point to which you are copying the entities. (You can specify a 2D or 3D point.) If you use a 2D point, the COPY command uses the current elevation setting for the Z value.

Example

The entities shown in figure COPY.1 represent a window, which you can duplicate by using the COPY command.

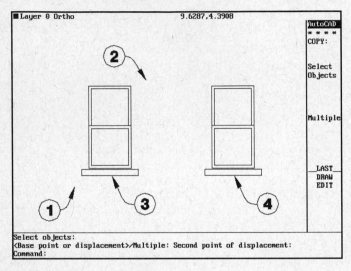

Figure COPY.1:
Using the COPY command to duplicate a group of entities.

```
Command: COPY↵
Select objects: W↵
First corner: Pick point ①
Other corner: Pick point ②
7 found
Select objects: ↵
<Base point or displacement>/Multiple: Pick point ③
Second point of displacement: Pick point ④
```

 Use Ortho mode, Snap mode, and object snap settings to simplify the copying process. Ortho mode enables you to copy orthogonally to (0, 90, 180, and 270 degrees) the original. Snap mode enables you to copy at precise increments. Object snap overrides enable you to copy in relation to other existing entities.

Related Commands

> **ARRAY**
> **OFFSET**

DBLIST

Screen **[INQUIRY] [DBLIST:]**

DBLIST (Data Base LIST) provides detailed information on every entity in a drawing. DBLIST switches your display to the text screen and then lists the drawing's entities. To pause the list, you can press Ctrl-S or the Pause key; press any key to continue. To cancel the list, press Ctrl-C.

 To print the listing on an attached printer, toggle the printer echo on by pressing Ctrl-Q before issuing the DBLIST command.

Example

This example demonstrates the type of information returned by the DBLIST command.

```
Command: DBLIST↵
              CIRCLE     Layer: NRPILLUS
                         Space: Model space
        center point, X= -56.3069  Y= -46.4808  Z=  0.0000
          radius   20.1769
  circumference 126.7754
        area 1278.9694
              CIRCLE     Layer: NRPILLUS
                         Space: Model space
        center point, X=  25.2901  Y= -48.2497  Z=  0.0000
          radius   18.0497
  circumference 113.4099
        area 1023.5092
```

Related Command

LIST

DDATTDEF

Screen **[DRAW] [ATTDEF:] [AttDef Dialogue]**

Pull down **[DRAW] [TEXT] [ATTRIBUTES] [DEFINE...]**

The DDATTDEF command creates attribute definitions—text entities included in blocks that can be assigned different values with each insertion. An attribute definition contains three parts: a tag that defines the type of information conveyed by the attribute, a prompt at which you supply a value when you insert the block, and a default value. Attributes appear on your screen as AutoCAD text; indeed, you will find that part of the attribute definition process involves specifying height, justification, style, rotation and position just as with AutoCAD's TEXT command.

AutoCAD also enables you to assign one or more modes to your attribute definitions: Invisible, so that AutoCAD renders attributes invisible on the screen; Constant, so that inserted attributes maintain a fixed, uneditable value; Verify, so that AutoCAD allows you to check and further edit a value you typed before inserting it; and Preset, so that AutoCAD automatically assigns the attribute's default value upon insertion. You can edit preset attributes with the ATTEDIT command after you insert them.

To reduce drawing clutter, make your attribute definitions invisible if you intend to insert a lot of them and do not need to see them on screen.

Prompts and Options

The DDATTDEF dialog box contains four areas in which you supply information about the attribute's definition (see fig. DDATTDEF.1):

- **Mode**. Click in one or more of the check boxes to make the attribute invisible, constant, verifiable or preset.

- **Attribute**. The Attribute section of the dialog box provides three edit boxes in which you type the attribute's Tag, Prompt, and default Value.

- **Insertion Point**. You supply a point at which AutoCAD draws the attribute. You can click on the <u>P</u>ick Pt. < button to pick a point on the screen with your digitizer or mouse, or you can click on the <u>X</u>, <u>Y</u> and <u>Z</u> edit boxes to type explicit coordinates.

- **Text Options**. In the text options area, you detail your attribute's appearance. Choose a desired justification and text style by clicking on the <u>J</u>ustification and <u>T</u>ext Style pop-up list boxes and selecting from the displayed lists. You can set text height and rotation by clicking on the <u>H</u>eight and <u>R</u>otation buttons and pointing with your mouse or digitizer, or you can click on the edit boxes that accompany the buttons and type specific values.

  If you have defined other attributes and you want the one you are currently creating to be aligned under the most recently created attribute, click on the check box beside the phrase that reads <u>A</u>lign below previous attribute. Click on the OK button to create the attribute.

Figure DDATTDEF.1:
The DDATTDEF dialog box.

Related Command

ATTDEF

DDATTE

Screen **[EDIT] [DDATTE:]**

DDATTE (Dynamic Dialog ATTribute Edit) enables you to edit attribute string values by using a dialog box. You can edit strings character by character or overwrite an entire line. If all of a block's attributes do not fit in a single dialog box screen, you can use the buttons in the dialog box to move through the various attributes.

Prompts and Options

- **Select block:**

  At this prompt, you choose a block that contains attributes you want to edit.

After a block with attributes is selected, a dialog box appears (see fig. DDATE.1). Each attribute is displayed along with an edit box that enables you to modify the attribute's value. In addition to the standard dialog box buttons, the following buttons appear within the dialog box:

- **Previous.** This button displays the previous group of attributes.
- **Next.** This button displays the next group of attributes.

Related Commands

ATTDEF
ATTEXT
BLOCK
DDATTDEF
DDATTEXT
INSERT

```
┌─────────────────────────────────────────────┐
│                Edit Attributes               │
│ Block name: CHAIR                            │
│                                              │
│ Enter furniture cost    ┌──────────────────┐ │
│                         │$300              │ │
│ Enter furniture fabric  ┌──────────────────┐ │
│                         │Cloth             │ │
│ Enter furniture manufac ┌──────────────────┐ │
│                         │Loth              │ │
│ Enter office number     ┌──────────────────┐ │
│                         │220               │ │
│                         ┌──────────────────┐ │
│        ⌖                ┌──────────────────┐ │
│                         ┌──────────────────┐ │
│                         ┌──────────────────┐ │
│                         ┌──────────────────┐ │
│                         ┌──────────────────┐ │
│                                              │
│  ┌────┐ ┌──────┐ ┌────────┐ ┌────┐ ┌─────┐ │
│  │ OK │ │Cancel│ │Previous│ │Next│ │Help.│ │
│  └────┘ └──────┘ └────────┘ └────┘ └─────┘ │
└─────────────────────────────────────────────┘
```

Figure DDATTE.1:
Using DDATTE to edit attributes within a drawing.

Related System Variables

ATTLISP
ATTDIA

DDATTEXT

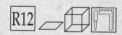

Screen **[UTILITY] [ATTEXT:] [Att Ext Dialogue]**

Pull down **[DRAW] [TEXT] [ATTRIBUTES] [EXTRACT...]**

The DDATTEXT command extracts attribute information from your drawing and stores it in a text file. You can analyze the extracted attribute data in a spreadsheet program, catalog it in a database program, or print it as a text report. DDATTEXT extracts information in one of three formats: Comma Delimited Format (CDF), Space Delimited Format (SDF), or Drawing Interchange Format (DXF). Use the format that is accepted by the program in which you want to use the extracted information.

Before you can extract attribute information, you must create a template file that tells AutoCAD how to format the information that it extracts. Each line in the template file defines a field. The template file contains two columns. The left column contains attribute tag names and information about the blocks from which AutoCAD extracts the attribute data. Block information can include block name, nesting level, rotation angle, counter, insertion layer, X, Y, and Z insertion point coordinates, scaling factors and extrusion directions, and entity handles.

The right column of the template file contains format information for the data that AutoCAD extracts. It takes the form Xwwwddd, where X can be N for numeric data or C for character data, www specifies the field's width, and ddd specifies the number of decimal places for numeric data. A sample template file might look like this:

```
BL:NAME   C008000
BL:X      N007001
BL:Y      N007001
BL:NUMBER N020000
OFFICE    N010000
FLOOR     N015000
NAME      C025000
```

Use an ASCII text editor to create the template file as a plain ASCII text file.

When you extract attribute data, AutoCAD prompts for the name of the template file to use and the name of the attribute extract file. You must use different file names for the template and extract files, or AutoCAD overwrites the template file.

Prompts and Options

At the top of the DDATTEXT dialog box (see fig. DDATTEXT.1), you see a group of three radio buttons, labeled File Format, with which you select the format for your attribute extract file: Comma Delimited File

(CDF), **S**pace Delimited File (SDF), or **D**rawing Interchange File (DXF). Beneath the File Format group, the Select **O**bjects button allows you to choose only those blocks from which you want attribute data to be extracted.

- Beneath the Select **O**bjects button, two buttons with companion edit boxes provide the means to specify or select template and output files. You may click on the edit boxes and type filenames, or you may click on the **T**emplate File or Output **F**ile buttons to select files from a list.

- **Template File** and **Output File**. When you click on the Template File or Output File button, a second dialog box appears (see fig. DDATTEXT.2). From this box you may search for and select existing template or output files.

- **Pattern**. In the **P**attern edit box at the top of the Template/ Output File dialog box, you can enter a file search pattern using alphanumeric characters and DOS wild-card characters like *.

  Beneath the Pattern edit box, AutoCAD displays the current drive and directory. Beneath the Directory display lie two list boxes from which you can select a different drive or directory or a specific file. Beneath the list boxes, the **F**ile edit box allows you to type a file name. When you select a file from the **F**iles list box, the file name automatically appears in the **F**ile edit box.

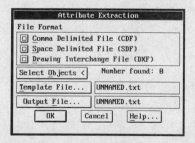

Figure DDATTEXT.1:
The DDATTEXT dialog box.

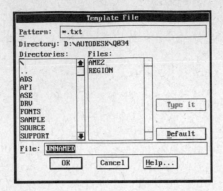

Figure DDATTEXT.2
The Template File dialog box.

Related Command

ATTEXT

DDCHPROP

Pull down   **[Modify] [Change] [Properties]**

The DDCHPROP command allows you to change drawing entities'
color, layer, linetype, and thickness properties. When you issue the
DDCHPROP command, AutoCAD prompts you to pick the objects you
wish to modify. Only after selecting these objects do you see the
DDCHPROP dialog box (see fig. DDCHPROP.1).

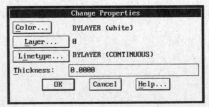

Figure DDCHPROP.1:
The DDCHPROP dialog box.

Prompts and Options

The Change Properties dialog box contains three buttons and an edit box. The buttons display dialog boxes with which to change color, layer, or linetype.

- **Color.** Clicking on the Color button displays the Select Color dialog box (see fig. DDCHPROP.2). The Select Color box contains four palette boxes from which to pick a new color. Click on one of the colored squares to pick a new color, or click on the BY**L**AYER or **B**YBLOCK buttons to set color by one of those methods. You may also click on the Color edit box and type a specific color name.

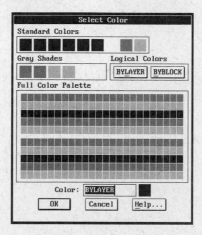

Figure DDCHPROP.2:
The Select Color dialog box.

- **Layer.** To change an entity's layer, click on this button to see the Select Layer dialog box, which features a list box containing the names of all of the layers in the drawing (see fig. DDCHPROP.3). A scroll bar appears on the list box if not all the layer names will fit on screen. To select a new layer, double-click on a layer name, or type a layer name in the **S**et Layer Name edit box.

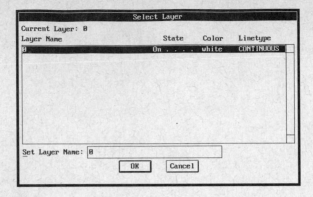

Figure DDCHPROP.3:
The Select Layer dialog box.

- **Linetype.** The Select Linetype dialog box that appears when you click on the Linetype button contains a list box that shows the currently loaded linetypes (see fig. DDCHPROP.4). If not all linetypes fit on screen, a scroll bar allows you to view and select from all of the loaded linetypes. To select a linetype, double-click on one of the linetype names in the list box or click on the Linetype edit box and type a linetype name.

Figure DDCHPROP.4:
The Select Linetype dialog box.

- **Thickness.** To change an entity's thickness, click on the Thickness edit box and type a new thickness.

Related Command

CHPROP

DDEDIT

Screen **[EDIT] [DDEDIT:]**

DDEDIT (Dynamic Dialog EDIT) is AutoCAD's easy-to-use text editor. With DDEDIT, you can add or replace characters, or even overwrite an entire string—all within a dialog box. DDEDIT enables you to edit existing text strings or attribute definitions.

 DDEDIT is good for editing text strings, but stops short of editing all of a text object's attributes. An AutoLISP-defined **TIP** command, CHTEXT, allows you to change text justification, perform search and replace abilities, change text height, width, style, and so on.

Prompts and Options

- **<Select a TEXT or ATTDEF object>/Undo:**

    The default option edits either text strings or attribute definitions. If you choose an attribute definition, you can change the attribute tag, prompt, and default values.

    Select the Undo option by entering **U**. DDEDIT undoes the edits performed on the previous text string.

    After you select a text string or attribute definition, a dialog box appears. The dialog box contains an edit box that enables you to modify the text string or attribute definition.

Related Commands

DDATTE
CHANGE

89

DDEMODES

Screen **[SETTINGS] [DDEMODES]**

Pull down **[Settings] [Entity Modes...]**

The DDEMODES command displays the Entity Creation Modes dialog box. From this dialog box you can set the color, linetype, elevation, text style, and thickness for any new entity. The DDEMODES command is also useful for checking the status of these entity-creation settings during an editing session.

Prompts and Options

DDEMODES issues no command-line prompts. Instead, this command provides a dialog box that features a number of buttons.

This dialog box's options perform the following functions:

- **Color.** This option controls the colors of new entities. When you select this option, AutoCAD displays a dialog box containing only color options. To select a new color, you can click on one of the colors in the dialog box or enter a valid AutoCAD color number from 1 to 255. If you select any color other than BYLAYER, you override the default entity color assigned to the current layer with the LAYER command.

- **Layer.** This option displays the Layer Control dialog box, which contains the names of all the currently defined layers and enables you to modify their properties. Refer to the dialog box description for the DDLMODES command for explanations of all the dialog box's options.

- **Linetype.** This option button displays a dialog box, which displays all currently loaded linetypes. You can select the linetype you want to use for all new entities from this dialog box.

- **Text Style.** This option is used to change the current text style. You choose your new text style from a dialog box that lists the currently defined text styles.

- **Elevation.** This option requires you to enter a valid Z value. By default, new entities are drawn in the X,Y plane of the current UCS.

- **Thickness.** This option requires you to enter a valid extrusion thickness. Applicable new entities are drawn with the new thickness.

Practice using the various DDEMODES options in an existing drawing. Note the differences between the capabilities of these options and the options of their more full-featured relatives.

Example

This example uses the TOOLPOST sample drawing to illustrate how the DDEMODES command works. The sequence uses the DDEMODES command to change the default linetype (see fig. DDEMODES.1), and then draw a line, which is shown in figure DDEMODES.2.

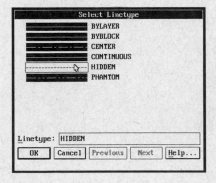

Figure DDEMODES.1:
Setting the default linetype to hidden.

Command: **DDEMODES** ↵
Press the Set Ltype *button*
Select the HIDDEN linetype
Click on the OK *button*
Click on the OK *button*

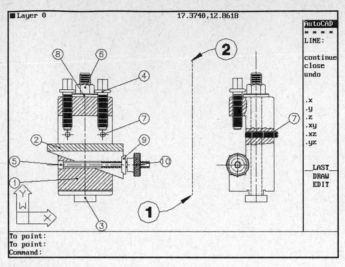

Figure DDEMODES.2:
Drawing a line after setting the default linetype.

```
Command: LINE↵
From point: Pick point ①
To point: Pick point ②
To point: ↵
```

Related Commands

> COLOR
> DDLMODES
> ELEV
> LAYER
> LINETYPE

Related System Variables

> CECOLOR
> CELTYPE
> CLAYER
> ELEVATION
> THICKNESS

DDGRIPS

Pull down **[Settings] [Grips...]**

Drawing entities in Release 12 might display *grips*, small squares located at strategic points on the entities. You can enable grips with the DDGRIPS command or by setting the GRIPS system variable to 1. With grips enabled, the drawing editor crosshairs snap automatically to a grip when the crosshairs pass over the grip. You can stretch, move, rotate, scale, or mirror the gripped entity by moving the grip. In addition to enabling or disabling grips, the DDGRIPS command also enables you to set the grips' color and size (see fig. DDGRIPS.1).

You can execute the DDGRIPS command transparently by preceding the command name with an apostrophe ('DDGRIPS).

Figure DDGRIPS.1:
The DDGRIPS dialog box.

Prompts and Options

At the top of the DDGRIPS dialog box, you see two check boxes. <u>E</u>nable Grips enables or disables grips on primitive entities. Enable Grips Within <u>B</u>locks enables or disables grips on entities contained within blocks.

- **Select Color.** Beneath the check boxes, the Unselected and Selected buttons display the Select Color dialog box (see fig. DDCHPROP.2, in the DDCHPROP listing), from which you can select colors for unselected and selected grips.

At the bottom of the DDGRIPS dialog box, a scroll bar enables you to adjust the grips' size dynamically. The small square to the right of the scroll bar grows and shrinks as you drag the scroll box, indicating the grips' size.

Related System Variables

GRIPS
GRIPBLOCK
GRIPCOLOR
GRIPHOT
GRIPSIZE

DDIM

Pull down **[Settings] [Dimension Style...]**

The DDIM dialog box (see fig. DDIM.1) provides access to all of AutoCAD's dimensioning system variables. Here you can also create custom system variable settings and save them under unique dimension style names for later recall.

 You can execute the DDIM command transparently by preceding the command name with an apostrophe ('DDIM).

Prompts and Options

The DDIM dialog box contains, on the left side, a Dimension Styles list box that shows the names of currently defined dimension styles. Double-click on a name to set its style. If not all defined styles fit on the current screen, a scroll bar appears with which you can display additional styles.

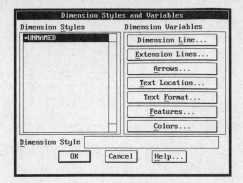

Figure DDIM.1:
The DDIM dialog box.

The Dimension Style edit box at the bottom of the dialog box provides a place to type a dimension style name for recall. On the right side of the DDIM dialog box, the Dimension Variables series of buttons provides access to various categories of dimension variables through the following dialog boxes:

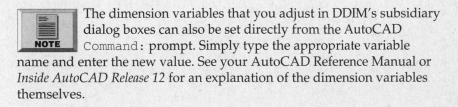

The dimension variables that you adjust in DDIM's subsidiary dialog boxes can also be set directly from the AutoCAD `Command:` prompt. Simply type the appropriate variable name and enter the new value. See your AutoCAD Reference Manual or *Inside AutoCAD Release 12* for an explanation of the dimension variables themselves.

- **Dimension Line.** The Dimension Line dialog box allows you to change the dimension line's appearance (see fig. DDIM.2). At the top of the dialog box, you see the name of the current dimension style.
- **Feature Scaling**. The Feature Scaling edit box lets you set the global dimension scaling factor.
- **Use Paper Space Scaling**. Clicking on the check box labeled Use Paper Space Scaling tells AutoCAD to compute an appropriate global dimension scaling factor based on the scaling between the current model space viewport and paper space, ignoring the value in the Feature Scaling box.

- **Dimension Line Color**. In the Dimension Line Color edit box, you can choose a color.

- **Force Interior Lines**. Beneath the Line Color box, the Force Interior Lines check box forces AutoCAD to draw a dimension line between the two extension lines even when the dimension text is placed outside the extension lines.

- **Basic Dimension**. If you check the Basic Dimension box, AutoCAD will draw a box around the dimension's text.

- **Text Gap**. The number that you type in the Text Gap edit box beneath the Reference Dimension box sets the spacing around the dimension text when AutoCAD breaks the dimension line to contain the dimension text.

- **Baseline Increment**. The Baseline Increment edit box specifies the distance to offset consecutive baseline dimensions, so that they do not overlap one another.

```
┌────────────────────────────────────────┐
│            Dimension Line               │
│ Style: *UNNAMED                         │
│ Feature Scaling:       │ 1.00000 │      │
│ ☐ Use Paper Space Scaling               │
│ Dimension Line Color: │ BYBLOCK │ ☐     │
│ Dimension Line                          │
│   ☐ Force Interior Lines                │
│   ☐ Basic Dimension                     │
│   Text Gap:           │ 0.0900 │        │
│   Baseline Increment: │ 0.3800 │        │
│    ┌──────┐  ┌────────┐  ┌───────┐      │
│    │  OK  │  │ Cancel │  │ Help...│      │
│    └──────┘  └────────┘  └───────┘      │
└────────────────────────────────────────┘
```

Figure DDIM.2:
The Dimension Line dialog box.

- **Extension Lines.** The Extension Lines dialog box controls the appearance of extension lines in much the same way that the Dimension Line box controls dimension lines (see fig. DDIM.3). Indeed, the first three lines you see in the Extension Line box are identical to those in the Dimension Line box. The fourth line contains an edit box in which you set the extension lines' color, as opposed to dimension line color. The rest of the box diverges from the Dimension Line box.

- **Extension Above Line**. In the **E**xtension Above Line edit box, you can type the distance that you want the extension lines to extend past the dimension line.

- **Feature Offset**. The value entered in the Feature **O**ffset edit box specifies the gap between the dimensioned entity and the beginning of the extension line.

- **Visibility**. The Visibilit**y** pop-up list box controls suppression of extension lines, whether both, only one, or neither.

- **Center Mark Size**. Beneath the Visibility box lies the **C**enter Mark Size edit box, where you set the size of center marks drawn by the CENTER, DIAMETER, and RADIUS dimensioning commands.

- **Mark with Center Lines**. If you click on the **M**ark with Center Lines check box, AutoCAD draws center marks rather than center lines.

```
╔══════════ Extension Lines ══════════╗
║ Style: *UNNAMED                      ║
║ Feature Scaling      │ 1.00000 │     ║
║ □ Use Paper Space Scaling            ║
║ Extension Line Color │BYBLOCK│ □     ║
║ Extension Lines                      ║
║   Extension Above Line │0.1800 │     ║
║   Feature Offset       │0.0625 │     ║
║   Visibility │Draw Both        │▼│   ║
║   Center Mark Size     │0.0900 │     ║
║   □ Mark with Center Lines           ║
║   ┌───┐  ┌──────┐  ┌──────┐          ║
║   │ OK│  │Cancel│  │Help..│          ║
║   └───┘  └──────┘  └──────┘          ║
╚══════════════════════════════════════╝
```

Figure DDIM.3:
The Extension Lines dialog box.

- **Arrows.** The Arrows dialog box (see fig. DDIM.4) controls how arrowheads are drawn at the ends of dimension lines. The first four lines are identical to those in the Dimension Lines dialog box (see fig. DDIM.2). At the top of the Arrows section of the dialog box, a row of four radio buttons specifies what kind of arrowheads are drawn: **A**rrow, Tic**k**, **D**ot or **U**ser.

- **Arrow Size**. Beneath the radio buttons, the Arrow Size edit box provides a place to enter the arrowheads' size.

- **User Arrow**. In the User Arrow edit box, you type the name of the block to use as the user customized arrowhead. The box is highlighted only if you have depressed the User radio button.

- **Separate Arrows**. If you click on the Separate Arrows check box, the First Arrow and Second Arrow edit boxes highlight so that you may enter the names of separate customized arrowheads for each end of the dimension line.

- **Tick Extension**. If you had selected the Tick radio button, the Tick Extension edit box highlights, enabling you to enter the distance which you want the dimension line to extend past the tick mark.

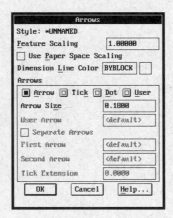

Figure DDIM.4:
The Arrows dialog box.

- **Text Location.** The Text Location dialog box governs the appearance of dimension text (see fig. DDIM.5). Again, the first four lines in the dialog box name the current style, set the global dimension scale factor, tell AutoCAD to use paper space scaling, and set dimension line color. Below the fourth line, you find the text settings. In the first two edit boxes, you set the height of dimension text and the height of tolerance text, respectively. The editing features in the rest of the dialog box, three pop-up list boxes and an edit box, govern dimension text placement in relation to the dimension line.

- **Horizontal**. The first pop-up list box, labeled **H**orizontal, controls the text's horizontal placement. This box offers three choices: Default, Force text inside, and Text, arrows inside. If you choose Default, AutoCAD places the text for Linear and Angular dimensions inside the extension lines, provided enough room exists. If not, AutoCAD places the text outside the extension lines. For Radius and Diameter dimensions, AutoCAD places the text outside of the arc or circle. If you choose the Force text inside option, AutoCAD places the text inside the extension lines regardless of the amount of space available. The Text, arrows inside option tells AutoCAD to place text and arrowheads inside the extension lines.

  If not enough room exists for both the arrowheads and the text (in which case AutoCAD normally places the arrowheads and dimension lines outside the extension lines), AutoCAD omits the arrowheads and dimension lines entirely, leaving only the dimension text inside the extension lines.

- **Vertical**. The second Text Placement pop-up list box, labeled **V**ertical, controls the dimensions text's vertical placement in relation to the dimension line. It, too, offers three choices: Centered, Above, and Relative. The Centered option causes AutoCAD to center the text on the dimension line, splitting the line in the process. The Above option tells AutoCAD to place the text above the dimension line a distance equal to the text's height, leaving the dimension line whole. The Relative option causes text to be placed some distance above or below the dimension line based upon the value in the Relative **P**osition edit box (the box is greyed out until you choose the Relative option in the Vertical pop-up list box).

  AutoCAD calculates the relative distance by dividing the relative position value by the text height value. A positive relative position value causes AutoCAD to place the text above the dimension line; a negative value causes text to be placed below the dimension line.

- **Alignment**. The third pop-up list box, titled Alignment, governs the text's alignment (or lack thereof) with the dimension line. The box provides four choices: Orient Text Horizontally, Align With Dimension Line, Align When Inside Only, and Align When Outside Only. When you choose to orient text horizontally, AutoCAD always draws the text horizontally, regardless of the dimension line's angle. Align With Dimension Line always causes AutoCAD to align the text at the dimension line's angle. The last two options cause AutoCAD to align text only when it places the text inside or outside of the extension lines, respectively.

```
┌─────────────────────────────────────┐
│            Text Location             │
│ Style: *UNNAMED                      │
│ Feature Scaling        [1.00000]     │
│ ☐ Use Paper Space Scaling            │
│ Dimension Text Color [BYBLOCK] [ ]   │
│ Text Position                        │
│  ┌─────────────────────────────────┐ │
│  │ Text Height       [0.1800]      │ │
│  │ Tolerance Height  [0.1800]      │ │
│  │ Text Placement                  │ │
│  │ Horizontal [Default]         [↓]│ │
│  │ Vertical   [Centered]        [↓]│ │
│  │ Relative Position [0.0000]      │ │
│  │ Alignment                       │ │
│  │ [Orient Text Horizontally]   [↓]│ │
│  └─────────────────────────────────┘ │
│   [  OK  ]  [ Cancel ]  [ Help... ]  │
└─────────────────────────────────────┘
```

Figure DDIM.5:
The Text Location dialog box.

- **Text Format.** The Text Format dialog box controls the way that AutoCAD displays dimension text (see fig. DDIM.6). The first three lines in the box display the current style name, let you set the global dimension scale factor, and let you choose to allow AutoCAD to calculate an appropriate scaling factor based on the scaling between the current model space viewport and paper space. The remainder of the dialog box consists of four groups that each govern a different aspect of dimension text formatting.

  Basic Units. The first area, titled Basic Units, contains four edit boxes and a check box. AutoCAD multiplies all linear dimensions

100

by the value stored in the Length Scaling edit box. If you want the length scaling factor applied to only dimensions created in paper space, click on the Scale in Paper Space Only check box. In the Round Off edit box, enter a value by which all dimensions should be rounded. Text strings entered in the Text Prefix and Text Suffix edit boxes will appear before and after, respectively, the dimension text.

The four check boxes in the Zero Suppression group of the Text Format dialog box allow you to suppress various parts of the dimension text. When you click on the 0 Feet check box, AutoCAD suppresses the feet portion of a feet-and-inch dimension. The 0 Inches box, when checked, causes AutoCAD to delete the inches portion of a feet-and-inch dimension. When checked, the Leading check box tells AutoCAD to suppress leading zeros in decimal dimensions. The Trailing check box causes AutoCAD to suppress trailing decimal zeros.

- **Tolerances.** In the Tolerances portion of the Text Format dialog box, you choose how AutoCAD displays dimension tolerances. If you click on the Variance radio button, AutoCAD appends the values entered in the Upper Value and Lower Value edit boxes. If the lower value equals the upper value, AutoCAD displays the tolerances as ±value appended to the dimension text. If the upper value does not equal the lower value, AutoCAD displays the tolerances as +upper value above -lower value. If you selected the Limits radio button, AutoCAD adds the upper value to the dimension and subtracts the lower value and displays both calculated values one above the other.

- **Alternate Units.** The Alternate Units group of the Text Format dialog box governs the display of alternate dimension units. If you click on the Show Alternate Units? check box, AutoCAD displays alternate as well as standard units in your dimensions. When you click on the check box, the Decimal Places, Scaling, and Suffix edit boxes highlight, allowing you to enter values in these boxes. In the Decimal Places box, type the number of decimal places with which you want the alternate units displayed. If you want alternate units

101

in linear dimensions scaled, enter the scaling factor in the Scaling edit box. If you want a suffix appended to the alternate units, type it into the Suffix edit box.

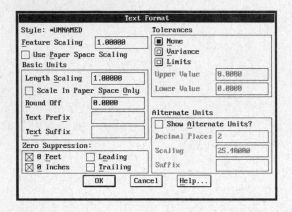

Figure DDIM.6:
The Text Format dialog box.

- **Features.** In the Features dialog box, you can edit the settings for dimension lines, extension lines, arrows, and text location, as discussed above for the individual dialog boxes that deal with these entities. Please see the respective discussions and figures for those dialog boxes for explanation.

- **Colors.** The Colors dialog box lets you set individual colors for dimension lines, extension lines and dimension text. You can also set the global dimension scale factor and instruct AutoCAD to calculate a scale factor based on the scaling in the current model space viewport and paper space. To set an entity color, click on that entity's edit box and type in a color name or number , or click on the adjacent color square to pick a color from the Colors dialog box (see fig. DDIM.7).

Related System Variables

See *Inside AutoCAD Release 12* for a list of dimensioning system variables.

```
┌─────────────────────────────────┐
│             Colors              │
├─────────────────────────────────┤
│ Style: *UNNAMED                 │
│ Feature Scaling    [1.00000]    │
│ ☐ Use Paper Space Scaling       │
│ Dimension Line Color [BYBLOCK] ☐│
│ Extension Line Color [BYBLOCK] ☐│
│ Dimension Text Color [BYBLOCK] ☐│
│  [  OK  ]  [ Cancel ]  [ Help...]│
└─────────────────────────────────┘
```

Figure DDIM.7:
The Colors dialog box.

DDINSERT

R12

Pull down **[DRAW] [INSERT...]**

The DDINSERT command (see fig. DDINSERT.1) displays a dialog box
for inserting blocks and drawing files into the current drawing.

Prompts and Options

The first two lines in the DDINSERT dialog box contain buttons and
companion edit boxes with which you select the block or file to insert.
In the edit boxes you can type specific names. A click on one of the
buttons reveals further dialog boxes with which you may select blocks
or files for insertion. These subsidiary boxes are discussed at length in
the following section.

In the bottom group of the dialog box, you specify the insertion point,
scale and rotation angle of the inserted block or file. At the top of this
group, the check box labeled **S**pecify parameters on screen lets you
toggle between entering insertion point, scale and rotation values in the
dialog box, or on the screen with your mouse or digitizer. The box is
checked by default, leaving the edit boxes greyed out. If you elect to
enter the insertion parameters in the dialog box, click on the check box.
The edit boxes become active.

In the Insertion Point group, click on the **X**, **Y**, or **Z** edit boxes and enter the insertion point coordinates. Do the same in the Scale group to select X, Y and Z scale factors. Click on the **A**ngle edit box in the rotation group and type a rotation angle, in degrees. Below the Options group, a check box lets you specify whether to insert the block exploded into its constituent entities, or as a single block entity. As in previous versions of AutoCAD, you cannot insert a block exploded if you have specified unequal X, Y, or Z scale factors.

```
┌──────────────────────────────────────────────────────┐
│                        Insert                          │
│ Select Block Name                                      │
│   ┌─────────┐ ┌──────────────────────────────────────┐│
│   │ Block...│ │                                      ││
│   └─────────┘ └──────────────────────────────────────┘│
│   ┌─────────┐ ┌──────────────────────────────────────┐│
│   │ File... │ │                                      ││
│   └─────────┘ └──────────────────────────────────────┘│
│ Options                                                │
│   ┌─┐ Specify Parameters on Screen                     │
│   └─┘                                                   │
│   Insertion Point   Scale           Rotation           │
│   X: 0.0000         X: 1.0000       Angle: 0           │
│   Y: 0.0000         Y: 1.0000                           │
│   Z: 0.0000         Z: 1.0000                           │
│   ┌─┐ Explode                                           │
│   └─┘    ┌──────┐   ┌────────┐   ┌────────┐            │
│          │  OK  │   │ Cancel │   │ Help...│            │
│          └──────┘   └────────┘   └────────┘            │
└──────────────────────────────────────────────────────┘
```

Figure DDINSERT.1:
The DDINSERT dialog box.

As mentioned earlier, the first two buttons in the DDINSERT dialog box summon subsidiary dialog boxes. From these you can select insertion blocks that you defined in the current drawing, or other drawing files.

- **Block.** To select a block defined in the current drawing, click on the Block button. The dialog box displayed (see fig. DDINSERT.2) contains, at the top, the **P**attern edit box, into which you may type a text pattern which the block name you are searching for may contain. Typing F*, for example, lists all block names beginning with the letter F. Below the Pattern box, a list box contains the names of all blocks currently defined in the drawing. If they do not all fit on a single screen, a scroll bar on the left side of the list box lets you scroll through the list until you find the needed block. Below the list box, the **S**election edit box provides a place where you may enter a block name directly.

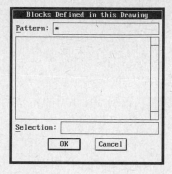

Figure DDINSERT.2:
The DDINSERT Select Block dialog box.

- **File.** To select a drawing file for insertion, click on the File button in the DDINSERT dialog box. The Select Drawing File dialog box (see fig. DDINSERT.3) also begins with a Pattern edit box where you may type a text pattern that the file you seek may contain. The pattern here, however, must end with the extension DWG, as only AutoCAD drawing files can be inserted. Beneath this edit box, AutoCAD informs you of the current directory, where the file search will take place. Next come two list boxes, equipped with scroll bars, if necessary. The list box on the left enables you to change to a different search directory. The box on the right lists drawing files contained in the current directory. You may select a directory on the left, or a drawing file on the right by double-clicking on the desired name, or by highlighting with the keyboard's arrow cursor keys and pressing Enter. To the right, the Type it and Default buttons remain greyed out, as they do not apply to this operation. Below the two list boxes, the File edit box allows you to type in a specific filename.

Related Commands

INSERT
MINSERT

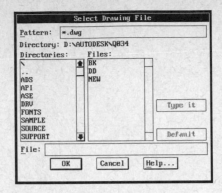

Figure DDINSERT.3:
The DDINSERT Select File dialog box.

Related System Variables

INSBASE
INSNAME

DDLMODES

Screen [LAYER...]

Pull down [Settings] [Layer Control...]

The DDLMODES (Dynamic Dialog Layer MODES) command uses the Layer Control dialog box to manage layer settings. DDLMODES also provides an easy way for you to check layer status. You can use the DDLMODES dialog box to turn layers on or off, lock or unlock layers, freeze or thaw layers, change color or linetype settings, and set a new current layer (see fig. DDLMODES.1).

Prompts and Options

DDLMODES provides no command-line prompts. When the Layer Control dialog box appears, it contains a list of the layers in the current drawing and a group of option buttons. These option buttons perform the following actions:

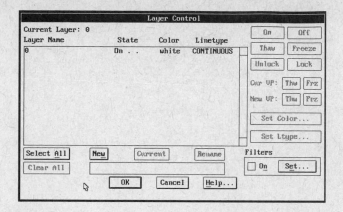

Figure DDLMODES.1:
The DDLMODES dialog box.

- **On.** This option turns selected layers on or off in the current viewport.
- **Off.** This option turns selected layers off in all viewports.
- **Thaw.** The Thaw option changes the status of selected layers from Frozen to Thawed. Layers that are thawed can be turned on and displayed on the screen.
- **Freeze.** This option changes the status of selected layers to Frozen. When a layer is frozen, it cannot be displayed on the screen.
- **Unlock.** Unlocking a layer reverses the Lock setting and enables editing of entities on the selected layer(s).
- **Lock.** Locking a layer prevents any editing of entities on the selected layer(s), as well as preventing any new entities from being placed upon the locked layer.
- **Cur VP Thw.** This option thaws the selected layers in the current viewport only. This option applies only to paper-space viewport entities.
- **Cur VP Frz.** This option freezes the selected layers in the current viewport. This option applies only to paper-space viewport entities.

- **New VP Thw.** This option controls whether the currently selected layers will be thawed in new viewports. This option applies only to paper-space viewport entities.

- **New VP Frz.** This option controls whether the currently selected layers will be frozen in new viewports. This option applies only to paper-space viewport entities.

- **Color.** Use this option to change a layer's color. When this option is selected, AutoCAD displays a dialog box containing color options. Any changes made to the color settings of external reference layers are not saved with the drawing.

- **Linetype.** Use this option to change a layer's linetype. When you select this option, AutoCAD displays a dialog box containing linetype options. Any changes made to the linetype settings of external reference layers are not saved with the drawing.

- **Select All.** This option highlights every layer in the layer list box, which is useful for making changes globally across all drawing layers.

- **Clear All.** This option dehighlights any layer that is currently highlighted in the layer list box.

- **New.** This option creates a new layer using the name you entered into the edit box below this button. If no name has been entered AutoCAD responds Null entry in edit box; or, if the layer exists, AutoCAD responds 1 layer name is duplicated.

- **Current.** This option makes the currently highlighted layer the current drawing layer. All new entities are drawn on this layer. Note that you cannot freeze the current layer from this dialog box, and you cannot make a frozen layer the current drawing layer.

- **Rename.** You can rename a layer by clicking on its existing name and then editing the name. You cannot rename a layer to an existing name, and you cannot rename external reference layer names.

- **Filters.** The Filters option controls which particular layers will be displayed in the Layer Control layer list box. This option has two controls, which perform the following actions:

On. This checkbox controls whether the layer name list box displays all the layers within the drawing or only those that match the selected filter set.

Set. This button displays the Set Layer Filters dialog box (see fig. DDLMODES.2). This dialog box narrows down the number of layers to be displayed in the Layer name list box. You can select only the layers that match a certain layer state (On/Off, Frozen/Thawed, Locked/Unlocked, etc.) or layer name/color/linetype.

```
                 Set Layer Filters
    On/Off:                    Both      ▼
    Freeze/Thaw:               Both      ▼
    Lock/Unlock:               Both      ▼
    Current Vport:             Both      ▼
    New Vports:                Both      ▼
    Layer Names:        *
    Colors:             *
    Ltypes:             *
    ┌─────────────────────────────────────┐
    │               Reset                 │
    └─────────────────────────────────────┘
    ┌────────┐  ┌────────┐   ┌────────┐
    │   OK   │  │ Cancel │   │ Help...│
    └────────┘  └────────┘   └────────┘
```

Figure DDLMODES.2:
The Set Layer Filters dialog box.

The COLOR and LINETYPE commands can override the values of layer color and linetype settings, respectively.

Example

This example uses the TROL1 sample drawing to illustrate how the DDLMODES command works.

Command: **DDLMODES** ↵
Click on the Select All *button*
Click on the Off *button*
Click on the Clear All *button*
Select the WHEEL-PH-2 *layer*
Click on the On *button*

Click on the Set Ltype *button*
Select the CENTER *linetype*
Click on the OK *button*
Click on the OK *button*

Related Commands

LAYER
VPLAYER

Related System Variable

CLAYER

DDMODIFY

Screen **[EDIT] [DDMODFY:]**

Pull down **[MODIFY] [ENTITY...]**

The DDMODIFY command enables you to change the characteristics of AutoCAD entities. At the top of the DDMODIFY dialog box, three buttons give you access to subsidiary dialog boxes, where you can change the chosen entity's color, layer and linetype (see figs. DDCHPROP.2, DDCHPROP.3, and DDCHPROP.4 in the DDCHPROP command summary). In this top section of the dialog box, you also find an edit box into which you can type a new entity thickness.

The rest of the DDMODIFY dialog box varies depending on the type of entity that you choose to modify. Figure DDMODIFY.1 shows the DDMODIFY dialog box that appears when you modify a line.

In the From point and To point edit boxes, you can specify new end-points. Click on the **P**ick Point button to pick a point on the screen with your pointing device, or click on the **X**, **Y**, or **Z** edit boxes to type explicit coordinates. You can modify the following properties of AutoCAD entities by using DDMODIFY:

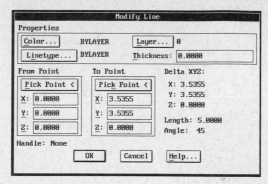

Figure DDMODIFY.1:
The DDMODIFY dialog box for modifying a line.

- **Blocks.** Insertion point; X, Y, and Z scale factors; rotation angle; number of columns and rows, and column and row spacing for blocks inserted with MINSERT.
- **Arcs.** Center point; radius; start angle and end angle.
- **Attdefs.** Tag; prompt; default value; origin point; height; rotation; width; obliquing angle; justification; style; upside down and/or backwards; invisible, constant, preset, and/or verify.
- **Circles.** Center point; radius.
- **Text.** Edit text; other properties same as for Attdefs.
- **Polylines.** Vertex locations; smoothing method; mesh structure; open or closed; application of linetypes.
- **Points.** Location.
- **Shapes.** Origin; size; rotation; width factor; obliquing angle.
- **Solids.** Corner locations.
- **Traces.** Corner locations.
- **3DFaces.** Corner locations, edge visibility.

Related Commands

CHANGE
CHPROP

DDOSNAP

Pull down **[Settings] [Object Snap]**

The DDOSNAP command enables you to set AutoCAD's running object snap modes. Object snaps enable you to manipulate objects and draw accurately by letting you specify points corresponding to the geometric features of a selected entity. To enter a point with object snap, you need only specify an object snap mode and pick any point on an existing entity. AutoCAD calculates the precise point coordinates according to the mode you specified and the object selected. You may set one or more modes to be applied to all point entry, or enter them on the fly at AutoCAD's command option prompts. AutoCAD provides the following object snap modes:

- **Endpoint.** Snaps to the endpoint of a line or arc.
- **Midpoint.** Snaps to the midpoint of a line or arc.
- **Center.** Snaps to the center of an arc or circle (you must pick the arc or circle on its circumference).
- **Node.** Snaps to a point entity.
- **Quadrant.** Snaps to the nearest 0, 90, 180, or 270 degree quadrant point of an arc or circle.
- **Intersection.** Snaps to the intersections of lines, arcs, and circles.
- **Insertion.** Snaps to the insertion point of a block, shape, attribute or text entity.
- **Perpendicular.** Snaps to the point on a line, circle, or arc that is perpendicular from that object to the last point.
- **Tangent.** Snaps to the point on a circle or arc that is tangent to that object from the last point.
- **Nearest.** Snaps to the point on a line, arc, or circle or to a point entity that is visually closest to the crosshairs.
- **Quick.** Snaps to the first point found that corresponds to one of the set of currently selected object snap modes.

Prompts and Options

The DDOSNAP dialog box contains a check box for each object snap mode (see fig. DDOSNAP.1). Click on one or more of the boxes to select the modes that you wish to remain active. At the bottom of the box, a horizontal scroll bar allows you to dynamically set the size of the *pickbox*, a small square that appears at the intersection of the crosshairs when you activate an object snap mode. An entity to which you want to snap must cross the boundary of the pickbox when you select the entity for the object snap to take affect.

DDOSNAP is a transparent command. You may run it by typing 'DDOSNAP while using another command. This **TIP** feature is convenient for setting object snap modes on the fly, when you do not know ahead of time which ones will be the most useful.

Figure DDOSNAP.1:
The DDOSNAP dialog box.

Related Command

OSNAP

Related System Variable

OSMODE

DDRENAME

Screen **[Utility] [Rename:] [Rename Dialogue]**

With the DDRENAME dialog box, you can rename blocks, dimension styles, layers, linetypes, text styles, UCS configurations, views, and viewport configurations.

Prompts and Options

At the top of the DDRENAME dialog box (see fig. DDRENAME.1) are two list boxes.

- **Named Objects.** On the left side, the **N**amed Objects list box shows the categories of objects you can rename.
- **Items.** On the right side, the **I**tems list box displays the name of each item in that category that the current drawing holds. For example, when you click on Layer in the Named Objects box, the Items box shows the name of every layer in the drawing. If the layer names do not all fit on one screen, use the scroll bar to view others.

  To rename an item, first pick the kind of item you want to rename from the Named Objects list box. Then pick a specific item from the Items list box. The name of the item that you just picked appears in the **O**ld Name edit box below the two list boxes. Click on the **R**ename To edit box and type the item's new name. AutoCAD accepts item names up to 31 characters in length, and their names may contain letters, digits, $ (dollar sign), - (hyphen), and _ (underscore).

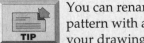 You can rename groups of items that contain the same text pattern with a single DDRENAME command. If, for example, your drawing contained a series of text styles called SIM-PLEX-1, SIMPLEX-2, SIMPLEX-3, SIMPLEX-4, and SIMPLEX-5, and you wanted to rename them all to ROMANS-1...ROMANS-5, you would type SIMPLEX* in the Old Name edit box and ROMANS* in the Rename To edit box.

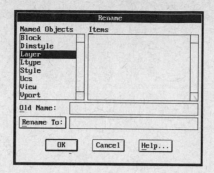

Figure DDRENAME.1:
The DDRENAME dialog box.

Related Command

RENAME

DDRMODES

Screen **[SETTINGS] [DDRMODES]**

Pull down **[Settings] [Drawing Aids...]**

DDRMODES (Dynamic Dialog dRawing MODES) controls drawing mode settings—snap, grid, blips, ortho, axis, and isoplane—by using a dialog box (see fig. DDRMODES.1). DDRMODES also is useful when you need to check the current status of the various drawing-mode settings.

Prompts and Options

DDRMODES provides no command-line prompts. Instead, you make selections from the following dialog box options:

- **Ortho.** This checkbox is used to turn Ortho mode on or off.
- **Solid Fill.** This checkbox is used to notify AutoCAD whether solids and thickened polylines are filled or only their edges are shown.

Figure DDRMODES.1:
The DDRMODES dialog box.

- **Quick Text**. This checkbox notifies AutoCAD to display text normally or as a boundary box showing the limits of the text. If the box is not checked, text displays normally.

- **Blips.** This checkbox is used to notify AutoCAD to place "blips" at every point where a point is picked in the drawing editor.

- **Highlight.** This checkbox is used to notify AutoCAD to display the entities chosen for selection sets with a temporary dashed linetype.

- **Snap.** The Snap options are used to turn Snap mode on or off, and to change the snap spacing (the default is 1), snap angle (default 0), and snap base (default 0,0).

- **Grid.** This option turns the drawing grid on or off (the default is off) and changes the grid spacing (the default is 0).

- **Isometric.** This option turns isometric drawing mode on or off and determines which isometric plane is currently in use. The default value is off.

Example

This example uses the TABLET-A sample drawing to illustrate how the DDRMODES command works.

Command: **DDRMODES** ↵
Press the Quick Text *button*
Press the OK *button*
Command: **REGEN** ↵

Related Commands

BLIPMODE
GRID
ORTHO
SNAP

Related System Variables

BLIPMODE
COORDS
GRIDMODE
GRIDUNIT
ORTHOMODE
SNAPANG
SNAPBASE
SNAPISOPAIR
SNAPMODE
SNAPSTYL
SNAPUNIT

DDSELECT

Pull down **[SETTINGS] [SELECTION SETTINGS...]**

The DDSELECT dialog box enables you to tell AutoCAD which entity selection modes to use when forming a selection set of entities that you want to edit (see fig. DDSELECT.1).

Prompts and Options

At the top of the DDSELECT dialog box, four check boxes appear beside the four entity selection options that AutoCAD offers. You may pick one, all, or any combination of these options.

- **Noun/Verb Selection**. If you pick the first option, **N**oun/Verb Selection, you can select entities in the drawing, and then select the command with which you wish to edit the entities. A small square, the *pickbox*, appears at the intersection of the crosshairs when this entity selection method is active.

- **Use Shift to Add**. **U**se Shift to Add dictates how additional entities are added to the selection set after you have chosen the first entity or entities. With Use Shift to Add selected, you hold down the Shift key to add more entities to the selection set. To remove entities from the selection set, hold down the Shift key and pick already selected entities. If you do not choose Use Shift to Add, you select entities as in previous versions of AutoCAD, although you can still use the Shift key method to remove entities from the selection set.

- **Click and Drag**. If you pick **C**lick and Drag, you can draw entity selection windows and crossing boxes by picking one corner and then dragging the mouse while continuing to depress the pointing device's button. When you have drawn the desired window, release the button and the entities contained within the window or that cross the window's boundaries are selected. With Click and Drag deactivated, you must make two picks with your pointing device to select the opposite corner of the window or crossing box.

 With Click and Drag activated, you can easily clear a selection set by clicking once on a blank area of the screen.

- **Implied Windowing**. If you activate **I**mplied Windowing, you can create either an entity selection window or crossing box at a Select objects: prompt. After you pick the first corner, drag the pointing device from left to right to form a window, or from right to left to form a crossing box. With Implied Windowing turned off, you must type a **w** or a **c** at the Select objects: prompt to initiate a window or a crossing box.

Beneath these four options, the button labeled **D**efault Selection Mode resets the modes to their default: Use Shift to Add and Implied Windowing selected. Beneath the default button, a horizontal scroll bar lets you dynamically adjust the size of the pickbox, from one to 20 pixels. Beneath the pickbox size scroll bar, the button labeled **E**ntity Sort Method displays a subsidiary dialog box where you may select the situations under which AutoCAD sorts entities in the order in which they appear in the drawing's database.

The **E**ntity Sort Method dialog box contains seven check boxes in which you may click to tell AutoCAD when to sort entities: **O**bject Selection, Object **S**nap, **R**edraws, S**l**ide Creation, R**e**gens, **P**lotting, and PostS**c**ript Output (see fig. DDSELECT.2).

Figure DDSELECT.1:
The DDSELECT dialog box.

Figure DDSELECT.2:
The Entity Sort Method dialog box.

Related Command

SELECT

Related System Variables

SORTENTS
TREEDEPH
TREEMAX

DDUCS

Screen [UCS:] [DDUCS:]

Pull down [Settings] [UCS >] [Named UCS...]

Pull down [Settings] [UCS >] [Preset...]

DDUCS (Dynamic Dialog User Coordinate Systems) controls User Coordinate Systems (UCSs) through a dialog box. You can change the current UCS, rename a previously defined UCS, list the specifications of a UCS, and delete a UCS through the DDUCS dialog box (see fig. DDUCS.1).

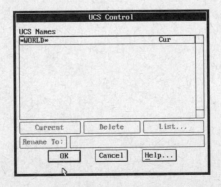

Figure DDUCS.1:
The DDUCS dialog box.

Prompts and Options

This command provides no command-line prompts. When the dialog box appears, it displays a list of currently defined user coordinate systems and several option buttons. The dialog box buttons perform the following options:

- **Current.** The currently highlighted UCS in the list box becomes the current UCS.
- **Delete.** Click on the Delete button to delete the currently highlighted UCS. Note that you cannot delete the *WORLD* or *PREVIOUS* coordinate systems.
- **List.** This option displays the coordinate system's origin and the direction of the X, Y, and Z axes in relation to the current UCS.
- **Rename To.** This option renames the currently highlighted UCS to the name you enter into the adjacent edit box. You cannot rename the *WORLD* or *PREVIOUS* coordinate systems.

Related Command

UCS

Related System Variables

UCSFOLLOW
UCSICON
UCSNAME.
UCSORG
UCSXDIR
UCSYDIR
WORLDUCS

DDUNITS

Screen **[SETTINGS] [next] [UNITS:] [DDUNITS]**

Pull down **[Settings] [Units Control...]**

121

AutoCAD allows for the display of coordinates, distances, and angles in several formats, so that, depending upon your trade, you can measure and notate in the most appropriate format. You set the format with the DDUNITS command. The main features of the DDUNITS dialog box (see fig. DDUNITS.1) are two sets of radio buttons. On the left, the Units buttons set the format used for distances and measurement. AutoCAD provides the following options:

- **S̲cientific.** Format 0.0000E+01, showing decimal distances with exponent.
- **De̲cimal.** Format 0.0000, showing distances in decimal with no associated units of measure.
- **E̲ngineering.** Format 0'-0.0000", showing feet and decimal inches.
- **A̲rchitectural.** Format 0'-0/0", showing feet and fractional inches.
- **F̲ractional.** Format 0 0/0, showing fractional distances with no associated units of measure.

Beneath the radio buttons, a pop-up list box enables you to set your desired level of precision.

The radio buttons on the right of the dialog box enable you to choose how AutoCAD measures angles. AutoCAD offers the following choices:

- **De̲cimal Degrees.** Format 0.0000, simple decimal numbers.
- **Deg/M̲in/Sec.** Format 0d0'0.0000', with 'd' indicating degrees, ''' indicating minutes, and '"' indicating seconds.
- **G̲rads.** Format 0.0000g, decimal numbers with the appended 'g' indicating grads.
- **R̲adians.** Format 0.0000r, decimal numbers with the appended 'r' indicating radians.
- **Sur̲veyor.** Format N or S 0d0'0.0000" E or W. The angle between N/S and E/W indicates the distance east or west from north or south. When the angle points in a cardinal direction, AutoCAD shows only the compass point, for example E for 0°.

As with the units section of the dialog box, a pop-up list box beneath the radio buttons enables you to set the precision of the angle's measurement.

Figure DDUNITS.1:
The DDUNITS dialog box.

Prompts and Options

At the bottom of the dialog box, the **D**irection button causes AutoCAD to display a subsidiary dialog box from which you choose the direction that equals angle 0 (see fig. DDUNITS.2). You may choose from **E**ast (default), **N**orth, **W**est, **S**outh, or **O**ther. If you choose Other, the **A**ngle edit box and **P**ick < button highlight. You may type an angle in the edit box, or show an angle with your pointing device by picking two points on-screen. Beneath the Pick < button, two additional radio buttons enable you to choose whether AutoCAD measures angles in the **C**ounter-Clockwise or C**l**ockwise direction.

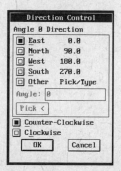

Figure DDUNITS.2:
The Direction Control dialog box.

The angle specified for object rotations is measured independently of the angle zero base. An unrotated object always has a zero rotation. Orientation angles are always measured from the angle zero base. If you choose angle zero to point south, a horizontal line of text is considered to be oriented to 180°.

Related Command

UNITS

Related System Variables

ANGDIR
AUNITS
AUPREC
ANGBASE
LUNITS
LUPREC

DDVIEW

Screen **[DISPLAY] [VIEW] [View Dialogue]**

Pull down **[View] [Set View] [Named View...]**

AutoCAD provides the means to save particular drawing views for later recall. This feature enables you to restore a precise display of a drawing or 3D viewpoint that you intend to use frequently. The DDVIEW command enables you to restore, create, delete, and obtain information about views.

Prompts and Options

The top of the dialog box (see fig. DDVIEW.1) contains a list box showing the names of all of the drawing's saved views. If not all views will fit on a single screen, a scroll bar appears with which you can see other view names.

Beneath the list box, the Restore View: line tells which view AutoCAD restores when you click on the **R**estore button. To restore a view, click on a view name in the list box. Then click on Restore, and, finally, click OK. You also can delete a saved view by clicking on the view name in the list box and then clicking on the **D**elete button. You are not warned before AutoCAD deletes the view, so be sure that you want the view deleted before you click on the button. The other two buttons in the dialog box display subsidiary dialog boxes in which you can create new views and view information about saved views.

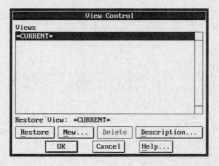

Figure DDVIEW.1:
The DDVIEW dialog box.

- **New.** In the dialog box that appears when you click on the New button, you configure and save new views. At the top of the dialog box, you type the name of the new view in the **N**ew Name edit box. Beneath the edit box, two radio buttons, **C**urrent Display and **D**efine Window, provide the choice to save the current drawing editor display as the new view, or to specify a window that constitutes the view. When you click on Define Window, the **W**indow < button and the First Corner and Other Corner boxes highlight. Click on the button to define the view's window. AutoCAD temporarily removes the dialog boxes so that you can draw the window. After the dialog boxes return, the First Corner and Other Corner boxes display the X and Y coordinates of the two corners. Click on **S**ave View to save the view (see fig. DDVIEW.2).

125

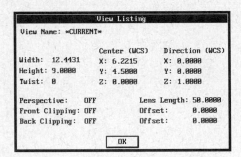

Figure DDVIEW.2:
The Define New View dialog box.

Description. When you click on the display button, an information dialog box appears showing information about the currently selected view (see fig. DDVIEW.3). This box shows the view name and the X, Y, and Z coordinates of the width, height, and twist values of the view's centerpoint and the view direction. Also displayed are the status of perspective, front clipping and back clipping, and the current lens length and the offset values for the front and back clipping planes.

Figure DDVIEW.3:
The View Listing dialog box.

Related Command

VIEW

Related System Variables

VIEWCTR
VIEWDIR
VIEWMODE
VIEWSIZE
VIEWTWIST

DELAY

DELAY is a special command for use with AutoCAD script files. DE-LAY programs a delay (measured approximately in milliseconds) in a script. You can cancel the delay by pressing any key.

Use the DELAY command as part of an AutoCAD script. Use the following command syntax:

`DELAY number`

In this generic syntax, **number** is the approximate length of the delay in milliseconds. The maximum delay number you can specify is 32,767.

For more information on DELAY, see the SCRIPT command, later in the Reference Guide.

Related Commands

SCRIPT

DIM/DIM1

Screen **[DIM:]**

Pull down **[Draw] [Dimensions>]**

The DIM and DIM1 commands enable you to enter AutoCAD's dimensioning mode, which is distinguished from the regular command mode

127

by the `Dim:` prompt. Dimensioning mode is used to draw dimensions in your drawings.

When you use the DIM command, you enter dimensioning mode and remain there until you issue the Exit dimensioning command or press Ctrl-C. When you use the DIM1 command, you remain in dimensioning mode only for a single dimensioning command and then immediately return to normal command mode. In dimensioning mode, AutoCAD's non-dimensioning commands (except for transparent commands, such as 'ZOOM and 'PAN) are not available.

While AutoCAD is in dimensioning mode, you can use any of AutoCAD's 27 dimensioning subcommands. The following pages of this Command Reference describe each dimensioning command in detail:

ALIGNED	HOMETEXT	RADIUS	TEDIT
ANGULAR	HORIZONTAL	REDRAW	TROTATE
BASELINE	LEADER	RESTORE	UNDO
CENTER	NEWTEXT	ROTATED	UPDATE
CONTINUE	OBLIQUE	SAVE	VARIABLES
DIAMETER	ORDINATE	STATUS	VERTICAL
EXIT	OVERRIDE	STYLE	

If you issue a single UNDO command at AutoCAD's `Command:` prompt after you exit dimensioning mode, you will cancel *all* the commands issued during a single dimensioning session. Therefore, if you enter dimensioning mode, draw several dimensions with dimensioning commands, exit from dimensioning mode, and issue the UNDO command, all the dimensions are undone. Similarly, you can issue a single REDO command to restore all the undone dimensions.

A few of the dimensioning commands have the same names as regular AutoCAD commands. You should be careful not to confuse these dimensioning commands with the general AutoCAD commands, such as REDRAW, SAVE, STATUS, STYLE, and UNDO. Some of the commands, such as REDRAW and UNDO, perform similar or identical functions in normal drawing mode and dimensioning mode. Others, however, are noticeably different.

AutoCAD creates dimensions in two types, *associative* and *non-associative*. Associative dimensions are special blocks that are linked to the entities in your drawing. If you stretch, scale, or modify dimensioned elements, the dimensions are automatically updated to reflect the new dimension value. Associative dimensions are enabled by setting the value of the DIMASO variable to 1 (ON). Non-associative dimensions are simply arrowheads, lines, and text, and they do not reflect any changes you make to the entities in your drawing. Non-associative dimensions are created when the DIMASO variable is set to 0.

When using paper space, you should keep associative dimensions in model space. No link exists between entities across the two areas of the drawing. Therefore, if your model changes, dimension entities created in paper space will not be updated along with your model.

Prompts and Options

After you issue the DIM or DIM1 command, the following prompt appears:

- `Dim:`

  At this prompt, enter the name of the DIM subcommand you want to use.

The Dimension Elements

Each dimension that is created by a dimension command contains certain elements. This is independent of whether the dimension is created as associative (DIMASO is set ON) or normal. As shown in figure DIM.1, there are four distinctive parts of a dimension. These parts are as follows:

① **Dimension Text.** Typically, this is the value measured by the dimension command. This text can be overridden by entering a different value, or it can be supplemented with prefix and suffix text. You can add prefix or suffix text by entering a new value and the characters "<>". These characters are used to indicate the dimension value retrieved by the dimension command.

129

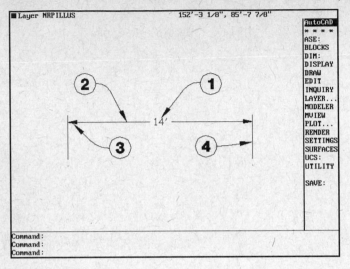

Figure DIM.1:
The basic dimension and its component parts.

②   **Dimension Line.** This line, or an arc for angular dimensions, delineates the extents of the distance.

③   **Dimension Arrow.** These are placed at both ends of the dimension line. You also can use a specialized block or a tick mark for your dimension arrows.

④   **Extension Line.** These lines lead from the points you choose to dimension, and extend beyond the dimension line.

Related Command

DDIM

Related System Variables

For a list of AutoCAD's dimensioning variables, see *Inside AutoCAD Release 12.*

Dim: ALIGNED

Screen **[DIM:] [Aligned]**

Pull down **[Draw] [Dimensions >] [Linear >] [Aligned]**

This dimensioning command draws a linear dimension parallel to a selected entity or parallel to two extension line origin points. Use this command when you need to dimension a feature that is not orthogonal and you want extension lines of equal length. When you pick an entity to dimension or two origin points, the ALIGNED command places the dimension line parallel to the entity or points and through a third point that you specify. You can abbreviate the ALIGNED command as AL.

To create angled dimensions with unequal extension lines or for dimensions at specific angles, use the ROTATED command to specify a dimension line angle.

Prompts and Options

- **First extension line origin or RETURN to select:**

  Pick a point at one end of the entity or feature that you want to dimension. AutoCAD prompts for the Second extension line origin. The extension lines are drawn perpendicular to the angle between the first and second extension line origins.

- **Select line, arc, or circle:**

  This prompt appears if you press Enter at the First extension line origin or RETURN to select: prompt. Select a line, polyline, arc, or circle; extension lines are located for you. If you select a line, polyline segment, or arc, AutoCAD dimensions the end points. If you select a circle, the diameter is dimensioned from the pick point to the diameter point on the opposite side. AutoCAD dimensions only the selected segment of a polyline.

- **Second extension line origin:**

  Pick a point at the opposite end of the entity or feature. The extension lines are drawn perpendicular to the angle between the first and second extension line origin points.

131

- **Dimension line location (Text/Angle):**

  Pick the point through which you want the dimension line to pass. AutoCAD uses the point to determine the offset distance between the selected object or pick points and the dimension line.

  If you use either of the (Text/Angle) options, one of the following prompts appears:

- **Enter text angle:**

  Your response to this prompt modifies the angle at which the dimension text is drawn. If you press Enter at this prompt, the text is drawn at the default text angle.

- **Dimension text <default>:**

  AutoCAD calculates the distance between the two extension line origin points you pick or between the two points derived from the object you select. AutoCAD then offers the distance (in the current drawing units and precision) as the default dimension text value. You can accept this value (press Enter), specify a new value, suppress any text by typing a space, or apply prefix or suffix text to the value (see the DIM/DIM1 command).

Example

AutoCAD offers two ways to create an aligned dimension: you can select an entity or pick both extension line origins. This example demonstrates both of these methods using the drawing shown in figure ALIGNED.1.

```
Command: DIM↵
Dim: ALIGNED↵
First extension line origin or RETURN to select: ↵
Select line, arc, or circle: Pick entity pointed to by ①
Dimension line location (Text/Angle): Pick point pointed to by ②
Dimension text <15'-4 1/4">: ↵
Dim: ALIGNED↵
First extension line origin or RETURN to select: Pick point ③
Second extension line origin: Pick point ④
Dimension line location (Text/Angle): A↵Pick point ⑤
Enter text angle: END of ③
Second point: END of ④
Dimension line location(Text/Angle):
Dimension text <15'-4 1/4">: ↵
```

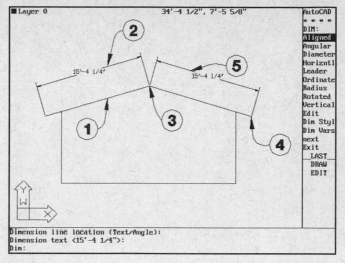

Figure ALIGNED.1:
The selection points used to create the aligned dimensions.

Related Commands

DDIM
Dim: ROTATED

Related System Variables

For a list of AutoCAD's dimensioning variables, see *Inside AutoCAD Release 12.*

Dim: ANGULAR

Screen [DIM:] [Angular]

Pull down [Draw] [Dimensions >] [Angular]

The ANGULAR dimensioning command dimensions the angle between two non-parallel lines, the angle swept by an arc or around part of a

133

circle, or the angle between any three points (one of which is a vertex of the angle to be dimensioned). The ANGULAR command creates a dimension arc instead of a dimension line, with non-parallel extension lines as needed. You can dimension either the inside or outside of major, minor, or complementary angles. You can abbreviate the ANGU-LAR command as AN.

Prompts and Options

- `Select arc, circle, line, or RETURN:`

  Pick an arc, circle, line, or polyline segment for AutoCAD to dimension. If you select an arc, AutoCAD automatically locates the end points for the origin of the extension lines. If you select a circle, the point by which you picked the circle becomes the first extension line origin, and then the `Second angle end point:` prompt appears. If you select a line, AutoCAD considers the line to be one side of an angle you want to dimension and prompts with `Second line:` for you to pick the second line of the angle to dimension.

  Press Enter at the `Select arc, circle, line, or RETURN` prompt to tell AutoCAD that you want to specify three points describing an angle for dimensioning. The three points do not need to be on existing geometry.

- `Angle vertex:`

  If you want to dimension an angle by three points, this prompt asks you to enter a point for the vertex of the angle.

- `First angle endpoint:`

  This prompt displays when you dimension an angle by three points. Pick a point along one side of the angle to dimension.

- `Second angle endpoint:`

  This prompt displays when you dimension an angle by three points or when you pick a circle at the initial prompt. Pick a point along the second side of the angle to dimension.

- **Second line:**

  If you pick a line at the initial prompt, this prompt asks you for the second line to describe the angle for dimensioning.

- **Dimension arc line location (Text/Angle):**

  For all angular dimension methods, pick the point through which you want the dimension line arc to pass. AutoCAD uses the point you pick to calculate the offset distance between your selected object or feature and the dimension line arc.

  You can dimension the angle between two lines or the complementary angle (180 degrees, less the angle between the lines), or the inside (minor—under 180 degrees) or outside (major—over 180 degrees) angle of an arc, three points, or points on a circle. The point you pick for the dimension arc location controls which angle is dimensioned.

  If you use either of the (Text/Angle) options, you will see one of the following prompts:

- **Dimension text <default>:**

  AutoCAD calculates the distance between the two extension line origin points you pick or between the two points derived from the object you select. AutoCAD then offers the distance (in the current drawing units and precision) as the default dimension text value. You can accept this value (press Enter), specify a new value, suppress any text by typing a space, or apply prefix or suffix text to the value (see the DIM/DIM1 command).

- **Enter text angle:**

  This prompt modifies the angle at which the dimension text is drawn. If you press Enter, the text is drawn at the default text angle.

- **Enter text location (or RETURN):**

  You can locate the text along the dimension arc or place it inside or outside the dimension arc. This prompt enables you to position the text as you require. If you press Enter, the text is placed along the dimension arc.

135

Examples

These examples demonstrate the steps needed to perform common angular dimensioning tasks. The drawing in figure ANGULAR.1 shows the points you pick to create an angular dimension by choosing line entities and by selecting three points that define an angle.

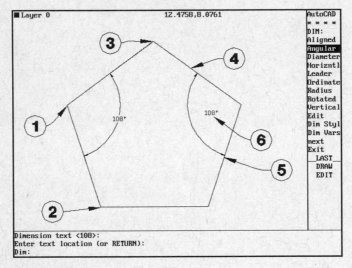

Figure ANGULAR.1:
Dimensioning inside a minor angle between two lines.

```
Command: DIM↵
Dim: ANGULAR↵
Select arc, circle, line, or RETURN: ↵
Angle vertex: END of ①
First angle endpoint: END of ②
Second angle endpoint: END of ③
Dimension arc line location (Text/Angle): MID of Pick line between ① and ②
Dimension text <108>: ↵
Enter text location: ↵
Dim: ANGULAR
Select arc, circle, line, or RETURN: ④
Second line: ⑤
```

```
Dimension arc line location (Text/Angle): ⑤
Dimension text <108>: ↵
Enter text location: ⑥
```

Related Command

DDIM

Related System Variables

For a list of AutoCAD's dimensioning variables, see *Inside AutoCAD Release 12*.

Dim: BASELINE

Screen **[DIM:] [next] [Baseline]**

Pull down **[Draw] [Dimensions >] [Linear >] [Baseline]**

The BASELINE dimensioning command enables you to use one existing linear dimension as the basis for one or more new dimensions. All new dimensions are based on the first extension line of the existing dimension. Each new dimension is created by specifying a new second extension line origin point. The BASELINE command offsets the new dimension line from the previous one and draws a new extended first extension line over the existing first extension line. You can abbreviate the BASELINE command as B.

Baseline dimensions can be created at any time after an initial linear dimension is created. You can select an existing linear dimension for the basis of new baseline dimensions. You must pick the dimension nearest to the end with the extension line you want used as the first extension line. The BASELINE command offsets each new dimension line by the dimension line increment value stored in the DIMDLI dimension variable. Changing the value of DIMDLI or updating existing dimensions with the UPDATE command has no effect on dimensions already placed in your drawing.

Prompts and Options

- **Second extension line origin or RETURN to select:**

  This prompt displays if the last dimension you created was a linear dimension or after you select a base dimension. The first extension line of the last dimension is considered the first extension line of subsequent dimensions unless you press Enter to select another extension line. Press Enter if you want to select a dimension other than the last one created.

- **Select base dimension:**

  This prompt displays if the last dimension created was not a linear dimension. To select the dimension to use as the base for subsequent dimensions, select it near the end that you want to use for the first extension line.

- **Dimension text <default>:**

  AutoCAD calculates the distance between the two extension line origin points you pick or between the two points derived from the object you select. AutoCAD then offers the distance (in the current drawing units and precision) as the default dimension text value. You can accept this value (press Enter), specify a new value, suppress any text by typing a space, or apply prefix or suffix text to the value (see the DIM/DIM1 command).

Example

This example demonstrates the steps necessary to create baseline dimensions from an existing horizontal dimension. The points used to create the dimensions are shown in figure BASELINE.1.

```
Command: DIM↵
Dim: HORIZONTAL↵
First extension line origin or RETURN to select: INT of ①
Second extension line origin: INT of ②
Dimension line location: ③
Dimension text <15'-4">: ↵
Dim: BASELINE ↵
Second extension line origin or RETURN to select: INT of ④
Dimension text <27'-4">: ↵
```

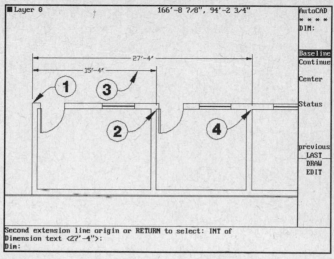

Figure BASELINE.1:
Baseline dimensions created using the BASELINE command.

Related Command

CONTINUE

Related System Variables

DDIM
DIMDLI

Dim: CENTER

Screen [DIM:] [next] [Center]

Pull down [Draw] [Dimensions >] [Radial >] [Center Mark]

The CENTER dimensioning command creates center marks or center lines at the center points of circles, arcs, or polyline arc segments. You can abbreviate the CENTER command as CE.

139

Center marks or lines created by the CENTER command are individual
line entities. Center marks are drawn twice the length of the positive
value of the dimension variable DIMCEN. If DIMCEN is set to a negative number, center lines are also drawn, extending the length of
DIMCEN beyond the circle or arc. If DIMCEN is set to 0, AutoCAD
disables center marks or center lines.

Prompts and Options

- **Select arc or circle:**

  Select the arc or circle to be dimensioned at any point.

Examples

The following example demonstrates the CENTER command for adding
center marks to an arc or circle. The mark created for a typical circle is shown
in figure CENTER.1.

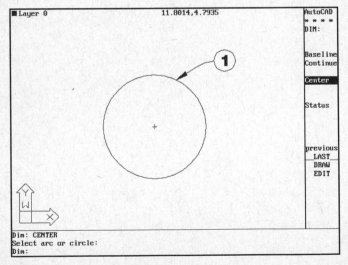

Figure CENTER.1:
The center mark created using the CENTER command.

```
Command: DIM↵
Dim: CENTER↵
Select arc or circle: Pick the circle
```

Related Commands

Dim: DIAMETER
Dim: RADIUS

Related System Variable

DIMCEN

Dim: CONTINUE

Screen [DIM:] [next] [Continue]

Pull down [Draw] [Dimensions >] [Linear >] [Continue]

The CONTINUE dimensioning command enables you to use one existing linear dimension as the basis for a set of dimensions aligned end-to-end (otherwise known as continuous dimensions). The CONTINUE command can be abbreviated as CO.

You can create continuous dimensions at any time after creating an initial linear dimension. If you start the CONTINUE command immediately after completing a linear dimension, AutoCAD treats the second extension line origin point of the previous dimension as the second extension line origin point of each new dimension. If you select an existing linear dimension for the basis of new continuous dimensions, you must pick the dimension nearest to the end with the extension line you want to use as the first extension line of subsequent dimensions.

In most cases, the CONTINUE command aligns each new dimension line with the last. If the dimension's text would otherwise overwrite the previous continued dimension's text, the CONTINUE command offsets the new dimension line by the dimension line increment value stored in the DIMDLI dimension variable.

141

Prompts and Options

- **Second extension line origin or RETURN to select:**

  This prompt displays if the last dimension you created is a linear dimension or after you select a base dimension. The second extension line of the last dimension becomes the first extension line of subsequent dimensions, unless you press Enter to select a different extension line. Press Enter also if you want to select a dimension other than the last one you created.

- **Select continued dimension:**

  This prompt displays if the last dimension you create is not a linear dimension. Select the dimension to use as the basis for subsequent dimensions near the end that you want to use for the first extension line.

- **Dimension text <default>:**

  AutoCAD calculates the distance between the two extension line origin points you pick or between the two points derived from the object you select. AutoCAD then offers the distance (in the current drawing units and precision) as the default dimension text value. You can accept this value (press Enter), specify a new value, suppress any text by typing a space, or apply prefix or suffix text to the value (see the DIM/DIM1 command).

Examples

This example demonstrates the steps necessary to create continuous dimensions (see figure CONTINUE.1).

```
Command: DIM↵
Dim: CONTINUE↵
Second extension line origin or RETURN to select: ↵
Select continued dimension: Pick point ①
Second extension line origin or RETURN to select: INT of ②
Dimension text <12'>: ↵
```

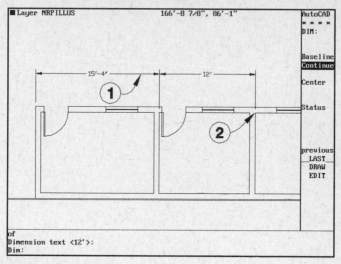

Figure CONTINUE.1:
Using the CONTINUE command.

Related Command

BASELINE

Related System Variables

DDIM
DIMDLI

Dim: DIAMETER

Screen **[DIM:] [Diameter]**

Pull down **[Draw] [Dimensions >] [Radial >] [Diameter]**

The DIAMETER dimensioning command dimensions the diameters of circles, arcs, and polyline arc segments. You can abbreviate the DIAMETER command as D.

143

AutoCAD can produce several variations of dimensions for diameters. These variations depend on the value of the system variables DIMTIX (Text Inside eXtension lines), DIMTOFL (Text Outside, Force dimension Line inside), and DIMCEN (CENter marks and lines). If both the DIMTOFL and DIMTIX variables are set to 0 (off), a leader is drawn to the dimension text from the point by which you picked the entity. The leader is drawn dynamically so that you can place the text for best readability. When DIMTOFL alone is on (1), AutoCAD places the dimension text outside the arc or circle, as in the previous style, and draws a dimension line through the diameter of the entity. When both DIMTOFL and DIMTIX are on, AutoCAD omits the leader and places the dimension text within the dimension line.

If the dimension variable DIMCEN is positive, a center mark is placed at the center point; if it is 0, no mark is placed; and if it is negative, center lines and marks are drawn. If the dimension text is placed at the center of the arc or circle, the center marks and lines are not drawn.

Dimension text for the DIAMETER command always begins with the diameter symbol (equivalent to %%c) by default.

Prompts and Options

- **Select arc or circle:**

  Pick the arc or circle to dimension. The point you pick determines the location of the dimension line or leader.

- **Dimension text <default>:**

  AutoCAD calculates the distance between the two extension line origin points you pick or between the two points derived from the object you select. AutoCAD then offers the distance (in the current drawing units and precision) as the default dimension text value. You can accept this value (press Enter), specify a new value, suppress any text by typing a space, or apply prefix or suffix text to the value (see the DIM/DIM1 command).

- **Enter leader length for text:**

  If dimension text is placed outside the circle or arc (as defined by the DIMTIX variable), you can drag the length of the dimension leader into place or enter a length at the keyboard. If you press Enter instead of dragging, AutoCAD draws a minimum length leader.

Examples

The following examples demonstrate the three styles of diameter dimensioning. The dimensions that these examples produce are shown in figure DIAMETER.1.

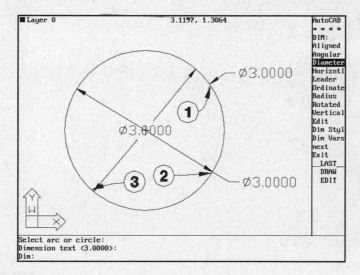

Figure DIAMETER.1:
Dimensioning with the DIAMETER command.

```
Command: DIM↵
Dim: DIMTIX↵
Current value <Off> New value: OFF
Dim: DIMTOFL
Current value <Off> New value: OFF
Dim: DIAMETER↵
Select arc or circle: Pick point ① (see fig. DIAMETER.1)
```

```
Dimension text <3.00>: ↵
Enter leader length for text: ↵
Dim: DIMTOFL↵
Current value <Off> New value: ON
Dim: DIAMETER↵
Select arc or circle: Pick point ② (see fig. DIAMETER.1)
Dimension text <3.00>: ↵
Enter leader length for text: ↵
Dim: DIMTIX↵
Current value <Off> New value: ON↵
Dim: DIAMETER↵
Select arc or circle: Pick point ③ (see fig. DIAMETER.1)
Dimension text <3.00>: ↵
```

Related Commands

CENTER
DDIM
RADIUS

Related System Variables

DIMTIX
DIMTOFL
DIMCEN

Dim: EXIT

Screen **[DIM:] [Exit]**

The EXIT dimensioning command terminates the dimensioning mode and restores command mode. You can also enter Ctrl-C at the DIM: prompt to terminate the dimensioning mode. The EXIT command can be abbreviated as E.

Example

The following example demonstrates how to use the EXIT command to return to AutoCAD's command mode.

```
Dim: EXIT↵
Command: ↵
```

Dim: HOMETEXT

Screen **[DIM:] [Edit] [HOMETEXT]**

Pull down **[Modify] [Edit Dims >] [Dimension Text >] [Home Position]**

The HOMETEXT dimensioning command restores one or more associative dimension text entities to their default (home) positions after they have been altered by the TEDIT, TROTATE, or STRETCH commands. If the dimension was not created with a named dimension style, AutoCAD updates the dimension with the current dimension variable settings. The HOMETEXT command can be abbreviated as HOM.

Prompts and Options

- **Select objects:**

  Select the dimension(s) to restore text to the default position(s). You can pick dimensions by any selection method and by any dimension component: extension lines, dimension line, arrowheads, or text.

Example

The following example takes the text of an associative dimension and return it to its original position. Figure HOMETEXT.1 shows the dimension text before using the HOMETEXT command (in the upper frame) and after using HOMETEXT.

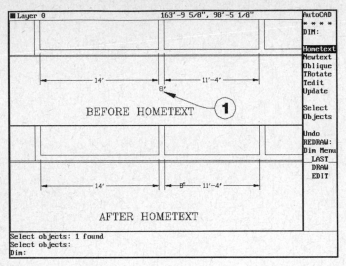

Figure HOMETEXT.1:
Dimension text being returned to its home position.

```
Command: DIM↵
Dim: HOMETEXT↵
Select objects: Pick point ①
Select objects: ↵
```

Related Command

NEWTEXT

Related System Variables

DIMASO
DIMSTYLE

Dim: HORIZONTAL

Screen [DIM:] [Horizntl]

Pull down [Draw] [Dimensions >] [Linear >] [Horizontal]

The HORIZONTAL dimensioning command draws dimensions with a horizontal dimension line. The extension line origin points need not have the same Y coordinates. The HORIZONTAL command can be abbreviated as HOR.

Prompts and Options

- **First extension line origin or RETURN to Select:**

  Pick a point at one end of the entity or feature to be dimensioned. AutoCAD prompts for the Second extension line origin:. The extension lines are offset from the points you pick by the current value of the dimension variable DIMEXO. The extension lines are drawn vertically, regardless of the angle between the first and second extension line origin points.

- **Select line, arc, or circle:**

  This prompt appears if you press Enter at the First extension line origin or RETURN to select: prompt. Pick a line, polyline, arc, or circle; extension lines are located for you. If you select a line, polyline segment, or arc, AutoCAD dimensions its end points. If you select a circle, the diameter is dimensioned between the 0- and 180-degree quadrant points. AutoCAD dimensions only the selected segment of an open polyline.

- **Second extension line origin:**

  Pick a point at the opposite end of the entity or feature to be dimensioned. AutoCAD offsets the second extension line from this point by the current value of the dimension variable DIMEXO. The extension lines are drawn vertically, regardless of the angle between the first and second extension line origin points.

- **Dimension line location (Text/Angle):**

  Pick the point through which you want the dimension line to pass. AutoCAD uses this point to determine the offset distance between the selected object or pick points and the dimension line.

149

If you use either of the (Text/Angle) options, you will see one of the following prompts:

- **Dimension text <default>:**

AutoCAD calculates the distance between the two extension line origin points you pick or between the two points derived from the object you select. AutoCAD then offers the distance (in the current drawing units and precision) as the default dimension text value. You can accept this value (press Enter), specify a new value, suppress any text by typing a space, or apply prefix or suffix text to the value (see the DIM/DIM1 command).

- **Enter text angle:**

This prompt modifies the angle at which the dimension text is drawn. If you press Enter, the text is drawn at the default text angle.

- **Dimension text <default>:**

AutoCAD determines the distance between the two extension line origin points you picked or between the two points derived from the object you selected. Then AutoCAD offers this distance (in the current drawing units and precision) as the default dimension text value. You can accept this value by pressing Enter, enter a new value, suppress any text by typing a space, or apply prefix or suffix text to the value.

Example

This example demonstrates how to use the HORIZONTAL command. The drawing in figure HORIZONTAL.1 shows the dimensions that are created in this example.

```
Command: DIM↵
Dim: HORIZONTAL↵
First extension line origin or RETURN to select: ↵
Select line, arc, or circle: Pick point ①
Dimension line location: Pick point ②
Dimension text <14'>: ↵
Dim: HORIZONTAL↵
First extension line origin or RETURN to select: END of ③
```

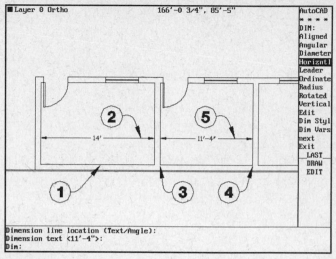

Figure HORIZONTAL.1:
Using the HORizontal command.

```
Second extension line origin: END of ④
Dimension line location (Text/Angle): ②
Dimension text <11'-4">: ↵
```

Related Commands

> **DDIM**
> **Dim: ALIGNED**
> **Dim: VERTICAL**

Related System Variables

For a list of AutoCAD's dimensioning variables, see *Inside AutoCAD Release 12.*

Dim: LEADER

Screen **[DIM:] [Leader]**

Pull down **[Draw] [Dimensions >] [Leader]**

The LEADER dimensioning command makes *callout notes* or *leader dimensions*, which are dimension lines leading from a line of text to a single arrowhead, which points at the feature to be described. You can abbreviate the LEADER command as L.

Horizontal leaders are made up of a single leader segment. Vertical or angled leader lines that are greater than 15 degrees automatically add a single horizontal segment (one arrowhead long) to the leader line adjacent to the dimension text. You draw a leader by picking an end point of the arrowhead and then dragging and picking any number of leader line segments, followed by pressing Enter. The leader text is then automatically middle-justified to the left or right depending upon the direction the last leader was drawn. LEADER dimensions are not associative, but consist of individual line and text entities and arrowheads (solid entities).

Prompts and Options

- **Leader start:**

  Pick the point where you want the leader to point. This point becomes the end point of the leader's arrowhead.

- **To point:**

  Pick any number of points for leader line segments. The first leader segment must be at least two arrowhead lengths long or the arrowhead is omitted. A leader can have any number of segments, although three is the traditional maximum. As with the LINE command, a rubber-band line stretches dynamically from each chosen point to the cursor to indicate the next segment's location. You can enter a U at this prompt to undo a leader segment. If you press Enter at this prompt after you enter one or more points, a final leader segment, one arrowhead long, is added automatically if the last segment was not within 15 degrees of horizontal.

- **Dimension text <default>:**

  Enter a single line of text for the leader. The dimension text of the last dimensioning command is presented as the default. You can add prefixes and suffixes to the default text, as with the other dimensioning commands.

Example

The following example demonstrates how simple it is to create callout notes in a drawing. The drawing shown in figure LEADER.1 shows the points used to create a note for the drawing.

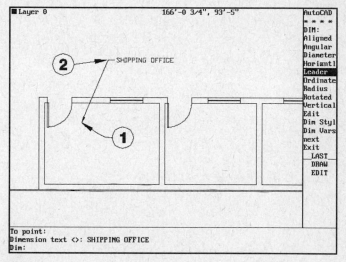

Figure LEADER.1:
A callout created using the LEADER command.

```
Command: DIM↵
Dim: LEADER↵
Leader start: Pick point ①
To point: Pick point ②
To point: ↵
Dimension text <>: SHIPPING OFFICE↵
```

Related Command

DDIM

Related System Variables

For a list of AutoCAD's dimensioning variables, see *Inside AutoCAD Release 12*.

Dim: NEWTEXT

Screen [DIM:] [Edit] [Newtext]

Pull down [Modify] [Edit Dims] [Dimension Text] [Change Text]

The NEWTEXT dimensioning command assigns a new text string to one or more existing associative dimensions. The current dimension variable settings are also applied, unless the selected dimensions were created with named dimension styles. Non-associative dimensions are not affected. The NEWTEXT command can be abbreviated as N.

Prompts and Options

- **Enter new dimension text:**

  At this prompt, you enter a new text string for the dimension. You can apply prefixes and suffixes or you can suppress text by entering a space character. If you press Enter without entering text, AutoCAD restores the default text strings of the selected associative dimension(s).

- **Select objects:**

  Select any part of an associative dimension or any number of associative dimensions by using AutoCAD's standard object-selection methods. If you choose more than one dimension, the text of each dimension is changed to the new value.

Example

The following example demonstrates how to use the NEWTEXT command to change existing associative dimension text. Figure NEWTEXT.1 shows the effects of using this command.

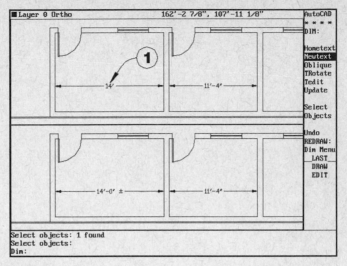

Figure NEWTEXT.1:
Dimension text modified using the NEWTEXT command.

```
Command: DIM↵
Dim: NEWTEXT↵
Enter new dimension text: 14'-0" %%P ↵
Select objects: Pickpoint ①
1 selected, 1 found
Select objects: ↵
```

Related Commands

> **DDIM**
> **HOMETEXT**
> **TEDIT**
> **TROTATE**
> **UPDATE**

Related System Variable

> **DIMASO**

Dim: OBLIQUE

Pull down **[Modify] [Edit Dims >] [Dimension Text >]
[Oblique Dimension]**

The OBLIQUE dimensioning command makes the extension lines of existing associative dimensions oblique with respect to their dimension lines. The OBLIQUE command is useful when dimensions in a dense drawing begin to interfere with one another or for special effects such as isometric dimensioning. The OBLIQUE command can be abbreviated as OB.

Prompts and Options

- **Select objects:**

  Use AutoCAD's normal object-selection methods to select the dimensions to edit. You can use the OBLIQUE command only with associative dimensions.

- **Enter obliquing angle (RETURN for none):**

  At this prompt, you enter the new obliquing angle for extension lines of the selected dimensions. This angle is measured in relation to the angle of the existing extension lines—positive in the counter-clockwise direction. The current dimension variable settings are applied to the selected dimension(s) unless the dimension(s) were created with a named dimension style. Pressing Enter gives the same result as entering an angle of zero degrees. The angle you enter does not affect subsequently created dimensions.

Example

This example demonstrates how to use the OBLIQUE command to apply an extension line angle to an existing vertical dimension. Figure OBLIQUE.1 shows the effects of using the OBLIQUE command.

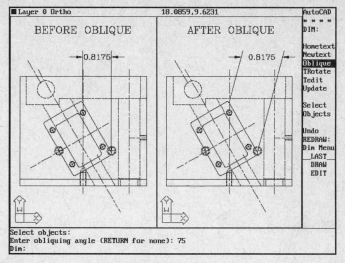

Figure OBLIQUE.1:
Dimension modified with the OBLIQUE command.

```
Command: DIM↵
Dim: OBLIQUE↵
Select objects: Pickpoint ①
1 selected, 1 found
Select objects: ↵
Enter obliquing angle (RETURN for none): 75↵
```

Related Commands

DDIM
Dim: TEDit
Dim: TROtate

Related System Variable

DIMASO

Dim: ORDINATE

Screen   **[DIM:] [ORDINATE]**

Pull down   **[Draw] [Dimensions >] [Ordinate >] [Automatic]**

The ORDINATE dimensioning command creates ordinate dimensions, also called datum dimensions. The ORDINATE command can be abbreviated as OR.

Ordinate dimensions denote either the X or Y distance from a common origin (0,0) point. This point is established by reorienting the current UCS origin. Ordinate dimensions consist of dimension text and a leader (without arrowhead) pointing to the feature dimensioned. If the angle between the first point (Select Feature:) and the second point (Leader endpoint...) is closest to the angle of the X axis, then the distance along the Y axis is dimensioned. If the angle between the points is closest to the angle of the Y axis, then the distance along the X axis is dimensioned. You can override the ORDINATE command's choice of axes by specifying the axis to dimension with the Xdatum or Ydatum options. The leader and dimension text are aligned perpendicular to the axis being dimensioned. You can enter ordinate dimension leaders more easily if Ortho mode is on.

Prompts and Options

* **Select Feature:**

  Pick the point you want to dimension. This becomes the start point of the ordinate dimension leader, offset by the current value of DIMEXO.

* **Leader endpoint (Xdatum/Ydatum):**

  Pick an end point for the leader or enter an **X** or **Y** to specify the dimension type. With Ortho off, if you can drag and pick the leader end point diagonally, an orthogonal break is automatically drawn in the middle of the leader. If you enter the Xdatum or

Ydatum options, the corresponding dimension types are drawn, regardless of the direction or location of the leader end point.

- **Dimension text <default>:**

  AutoCAD calculates the distance between the two extension line origin points you pick or between the two points derived from the object you select. AutoCAD then offers the distance (in the current drawing units and precision) as the default dimension text value. You can accept this value (press Enter), specify a new value, suppress any text by typing a space, or apply prefix or suffix text to the value (see the DIM/DIM1 command).

Example

The following example uses the ORDINATE command to dimension the part shown in figure ORDINATE.1.

```
Command: DIM↵
Dim: ORDINATE↵
Select Feature: CEN of Pick point ①
```

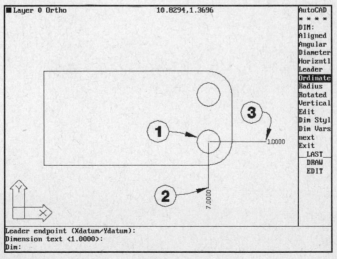

Figure ORDINATE.1:
Ordinate (datum dimensions) used to locate a part feature.

```
Leader endpoint (Xdatum/Ydatum): Pick point ②
Dimension text <7.0000>: ↵
Dim: ORDINATE↵
Select Feature: CEN of ①
Leader endpoint (Xdatum/Ydatum): Pick point ③
Dimension text <1.0000>: ↵
```

Related Commands

DDIM
UCS

Related System Variables

For a list of AutoCAD's dimensioning variables, see *Inside AutoCAD Release 12*.

Dim: OVERRIDE

Screen **[DIM:] [Dim Styl] [Override]**

The OVERRIDE dimensioning command modifies selected dimensions to use new values for one or more dimension variables. The OVERRIDE command differs from the UPDATE command, in that it updates specific dimension variables; the UPDATE command applies all the current dimension variable settings to the selected dimension(s). The OVERRIDE command can be abbreviated as OV.

Prompts and Options

- **Dimension variable to override:**

  You enter the name of a dimension variable to change.

- **Current value <*default*> New value:**

  You enter a new value for each dimension variable specified. Press Enter to proceed with object selection. The variables you override affect only selected dimensions; they do not affect the current dimension style or subsequently created dimensions.

- **`Select objects:`**

  Use any of AutoCAD's object-selection methods to select the existing associative dimensions you want to override. The settings you specified above are applied to each.

- **`Modify dimension style "current"? <N>`**

  If a selected dimension was defined with a named style, you can enter **Y** to update the style or press Enter to leave the style unchanged. If you enter **Y**, the selected dimension is modified and retains the named style. If you enter **N** or press Enter, the dimension is modified and its style becomes *UNNAMED.

Example

This example demonstrates how the OVERRIDE command can be used to adjust selected dimensions within a drawing. Figure OVERRIDE.1 shows the original dimension and its appearance after overriding its original settings.

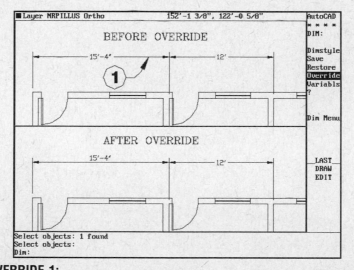

Figure OVERRIDE.1:
Linear dimension before and after overriding DIMTAD.

```
Command: DIM↵
Dim: OVERRIDE↵
Dimension variable to override: DIMTAD↵
Current value <Off> New value: ON
Dimension variable to override: ↵
```
Pick point ①
```
Select objects: 1 selected, 1 found
Select objects: ↵
```

Related Commands

> DDIM
> Dim: UPDATE

Related System Variables

For a list of AutoCAD's dimensioning variables, see *Inside AutoCAD Release 12*.

Dim: RADIUS

Screen **[DIM:] [Radius]**

Pull down **[Draw] [Dimensions >] [Radial >] [Radius]**

The RADIUS dimensioning command is used to dimension the radius of circles, arcs, and polyline arc segments. You can abbreviate the RADIUS command as RA.

AutoCAD can produce several variations of dimensions for radii. These variations depend on the value of the system variables DIMTIX (Text Inside eXtension lines), DIMTOFL (Text Outside, Force dimension Line inside), and DIMCEN (CENter marks and lines). If both the DIMTIX and DIMTOFL variables are set to 0 (off), a leader is drawn to the dimension text from the point by which the entity was picked. The leader is drawn dynamically so you can place the text for best readability. When DIMTOFL alone is on (1), AutoCAD places the dimension text outside the arc or circle, as in the previous style, and draws a dimension line from the center of the entity. When both DIMTOFL and DIMTIX are on, AutoCAD omits the leader and places the dimension text within the dimension line.

If the dimension variable DIMCEN is positive, a center mark is placed at the center point; if DIMCEN is 0, no mark is placed; and if DIMCEN is negative, center lines are drawn.

Dimension text for the RADIUS command always begins with the symbol R (for RADIUS) by default.

Prompts and Options

- **Select arc or circle:**

  Pick the arc or circle to dimension. The point by which you pick the entity determines the end point of the dimension line or leader and the general location of dimension text.

- **Dimension text <** *default* **>:**

  AutoCAD calculates the distance between the two extension line origin points you pick or between the two points derived from the object you select. AutoCAD then offers the distance (in the current drawing units and precision) as the default dimension text value. You can accept this value (press Enter), specify a new value, suppress any text by typing a space, or apply prefix or suffix text to the value (see the DIM/DIM1 command).

- **Enter leader length for text:**

  If dimension text is forced outside the arc or circle by the DIMTIX variable, you can drag the length of the dimension leader or enter a length at the keyboard. If you press Enter at this prompt, AutoCAD draws a minimum length leader.

Example

This example creates several types of radial dimensions. Each one is different, due to changes in the three key dimensioning variables. Figure RADIUS.1 shows each type of dimension.

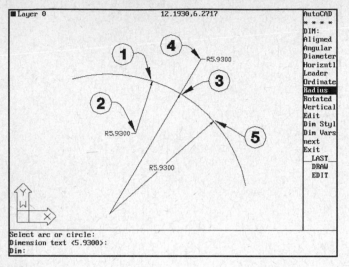

Figure RADIUS.1:
Dimensioning with the RADIUS command.

```
Command: DIM↵
Dim: RADIUS↵
Select arc or circle: Pick point ①
Dimension text <5.9300>: ↵
Enter leader length for text: Pick point ②
Dim: DIMTOFL↵
Current value <Off> New value: ON↵
Dim: RADIUS↵
Select arc or circle: Pick point ③
Dimension text <5.9300>:
Enter leader length for text: Pick point ④
Dim: DIMTIX↵
Current value <Off> New value: ON↵
Dim: RADIUS↵
Select arc or circle: Pick point ⑤
Dimension text <5.9300>: ↵
```

Related Commands

DDIM
Dim: CENTER
Dim: DIAMETER

Related System Variables

DIMTIX
DIMTOFL
DIMCEN

Dim: REDRAW

The REDRAW dimensioning command repaints the current viewport in the same fashion as the normal REDRAW command does. Any blips are removed and all entities are redrawn. The REDRAW command can be abbreviated as RED.

Related Commands

REDRAW
REDRAWALL

Dim: RESTORE

Screen **[DIM:] [Dim Styl] [Restore]**

The RESTORE dimensioning command restores the dimension variable settings saved as a named dimension style, making it the current style. The new settings remain in effect until a setting is changed or until another style is restored. If an existing associative dimension has a named style, you can quickly restore the settings used by that dimension by picking that dimension at the first prompt. The RESTORE command can be abbreviated as RES.

Prompts and Options

- `Current dimension style: NAME`
  `?/Enter dimension style name or RETURN to select`
  `dimension:`

165

This prompt lists the current dimension style name. If a named style is not current, the style is listed as *UNNAMED.

You can enter a question mark to display named dimension styles in the current drawing or enter a style name to restore. To select an existing associative dimension entity, press Enter and AutoCAD prompts with `Select dimension:`. If you enter a dimension style name preceded by a tilde (~), AutoCAD displays the differences in values of dimension variables between the specified style and the current settings.

- **`Dimension style(s) to list <*>:`**

  If you entered a question mark at the previous prompt, this prompt displays. Enter the names of dimension styles for listing (separated by commas) or use wild-card characters to match. If you press Enter or enter an asterisk, AutoCAD lists all the named styles within the current drawing.

- **`Select dimension:`**

  If you press Enter at the `?/Enter dimension style name or RETURN to select dimension:` prompt, this prompt displays. Select a dimension by using AutoCAD's object-selection methods. If the dimension is defined with a named dimension style, that style is restored as the current style. If the dimension is not defined with a named style, the RESTORE command terminates without affecting the current style.

Example

This example demonstrates the options of the RESTORE command to list, compare, and restore dimension styles.

```
Dim: RESTORE↵
Current dimension style: *UNNAMED
?/Enter dimension style name or RETURN
to select dimension: ?↵
Dimension style(s) to list <*>: ↵
Named dimension styles:
  DIM-16
  DIM-8
```

```
?/Enter dimension style name or RETURN to select dimension: ~DIM-8↵
Differences between DIM-8 and current settings:
          DIM-8              Current Setting
DIMASZ   0.0625              0.1800
DIMBLK   ARCARROW
DIMDLE   0.0625              0.0000
DIMDLI   0.0000              0.3800
DIMEXE   0.0313              0.1800
DIMGAP   0.0000              0.0900
DIMSCALE 96.0000             1.0000
DIMTAD   On                  Off
DIMTIH   Off                 On
DIMTIX   On                  Off
DIMTXT   0.0938              0.1800
DIMZIN   1                   0
?/Enter dimension style name or RETURN to select dimension: DIM-8↵
```

Related Commands

DDIM
Dim: OVERRIDE
Dim: SAVE
Dim: STATUS
PURGE

Related System Variable

DIMSTYLE

Dim: ROTATED

Screen   **[DIM:] [Rotated]**

Pull down   **[Draw] [Dimensions >] [Linear >] [Rotated]**

The ROTATED dimensioning command draws a dimension line at a specified angle, regardless of the angle of the feature or object dimensioned. Extension lines are drawn perpendicular to the dimension line. Otherwise, the ROTATED command operates in the same way as the other linear dimensioning commands, such as HORIZONTAL and VERTICAL. The ROTATED command can be abbreviated as RO.

Prompts and Options

- **Dimension line angle <0>:**

  You enter an angle for the dimension line. AutoCAD measures the angles with its standard method, counterclockwise 0 degrees in the east direction. You can show AutoCAD an angle by picking two points.

- **First extension line origin or RETURN to select:**

  Pick a point at one end of the entity or feature to be dimensioned. AutoCAD prompts for the Second extension line origin: . The extension lines are offset from the points you pick by the current value of the dimension variable DIMEXO. The extension lines are drawn perpendicular to the dimension line angle.

  If you press Enter, the following prompt appears.

- **Select line, arc, or circle:**

  This prompt appears if you press Enter at the First extension line origin or RETURN to select: prompt. Pick a line, polyline, arc, or circle; extension lines are located for you. If you select a line, polyline segment, or arc, AutoCAD dimensions its end points, projecting extension lines to the specified dimension line angle. If you select a circle, the diameter is dimensioned at the dimension line angle specified. AutoCAD dimensions only the selected segment of a polyline.

- **Second extension line origin:**

  Pick a point at the opposite end of the entity to be dimensioned. AutoCAD automatically offsets the second extension line from this point by the current value of the dimension variable DIMEXO. The extension line is drawn perpendicular to the dimension line.

- **Dimension line location (Text/Angle):**

  Pick the point through which you want the dimension line to pass. AutoCAD uses the point to determine the distance between your selected object, feature, or pick points and the dimension line.

If you use either of the (Text/Angle) options, the following prompt appears:

- **Enter text angle:**

  This prompt modifies the angle at which the dimension text is drawn. If you press Enter, the text is drawn at the default text angle.

- **Dimension text <*default*>:**

  AutoCAD determines the distance between the two extension line origin points you picked or between the two points derived from the object you selected. AutoCAD then offers this distance in the current drawing units and precision as the default dimension text value. You can accept this value by pressing Enter, enter a new value, suppress any text by typing a space, or apply prefix or suffix text to the value (see Chapter 5).

Example

This example demonstrates the two methods of creating a rotated dimension. Figure ROTATED.1 illustrates the points chosen for this example.

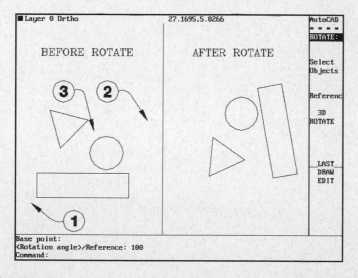

Figure ROTATED.1:
Dimensions created using the ROTATED command.

```
Command: DIM↵
Dim: ROTATED↵
Dimension line angle <0>: 30↵
First extension line origin or RETURN to select: INT of Pick point ①
Second extension line origin: INT of Pick point ②
Dimension line location (Text/Angle): Pick point ③
Dimension text <5.7956>: ↵
Dim: ROTATED↵
Dimension line angle <0>: 60↵
First extension line origin or RETURN to select: ↵
Select line, arc or circle: Pick point ④
Dimension line location (Text/Angle): A↵
Enter text angle: 60↵
Dimension line location (Text/Angle): Pick point ⑤
Dimension text <5.7956>: ↵
```

Related Commands

DDIM
Dim: ALIGNED
Dim: OBLIQUE

Related System Variables

For a list of AutoCAD's dimensioning variables, see *Inside AutoCAD
Release 12.*

Dim: SAVE

Screen **[DIM:] [Dim Styl] [Save]**

The SAVE dimensioning command stores the current settings of all
dimension variables in the current drawing as a named dimension style.
This named style remains current until you change a dimension variable, save it under another name, or restore another named style with
the RESTORE command. You can abbreviate the SAVE command as
SA.

Prompts and Options

- **`?/Name for new dimension style:`**

  You enter a name for the current style. The name must conform to the general AutoCAD rules for named objects: it can contain as many as 31 letters or digits and it can include dollar signs ($), hyphens (-), or underscore characters (_). If you enter a question mark, AutoCAD produces a listing of the named dimensioned styles in the current drawing.

- **`Dimension style(s) to list <*>:`**

  If you enter a question mark at the previous prompt, this prompt appears. Enter the names of dimension styles for listing (separated by commas) or use wild-card characters to match. If you press Enter or enter an asterisk, AutoCAD lists all the named styles within the current drawing.

- **`That name is already in use, redefine it? <N>`**

  This prompt displays if the specified style name already exists. If you answer **N**, the first prompt repeats; if you answer **Y**, the existing style is overwritten and all associative dimensions defined with that style regenerate to reflect any changes in variable values.

Example

The following example demonstrates the SAVE command options. To save a new dimension style, proceed as follows:

```
Command: DIM↵
Dim: SAVE↵
?/Name for new dimension style: TEST↵
Dim: SAVE↵
?/Name for new dimension style: TEST That name is already in use,
redefine it? <N> Y↵
Dim: SAVE↵
?/Name for new dimension style: ?↵
Dimension style(s) to list <*>: ↵
Named dimension styles: TEST↵
?/Name for new dimension style:
Press Ctrl-C
*Cancel*
```

Related Commands

DDIM
OVERRIDE
RESTORE

Related System Variable

DIMSTYLE

Dim: STATUS

?

The STATUS dimensioning command lists the current settings of all dimension variables with a short description of each variable. The STATUS dimensioning command is not the same as the normal STATUS command, which displays other drawing parameters. The STATUS command can be abbreviated as STA.

Example

```
Command: DIM
Dim: STATUS
DIMALT   Off              Alternate units selected
DIMALTD  2                Alternate unit decimal places
DIMALTF  25.4000          Alternate unit scale factor
DIMAPOST                  Suffix for alternate text
DIMASO   On              Create associative dimensions
DIMASZ   0.1800           Arrow size
DIMBLK                    Arrow block name
DIMBLK1                   First arrow block name
DIMBLK2                   Second arrow block name
DIMCEN   0.0900           Center mark size
DIMCLRD  BYBLOCK          Dimension line color
DIMCLRE  BYBLOCK          Extension line & leader color
DIMCLRT  BYBLOCK          Dimension text color
DIMDLE   0.0000           Dimension line extension
DIMDLI   0.3800           Dimension line increment for
continuation
```

```
DIMEXE   0.1800         Extension above dimension line
DIMEXO   0.0625         Extension line origin offset
DIMGAP   0.0900         Gap from dimension line to text
DIMLFAC  1.0000         Linear unit scale factor
— Press RETURN for more —
```
You can press Enter to continue the listing or press Ctrl-C to cancel.

Related Commands

DDIM
Dim: RESTORE

Related System Variables

For a list of AutoCAD's dimensioning variables, see *Inside AutoCAD Release 12.*

Dim: STYLE

Screen **[DIM:] [Dim Style] [Dimstyle]**

The STYLE command changes the current text style in use for dimension text. The STYLE command can be abbreviated as STY.

The style you set affects dimensioning, as well as the TEXT, DTEXT, and ATTDEF commands. The STYLE dimensioning command is not the same as the normal STYLE command. Both commands set the current text style, but the normal STYLE command can also list defined text styles and create new text styles. Do not confuse text styles with dimension styles, which are created with the SAVE and DDIM dimensioning commands.

Prompts and Options

- **New text style <default>:**

    You enter the name of an existing text style to make it the style for new dimensions. The current text style is presented as the default.

Example

The following example demonstrates changing text styles with the STYLE command. ROMANC becomes the current text style upon completion of the example.

```
Command: DIM⏎
Dim: STYLE⏎
New text style <STANDARD>: ROMANC ⏎
```

Related Commands

DDIM
STYLE

Related System Variables

DIMSCALE
DIMTXT

Dim: TEDIT

Screen **[DIM:] [Edit] [TEDIT]**

Pull down **[Modify] [Edit Dims >] [Dimension Text >] [Move Text]**

The TEDIT command edits the location or angle of the text of a single existing associative dimension entity. The TEDIT command can be abbreviated as TE.

The TEDIT command includes options to:

- Shift dimension text as far to the left or right as possible along its associated dimension line (only for linear, radius, or diameter dimensions)
- Restore its default position (similar to the HOMETEXT command)
- Alter the text angle (similar to the TROTATE command)

If the dimension was created with a named dimension style, it is regenerated with the dimension variable settings of that style. If the dimension was not created with a named dimension style, the current dimension variable settings are applied to the dimension.

Prompts and Options

- `Select dimension:`

  Select the dimension to edit with any of AutoCAD's general object-selection methods.

- `Enter text location (Left/Right/Home/Angle):`

  Drag the dimension text into the desired position or specify one of the options. If the dimension variable DIMSHO is on (1), the text displays dynamically as you drag it.

- `Left.` The Left option moves the dimension text as far to the left along the dimension line as possible with a two-arrowhead length leader to the left of the text.

- `Right.` The Right option moves the dimension text as far to the right along the dimension line as possible with a two-arrowhead length leader to the right of the text.

- `Home.` The Home option returns the dimension text to its home position, centered along the length of the dimension line.

- `Angle.` The Angle option prompts for a new dimension text angle. If you select this option, the `Text angle:` prompt displays:

- `Enter text angle:`

  You enter a new text angle or pick two points to show the angle. The text is rotated about its center point. Angles are measured counterclockwise, according to the standard AutoCAD orientation of 0 degrees in the east direction. If you enter **0**, AutoCAD restores the text to its default angle; if you press Enter, the current angle is unchanged.

Example

This example demonstrates each of the TEDit options. Figure TEDIT.1 shows a series of typical horizontal dimensions relocated by using TEDIT.

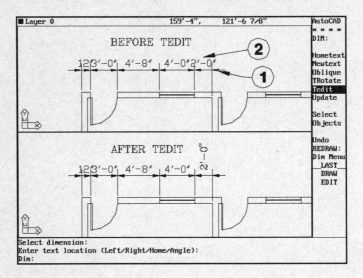

Figure TEDIT.1:
Crowded horizontal dimensions.

```
Command: DIM↵
Dim: TEDIT↵
Select dimension: Pick point ①
Enter text location (Left/Right/Home/Angle): A↵
Enter text angle: 90↵
Command: DIM↵
Dim: TEDIT↵
Select dimension: Pick point ②
```

Related Commands

   Dim: HOMETEXT
   Dim: TROTATE

Related System Variables

DIMSHO
DIMTAD
DIMTVP
DIMTIH
DIMTOH

Dim: TROTATE

Pull down **[Modify] [Edit Dims >] [Dimension Text >] [Rotate Text]**

The TROTATE dimensioning command alters the rotation angle of dimension text for selected existing associative dimensions. TROTATE functions like the Angle option of the TEDIT command. The TROTATE command can be abbreviated as TR.

If a selected dimension was created with a named dimension style, it is regenerated with the dimension variable settings of that style. If a selection dimension was not created with a named style, the current dimension variable settings are applied to that dimension.

Prompts and Options

- **Enter text angle:**

  You enter a new angle for dimension text, either from the keyboard or by picking two points. If you enter **0**, AutoCAD restores the dimension text to its default angle. AutoCAD measures the angle counterclockwise, according to its standard of 0 degrees in the east direction.

- **Select objects:**

  Use AutoCAD's normal object-selection methods to select all the dimensions to receive the new dimension text angle setting. Only associative dimensions are affected.

Example

This example rotates the dimension text shown in figure TROTATE.1, so that it fits better between the extension lines.

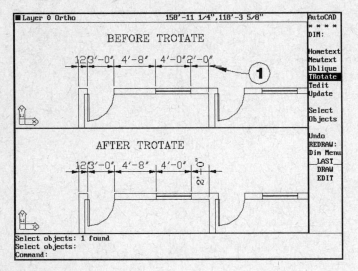

Figure TROTATE.1:
Dimension text before and after rotation.

```
Command: DIM↵
Dim: TROTATE↵
Enter text angle: 90↵
Select objects: Pick point ①
1 selected, 1 found
Select objects: ↵
```

Related Commands

> **Dim: HOMETEXT**
> **Dim: TEDIT**

Related System Variables

DIMTIH
DIMTOH

Dim: UNDO

Screen **[DIM:] [Edit] [Undo]**

The UNDO dimensioning command undoes the last dimension operation. The command can be repeated back to the beginning of the current dimensioning session. No redo command exists for Dim mode. The UNDO command can be abbreviated as U.

Related Commands

REDO
UNDO

Dim: UPDATE

Screen **[DIM:] [Edit] [Update]**

Pull down **[Modify] [Edit Dims >] [Update Dimension]**

The UPDATE dimensioning command regenerates selected existing associative dimensions using the current dimension style, units parameters, and text style. UPDATE overrides any dimension style reference a dimension may have, redefining it with the current dimension style. If the current dimension style is *UNNAMED, the dimensions lose their style and are regenerated with the current dimensioning variable settings. The UPDATE command can be abbreviated as UP.

Prompts and Options

- `Select objects:`

  Use AutoCAD's normal object-selection methods to select existing associative dimensions to be updated.

Example

This example modifies an existing dimension with UPDATE to reflect a change in the DIMTAD variable. Figure UPDATE.1 shows the effects of the UPDATE command.

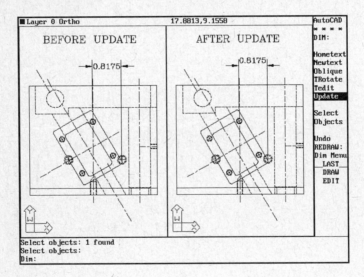

Figure UPDATE.1:
The original horizontal dimensions.

```
Dim: UPDATE ↵
Select objects: Pick the dimension at ①
Select objects: ↵
```

Related Commands

Dim: HOMETEXT
Dim: NEWTEXT
Dim: OBLIQUE
Dim: TEDIT
Dim: TROTATE
SCALE
STRETCH

Related System Variables

For a list of AutoCAD's dimensioning variables, see *Inside AutoCAD Release 12.*

Dim: VARIABLES

Screen [DIM:] [Dim Styl] [Variabls]

The VARIABLES dimensioning command lists all dimension variable settings for a specified named style or compares the differences between a named style and the current style. You cannot change dimension variables or make a style current with this command. The desired style may be specified by name or by picking a dimension defined with that style. The VARIABLES command can be abbreviated as VAR.

Prompts and Options

- `Current dimension style: CURRENT`
  `?/Enter dimension style name or RETURN to select`
  `dimension:`

  You enter a question mark to display named dimension styles in the current drawing or to enter a style name to list. To select an existing associative dimension created with the desired style, press Enter and AutoCAD prompts with `Select dimension:`. Enter a dimension style name preceded by a tilde (~) to view the differences in values of dimension variables between the specified style and the current settings.

- **Dimension style(s) to list <*>:**

  This prompt appears if you enter a question mark at the ?/Enter dimension style name prompt. Enter the names of dimension styles for listing (separated by commas), or use wild-card characters to match. If you press Enter or enter an asterisk, AutoCAD lists all the named styles within the current drawing.

- **Select dimension:**

  Use AutoCAD's normal object-selection methods to select a dimension created with the dimension style you want to list or compare. The selected dimension need not be defined with a named style for its variables to be listed.

Examples

This example demonstrates the steps for displaying the variables stored within a named style.

```
Command: DIM↵
Dim: VARIABLES↵
Current dimension style: *UNNAMED
?/Enter dimension style name or RETURN to select dimension: ?↵
Dimension style(s) to list <*>: ↵
Named dimension styles: ↵
  ARCH
?/Enter dimension style name or RETURN to select dimension: ARCH↵
Status of ARCH:
DIMALT    Off                  Alternate units selected
DIMALTD   0                    Alternate unit decimal places
DIMALTF   25.4000              Alternate unit scale factor
DIMAPOST                       Suffix for alternate text
DIMASO    On                   Create associative dimensions
DIMASZ    0.0625               Arrow size
DIMBLK    ARCARROW             Arrow block name
DIMBLK1   ARCARROW             First arrow block name
DIMBLK2   ARCARROW             Second arrow block name
DIMCEN    0.0900               Center mark size
```

```
DIMCLRD  1 (red)          Dimension line color
DIMCLRE  1 (red)          Extension line & leader color
DIMCLRT  BYBLOCK          Dimension text color
DIMDLE   0.0000           Dimension line extension
DIMDLI   0.0000           Dimension line increment for con-
tinuation
DIMEXE   0.0313           Extension above dimension line
DIMEXO   0.0625           Extension line origin offset
DIMGAP   0.0000           Gap from dimension line to text
DIMLFAC  1.0000           Linear unit scale factor
— Press RETURN for more —
```

Related Commands

DDIM
Dim: RESTORE
Dim: SAVE

Related System Variables

For a list of AutoCAD's dimensioning variables, see *Inside AutoCAD Release 12.*

Dim: VERTICAL

Screen **[DIM:] [Vertical]**

Pull down **[Draw] [Dimensions >] [Linear >] [Vertical]**

The VERTICAL dimensioning command draws dimensions with a vertical dimension line. The extension line origin points need not have the same X coordinates. The VERTICAL command can be abbreviated as VE.

Prompts and Options

- **First extension line origin or RETURN to Select:**
  Pick a point at one end of the entity or feature to be dimensioned. AutoCAD prompts for the `Second extension line origin:`.

The extension lines are offset from the points by the current value of the dimension variable DIMEXO. The extension lines are drawn horizontally, regardless of the angle between the first and second extension line origin points.

If you press Enter, the following prompt appears.

- **Select line, arc, or circle:**

  This prompt appears if you press Enter at the `First extension line origin or RETURN to select:` prompt. Pick a point to select a line, polyline, arc, or circle; extension lines are located for you. If you select a line, polyline segment, or arc, AutoCAD dimensions its end points. If you select a circle, the diameter is dimensioned between the 90- and 270-degree quadrant points. AutoCAD dimensions only the selected segment of an open polyline.

- **Second extension line origin:**

  Pick a point at the opposite end of the entity or feature to be dimensioned. AutoCAD offsets the second extension line from this point by the current value of the dimension variable DIMEXO. The extension lines are drawn horizontally, regardless of the angle between the first and second extension line origin points.

- **Dimension line location (Text/Angle):**

  Pick the point through which you want the dimension line to pass. AutoCAD uses this point to determine the offset distance between your selected object, feature, or pick points and the dimension line.

  If you use either of the (Text/Angle) options, the following prompt appears:

- **Enter text angle:**

  This prompt modifies the angle at which the dimension text is drawn. If you press Enter, the text is drawn at the default text angle.

- **Dimension text <default>:**

  AutoCAD calculates the distance between the two extension line origin points you pick or between the two points derived from the object you select. AutoCAD then offers the distance (in the current drawing units and precision) as the default dimension text value. You can accept this value (press Enter), specify a new value, suppress any text by typing a space, or apply prefix or suffix text to the value (see the DIM/DIM1 command).

Examples

This example uses the VERTICAL command to dimension a part using various options. Figure VERTICAL.1 illustrates the points used in this example.

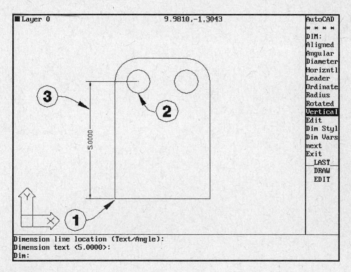

Figure VERTICAL.1:
Dimensioning with the VERTICAL command.

```
Command: DIM↵
Dim: VERTICAL↵
First extension line origin or RETURN to select: END of Pick point ①
Second extension line origin: CEN of Pick point ②
Dimension line location (Text/Angle): A↵
Enter text angle: 90↵
Dimension line location (Text/Angle): Pick point ③
Dimension text <5.0000>: ↵
```

185

Related Commands

DDIM
Dim: HORIZONTAL

Related System Variables

For a list of AutoCAD's dimensioning variables, see *Inside AutoCAD Release 12*.

DIST

Screen **[INQUIRY] [DIST:]**

Pull down **[Assist] [Inquiry >] [Distance]**

DIST measures the distance between two 2D or 3D points. You can enter the coordinates of the points at the keyboard or choose them on screen with a pointing device. The DIST command also provides information about the angle in the X,Y plane, the angle from the X,Y plane of an imaginary line between the two points, and the difference in X, Y, and Z values between the two points.

You can execute the DIST command transparently by preceding the command name with an apostrophe (**'DIST**).

Prompts and Options

- **First point:**

  At this prompt, specify the first point.
- **Second point:**

  At this prompt, specify the second point.

Example

The following example uses the DIST command to measure the distance between two points:

```
Command: DIST↵
First point: 1,1↵
Second point: 5,5↵
```
AutoCAD displays the following information:

```
Distance = 5.6569, Angle in XY Plane = 45, Angle from XY Plane = 0
Delta X = 4.0000, Delta Y = 4.0000, Delta Z = 0.0000
```

 Use the object snap modes to help measure the distance between specific points on existing entities.

Related System Variable

DISTANCE

DIVIDE

Screen **[EDIT] [DIVIDE:]**

Pull down **[Construct] [Divide]**

The DIVIDE command places points or blocks along the length of an entity, dividing it into a specified number of equal segments. You can divide lines, circles, arcs, and polylines. The divided entity, however, is not actually broken into individual segments.

Prompts and Options

- **Select object to divide:**

  When AutoCAD displays this prompt, you can use the standard object-selection methods to pick a line, circle, arc, or polyline.

- **<*Number of segments* >/Block:**

  At this prompt, you can either enter the number of equal segments to create, or select the Block option. The Block option enables you to insert a block at the dividing points. Note that you must define the block in the current drawing prior to selecting the Block option.

  When you select the Block option, the following prompts appear:

- **Block name to insert:**

  Enter the name of a block already defined in the current drawing.

- **Align block with object? <Y>:**

  If you accept the default answer of yes, the block is aligned with the divided entity. An aligned block is rotated around its insertion point parallel with the divided entity. If you answer **N**, the block is inserted with a rotation angle of 0.

- **Number of segments:**

  At this prompt, enter the number of equal segments to create.

Example

This example shows how the DIVIDE command is typically used in a real-world situation. Figure DIVIDE.1 shows a wall line that needs to be broken into seven even sections for placement of windows.

```
Command: DIVIDE┘
Select object to divide: Pick point ①
<Number of segments>/Block: 7 ┘
```

Related Command

MEASURE

DLINE

Pull down **[Draw] [Line>] [Double Lines]**

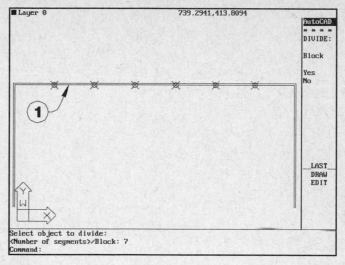

Figure DIVIDE.1:
A wall line showing the locations for a few windows.

The DLINE command draws double lines and arcs. DLINE is defined by AutoLISP in the file DLINE.LSP and loaded by the default AutoCAD menu. With DLINE, you can choose to snap double line starting points to other objects, break intersecting objects, and cap double line segments automatically. DLINE gives you complete control over the width of double lines and how they are drawn from a center line used to locate segment end points.

Prompts and Options

The following prompt appears when DLINE is first executed and before a start point is specified:

```
Break/Caps/Dragline/Offset/Snap/Undo/Width/<start point>:
```

This prompt is displayed after a start point is specified:

```
Arc/Break/CAps/CLose/Dragline/Snap/Undo/Width/<next point>:
```

In Arc mode, you are presented with a slightly different prompt:

```
Break/CAps/CEnter/CLose/Dragline/Endpoint/Line/Snap/Undo/Width/
<second point>:
```

Descriptions for each of DLINE's options follow. The options available to you depend on which of the DLINE prompts you just received.

- **Arc.** After you enter a start point, you can enter Arc mode with this option. DLINE draws double arcs through combinations of Start point, Center point, Endpoint or Start point, Second point, Endpoint.

- **Break.** The Break option causes DLINE to remove a section of the entity between double line end points when the Snap option is used. The Break option issues the prompt `Break Dline's at start and end points? OFF/<ON>:`

- **Caps.** The Caps option causes DLINE to close the specified ends of double line segments automatically. The Caps option issues the prompt `Draw which endcaps? Both/End/None/Start/<Auto>:` The Both option caps both end points, End caps only the ending segment, None disables capping, Start caps only the beginning segment, and Auto caps segments not snapped to other objects with the Snap option.

- **Center.** The Center option enables you to specify the center point of double line arcs when in Arc mode.

- **Close.** The Close option closes double lines or arcs created during the current invocation of DLINE with double lines or double arcs, respectively. Two double line segments or one double arc segment must exist before closing.

- **Dragline.** The Dragline option sets the location of double lines with respect to the rubber band line used to specify points. The Dragline option issues the prompt `Set dragline position to the Left/Center/Right/<Offset from center = default>:` The Left and Right options set the dragline to the left or right edge of the double line from the perspective of looking from the start point toward the end point. Center places the double lines equidistant from the dragline. Offset allows specification of an offset distance.

- **Endpoint.** You specify an end point for double line arcs with this option.

- **Line.** The Line option returns to Line mode from Arc mode.

- **Offset.** The Offset option begins double lines in a specified direction and distance from a base point. This option issues the prompt `Offset from:` to request the base point. At the `Offset toward:` prompt, specify a point to define the direction of the new double lines. The `Enter offset distance:` prompt accepts a distance from the base point, in the direction previously specified, to begin double lines. The distance between the base point and the point specified as the direction is offered as the default offset distance.

- **Second point.** The Second point option appears only during Arc mode and accepts a second point through which DLINE draws double arcs.

- **Snap.** When Snap is on, DLINE searches near pick points for objects to attach its double lines or arcs similar to Osnap. DLINE issues the prompt `Set snap size or snap On/Off. Size/ OFF/<ON>:` The On and Off options enable or disable Snap, respectively. You can control the distance (in pixels) that Snap searches with the Size option, which prompts `New snap size (1-10)<default>:`. If the Break option (above) is on, objects found by Snap will be broken and intersections with DLINE segments will be cleaned up automatically.

- **Start point.** This option, which is the default, asks you to specify a starting point for double lines or arcs.

- **Undo.** The Undo option voids the last picked point in Line or Arc mode.

- **Width.** This option prompts `New DLINE width <default>:`. You enter a distance or pick two points to specify the distance between double lines.

Example

The following example uses DLINE in several steps to draw shapes using some of the available options and defaults. The results are shown in figure DLINE.1

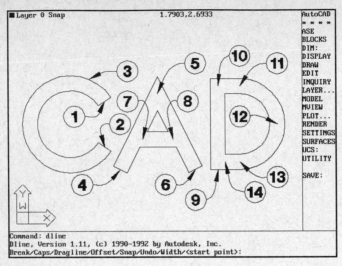

Figure DLINE.1:
Shapes created with DLINE.

```
Command: DLINE ↵
Dline, Version 1.11, (c) 1990-1992 by Autodesk, Inc.
Break/Caps/Dragline/Offset/Snap/Undo/Width/<start point>: Pickpoint ①
Arc/Break/CAps/CLose/Dragline/Snap/Undo/Width/<next point>: A ↵
Break/CAps/CEnter/CLose/Dragline/Endpoint/Line/Snap/Undo/Width/
<second point>: E ↵
Endpoint: Pick point ②
Angle/Direction/Radius/<Center>: D ↵
Tangent direction: Pick point ③
Break/CAps/CEnter/CLose/Dragline/Endpoint/Line/Snap/Undo/Width/
<second point>: ↵
Command: ↵
Dline, Version 1.11, (c) 1990-1992 by Autodesk, Inc.
Break/Caps/Dragline/Offset/Snap/Undo/Width/<start point>: Pickpoint ④
Arc/Break/CAps/CLose/Dragline/Snap/Undo/Width/<next point>: Pick
point ⑤          ·
Arc/Break/CAps/CLose/Dragline/Snap/Undo/Width/<next point>: Pick
point ⑥
Arc/Break/CAps/CLose/Dragline/Snap/Undo/Width/<next point>: ↵
Command: ↵
Dline, Version 1.11, (c) 1990-1992 by Autodesk, Inc.
```

```
Break/Caps/Dragline/Offset/Snap/Undo/Width/<start point>: Pick
point ⑦
Arc/Break/CAps/CLose/Dragline/Snap/Undo/Width/<next point>: Pick
point ⑧
Command: ↵
Dline, Version 1.11, (c) 1990-1992 by Autodesk, Inc.
Break/Caps/Dragline/Offset/Snap/Undo/Width/<start point>: Pick point ⑨
Arc/Break/CAps/CLose/Dragline/Snap/Undo/Width/<next point>: Pick
point ①0
Arc/Break/CAps/CLose/Dragline/Snap/Undo/Width/<next point>: Pick
point ①1
Arc/Break/CAps/CLose/Dragline/Snap/Undo/Width/<next point>: A ↵
Break/CAps/CEnter/CLose/Dragline/Endpoint/Line/Snap/Undo/Width/
<second point>: Pick point ①2
Endpoint: Pick point ①3
Break/CAps/CEnter/CLose/Dragline/Endpoint/Line/Snap/Undo/Width/
<second point>: L ↵
Arc/Break/CAps/CLose/Dragline/Snap/Undo/Width/<next point>: Pick point
①4
```

Related Commands

> **ARC**
> **BREAK**
> **EXTEND**
> **LINE**
> **OFFSET**
> **SNAP**
> **TRIM**
> **UNDO**

DONUT or DOUGHNUT

Screen **[DRAW] [DONUT:]**

Pull down **[Draw] [Donut]**

The DONUT command draws filled rings and circles by using wide-polyline arc segments. You must provide the inside diameter, outside diameter, and center point for the polyline.

Prompt and Options

- **Inside diameter <0.5000>:**

  This prompt requires you to enter a value or two points for the size of the donut's hole. The default value is 0.5 units.

- **Outside diameter <1.0000>:**

  This prompt requires you to enter a value or two points to create the donut's outer diameter. The outside diameter must be greater than the inside diameter. The default value is 1.0 units.

- **Center of doughnut:**

  At this prompt, specify the donut's center point. You can enter the point's coordinates or pick the point on-screen. This prompt repeats until you press Enter, enabling you to make multiple donuts of the same size.

Example

The following example creates two donut objects with the DONUT command.

```
Command: DONUT↵
Inside diameter <0.5000>: 3↵
Outside diameter <1.0000>: 4↵
Center of doughnut: Pick a point ①
Center of doughnut: ↵
```

Related Commands

FILL
PLINE
PEDIT

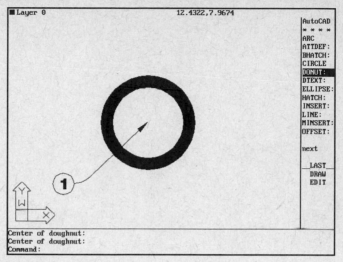

```
■Layer 0                    12.4322,7.9674
                                              AutoCAD
                                              * * * *
                                              ARC
                                              ATTDEF:
                                              BHATCH:
                                              CIRCLE
                                              DONUT:
                                              DTEXT:
                                              ELLIPSE:
                                              HATCH:
                                              INSERT:
                                              LINE:
                                              MINSERT:
                                              OFFSET:

                                              next

                                              _LAST_
                                              DRAW
                                              EDIT




Center of doughnut:
Center of doughnut:
Command:
```

Figure DONUT.1:
The polyline entity created by the DONUT command.

Related System Variables

> DONUTID
> DONUTOD

DRAGMODE

Screen **[SETTINGS] [DRAGMOD:]**

The DRAGMODE command controls dragging when you draw or move objects. Some drawing commands (such as CIRCLE, ARC, IN-SERT, and SHAPE) enable you to drag objects so that you can see the size, shape, or position of the entity. Some editing commands, such as MOVE, COPY, and STRETCH, also take advantage of this dragging capability.

You can execute the DRAGMODE command transparently by preceding the commmand name with an apostrophe ('**DRAGMODE**).

 Most of the time, you will want to take advantage of AutoCAD's dragging capabilities to make drawing and editing easier. If you use DRAGMODE during large selection-set manipulations, however, such as when moving or copying complex blocks, screen performance may suffer. Turn off DRAGMODE temporarily during such operations for smoother cursor movement on slower systems.

You can control DRAGMODE's default setting in new drawings by modifying the state of DRAGMODE in the default prototype drawing. You also can use the DRAGMODE system variable to control dragging.

Prompts and Options

- **ON:**

  This option enables object dragging when requested by the user or by a menu macro, and the keyword **drag** is used at the appropriate prompts.

- **OFF:**

  This option disables object dragging.

- **Auto:**

  This option initiates object dragging automatically for all commands that allow object dragging.

Related System Variables

DRAGMODE
DRAGP1
DRAGP2

DTEXT

Screen **[DRAW] [DTEXT:]**

Pull down **[Draw] [Text] [Dynamic]**

DTEXT (Dynamic TEXT) enables you to enter text strings into your drawing. DTEXT produces the same results as the TEXT command but offers several advantages:

- You can see the text in the drawing as you type.

- You can move the cursor to a different part of the screen to begin a new text line.

- When starting a second line of text, you press Enter only once. With the TEXT command, you must press Enter twice to start a second line of text.

Prompts and Options

- **Justify/Style/<Start point>:**

  At this prompt, you have three choices. First, you can select Justify to change the text justification. The default value is left justification. Second, you can select Style to change the current text style. Note that the style must already be defined using the STYLE command. Third, you can enter the starting point of a left-justified text string, which is the default choice at this prompt. If you know the justification option you want to use, you can enter it at this prompt without selecting Justify first. The DTEXT justification options are described later.

- **Height:**

  At this prompt, specify the text's height. You see this prompt only when the current style does not have a predefined text height.

- **Rotation angle:**

  At this prompt, enter the text's rotation angle.

- **Text:**

  At this prompt, type the text string. This prompt is repeated so that you can type additional text strings. Press Enter at a blank `Text:` prompt to end the DTEXT command.

  If you press Enter, AutoCAD highlights the last text entered and prompts for a new string. The new string is placed directly below the highlighted text and has the same text style, height, and rotation as the highlighted text.

Justification Options

You can choose among the following justification options for your text:

- **Align.** You specify the start point and end point of the text string. AutoCAD adjusts the text's height so that the text fits between the two points.
- **Fit.** You specify the start point, end point, and height of the text string. AutoCAD fits the text between the two points by adjusting the width factor.
- **Center.** You specify the center of the text string horizontally and the base of the text string vertically.
- **Middle.** You specify the center of the text string horizontally and vertically.
- **Right.** You specify the right end point of the text string at the base.
- **TL.** Text justification is at the top left corner of the first character's text cell. A *text cell* is the rectangular area into which all characters of a font fit. You can visualize this area by imagining a character with both ascenders and descenders or an uppercase letter with a descender.
- **TC.** Text justification is at the top of a string's text cells; the string itself is centered horizontally.
- **TR.** Text justification is at the top right corner of the last text cell of a string.
- **ML.** Text justification is at the vertical middle of an uppercase text cell and at the left of the first character. Regardless of the text

string's composition, ML justification is calculated as if the first character is uppercase without descenders.

- **MC.** Text justification is at the vertical middle of an uppercase text cell and at the horizontal center of the text string. Regardless of the text string's composition, MC justification is calculated as if the entire string is uppercase without descenders.
- **MR.** Text justification is at the vertical middle of an uppercase text cell and at the horizontal right of the last character. Regardless of the text string's composition, MR justification is calculated as if the last character is uppercase without descenders.
- **BL.** Text justification is at the bottom left of the first character's text cell.
- **BC.** Text justification is at the bottom of a string's text cells; the string itself is centered horizontally.
- **BR.** Text justification is at the bottom right corner of the last text cell of a string.

Example

This example shows the simplicity of using the DTEXT command. The text entity that is drawn is shown in figure DTEXT.1, along with the box that shows the position of all new letters before you type them.

```
Command: DTEXT↵
Justify/Style/<Start point>: Pickpoint ①
Height <0.2000>: .5↵
Rotation angle <0>: ↵
Text: THIS IS A LINE↵
Text: OF TEXT↵
Text: ↵
```

Related Commands

CHANGE
DDEDIT
QTEXT
STYLE
TEXT

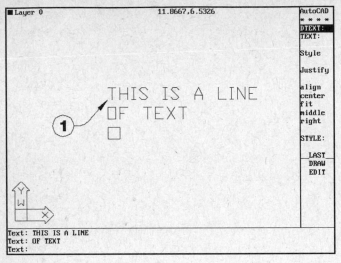

Figure DTEXT.1:
The text string entered with the DTEXT command.

Related System Variables

TEXTSIZE
TEXTSTYLE

DVIEW

Screen **[DISPLAY] [DVIEW:]**

Pull down **[View] [Set View >] [Dview]**

DVIEW, which stands for Dynamic VIEW, is used to set up views of three-dimensional models interactively from any point in space. The DVIEW command uses a camera-and-target metaphor to help you visualize and set up a view.

DVIEW also creates perspective projections of three-dimensional models. In perspective mode, objects that are close to the camera appear larger than objects that are farther away. The default projection mode is parallel projection. In parallel-projection mode, objects appear to be their true size regardless of their distance from the camera.

Prompts and Options

- **Select objects:**

  The objects selected for DVIEW are used to give you a preview of how the entire three-dimensional model will look in the new view. Selected objects are dragged on the screen as the view is dynamically changed. Be careful not to select too many objects to drag. Depending on your graphics system and the speed of your computer, dragging of objects may become sluggish and awkward.

  If you press Enter at this prompt, AutoCAD utilizes a user-defined block named DVIEWBLOCK as the view indicator. DVIEWBLOCK must be scaled to fit into a one-unit cube. DVIEWBLOCK is shown aligned with the X, Y, and Z axes of the current UCS. If DVIEWBLOCK does not exist, AutoCAD uses a small house as the view indicator.

- **CAmera/TArget/Distance/POints/PAn/Zoom/TWist/CLip/ Hide/Off/Undo/<eXit>:**

- **CAmera.** The CAmera option rotates the camera about the target. When you select this option, AutoCAD prompts for the angle from the Z,Y plane and the angle in the X,Y plane from the X axis, relative to the target point.

- **TArget.** The TArget option rotates the target about the camera. When you select this option, AutoCAD prompts for the angle from the X,Y plane and the angle in the X,Y plane from the X axis, relative to the target point.

- **Distance.** The Distance option switches from parallel to perspective view and changes the camera's distance from the target along the current line of sight. When you select this option, AutoCAD prompts for the camera-to-target distance.

- **POints.** The POints option sets the camera and target points. These are the points you are looking from and to. When you select this option, AutoCAD prompts for camera and target points.

- **PAn.** The PAn option moves both the camera and target points parallel to the current view plane. When you select this option, AutoCAD prompts for a displacement base point and the second point of displacement.

- **Zoom.** The Zoom option zooms the image in and out but does not change the perspective. This option works in much the same manner as a camera's zoom lens. When you select this option, AutoCAD prompts for a zoom scale factor in parallel projection mode and lens length in perspective projection mode.

- **TWist.** The TWist option rotates a view about the line of sight. When you select this option, AutoCAD prompts for a view twist angle.

- **CLip.** The CLip option moves a cutting plane, which removes objects from the view. The back cutting plane removes objects behind the plane; the front cutting plane removes object in front of the plane. The front and back cutting planes may be independently moved in relation to one another. When you select this option, AutoCAD prompts for front or back clipping and then prompts for the distance from the target to place the cutting plane.

- **Hide.** The Hide option removes hidden lines from the selected objects while within the DVIEW command.

- **Off.** The Off option turns off perspective projection mode and turns on parallel projection mode.

- **Undo.** The Undo option undoes the effects of the other DVIEW command options one at a time.

- **eXit.** The default option, eXit, returns you to the `Command:` prompt and regenerates the view based on the settings of the other options.

Example

This example shows how the DVIEW command is used to dynamically view the house in the DHOUSE drawing. Figure DVIEW.1 shows the selection points for choosing the entities in the drawing. Figure DVIEW.2 displays the house model in its dynamic view.

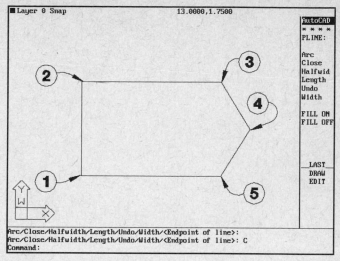

Figure DVIEW.1:
The selection points for choosing the house entities.

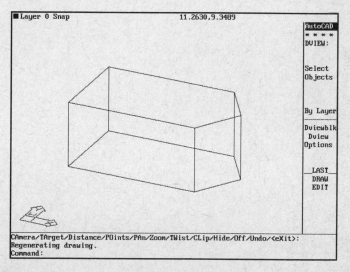

Figure DVIEW.2:
The house model after the dynamic view options have been set.

```
Command: DVIEW↵
Select objects: W
First corner: Pick point ①
Other corner: Pick point ②
20 found
Select objects: ↵
CAmera/TArget/Distance/POints/PAn/Zoom/TWist/CLip/Hide/Off/Undo/
<eXit>: D↵
New camera/target distance <1.0000>: 50↵
CAmera/TArget/Distance/POints/PAn/Zoom/TWist/CLip/Hide/Off/Undo/
<eXit>: CA↵
[T]oggle angle in/Enter angle from XY plane <90.00>: 25↵
[T]oggle angle from/Enter angle in XY plane from Xaxis <-90.00>:
-100↵
CAmera/TArget/Distance/POints/PAn/Zoom/TWist/CLip/Hide/Off/Undo/
<eXit>: ↵
Regenerating drawing.
```

Related Commands

VIEW
VPOINT

Related System Variables

BACKZ
FRONTZ
LENSLENGTH
TARGET
VIEWDIR
VIEWMODE
VIEWSIZE
VIEWTWIST
WORLDVIEW

DXBIN

Screen **[UTILITY] [DXF/DXB] [DXBIN:]**

Pull down **[File] [Import/Export >] [DXB In...]**

The DXBIN command imports DXB files, which are binary drawing exchange files. DXB files are limited in the types of entities and other drawing data they can contain. Unlike binary DXF files, binary DXB files are not a complete representation of the AutoCAD drawing file. DXB files are used by programs such as AutoShade to export simple drawing data, which then can be imported by the AutoCAD DXBIN command.

> **TIP** DXB files are useful for creating flat drawings of three-dimensional models created in AutoCAD. To create a DXB file, configure for file output format, selecting the AutoCAD DXB file output option. A DXB file contains only line entities. In a DXB plot file, circles, arcs, and text are composed of many short lines.

Prompts and Options

- When you execute the DXB command, it displays a file selection dialog box for you to specify the file to import.

Related Commands

DXFIN
DXFOUT
FILMROLL
IGESIN
IGESOUT
PSIN
PSOUT

DXFIN

Screen **[UTILITY] [DXF/DXB] [DXFIN:]**

Pull down **[File] [Import/Export] [DXF In...]**

The DXFIN command imports a file—which conforms to the Drawing Interchange File (DXF) standard—into the current drawing. DXF files often are used to transfer drawing files between CAD packages.

The DXFIN command imports some or all of a DXF file into the current drawing, depending on whether any entities exist in the current drawing. If you want to import a complete DXF file, including defined layers, linetypes, text styles, blocks, and so on, the current drawing must be new and completely empty.

You may create a new and empty drawing file using two methods. First, you can enter the new drawing name at the OPEN command's File edit box as *filename=*, where *filename* is the name of the new drawing. This sets the new drawing equal to no prototype, which begins it as an empty drawing. Second, you can check the No Prototype box of the Create New Drawing dialog box. Regardless of how you create the new and empty drawing file, you must use DXFIN before any command that creates entities or defines named layers, linetypes, text styles, and so on. When the DXFIN command successfully imports a complete DXF file, AutoCAD automatically performs a ZOOM All command.

If a drawing file is not new and empty, DXFIN will import only the entities section of a DXF file, ignoring all named objects in the DXF file, such as layers, linetypes, text styles, and blocks. A DXF file, however, does not need to be a complete drawing file containing named definitions; it can be as simple as a single entity. Some third-party AutoCAD application programs create new entities as DXF files and use DXFIN to insert them into a drawing.

The following prompt appears if you use DXFIN in a drawing that is not new and empty:

```
Not a new drawing – only ENTITIES section will be input.
```

Prompts and Options

When you execute the DXFIN command, it displays a file selection dialog box listing files with the extension DXF. Select a file or enter the path and file name of an existing file to import.

Related Commands

DXBIN
DXFOUT
FILMROLL
IGESIN
IGESOUT
PSIN
PSOUT

Related System Variable

FILEDIA

DXFOUT

Screen [UTILITY] [DXF/DXB] [DXFOUT:]

Pull down [File] [Import/Export] [DXF Out...]

The DXFOUT command creates a file in the Drawing Interchange File (DXF) standard. This file standard directly represents your drawing and often is used to convert AutoCAD files to other CAD-related packages and prepare it for machine tool devices, rendering packages, or other CAD programs that support the DXF format.

The DXFOUT command enables you to adjust the precision of the DXF file, write only entities, or create a binary version of the DXF file. AutoCAD automatically attaches the extension DXF to the file name you specify.

NOTE A DXF file typically takes two to three times more disk space than the original drawing file. Whereas the default format created by DXFOUT is an ASCII file, the binary format is more compact, efficient, and precise; it also loads several times faster. Do not confuse the Binary DXF file with a Drawing Interchange Binary (DXB) file used in the DXBIN command.

By default, the DXFOUT command creates a complete ASCII DXF file, which fully describes the drawing, including all named definitions such as layers, linetypes, text styles, and blocks. The default precision is six decimal places, which often is sufficient. You can specify the accuracy between 0 and 16 places. The more decimal places you instruct AutoCAD to use, the larger your DXF file will be. Binary DXF files are created with the full precision of the AutoCAD drawing and are not affected by the precision you specify.

If you want to write specific entities to the DXF file, use the DXFOUT command's Entity option. You then are prompted to specify the desired accuracy.

Prompts and Options

When you execute the DXFOUT command, it displays the Create DXF File dialog box listing files with the extension DXF. Select an existing file to overwrite or specify a new path and file name.

- `Enter decimal places of accuracy (0 to 16)/Entities/Binary <6>:`

  Accept the default or enter the number of decimal places of accuracy if you want AutoCAD to write a full ASCII DXF file.

  The Entities option issues the standard `Select Objects:` prompt, then reprompts for the number of decimal places of accuracy and again offers the binary option.

  The Binary option creates a smaller yet more precise file than the standard ASCII format. This binary file has the same DXF extension as the ASCII format. After the Binary option is specified, AutoCAD immediately begins writing the DXF file.

- **Select objects:**

  Use any of AutoCAD's standard object-selection methods to select the entities to write in the DXF file.

Related Commands

DXBIN
DXFIN
FILMROLL
IGESIN
IGESOUT
PLOT
PSIN
PSOUT

Related System Variable

FILEDIA

EDGESURF

Screen [DRAW] [next] [3D Surfs] [EDGSURF:]

Pull down [Draw] [3D Surfaces >] [Edge Defined Patch]

The EDGESURF command is one of six commands that create a 3D polygon mesh. EDGESURF creates a four-sided mesh that can be defined by arcs, lines, and open polylines (either 2D or 3D).

The EDGESURF command creates a *Coons surface patch* between the four edge entities. To picture this form of mesh, envision a fishing net. The net can be a four-sided shape of virtually any size, and its holes can be any size.

The two axes of the mesh are called the M and N directions of the surface. The AutoCAD system variables SURFTAB1 and SURFTAB2 define the number of tabulation lines along the M and N directions of the surface.

Large SURFTAB settings create smoother surfaces at the expense of file size, entity regeneration, and hidden-line removal. When you are setting the variables, consider the application of the mesh. If large settings are needed for the final product, construct two meshes with the same boundaries: a temporary mesh with a moderate number of faces and a final mesh (kept on a frozen layer until needed) that has more faces. By using the temporary mesh, you can save time during the drawing and editing stages of your project. Replace the temporary mesh with the final mesh before final plotting and presentation.

As with other polygon meshes, you can edit the completed mesh by using most of AutoCAD's editing commands. These include the PEDIT command for fitting smooth curves through each vertex. If you use the EXPLODE command to break the mesh apart, the mesh is replaced with 3Dface entities.

The end points of boundary entities must intersect, and the entities must form a closed region. If not, AutoCAD returns the following message:

```
Edge n does not touch another edge.
```

In this message, the n signifies the number of the entity that does not coincide with the next.

Prompts and Options

- **Select edge** n:

  Select each of the four boundary edges for the polygon mesh in any order. Remember that the first edge selected determines the M direction of the mesh and that the endpoints of each edge must intersect. The end of the first edge nearest the pick point is the origin of the mesh, with the M direction extending toward the opposite end of the edge. The other axis of the mesh is the N direction. The number of tabulation lines in the M and N directions is determined by the value of the variables SURFTAB1 and SURFTAB2. The default values for SURFTAB1 and SURFTAB2 create a 6×6 mesh.

Example

This example creates a mesh between four entities in 3D space. The entities shown in figure EDGESURF.1 are a combination of arcs and lines positioned in 3D space.

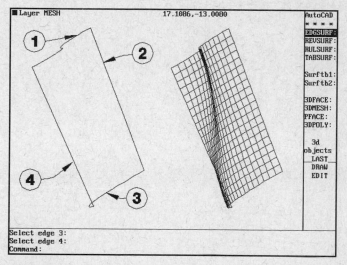

Figure EDGESURF.1:
The edgesurf edges and the polygon mesh created using EDGESURF.

```
Command: EDGESURF↵
Select edge 1: ①
Select edge 2: ②
Select edge 3: ③
Select edge 4: ④
```

Related Commands

PEDIT
PFACE
REVSURF
RULESURF

TABSURF
3DFACE
3DMESH

Related System Variables

SURFTAB1
SURFTAB2

ELEV

Screen **[SETTINGS] [ELEV:]**

The ELEV command sets the elevation of the current *construction plane* for subsequently created drawing entities. This elevation is a distance along the Z axis above or below the current User Coordinate System (UCS) origin. The construction plane is a plane located at the specified elevation above or below the X,Y plane of the current UCS. The Z coordinates of points and new entities default to lie in the construction plane, unless otherwise specified when the points are input or the entities are created.

The ELEV command also sets the *extrusion* thickness for subsequently drawn entities. The term *extrusion* refers to the distance an entity is projected along the Z axis. An extruded circle, for example, resembles a cylinder when viewed from an oblique viewpoint.

 The DDEMODES command dialog box has edit boxes for setting the elevation and thickness of all new entities, and it can be used transparently within other commands.

 The use of the ELEV command is not recommended. Setting elevation to a nonzero height is confusing and can lead to errors when combined with a UCS located above or below the WCS origin. It is easier and less confusing to leave the elevation set to zero and to use the UCS to control the location of the construction plane.

Use the THICKNESS system variable or the DDEMODES dialog box to control extrusion thickness. The ELEV command will probably be deleted in a future release of AutoCAD.

Entities not affected by the current thickness setting are meshes, 3D faces, 3D polylines, viewports, dimensions, and text. You can assign a thickness to text after it has been created, however, by using the CHANGE or CHPROP command.

Prompts and Options

- **New current elevation <0.0000>:**

  At this prompt, you enter a value or pick two points to show a distance to define the new elevation. A negative value specifies an elevation below the current UCS. If you pick a point at this prompt, AutoCAD prompts for a second point.

- **New current thickness <0,0000>:**

  You can enter a value or pick two points to show a distance to define the extrusion value for entities. A negative value extrudes entities along the negative Z axis. If you pick a point at this prompt, AutoCAD prompts for a second point.

Example

This example shows the effects of elevation and thickness on the creation of new entities. The result is shown in figure ELEV.1.

```
Command: ELEV↵
New current elevation <0.0000>: 2↵
New current thickness <0.0000>: 2↵
```

Related Commands

CHANGE
DDEMODES
DDUCS
UCS

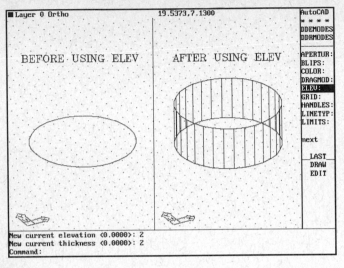

Figure ELEV.1:
An extruded circle at an elevation of 2 above the UCS.

Related System Variables

ELEVATION
THICKNESS

ELLIPSE

Screen **[DRAW] [ELLIPSE:]**

Pull down **[Draw] [Ellipse >]**

The ELLIPSE command draws an ellipse. This ellipse is constructed of polyline arcs and is a single closed polyline. You can use the PEDIT command to modify an ellipse.

You can specify ellipses by any one of several combinations of axis end points (the default), axis distances, rotation, or a center point. If the Snap Style option is set to isometric mode, the ELLIPSE prompt includes an isometric option, which creates an isometric circle in the current isometric plane. See the SNAP command for details on isometric mode.

Prompts and Options

- **`<Axis endpoint 1>/Center/Isocircle:`**

  The default option is to specify one end point of the first axis. If you enter **C** for the Center option, ELLIPSE displays the `Center of ellipse:` prompt. If Snap mode is set to isometric, you can enter **I** for the Isocircle option and ELLIPSE prompts `Center of circle:` and `<Circle radius>/Diameter:`. The Isocircle option draws a 2D ellipse that looks like a circle drawn in the current isometric plan.

- **`Axis endpoint 2:`**

  You enter the second end point of the first axis.

- **`<Other axis distance>/Rotation:`**

  After you specify the major axis, you enter a distance value or pick a point to show a distance for the half width of the ellipse. If you enter **R** for the Rotation option, the ELLIPSE command displays the `Rotation around major axis:` prompt.

- **`Rotation around major axis:`**

  At this prompt, you enter an angle value or pick a point to show the angle to rotate the ellipse around the first axis. The Rotation option is similar to specifying the second axis end point by rotating a perfect circle around the first axis in 3D. The Rotation option, however, does not actually rotate the ellipse in 3D. The ellipse is drawn as a two-dimensional oval in the current UCS. An angle of 0 degrees creates an ellipse that looks like a circle in plan view.

- **`Center of ellipse:`**

  The Center option displays this prompt. You specify a point for the center of the ellipse. The ELLIPSE command then prompts for the end point of the first axis.

- **Axis endpoint:**

  If you specify a center point for the ellipse, this prompt displays. You specify a point for one end of the first axis. The point defines the length of the axis from the center point. AutoCAD then displays the `<Other axis distance>/Rotation:` prompt.

Figure ELLIPSE.1 shows an example of the three points selected by the preceding method and the axes they define.

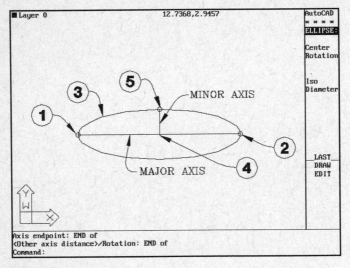

Figure ELLIPSE.1:
The ellipse axes and the three points.

Example

This example demonstrates two common methods for creating an ellipse. The first method defines the major and minor axes of the ellipse. The second method specifies the ellipse center, and then defines its axes. The results are shown in figure ELLIPSE.1.

```
Command: ELLIPSE↵
<Axis endpoint 1>/Center: Pick point ①
Axis endpoint 2: Pick point ②
```

```
<Other axis distance>/Rotation: Pick point ③
Command: ELLIPSE↵
<Axis endpoint 1>/Center: C↵
Center of ellipse: Pick point ④
Axis endpoint: Pick point ⑤
<Other axis distance>/Rotation: Pick point ①
```

Related Commands

> **CIRCLE**
> **ISOPLANE**

END

Screen **[UTILITY] [next] [END:]**

The END command finishes your drawing session by saving your work. If you have an existing drawing in the same directory as the current drawing, and that file has the same name as the current drawing, the existing drawing file is renamed with a BAK extension. If a file with the same name as the current drawing and a BAK extension already exists in the same directory as the current drawing, that file is deleted.

Related Commands

> **QUIT**
> **SAVE**

ERASE

Screen **[EDIT] [ERASE:]**

Pull down **[Modify] [Erase >]**

The ERASE command deletes selected entities from a drawing.

217

Prompts and Options

- `Select objects:`

  Use any of AutoCAD's standard object-selection methods to select the objects that you want this command to erase. Press Enter to terminate object selection and erase the selected entities.

Example

The following example shows how the ERASE command deletes entities from a drawing. Figure ERASE.1 shows the results of the ERASE command.

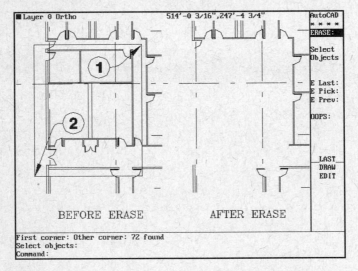

Figure ERASE.1:
Selecting the entities to be erased.

```
Command: ERASE↵
Select objects: W↵
First corner: Pick point ①
Other Corner: Pick point ②
Select objects: ↵
```

Related Commands

UNDO
OOPS

EXPLODE

Screen **[EDIT] [EXPLODE:]**

Pull down **[Modify] [Explode]**

The EXPLODE command reduces a complex entity (inserted blocks, polylines, associative dimensions, and meshes) into its component parts. Complex entities are made up of simpler entities, such as lines, arcs, text, 3Dfaces, and other entities.

When polylines are exploded, they are reduced into lines and arcs. Polylines that are curve-fit or spine-fit lose their original geometry and are exploded into lines and arcs that approximate the curve or spline. Tangent and width information also is lost when polylines are exploded.

Polygon meshes are exploded into three-dimensional faces. Polyface meshes are exploded into three-sided faces, lines, and points. If a polyline or mesh contains component parts with differing layers, colors, or linetypes, all component parts receive the layer, color, and linetype of the first component part in the polyline or mesh when exploded. Associative dimensions are exploded into lines, text, and points, and their arrowheads are exploded into blocks or solids.

Block references (inserted blocks) are exploded into the entities contained in their block definitions. You cannot explode external references (Xrefs) and their dependent blocks, mirrored blocks, or blocks with unequal X, Y, or Z scales. Attributes in exploded blocks are deleted and replaced with their attribute definition entities.

If complex entities are nested, such as a block containing other blocks or other complex entities, only the outer entity is exploded. After you

219

explode the outer block, you can select and explode the entities that had been contained within it.

Prompts and Options

- **Select objects:**

Use any of AutoCAD's standard object-selection methods to select the objects that you want to explode. You can press Enter to terminate object selection and explode the selected entities into their component parts.

Example

The following example shows how to use the EXPLODE command to explode the polyline shown in figure EXPLODE.1 into lines and arcs.

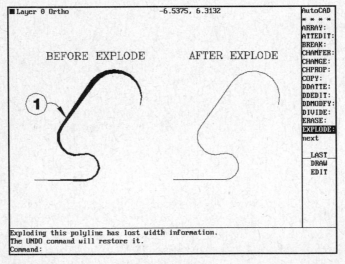

Figure EXPLODE.1:
A polyline that has been exploded.

```
Command: EXPLODE ↵
Select objects: Pickpoint ①
Select objects: ↵
```

Related Commands

BLOCK
INSERT
UNDO

EXTEND

Screen **[EDIT] [EXTEND:]**

Pull down **[Modify] [Extend]**

The EXTEND command increases the length of lines, open polylines, and arcs so that they intersect a boundary edge. The edge may be any entity, such as a line, circle, arc, sketch line, viewport entity, or an open or closed polyline (both 2D and 3D). You also can extend associative dimensions; when you extend an associative dimension, it updates automatically. Hatch entities cannot be extended, nor can you select a hatch as a boundary edge. Other entities that cannot be extended or used as a boundary edge include blocks, shapes, meshes, 3D faces, text, traces, and points.

AutoCAD enables you to select multiple boundary edges, but you can choose entities to be extended only one at a time. The EXTEND command offers an Undo feature, which returns the most recently extended entity to its former length.

 The EXTEND command can be used only on entities that are parallel to the current UCS. You can easily overcome this restriction, however, by setting the UCS to Entity, invoking the EXTEND command, and then setting the UCS to Previous.

Prompts and Options

- `Select boundary edge(s)...`
  `Select object(s):`

Select the boundaries to which you want to extend the entities. Boundaries can be lines, arcs, circles, open or closed polylines, viewport borders, or sketched lines.

- **<Select object to extend>/Undo:**

Pick the entities you want to extend. The point at which you pick the entity determines the direction of the extension. AutoCAD extends the entity from the end point that is closest to the picked location.

If you wish to reverse the effects of the EXTEND command on the last entity, enter **U** to return the previously extended entity to its original length.

Example

The following example demonstrates the EXTEND command with lines and arcs (see fig. EXTEND.1). Note that the line pointed to by ④ will not be extended because it does not intersect the EXTEND command boundary.

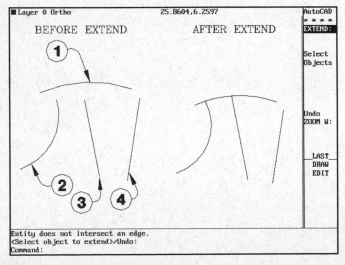

Figure EXTEND.1:
The lines and arcs before and after using the EXTEND command.

```
Command EXTEND↵
Select boundary edge(s)...
Select object(s): ①
Select object(s): ↵
<Select object to extend>/Undo: ②
<Select object to extend>/Undo: ③
<Select object to extend>/Undo: ④
The entity does not intersect an edge.
<Select object to extend>/Undo:
```

Related Commands

CHAMFER
CHANGE
FILLET
STRETCH
TRIM

FILES

Screen **[UTILITY] [FILES:]**

Pull down **[File] [Utilities...]**

The FILES command enables you to perform file maintenance from within AutoCAD. You can list drawing files, list other files, delete files, rename files, copy files, and unlock files.

The FILEDIA system variable controls the method of file specification with the FILES command. If FILEDIA is set to 1, each of the command options is performed through dialog boxes (see fig. FILES.1). If the FILEDIA variable is set to 0, AutoCAD issues the text-only prompts.

R12 You can execute the FILES command transparently by preceding the command name with an apostrophe ('FILES).

Figure FILES.1:
The FILES command dialog box.

 You should be careful not to delete any files in use or AutoCAD's temporary files when you are using the FILES command. Temporary files are designated with the extensions $A, $AC, and AC$. Files used for file locking are given an extension of ??K. AutoCAD may crash if you delete temporary files. If lock files are deleted, anyone can access the file in use on a network system. A loss of data is inevitable when two people edit the same file on two different machines.

Prompts and Options

If the FILEDIA variable is set to 1, each of the five FILES command options (List files, Copy file, Rename file, Delete File, and Unlock file) displays a second dialog box. This dialog box, shown in figure FILES.2, displays available files and the standard dialog box buttons OK, Cancel, and **H**elp. The FILES command options perform the following operations:

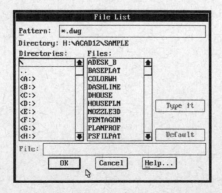

Figure FILES.2:
The typical FILES command dialog box.

- **List files...** The File List dialog box appears, listing all the drawing files in the current directory. To change the file types that are displayed in the list box, change the wild-card pattern to the files you want to see. For example, you could change the pattern to *.* to see all the files in the current directory.

- **Copy file...** Initially, the Source File dialog box appears. You should select the file to copy from by navigating the Directories: and Files: list boxes. When the file appears, highlight it in the Files: list box and click on the OK button. You can also type the full path and name of the source file in the File: edit box.

  After selecting the source file, you need to supply a location and name for the copy. The Destination File dialog box appears and requests this information. You can navigate the Directories: list box to choose a location for the file. To change the destination file's name, type in a new name, including extension, into the File: edit box. Click on the OK button when you are finished. AutoCAD displays the status of the copy at the bottom of the dialog box.

- **Rename files.** The Old File Name dialog box appears, requesting the name of the original file. You may select the file name from the Directories: and Files: list boxes or type in the full path and name from the File: edit box. Click on the OK button when you are finished.

  The New File Name dialog box appears next, requesting the new name for the file. You may select the file name from the Directories: and Files: list boxes or type the full path and name in the File: edit box. If you select an existing file name, you are prompted to verify that you want to replace the existing file. Press the OK button when you are finished. The success or failure of the operation is reported at the bottom of the dialog box.

- **Delete files.** The File(s) to Delete dialog box appears, requesting the names of the files you want erased from your disk. You may select the file names from the Directories: and Files: list boxes or type the full path and name in the File: edit box. If you want to list a specific group of files, such as all the backup drawing files, you can enter the appropriate pattern at the Pattern edit box.

When the files you want to erase are displayed in the Files: list box, you must highlight each file you want to delete. To delete all listed files, click on the Select All button. To dehighlight a group of files, click on the Clear All button. Click on the OK button when you are finished. AutoCAD displays the number of files that it deletes at the bottom of the dialog box. Any files that are currently locked by AutoCAD are not deleted.

- **Unlock files**. This option is used to remove the file locks set by AutoCAD in any configuration with file locking enabled. The Files to Unlock dialog box displays, requesting the names of the files you want to unlock. You specify the names of the actual files you want to unlock, not the names of lock files (#.??K) themselves. You can list specific files by using the Pattern: edit box (such as any file matching the *.DWG template). Select the files individually from the Directories: and Files: list boxes, use the Select all button, or type the names of the exact files you want to unlock.

  AutoCAD attempts to unlock any locked files you specify. If a file is already in use by someone, a message appears at the bottom of the dialog box, informing you that the file is in use, and inquiring if you still want the file to be unlocked. When files are unlocked, AutoCAD displays the total number at the bottom of the dialog box.

- **Exit**. This option returns you to the drawing editor.

If the FILEDIA variable is set to 0, the FILES command presents the following prompts and options:

- **Exit File Utility Menu**

  When you select this option, you return to the drawing editor.

- **List Drawing files:**

  AutoCAD presents a list of all files with the extension DWG in the specified drive or directory. (The list is similar to the results of the DOS command DIR *.DWG /W/P.) After you select this option, AutoCAD displays the following prompt:

      Enter drive or directory:

Press Enter if you want to see a list of the drawing files in the current directory. Otherwise, you can enter an alternative drive or directory.

- **List user specified files:**

  When you select this option, AutoCAD lists files according to a file-name specification you supply. Wild cards are allowed. You can restrict the list to just the backup files (*.BAK), for example, or to all the drawings with file names beginning with the letter F (F*.DWG). When you select this option, AutoCAD displays the following prompt:

  ```
  Enter file search specification:
  ```

  You should enter a valid file-search specification for your operating system. Include a drive and path prefix if necessary.

- **Delete files:**

  When you select this option, AutoCAD erases files from a disk. The following prompt appears, asking you to specify the files to be deleted:

  ```
  Enter file deletion specification:
  ```

  You can enter a drive, path, and file-name specification. Wild cards are allowed. If you specify a file that is locked, AutoCAD displays the following messages:

  ```
  Deletion denied, file: filename was locked by
  login name at time on date
  0 files deleted.
  Press RETURN to continue:
  ```

  If the file is not in use, you can unlock the file and then delete it.

- **Rename files:**

  By selecting this option, you can rename existing files from within AutoCAD. This option does not accept wild-card characters. AutoCAD displays the following prompt:

  ```
  Enter current filename:
  ```

Now you enter the name of the file to rename. Include a drive and path prefix if necessary. AutoCAD then prompts for the file's new name, as follows:

```
Enter new filename:
```

You should enter a new name for the file. Do not include a drive or path. If you specify a file that is locked, AutoCAD displays the following messages:

```
Rename denied, file: filename was locked by login
name at time on date

0 files renamed.

Press RETURN to continue:
```

If the file is not in use, you can unlock the file and then rename it.

- **Copy files:**

When you select this option, you can make a copy of one or more specified files from within AutoCAD. The original file is called *source*, and the copy is called *destination*. You can place the copy on a separate drive or in a different directory. AutoCAD displays the following prompts:

```
Enter name of source file:

Enter name of destination:

Copied xxxxxx bytes.

Press RETURN to continue:
```

The *xxxxxx* will be replaced with a number that represents the size of the file copied.

If you specify a file that is locked, AutoCAD displays the following message:

```
Copy denied, file: filename was locked by login
name at time on date

0 files copied.

Press RETURN to continue:
```

If the file is not in use, you can unlock the file and then copy it.

228

- **Unlock files:**

  If you try to open a file that is locked, you receive the following message:

  ```
  Waiting for file: filename.dwg
  Locked by user: login name at time on date
  Press Ctrl-C to Cancel
  ```

  If you press Ctrl-C, or if 12 attempts to retrieve the file have failed, AutoCAD displays the following prompt:

  ```
  Access denied: filename.dwg is in use.
  Press Return to Continue:
  ```

  These prompts indicate that the file is locked. (If a user turns off his computer or if it crashes while editing a locked file, the file remains locked.) If you select the Unlock files option of the Files command, the following prompt appears:

  ```
  Enter locked file(s) specification:
  ```

  You enter the locked drawing's name with the extension DWG, and AutoCAD responds with the following prompt:

  ```
  The file: filename.dwg was locked by login name
  at time on date.
  Do you wish to unlock it <Y>
  ```

  After you verify that the file is not actually in use, press Enter to accept the default of Yes, and the following messages appear:

  ```
  Lock was successfully removed.
  1 files unlocked.
  Press RETURN to continue:
  ```

  If the drawing file has been deleted, and the lock file still exists, the following messages appear:

  ```
  ORPHAN lock file filename was locked by login
  name at time on date.
  Do you still wish to unlock it? <Y>
  ```

229

Example

This example demonstrates how to use the FILES command to remove all backup files in the current directory.

Command: **FILES** ↵
Click on the Delete file... *button*
Double-click in the Pattern *edit box and enter* ***.BAK**, *then press the OK button. All files matching the selected pattern are shown in the* Files: *list box*
Click on the Select all *button to highlight the files*
Press the OK *button to delete the selected files and return you to the FILES command dialog box*
Press the Exit *button*

Related Commands

> **CATALOG**
> **DEL**
> **DIR**
> **SH**
> **SHELL**

Related System Variable

> **FILEDIA**

FILL

Screen **[DRAW] [PLINE:]** *or* **[SOLID:]** *or* **[TRACE:]**

then **[FILL ON]** *or* **[FILL OFF]**

The FILL command controls the display of wide polylines, solids, and traces. The default, On, displays these entities filled in. When FILL is turned off, AutoCAD displays only the outlines of these entities (see fig. FILL.1). This setting affects both the screen display and the printed or plotted output. Solid filled entities also display only as outlines when hidden lines are removed with the HIDE command.

Filled entities are regenerated faster when the FILL command is off. A regeneration is necessary in order to see the results of changing the Fill mode setting on existing entities.

 You can execute the FILL command transparently by preceding the command name with an apostrophe ('**FILL**).

Prompts and Options

- **ON/OFF <*default*>**
- **ON:**

  When you specify the On option, AutoCAD displays wide polylines, solids, and traces as solid (filled in). Existing entities are not affected until the next regeneration.

- **OFF:**

  When the Off option is specified, AutoCAD displays wide polylines, solids, and traces as outlines.

Related Commands

> **PLINE**
> **SOLID**
> **TRACE**

Related System Variable

> **FILLMODE**

FILLET

Screen **[EDIT] [next] [FILLET:]**

Pull down **[Construct] [Fillet]**

The FILLET (pronounced FILL-it) command joins the closest end points of two entities, with an arc. The two entities are trimmed or extended so that the arc fits precisely between them. The arc is placed on the current layer if the two entities are on different layers. Otherwise, the arc is placed on the same layer as the filleted entities.

The FILLET command can be used only with line, arc, circle, or polyline entities. Filleting occurs only when enough distance exists between vertices or end points to accommodate the full fillet radius. When used with a fillet radius of 0, the FILLET command is useful for joining entities at their intersection.

You can fillet an entire polyline or two straight 2D polyline segments. Segments must be contiguous or separated by another segment, which is removed to produce the fillet. You cannot fillet one polyline segment with another entity.

Prompts and Options

- `Polyline/Radius/<select first object>:`

  The default option—select first object—immediately fillets two entities, which can be lines, circles, or arcs. Circles and arcs must be selected by picking or by coordinate entry and are filleted depending on the points you supply. Circles are not trimmed. You can select multiple objects by a window or crossing selection set, but only two objects will be filleted, sometimes with unexpected results. If you select a polyline without first using the Polyline option, AutoCAD displays an error message. When the first entity is chosen, it is highlighted.

- `Select second object:`

  You select the second entity to be filleted. The two entities are trimmed or extended until they intersect the fillet arc. Lines that are parallel to each other cannot be filleted.

- `Select 2D polyline:`

  This option fillets all the valid vertices of a 2D polyline. The fillet radius is applied to each vertex. Vertices that have enough distance between the following and preceding vertices are filleted with the set radius. The command reports the number of vertices that could or could not be filleted.

- **Enter fillet radius <0.000>:**

  You enter the radius of the arc to join the selected entities. A value of **0** forces the entities' end points to intersect each other. A positive value joins the chosen entities with an arc.

Example

The following example shows you how the FILLET command can be used on lines and polylines (see fig. FILLET.1).

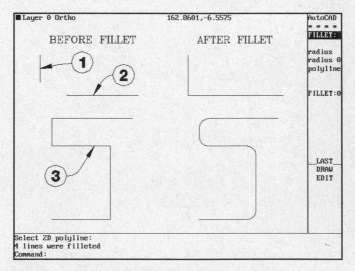

Figure FILLET.1:
The entities before and after using the FILLET command.

```
Command: FILLET↵
Polyline/Radius/<Select first object>: R↵
Enter fillet radius <0.0000>: 0 ↵
Command: FILLET↵
FILLET Polyline/Radius/<Select first object>: Pickpoint ①
```

233

```
Select second object: Pick point ②
Command: FILLET↵
Polyline/Radius/<Select first object>: R↵
Enter fillet radius <0.0000>: 6↵
Command: FILLET↵
FILLET Polyline/Radius/<Select first object>: P↵
Select 2D polyline: Pick point ③
4 lines were filleted
```

Related Command

CHAMFER

Related System Variable

FILLETRAD

FILMROLL

Screen **[RENDER] [RMAN] [FILMROL:]**

Pull down **[File] [Import/Export >] [Filmroll]**

The FILMROLL command creates a file for use by AutoShade or 3D Studio, which are Autodesk programs that render three-dimensional models. The file is given the extension FLM. After the filmroll file is created, you can load it into AutoShade or 3D Studio for rendering and animating. This file contains information about all surfaces within the drawing, independent of the current UCS or view, the last view used in the drawing, and data stored in any AutoShade or Autodesk RenderMan blocks placed in the drawing (lights, cameras, scenes, and surface finishes). The filmroll-file format is described in more detail in the *AutoShade User Guide*.

Prompts and Options

If the FILEDIA variable is set to 0, the FILMROLL command presents the following prompts and options.

- **Enter the filmroll file name < *default*>:**

    You enter a valid name for the file, including a drive and path specification, if necessary. AutoCAD assumes the current drawing's name as the default. The extension FLM is automatically added to the file name.

    After the filmroll file's name is entered, the following messages report the progress of the command:

    ```
    Creating the filmroll file
    Filmroll file created
    ```

If the FILEDIA variable is set to 1, the FILMROLL command presents a dialog box, requesting the name to be given to the filmroll file. You can choose the exact location where you want the file to be stored by navigating the Directories: and Files: list boxes. Enter a valid file name in the File: edit box and click on the OK button. The filmroll file is created, and AutoCAD displays a message to let you know that the file is created.

Related System Variable

FILEDIA

FILTER

Screen **[EDIT] [next] [SELECT:] [Filters]**

Pull down **[Assist] [Object Filters]**

The FILTER command displays the Entity Selection Filters dialog box (see fig. FILTER.1) and enables you to create filters to aid in creating select sets. FILTER can be used at the Command: prompt to create select sets for later use, or it can be transparently at a Select objects: prompt to select objects for the current command. FILTER creates a list of properties that an entity must have to be selected. Entity properties include color, linetype, layer, entity type, coordinates, and so forth.

NOTE For the FILTER command to work, entity color and linetype must be assigned directly to an entity with the COLOR, LINETYPE, or CHPROP commands. Entities with properties set to BYLAYER are not filtered.

The Entity Selection Filters dialog box is divided into three groups of options: the Entity Selection Filter List Box, the Select Filter group, and the Named Filters group. FILTER enables you to use relational operators (<,>,and !=) and Boolean operators (AND, OR, XOR, and NOT) when defining filters.

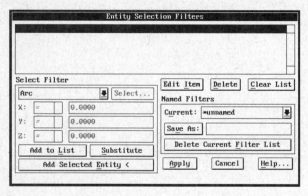

Figure FILTER.1:
The Entity Selection Filters dialog box.

Prompts and Options

- `Select Objects:`

  You select the objects to which you want to apply the filter. This prompt appears after you click on **A**pply in the Entity Selection Filters dialog box.

You can use the following options with the FILTER command.

- `Edit Item.` This option moves the filter highlighted in the Filters List Box to the Select Filter group for editing.

- `Delete`. This option deletes the filter highlighted in the Filters List Box.

- **Clear List**. This option deletes all of the filters in the Filters List Box.
- **Select Filter Drop-down list box**. This option displays a list of all of the filter types available. If you are editing an existing filter, this option shows the current filter's type.
- **Select**. This option displays a dialog box with all the available items of the filter type being edited. Valid types for the select are Xdata ID, Block Name, Color, Dimension Style, Layer, Linetype, or Text Style Name.
- **X:** This option displays the relational operators you can choose from. The relational operators are =, !=, <, <=, >, >=, *. X displays an X value in the edit box when working with coordinates, such as the starting point of a line. X displays the selected attribute when working with types such as the color of layer.
- **Y:** Y displays the relational operators you can choose from. The relational operators are =, !=, <, <=, >, >=, *. This option displays a Y value in the edit box when working with coordinates.
- **Z:** Z displays the relational operators you can choose from. The relational operators are =, !=, <, <=, >, >=, *. This option displays a Z value in the edit box when working with coordinates.
- **Add to List**. This option adds the current Select Filter settings to the Filters list box above the highlighted filter.
- **Substitute**. This option replaces the filter highlighted in the Filter List Box with the Select Filter settings.
- **Add Selected Entity**. This option adds the properties of a selected entity to the Filter List Box.
- **Current**. This option displays a drop-down list box of the available named filter lists.
- **Save as**. This option saves the current set of filters in the Filter List Box to the name entered in the Save As edit box. This creates a named filter list.
- **Delete Current Filter List**. This option deletes the current filter from the list of available named filters.
- **Apply**. This option exits the Entity Selection Filters dialog box and performs the filter on all items you select.

237

Commands

Example

The following example uses FILTER transparently to select entities to ERASE. See figure FILTER.2.

```
Command: ERASE ↵
Select Objects: 'FILTER ↵
```
Click on the Select Filter *pop-up list*
Select Color
Click on Select
Type **Blue** *or* **5** *and click on* OK
Click on the X: *pop-up list and select* !=
Click on Add to List
Click on Add selected Entity *and pick the line at* ①
Highlight Color = BYLAYER *in the Filters List Box*
Click on Delete
Highlight Line Start *and click on* Edit Item
Set the X: *and* Y: *pop-up lists to* >= *and click on* Substitute
Delete the Line End *filter*
Delete the Normal Vector *filter*
Type **FILTER1** *in the* Save As *edit box and click on* Save As
Click on Apply *and select all of the entities*
```
6 found
4 were filtered out
Select objects: ↵
```

Once an item is selected using a filter, you can change the filter without affecting the selected entities.

Related Command

SELECT

FINISH

Pull down **[Render] [Finishes]**

Screen **[RENDER] [FINISH]**

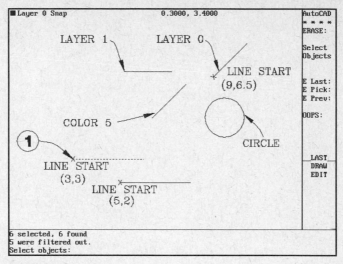

```
■ Layer 0 Snap          0.3000, 3.4000        AutoCAD
                                               * * * *
                                              ERASE:
     LAYER 1         LAYER 0
                                              Select
                                              Objects
                            LINE START
                            (9,6.5)            E Last:
                        ×                      E Pick:
                                               E Prev:

                                              OOPS:
      COLOR 5

    ①                                          LAST
                      ×............            DRAW
    LINE START                                 EDIT
      (3,3)      ×
            LINE START
              (5,2)

6 selected, 6 found
5 were filtered out.
Select objects:
```

Figure FILTER.2:
Objects selected by using the FILTER command.

The FINISH command enables you to assign and control surface finish characteristics of three-dimensional objects for rendering. The surface finish characteristics you can control with the FINISH command are name, color, ambiance, diffusion, shininess, and roughness. The FINISH command also enables you to share finishes between drawings with the import and export options.

A finish is assigned to an object in one of two ways. The first way is to assign a finish directly to an object. The second way assigns the finish to an AutoCAD Color Index (ACI). All objects with the same ACI share the same finish.

The FINISH command has four dialog boxes. The dialog boxes are Finishes, New/Modify Finish, Import Preset Finish, and Attach by AutoCAD Color Index.

Prompts and Options

The Finishes dialog box is the main dialog box for the FINISH command; all other FINISH dialog boxes and options are accessed through this dialog box. The Finishes dialog box is shown in figure FINISH.1.

Figure FINISH.1:
The Finishes dialog box.

The Finishes Dialog Box

- **Finishes.** The Finishes list box shows the currently defined finishes. A period or a number appears after the name of the finish in the list box. The number is an AutoCAD Color Index (ACI). Finishes with an ACI number after them are attached to that ACI, and all objects with that ACI share the attached finish.

  The *GLOBAL* finish is the default finish template. If you want to define several new finishes with common values for specific finish characteristics, set the *GLOBAL* finish to the common values shared between finishes. All new finishes will have the values defined in the *GLOBAL* finish.

  To modify, delete, export, or attach a finish, first highlight it in the Finishes list box and then pick the appropriate button.

- **New.** The New button displays the New Finish dialog box so that you can define a new finish. The *GLOBAL* finish defines the default characteristics for new finishes. The New Finish and the Modify Finish dialog boxes are identical in appearance and features.

- **Modify.** The Modify button displays the Modify Finish dialog box so that you can change the characteristics of a finish. Highlight the finish you want to modify in the Finishes list box, then click on the Modify button.

- **Delete**. The <u>D</u>elete button deletes a highlighted finish from the list of defined finishes.

- **Import.** The <u>I</u>mport button displays the Import Preset Finish dialog box, enabling you to select a pre-defined finish from a list box for import into the current drawing. You can also preview the finish before importing it by highlighting a finish and then clicking on the Preview Finish icon. The pre-defined finishes are stored in the NULLSURF.SP3 file.

- **Export.** The E<u>x</u>port button writes the highlighted finish to the NULLSURF.SP3 file. Only exported finishes can be imported into other drawings.

Currently, AutoCAD does not offer a way to delete a preset finish from within the AutoCAD program. However, the NULLSURF.SP3 file is an ASCII text file and it can be modified with any ASCII text editor. Use your text editor to delete any unwanted finishes.

- **Pick.** The <u>P</u>ick button enables you to pick the finishes block in your drawing to modify, delete, export, or attach. The Finishes dialog box disappears momentarily to let you pick the block and reappears after you pick, highlighting the finish name in the Finishes list box.

- **Entities.** The <u>E</u>ntities button in the Attach group assigns a highlighted finish to a specific entity. When the Finishes dialog box disappears, pick the object to assign the finish.

- **ACI.** The <u>A</u>CI button in the Attach group displays the Attach by AutoCAD Color Index dialog box, enabling you to assign a highlighted finish to an AutoCAD Color Index (ACI). The ACI is the same as the AutoCAD color number. All objects that have the same ACI will also have the same finish.

  The color of the finish can be set independently from the actual entity color. This means that you do not need to know the rendering color at the time the object is drawn, and you do not need a display device that is capable of displaying all AutoCAD colors to draw objects that will be rendered later.

The ACI method for attaching a finish is more efficient when there are many objects sharing the same finish because you do not have to pick each object requiring the same finish.

To assign a color to an ACI, highlight a finish in the Finishes dialog box, and then click on ACI. When the Attach by AutoCAD Color Index dialog appears, pick an index number. The ACI that you pick will be removed from the list; therefore, it cannot be used more than once.

New and Modify Finish Dialog Boxes

Finish characteristics are set in the New and Modify Finish dialog boxes. You can name a finish, change the name of a finish, specify a specific color for the finish, alter a finish's settings, or preview a finish. Both the New Finish and Modify Finish dialog boxes are explained here because their features are identical. The Modify Finish dialog box is shown in figure FINISH.2.

Figure FINISH.2:
The Modify Finish dialog box.

- **Finish Name:** The Finish Name edit box is used to assign or alter the name of a finish. You cannot change the name of the *GLO-BAL* finish. The name of the finish is limited to eight characters.

- **Use Entity Color.** The Use Entity Color button in the Color group causes objects to be rendered with the color of the entities in the AutoCAD drawing. When a finish uses the entity's color, Current Color in the color group will display `<entity color>`.

- **Set Color.** The Set Color button in the Color group displays the color dialog box, allowing you to explicitly specify the color of a finish. The explicit color setting overrides the entity color. You can set the color numerically by specifying the color by red, green, and blue (RGB) values or hue, luminance, and saturation (HLS) values. You also can set the color visually by picking the color from the color wheel. Current Color in the Color group displays the RGB or HLS values of the specified color.

- **Ambient:** The Ambient edit box in the Settings group adjusts the amount of ambient light that is reflected by a finish. Ambient light is light that does not have a source or direction and illuminates everything evenly. Values must range from zero to one.

- **Diffuse:** The Diffuse edit box in the Settings group specifies the amount of light hitting an object that is dispersed in all directions by a finish. Values must range from zero to one.

- **Specular:** The Specular edit box in the Settings group specifies the shininess of a finish. The shinier a finish is, the more pronounced the highlights become. Values must range from zero to one.

- **Roughness:** The Roughness edit box in the Settings group specifies the size of the specular highlight. The roughness setting will only have an effect if Specular is greater than zero. Values must range from 0 to one.

- **Preview Finish.** The Preview Finish button in the Preview group shows you the approximate effects of the settings and color characteristics. You can also click on the Preview Finish icon to preview the finish.

Example

This example of the FINISH command uses a 3D torus and a single point light to create and apply a gold finish to the torus, as in figure FINISH.3.

Choose Render, *then* Finish
Click on **N**ew, *and then in the* Finish **N**ame *edit box, enter* **GOLD**
Click on Set **C**olor *in the* Color *group*
In the Color *dialog box, set* Red *to 1,* Green *to .83, and* Blue *to 0, and then click on* OK
Set **A**mbient *to .40,* **D**iffuse *to .53,* **S**pecular *to .93, and* **R**oughness *to .02*
Click on the preview finish icon
Note the effects of the settings on the sphere. The actual finish will appear slightly different, depending on lighting conditions.

Click on OK
`Enter New Finish location <current>:` *Pick any point*
Click on Entities *in the Attach group*
`Gathering objects...`
`Select objects to attach "GOLD" to:` *Pick the torus*
`1 found`
`Select objects:` ↵
`Updating drawing...done.`
Click on OK in the Finishes dialog box
Use the RENDER command to render the torus and view the new finish

Related Commands

LIGHT
RPREF

GIFIN

The GIFIN command imports a Graphics Interchange Format raster file into AutoCAD. AutoCAD scans the raster image and creates a block consisting of a rectangular colored solid for each pixel in the GIF file. Once a raster image is imported into AutoCAD, you can trace over the raster image with AutoCAD geometry to create an AutoCAD drawing of the raster image. When you are through, you can erase the raster image. Raster images can be scaled, mirrored, and rotated like regular entities.

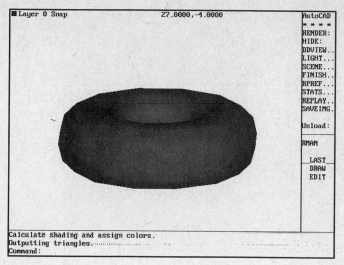

Figure FINISH.3:
The rendered torus with a gold finish.

 Do not explode the block representation of a raster file. If you do, the resulting entities will use large quantities of disk space and memory.

 The system variable GRIPBLOCK should be set to 0 to avoid highlighting all the solid entities in the block.

Prompts and Options

- `GIF file name:`

  At this prompt, you enter the name of the GIF file you want to import (you do not need to include the extension).

- `Insertion point <0,0,0>:`

  At this prompt, you enter the X, Y, and Z coordinates or pick the insertion point for the raster file.

- **Scale Factor:**

  You enter a number or drag the crosshairs to scale the raster file from the insertion point.

- **New length:**

  If you press Enter at the Scale Factor prompt, you will be prompted to pick a point to specify the scale factor.

The following options actually function as separate commands that control how a raster file will be imported. (These same options are also available under the PCXIN and TIFIN commands.)

- **RIASPECT**. You enter a real number to control the aspect ration of the raster image.

   To display VGA or MCGA images in 320 X 200 mode, use an RIASPECT of 0.8333.

- **RIBACKG**. This command sets the background color of the raster image. Areas of the raster image that are the same color as RIBACKG are not converted to solid entities in a block.

   To reduce the size of an imported image, set RIBACKG to the most common color in your raster image.

- **RIEDGE**. RIEDGE controls the amount of the image imported. Enter **0** (the default) to disable edge detection; enter **1** to 255 to increase edge detection. The higher the RIEDGE number, the more prominent an image must be to be imported.

   Use RIEDGE to import just the edges of an image if you want to trace over it with vectors.

- **RIGAMUT.** RIGAMUT controls the number of colors that are imported from a raster image. The value reflects the number of colors starting with 0 (black) through 256. If you enter **3**, you import the black, red, and yellow areas of the raster file. Use RIEDGE and RITHRESH to control importing on a monochrome display.
- **RIGREY.** If RIGREY is set to a non-zero number, the raster file is imported in shades of grey. The default is 0.
- **RITHRESH.** RITHRESH controls the amount of raster image imported based in the brightness of the image area. The default is 0. Enter a number to import only pixels with a brightness over the number.

Example

The following example imports a GIF file called TEST.GIF into AutoCAD at 3,3,0.

```
Command: GIFIN↵
GIF file name: TEST ↵
Insertion point <0,0,0>: 3,3,0↵
Scale factor: 2 ↵
```

Related Commands

PCXIN
TIFFIN

Related System Variable

GRIPBLOCK

GRAPHSCR

Enter **GRAPHSCR** *or* **'GRAPHSCR**

The GRAPHSCR command switches a single-screen AutoCAD system from the text screen to the graphics screen. On systems with windowing environments, the switch is between the graphics window and the text window. You can press F1 to switch between the two types of screen display. This command has the opposite effect of the TEXTSCR command. Neither of these commands affects an AutoCAD system with dual screens. The GRAPHSCR command often is used to return to the drawing editor after commands such as LIST, STATUS, TIME, or TYPE are invoked. The GRAPHSCR command can be used transparently.

Related Command

TEXTSCR

Related System Variable

SCREENMODE

GRID

Screen [SETTINGS] [GRID:]

The GRID command displays a rectangular array of reference points, which are aligned with the current UCS. You can turn the grid on or off by pressing F7 or Ctrl-G. You can change the grid's spacing in both axes, set the spacing so that it is equal to the current Snap increment, and adjust the grid aspect ratio for special needs (such as isometric drafting). You also can turn the grid on and off and alter its appearance for each viewport. The grid is a visual tool on the display and, therefore, is not plotted.

Prompts and Options

- Grid spacing(X) or ON/OFF/Snap/Aspect <0.0000>:

    The default option is to enter a number at this prompt. AutoCAD sets the grid spacing to that number of drawing units. If you enter a number followed by an **X**, the grid spacing is adjusted to a multiple of the current snap spacing. If you set the snap, for example, to a spacing of one drawing unit, you can display a grid point at every 10 snap points by entering **10X**. If the grid is turned on but cannot be seen because the spacing between dots is not great enough, you see the following prompt: `Grid too dense to display`.

On and Off. The On and Off options are used to set the display of the grid. The most recent settings for spacing and aspect are used. You can toggle the grid on and off by pressing Ctrl-G or F7.

Snap. The Snap option sets the grid spacing to the current snap increment value.

Aspect. The Aspect option enables you to display a grid that has different X and Y spacing. This feature is detailed in the following example.

Example

In this example, a grid is displayed with an X (horizontal) spacing value of .5 drawing units and a Y (vertical) spacing of 1 drawing unit. The grid that AutoCAD draws in shown in figure GRID.1.

```
Command: GRID↵
Grid spacing(x) or ON/OFF/Snap/Aspect <0.0000>: A↵
Horizontal spacing(x) <0.0000>: .5↵
Vertical spacing(x) <0.0000>: 1 ↵
```

Related Commands

DDRMODES
LIMITS
SNAP

Related System Variables

GRIDMODE
GRIDUNIT

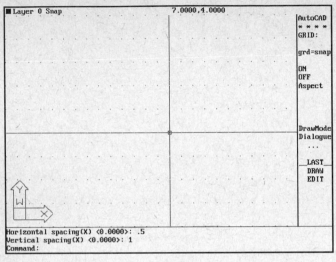

Figure GRID.01:
The grid set so that the X and Y aspects have different values.

HANDLES

Screen **[SETTINGS] [HANDLES:]**

The HANDLES command enables and disables the assigning of entity handles. When an entity is added to a drawing, it is given an entity name and, if handles are enabled, a unique entity identifier called an *entity handle*. The entity names change from session to session in the drawing editor, but the entity handle always remains the same. This ensures continuity between entities within the drawing editor and external programs that reference them.

Entity handles are used by external programs to directly access drawing entities. When a program needs information about an entity, it can use the entity handle to refer to the entity state. The PTEXT AutoLISP program, which comes with Release 12, uses entity handles to keep track of the correct text entities as it performs text entry and editing.

Prompts and Options

- **ON/DESTROY:**

  The only two options are to turn on the entity handles or to destroy all the handles that are associated with existing entities. At this prompt, type the entire keyword **On** or **Destroy**. The Destroy process also causes AutoCAD to discontinue assigning handles to new entities.

- **Proceed with handle destruction <NO>:**

  Due to the severity of destroying entity handles, AutoCAD displays a prompt to confirm your intention. You can type **No** or press Enter to abort the handle-destruction process; otherwise, enter the key phrase shown to complete the destruction of the entity handles. The *key phrase* is one of five possible phrases that are randomly chosen to complete the destruction process. After you correctly type in the key phrase, all handles are removed from the drawing database.

Example

The following example shows how to destroy the entity handles within a drawing. The warning text and key phrase are shown in figure HANDLE.1.

```
Command: HANDLES↵
ON/DESTROY: DESTROY↵
Proceed with handle destruction <NO>: DESTROY HANDLES ↵
```

Related System Variable

HANDLES

HATCH

Screen [DRAW] [HATCH:]

Pull down [Draw] [Hatch]

```
***** W A R N I N G  *****

Completing this command will destroy ALL
database handle information in the drawing.
Once destroyed, links into the drawing from
external database files cannot be made.

If you really want to destroy the database
handle information, please confirm this by
entering `GO AHEAD' to proceed or `NO'
to abort the command.

Proceed with handle destruction <NO>: GO AHEAD
Database handles removed.

Command:
```

Figure HANDLE.1:
The warning message and key phrase for entity-handle destruction.

The HATCH command fills areas of your drawing with patterns. In the crosshatching process, you select a boundary that AutoCAD fills with the pattern you specify. The resulting hatch region is saved as an unnamed block definition that can be moved, copied, colored, and manipulated in much the same manner as other blocks. Hatches, like all other AutoCAD 2D entities, can be created in any definable construction plane. This versatility makes hatches very desirable for adding textures to three-dimensional models such as buildings.

AutoCAD offers more than 50 predefined hatch patterns in the file ACAD.PAT. These patterns include brick, stone, wood, grass, and other textures. The HATCH command also enables you to create simple patterns directly at the Command: prompt.

Prompts and Options

- **Pattern (? or name/U,style)<** *default***>:**

  At this prompt, you enter a pattern name or type **?** to see a list of available patterns. The default is the current pattern. If no pattern has yet been used, you can enter its name with an optional style, or you can use the U option to create a user-defined pattern. Hatch pattern styles are explained later in this section.

The specified hatch pattern must be defined in the file ACAD.PAT or stored in a file with the pattern name and a PAT extension. If you want to use a hatch pattern named GLASS, for example, it must be in the ACAD.PAT file or a file named GLASS.PAT.

- `Pattern(s) to list <*>:`

  You enter the names of patterns you want to list, using wild cards if desired. All hatch-pattern definitions stored in the ACAD.PAT file are listed. This option does not list patterns that are defined in other files.

  To view examples of the supplied hatch patterns, use the new BHATCH command.

- `Angle for crosshatch lines <0>:`

  The U option, for defining a user-specific hatch pattern, presents this prompt. This pattern is a simple repeating-line pattern with a set distance between each line. You can enter a value for the pattern angle or pick two points that describe the angle of the pattern.

- `Spacing between lines <1>:`

  You enter the number of drawing units for the spacing between each line in the user-defined pattern.

- `Double hatch area? <N>:`

  The user-defined hatch is a single series of repeating lines. This option adds another set of repeating lines drawn perpendicular to the first set of lines using the same spacing.

- `Scale for pattern <1>:`

  This prompt is displayed after you enter a valid pattern name at the first HATCH command prompt. You enter a scale factor to be applied to the pattern definition to enlarge or reduce the hatch drawn.

- **Angle for pattern <0>:**

  At this prompt, you enter an angle to rotate the pattern. Note that some hatch patterns are angled by default.

- **Select objects:**

  You select the entities to form the hatch boundary. The boundary forms the limits within which the pattern will be created. The boundary objects chosen affect the accuracy of the hatching. If the entities do not form a closed area (their end points do not meet), the hatch may be incomplete (see figure HATCH.1).

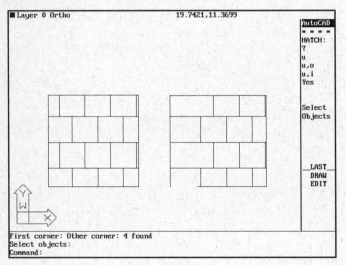

Figure HATCH.1:
Incomplete and complete boundaries for hatch patterns.

To hatch a region bounded by entities that extend beyond the desired area, you can use the PLINE command to create a temporary hatch boundary. Hatch the closed polyline, and then delete it. The hatch block remains within the drawing.

To re-create the boundary for a hatch pattern semi-automatically, use the new BPOLY command. To create boundaries, preview hatches, and better control hatching, use the BHATCH command.

Hatching Styles

Hatching styles, which you specify by placing a comma and the style letter after the pattern name, affect the manner in which hatching occurs. The hatch boundary forms the limits within which the hatch will fill. If entities are within the outermost boundary that is chosen, and those entities form another boundary, the hatching stops at that inner boundary. Hatch styles determine how AutoCAD regards these inner boundaries.

The first hatch style, N (Normal), tells the HATCH command that all boundaries found are valid. AutoCAD fills every other closed region found within the selected boundary objects. This style has the same effect as using no style name at all. The second style type, O (fill Outermost), fills only the area defined by the outermost set of boundaries. The final hatch style, I (ignore Internal boundaries), completely fills the area defined by the outermost boundary, regardless of any other possible boundaries found.

Finally, different entities are hatched differently by the HATCH command. Text, attributes, and shape entities have a rectangular boundary that follows the outline of the letters or the shape. AutoCAD recognizes solids and trace entities and does not perform hatching within their boundaries. Blocks are hatched according to the arrangement of entities within the blocks. If the entities form boundaries, those boundaries are treated as normal entity boundaries. Paper-space viewports are considered valid boundaries, so the HATCH command fills the viewport with the selected pattern.

Example

This example shows how to use the HATCH command to fill in the wall shown in figure HATCH.2.

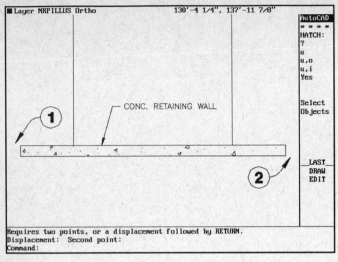

Figure HATCH.2:
Filling a wall with the concrete hatch pattern.

```
Command: HATCH⏎
Pattern (? or name/U,style): AR-CONC⏎
Scale for pattern <1>: 5⏎
Angle for pattern <0>: ⏎
Select objects: W⏎
First corner: Pick point at ①
Second corner: Pick point at ②
```

Related Commands

> BHATCH
> BPOLY

Related System Variables

> HPANG
> HPDOUBLE
> HPNAME
> HPSCALE
> HPSPACE
> SNAPBASE

HELP

Screen   **[INQUIRY] [HELP:]**

Screen   **[* * * *] [HELP]**

Pull down   **[Assist] [Help!]**

The HELP command provides information on the commands available within the AutoCAD program. You can issue the HELP command transparently by preceding the command with an apostrophe ('HELP). A question mark (?) also invokes help. If HELP is used transparently, it provides information about the command that is currently in process.

When you enter HELP at the `Command:` prompt, AutoCAD displays the Help dialog box shown in figure HELP.1. This dialog box displays help for the current command in use as well as providing a comprehensive index from which you can select other commands. The Help information is cross-referenced to the *AutoCAD Reference Manual*.

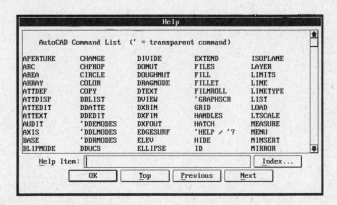

Figure HELP.1:
The AutoCAD Help dialog box.

Prompts and Options

The HELP command dialog box has an edit box where you can type the particular command on which you want information. In addition to standard dialog box buttons, the dialog box also contains buttons that perform the following functions:

- **Index.** This button displays an alphabetized list of all items that you may request help about. If you pick one of the items, its help information will be displayed.
- **Top.** This button displays lists of AutoCAD commands and system variables.
- **Previous.** This button displays the previous item of help information in relation to the information shown in the dialog box.
- **Next.** This button displays the next item of help information in relation to the information shown in the dialog box.

HIDE

Screen **[DISPLAY] [HIDE:]**

Pull down **[Render] [Hide]**

The HIDE command temporarily suppresses the display of any lines or edges that are hidden behind a surface. A *surface* can be a circle, solid, trace, wide polyline, polygon mesh, extruded edge, or 3D face. The HIDE command gives an opaque top and bottom face to extruded circles, solids, traces, and wide polylines. This command typically is used to present a three-dimensional model. HIDE also is useful for verifying the accuracy of a model's surfaces.

The command is completely automatic unless issued from the screen or pull-down menus, in which case you are prompted to confirm the hide operation. A hidden-line removal may take time, depending on the complexity of the model. You can reduce this time by using the ZOOM command to fill the display with only the desired geometry. AutoCAD hides only the information that appears within the boundaries of the current display. The HIDE command also works more quickly if unneeded layers are frozen.

After hidden lines are removed, the entire drawing can be displayed only after a regeneration of the drawing, caused by using any display command. To save a hidden-line view for later display, use the MSLIDE command.

The HIDE command affects only the current viewport, and you can hide only one viewport at a time. Also, only entities on layers that are turned on and thawed will be used for hidden-line removal. Displays made by the command are lost after the drawing session ends or the viewport is regenerated. The SHADE command performs similar results by filling the faces with color. The SHADE command is quicker than the HIDE command, but not always as accurate. The HIDE command does not affect plotting. The PLOT command includes an option for hiding entities.

Example

This example demonstrates the effects of the HIDE command in two viewports. Figure HIDE.1 shows the objects in the right-hand viewport after the HIDE command .

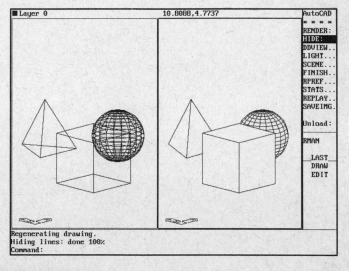

Figure HIDE.1:
The right viewport displays entities of the left viewport after hidden lines are removed.

```
Command: HIDE ↵
Regenerating Drawing.
Hiding lines: done nn%
Removing Hidden Lines: xxx
```

Related Commands

RENDER
SHADE

ID

Screen **[INQUIRY] [ID:]**

Pull down **[Assist] [Inquiry >] [ID Point]**

The ID command identifies the absolute X,Y,Z coordinates of a single point within 3D space. You pick a point within the drawing editor, and AutoCAD displays the point's coordinates. The ID command is useful for finding the location of points along entities that do not lie parallel to the WCS.

 You can execute the ID command transparently by preceding the command name with an apostrophe ('ID).

Prompts and Options

- **Point:**
  You specify a point in the drawing editor for which you want to retrieve the coordinates. You can use object snap overrides or any other method of point selection.

Example

This example illustrates how to use the ID command. The ID command displays the coordinates of the point shown in figure ID.1.

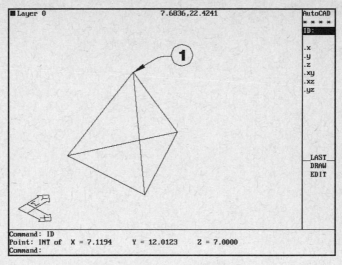

Figure ID.1:
Coordinates retrieved by the ID command.

```
Command: ID ↵
Point: INT of Pick point ①
```

Related System Variable

LASTPOINT

IGESIN

Screen **[UTILITY] [IGES] [IGESIN:]**

Pull down **[File] [Import/Export >] [IGES In]**

The IGESIN command imports drawing information from a file that conforms to the *Initial Graphics Exchange Specification* (IGES). IGES enables the accurate exchange of data between CAD systems that support the IGES specification. IGES is an international standard that is used by many larger CAD systems as well as PC-based CAD systems, such as AutoCAD. When you register your AutoCAD software, you

261

receive a copy of the current IGES Interface Specification, which details which features of AutoCAD are supported in the most recent release of the IGES specification.

Prompts and Options

By default, IGESIN displays a dialog box for you to select the IGES file you want to import. If the FILEDIA variable is set to 0, you will instead receive the `File name:` prompt, at which you enter the path and file name of a valid IGES file. The Select IGES File dialog box (see fig. IGESIN.1) initially displays the names of any files with an IGS extension. If the file you want to import is in the list, you can highlight it and click on the OK button. You also can navigate the Directories list box if the file is in a different drive or directory. In addition to the standard OK, Help, and Cancel buttons, the dialog box presents the following buttons:

- **Type it.** This dialog box button produces a prompt in the AutoCAD command line area for you to manually enter the name of the IGES import file.

- **Default.** This button resets the default options such as filename pattern and directory location if they have been changed.

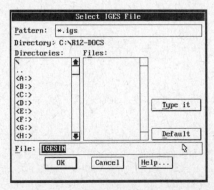

Figure IGESIN.1:
The dialog box for importing an IGES file.

Related Command

    IGESOUT

Related System Variable

    FILEDIA

IGESOUT

Screen **[UTILITY] [IGES] [IGESOUT:]**

Pull down **[File] [Import/Export >] [IGES Out]**

The IGESOUT command exports AutoCAD drawing information to a file that conforms to the Initial Graphics Exchange Specification. Other CAD programs that support the IGES interface then can read in the entity information created by AutoCAD. When you register your AutoCAD software, you receive a copy of the current IGES Interface Specification, which details which features of AutoCAD are supported in the most recent release of the IGES specification.

Prompts and Options

By default, the IGESOUT command displays a dialog box that enables you to name the IGES file you want to create. If the FILEDIA variable is set to 0, you instead see the `File name:` prompt, on which you enter a valid file name. The Create IGES File dialog box (see fig. IGESOUT.1) initially displays the name of the current drawing file. To use this name for the export file, click on the OK button. You may also navigate the Directories list box if you want to store the file in a different drive or directory. In addition to the standard OK, Help, and Cancel buttons, the dialog box has the following buttons:

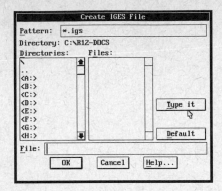

Figure IGESOUT.1:
The dialog box for exporting an IGES file.

- **Type it.** This dialog box button produces a prompt in the AutoCAD command line area for you to enter the name of the IGES export file.
- **Default.** This button resets the default options such as filename pattern and directory location if they have been changed.

Related Commands

> **DXFIN**
> **DXFOUT**
> **IGESIN**

Related System Variable

> **FILEDIA**

INSERT

Screen **[DRAW] [INSERT:]**

Screen **[BLOCKS] [INSERT:]**

Pull down **[Draw] [Insert]**

The INSERT command places blocks created with the BLOCK command into the current drawing. INSERT enables you to specify how blocks are located, scaled, and rotated when added to your drawing. If a block name that you specify is not currently defined in the drawing, INSERT attempts to load the block from disk.

Prompts and Options

- **Block name (or ?) <default>:**

  At this prompt, you enter a block name to insert or accept the default name of the last block inserted. If the name you supply is not a block defined in the current drawing, the program attempts to find a file with a matching name along the AutoCAD search path. If no match is found, the command is aborted, and you receive an error message. To see a list of the blocks defined in the current drawing, enter a question mark at this prompt. If you want to enter a drawing file from disk, enter a tilde (~) to display the Select File dialog box.

  If you type an asterisk before the name of the block to insert, AutoCAD automatically explodes the block when it places it into your drawing.

- **Insertion point:**

  You specify an insertion point for the block. This insertion point is used to place, scale, and rotate the block in the drawing editor.

  Until you specify a point for the block you insert, the block is highlighted so you can drag it on-screen and have an idea of how the block will look when placed. If you know in advance the various insertion parameters (X, Y, and Z scales and rotation), you can preset the parameters so the highlighted image is more accurate before being inserted. You can enter these preset parameters at this prompt before you choose the insertion point. A description of each parameter option follows:

- **Scale**. The Scale option presets the scale in each axis (X, Y, and Z) to the same value. The highlighted block is updated, and then you can choose its insertion point. After the block is located in the drawing, you are not prompted to enter a value for the scale factors.

- **Xscale.** The Xscale option presets the scale in the X axis only. Insertion then proceeds as with Pscale (see note following).

- **Yscale.** The Yscale option presets the scale in the Y axis only. Insertion then proceeds as with Pscale.

- **Zscale.** The Zscale option presets the scale in the Z axis only. Insertion then proceeds as with Pscale.

- **Rotate.** The Rotate option presets the block rotation value. The highlighted block is updated, and insertion can proceed. After the block is located, this angle is used and you are not prompted to supply this value.

 The following five options enable you to preset the high-lighted block's values, but then you must answer the INSERT command's usual prompts about scale factors and rotation.

- **Pscale.** The Pscale option presets all three axes' scales, but after the block is located, you still are prompted for a block scaling factor.

- **Pxscale.** The Pxscale option presets the block's X axis scale factor, but after the block is located, you still are prompted for the scale along this axis.

- **Pyscale.** The Pyscale option presets the block's Y axis scale factor, but after the block is located, you still are prompted for the scale along this axis.

- **Pzscale.** The Pzscale option presets the block's Z axis scale factor, but after the block is located, you still are prompted for the scale along this axis.

- **Protate.** The Protate option presets the highlighted block's rotation. After the block is located in the drawing editor, you again are prompted for a final rotation angle.

- **X scale factor <1>/Corner/XYZ:**

  You enter a number for the X-scale factor, accept the default value, or enter an option. You receive this prompt when none of the scale factors is preset. A positive scale factor creates an inserted block in the same orientation as the original block definition. If you enter a negative value, the block appears mirrored about the Y axis. You also can specify a scale factor by dragging your pointing device or by using the Corner option. For either of these choices, the distance between the two specified points are used as the scale factors for both the X and Y axes.

- **Y scale factor (default=X):**

  You enter a number for the Y-scale factor or accept the default. By default, this value is the same as the X-scale factor.

- **Rotation angle <0>:**

  At this prompt, you enter a number for the rotation angle to be used when inserting the block. You can specify a point either by coordinates or by dragging the pointing device, and the angle between this point and the insertion point will be used as the rotation angle.

- **X scale factor <1>/Corner:**

  This prompt appears if you use the XYZ option. You will be prompted for scale factors for each of the three axes, beginning with the X axis. The corner option works the same as in the first prompt.

- **Y scale factor (default=X):**

  This second prompt of the XYZ option enables you to specify a scale factor for the Y axis. By default, this value is set to the same scale as the one for the X axis.

- **Z scale factor (default=X):**

  This last prompt of the XYZ option enables you to specify a scale factor for the Z axis. By default, this value is set to the same scale as that for the X axis.

To change the scale factors of a block after it is inserted, use the DDMODIFY command. You cannot use the EXPLODE command to explode blocks with unequal X, Y, and Z scale factors.

Example

The following example uses the INSERT command to insert a block of a chair as illustrated in figure INSERT.1. This exercise demonstrates the effects that uneven scale factors can have upon a block.

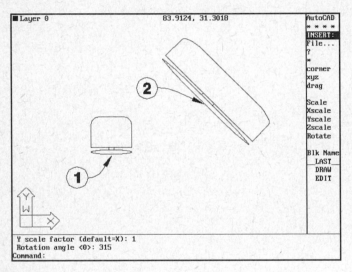

Figure INSERT.1:
A chair block inserted with various scaling and rotation factors.

```
Command: INSERT↵
Block name (or ?): CHAIR↵
Insertion point: Pick point ①
X scale factor <1> / Corner / XYZ: ↵
Y scale factor (default=X): ↵
Rotation angle <0>: ↵
Command: INSERT↵
Block name (or ?): CHAIR↵
Insertion point: Pick point ②
X scale factor <1> / Corner / XYZ: 3 ↵
```

```
Y scale factor (default=X): 1↵
Rotation angle <0>: 315 ↵
```

Related Commands

DDINSERT
DDMODIFY
EXPLODE
MINSERT
XREF

Related System Variables

INSBASE
INSNAME

ISOPLANE

The ISOPLANE command is used in conjunction with the STYLE option of the SNAP command to create isometric drawings that resemble 3D objects. The ISOPLANE command is a drawing aid (similar to the GRID, SNAP, and ORTHO commands) that enables you to draw in the three isometric drafting planes.

Setting the Style option of the SNAP command to Isometric forces the crosshair cursor to align with the 30, 90, and 150 degree axes used in isometric drafting. If Grid mode is turned on, it too will display as isometric. When Ortho mode is on in Isometric mode, lines can be drawn only in the two axes of the current isometric plane.

Figure ISOPLANE.1 demonstrates how a 2D isometric drawing appears to be three-dimensional. The figure contains three distinct isometric planes at 30, 90, and 150 degrees. The ISOPLANE command enables you to specify which plane to work in and should be used in conjunction with the ORTHO command to restrict drawing to a single plane at one time. When you are drawing in one of the isometric planes, the crosshairs align parallel to that plane.

Use the Ctrl-E control-key sequence to quickly switch between the three isometric planes.

Prompts and Options

- **Left/Top/Right/<Toggle>:**

  The Left option sets the current isometric plane to the left plane
  (see fig. ISOPLANE.1). After you select this or any other option at
  this prompt, the crosshairs are rotated to reflect the plane you
  chose.

  The Right option sets the current isometric plane to the right plane.

  The Top option sets the current isometric plane to the top plane.

  Accepting the default option, Toggle, cycles among the left, top,
  and right isometric planes. If your current plane is top, it is
  changed to right, and so on. After pressing Enter at the prompt,
  you return to AutoCAD's Command: prompt.

Example

This example demonstrates how to use the ISOPLANE and SNAP commands to prepare to draw in the left isometric plane. The drawing shown in
figure ISOPLANE.1 shows the crosshairs aligned to the left plane.

```
Command: SNAP ↵
Snap spacing or ON/OFF/Aspect/Rotate/Style <1.0000>: S↵
Standard/Isometric <S>: i↵
Vertical spacing <1.0000>: ↵
Command: ISOPLANE ↵
Left/Top/Right/<Toggle>: ↵
Current Isometric plane is: Top
```

Related Commands

DDRMODES
ELLIPSE
SNAP

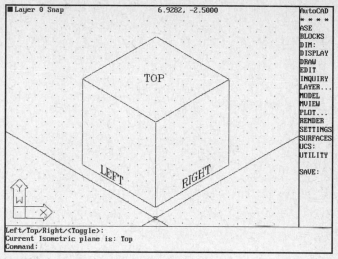

Figure ISOPLANE.1:
A sample of 2D entities that appear to be three dimensional.

Related System Variable

SNAPISOPAIR

LAYER

The LAYER command enables you to control layers used for the drawing, displaying, and plotting of entities. Layers enable you to group similar types of information in a drawing for easier editing and creation. Layers, similar to sheets of mylar used for overlay drafting, ease the burden of keeping track of the various elements in your drawing. The LAYER command enables you to set the color, linetype and visibility of each layer, make new layers, set the current layer, freeze or thaw layers, or lock and unlock layers.

You also can use the DDLMODES command to modify layer properties. Instead of working from the command line, as the LAYER command works, the DDLMODES command uses a dialog box to display all layers and modify their properties.

Prompts and Options

- **?/Make/Set/New/ON/OFF/Color/Ltype/Freeze/Thaw/ LOck/Unlock:**

  This prompt presents all of the LAYER command's options. The following paragraphs explain each option.

  The ? option lists all of the layers defined within the current drawing. This list contains the full name of the layer, its color and linetype, and its state of visibility. When using this option, you get an additional prompt, `Layer name(s) to list <*>:`, that enables you to specify which layer name(s) you want listed. The default lists all the layers; but, if you are looking for information about particular layers only, you can type each layer's name, separated by commas, or use wild-card searches to narrow down the layers listed.

- **New current layer <default>:**

  Both the Make and Set options use this prompt. Enter the name of a layer to set as the current layer. The Make option creates a new layer with the name entered and then sets it as the current layer. Set establishes the layer name as the current layer only if that layer already exists. The current layer is where new entities that you draw are placed. These new entities take on the color and linetype characteristics of the layer on which they reside.

- **New layer name(s):**

  The New option prompts you to enter the names of new layers that you want to add to the current drawing. If you want to enter more than one layer name, separate each name with a comma. The layer name can be up to 31 characters in length and can include numbers, letters, and special characters, such as $, -, and _.

- **Layer name(s) to turn Off:**

  The Off option affects the visibility of layers, which governs how they are considered during screen redraws. A layer that is turned off is not visible on-screen, but the layer's entities are calculated during any screen regenerations. To have layers ignored during screen regenerations, use the Freeze option. The Layer command warns you if you attempt to turn off the current layer.

- **Layer name(s) to turn On:**

  Enter the names of layers to turn on. As with the other LAYER options, if you need to turn on more than one layer, separate each layer name with a comma.

  Color

  The Color option is used to assign the color to display entities. Enter a color number or name for layers you specify. Then, at the `Layer name(s) for color` *number* `<default>:` prompt, enter the name(s) of the layers you want that color assigned to. Any entity whose color is set to BYLAYER (the default for new entities) assumes the color assigned to the layer on which it resides. The color you enter can be any valid color number for your graphics card, or the name of one of the first seven colors: red, yellow, green, cyan, blue, magenta, or white.

- **Linetype (or ?) <CONTINUOUS>:**

  Enter a linetype name to set for layers you specify. This linetype is applied to all entities on the specified layers. If you use the ? option, a list of the linetypes currently loaded in the current drawing is displayed. Any entity whose linetype is set to BYLAYER (the default for new entities) assumes the linetype of the layer on which it resides. The linetype you enter can be any valid linetype defined within the drawing or within the ACAD.LIN file, used for storing linetype definitions.

  After you specify a linetype, you must indicate which layers that linetype is to be used for, at the `Layer name(s) for linetype` *name* `<default>:` prompt. The default sets the current layer to the new linetype, but you also can enter other layer names as

needed. You may need to regenerate the drawing to see the change take effect.

- **Layer name(s) to Freeze:**

  Enter the name(s) of layers to freeze. Freezing a layer is similar to turning off a layer, except that entities on frozen layers are not calculated during regenerations. Therefore, regenerations can proceed faster than with layers that are only turned off. Frozen layers also are not displayed, but they can be turned on. Note that, unlike with the Off option, the current layer cannot be frozen.

- **Layer name(s) to Thaw:**

  Enter the name(s) of layers to thaw. Thawing a layer reverses the freezing process. Layers that have been thawed are not necessarily turned on; whether the layers are turned on depends on the On/Off state of the layer. If the layer is turned on, you may need to perform a regeneration before the thawed entities become visible on-screen.

- **Layer name(s) to Lock:**

  Enter the name(s) of layers to lock. The locking process prevents any changes to entities on layers designated as locked.

- **Layer name(s) to Unlock:**

  Enter the name(s) of layers to unlock. Layers that are currently locked are unlocked, and you can then make changes to the entities that reside upon those layers.

Example

This example uses the LAYER command to change the linetype of the entities on the LINES layer, which is shown in the figure LAYER.1.

```
Command: LAYER↵
?/Make/Set/New/ON/OFF/Color/Ltype/Freeze/
Thaw/LOck/Unlock: LT↵
Linetype (or ?) <CONTINUOUS>: HIDDEN↵
Layer name(s) for linetype HIDDEN
<0>: LINES↵
?/Make/Set/New/ON/OFF/Color/Ltype/Freeze/
Thaw/LOck/Unlock: ↵
Regenerating drawing.
```

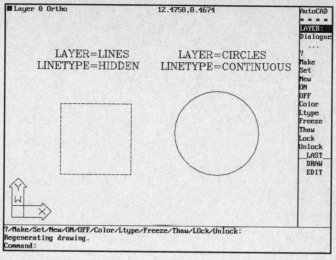

Figure LAYER.1:
Using the LAYER command to set the linetype of a layer.

Related Commands

> CHANGE
> COLOR
> LINETYPE
> DDEMODES
> DDLMODES
> REGEN
> REGENALL
> VPLAYER

Related System Variables

> CLAYER
> CECOLOR
> CELTYPE

LIGHT

Screen **[RENDER] [LIGHT]**

Pull down **[Render] [Lights]**

The LIGHT command enables you to specify, place, and control lighting for rendering. The three types of lights you can place anywhere in model space are point, distant, and spot. You also can control the amount of ambient light that shines on all surfaces.

You can control the position and intensity of all types of lighting. However, to control the color of lights and render spotlights, AutoShade Version 2 must be installed and operational.

Prompts and Options

The LIGHT command has four dialog boxes. They are Lights, New Light Type, New and Modify Light, and New Spotlight.

The Lights Dialog Box

The Lights dialog box (see fig. LIGHT.1) is the main dialog box for the LIGHT command. All other LIGHT dialog boxes and options are accessed through this dialog box. You can select the following options from this dialog box:

- **Lights.** The **L**ights list box shows the names of the lights in the current drawing.
- **New.** The **N**ew button displays the New Light Type dialog box, enablng you to select a new light type and add it to a drawing. You can choose one of three types of lights to add to your drawing: point, distant, and spotlight. After a new light type is chosen, the New Light dialog box appears. New lights are positioned at the current viewpoint and, in the case of distant lights and spotlights, are parallel to the current line of sight.

  A *point* light emits beams uniformly in all directions. A point light is analogous to a bare light bulb.

A *distant* light emits parallel beams from a plane at the light source. A distant light behaves similar to sunlight. Distant lights do not have fall-off parameters.

A *spot* light emits beams in the shape of a cone originating at the light source. The spread of the beam, as well as other beam parameters, can be changed to alter the characteristics of the spot. Although you can define spotlights with AVE Render (if RMan Prompting is turned on in the Rendering Preferences dialog box), spotlights can be rendered only with AutoShade Version 2 with Autodesk RenderMan.

- **Modify.** The Modify button displays the Modify Light dialog box, enabling you to change parameters of a light highlighted in the Lights list box. If you double-click on a light name in the Lights list box, the Modify Light dialog box automatically appears, enabling you to edit the selected light.

- **Delete.** The Delete button enables you to delete a light from the drawing. Highlight the light you want to delete, and then click on Delete.

- **Pick.** The Pick button causes the Lights dialog box to disappear, enabling you to pick a light icon to modify from the drawing.

- **Ambient Light.** The Ambient Light edit box specifies the amount of background light that shines on all object surfaces. The value range for ambient light is from zero (off) to one (brightest). Use the slider bar to interactively specify a value.

- **None.** The None option of the Point Light Fall-off group causes a light's intensity to illuminate all objects uniformly, regardless of distance from the point light source. Normally, the intensity of light reaching an object decreases as the distance from the light source increases. This phenomenon is called *fall-off*.

- **Inverse Linear.** The Inverse Linear option of the Point Light Fall-off group causes a point light's intensity to fall off inversely to the distance from the light source. This means that an object that is 10 units from a point light source will be illuminated at 1/10 the intensity of the source.

- **Inverse Square.** The Inverse **S**quare option of the Point Light Fall-off group causes a point light's intensity to fall off inversely to the square of the distance from the light source. This means that an object that is 10 units from a point light source will be illuminated at 1/100 the intensity of the source.

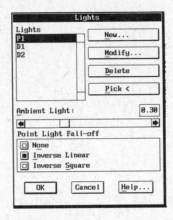

Figure LIGHT.1:
The Lights dialog box.

The New and Modify Light Dialog Boxes

The New and Modify Light dialog boxes enable you to specify light characteristics. In the New and Modify dialog boxes, you can name or rename a light, position it, set its intensity, alter its color, and control its shadows.

Because many of the New and Modify Light dialog options are common to all light types, each option that follows applies to all light types. Specific differences are discussed where appropriate. The Modify Light dialog box is shown in figure LIGHT.2.

The dialog box offers the following options:

- **Light Name.** The Light **N**ame edit box is used to assign or change the name of a light. Light names are limited to eight characters.

Figure LIGHT.2:
The Modify Light dialog box.

- **Intensity.** The **I**ntensity edit box specifies the brightness of the light. Distant lights have a maximum intensity of 1 because they do not have a fall-off parameter. Use the slider bar to interactively specify a value.

- **Modify.** The **M**odify button in the Position group allows repositioning of the light. For point lights, you are prompted to enter the light location. For distant lights and spotlights, you are prompted for the light target in addition to the light location. Specify a 3D point or pick a new point.

- **Show.** The **S**how button in the Position group displays the X, Y, and Z location of the light position (if applicable) and target.

- **Modify Light Color.** The Modify **L**ight Color button displays the Color dialog box and allows you to specify a color for a light. This button is enabled only if RMan Prompting has been turned on in the Rendering Preferences dialog box. You can specify the color of the light by its red, green, and blue (RGB) values, or hue, luminance, and saturation (HLS) values, or pick the color visually.

- **Depth Map Size.** The **D**epth Map Size edit box allows you to specify how shadows from lights are rendered in AutoShade Version 2 with Autodesk RenderMan. Enter a value between zero and six. Zero produces no shadows, and a value of 6 produces sharp-edged shadows. Use the slider bar to interactively specify a value.

The following three parameters are for spotlights only:

- **Cone Angle.** The **C**one Angle edit box specifies the angle from the spotlight's line of sight to the outer edge of the beam cone. Use the slider bar to interactively specify a value.

- **Cone Delta Angle.** The Cone Delta **A**ngle edit box specifies the angle from the edge of the beam cone to the outer edge of the fall-off cone. This area is also know as the area of rapid decay. Use the slider bar to interactively specify a value.

- **Beam Distribution.** The **B**eam Distribution edit box specifies the rate of rapid decay fall-off.

Example

The following example uses the LIGHT command to create a new point light source in the PINS2.DWG that is located in \ACAD\TUTORIAL. If you do not have this drawing, you can install it from your AutoCAD distribution disks by installing the AVE Render tutorial files. Render the PINS2 drawing before and after adding the new light.

Choose Render, *then* Lights
Click on the New *button in the* Lights *dialog box,*
then click on OK *in the* New Light Type *dialog box*
In the Light **N**ame *text box, enter* **P1** ↵
Set Intensity *to 10.00*
Click on Modify *in the* Position *group*
`Enter light location <current>:` **4.5,-3**↵
Click on OK *in the two consecutive dialog boxes*
to return to the AutoCAD command prompt

Related Command

FINISH

LIMITS

Screen **[SETTINGS] [LIMITS:]**

Pull down **[Settings] [Drawing Limits]**

The LIMITS command defines a rectangular boundary within which you can draw. You can exceed or redefine the boundary at any time. The boundary limits have a lower left corner and an upper right corner in the X-Y plane, but no limit in the Z axis.

The drawing's limits also are used for displaying the extent of the grid when Grid mode is turned on, and as an area specification for plotting. Model space and paper space each have their own drawing limits, and when you issue the ZOOM command's All option, ZOOM displays the drawing's limits or extents, whichever is greater.

Prompts and Options

- **ON/OFF/<Lower left corner><0.0000,0.0000>:**

  The On option turns on limits checking. While turned on, any coordinate entry that does not fall within the drawing limits is not accepted. If you try to enter coordinates outside of these boundaries, the following message appears:

      **Outside limits.

  Note that this checking is not absolute. For example, you can define a circle whose perimeter exceeds the drawing's limits.

  The Off option disables limits checking. Limits checking is off by default; even after you set the drawing's limits.

  The Lower left corner option is the default and defines the lower left corner of a rectangular area that represents the drawing's limits. Enter a 2D coordinate or pick a point on-screen. The default is 0,0, unless otherwise specified in a prototype drawing.

- **Upper Right Corner<12.0000,9.0000>:**

  After specifying the lower left corner of the drawing's limits, you are prompted for the upper right corner. This point represents the

281

opposite corner of the rectangular area of the drawing's limits. The default setting is governed by the prototype drawing.

Example

This example demonstrates the effects of setting a drawing's limits with the LIMITS command. The points describing the drawing's limits are shown in figure LIMITS.1.

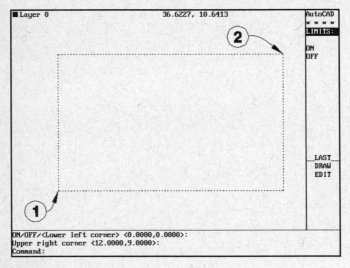

Figure LIMITS.1:
The grid turned on to show the drawing limits.

```
Command: LIMITS↵
ON/OFF/<Lower left corner><0.0000,0.0000>: Pick①
Upper Right Corner<12.0000,9.0000>: Pick②
```

Related Commands

PLOT
ZOOM

Related System Variables

LIMCHECK
LIMMAX
LIMMIN

LINE

Screen **[DRAW] [LINE:]**

Pull down **[Draw] [Line >]**

The LINE command draws straight lines between two specified points.
These points may have any 2D or 3D coordinate location. The command
repeats, enabling many lines to be created, until you press Enter or type
Ctrl-C. After lines have been drawn, you can type C to create a closed
polygon. You can draw lines at right angles by using Ortho mode. You
also can use the TRACE or POLYLINE commands for wide lines.

Prompts and Options

- **From point:**

  Specify a starting point for the line segment. The point may have
  any X, Y, and Z coordinates and can be preceded with any Osnap
  overrides or point filters. If you press Enter at this prompt,
  AutoCAD begins the line by using the end point of the last line or
  arc created.

- **To point:**

  Enter an end point for the segment and a line is drawn. This
  prompt repeats until you press Enter or Ctrl-C.

- **Close.** Enter **C** at any `To point:` prompt to connect the end of
  the last line with the beginning of the first line and complete the
  command. You must have drawn at least two previous lines to use
  the Close option.

- **Undo.** Enter **U** while within the command to remove the last end point specified. You can use the Undo option to remove previous line segments back to the initial `From point:` location.

Example

This example shows the simplicity of using the LINE command. The lines drawn are shown in figure LINE.1.

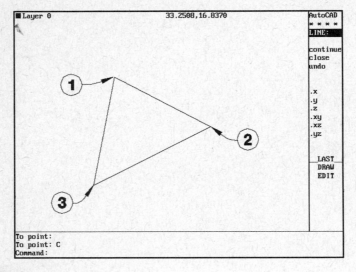

Figure LINE.1:
Simple shape drawn with the *LINE* command.

```
Command: LINE↵
From point: Pick①
To point: Pick②
To point: Pick③
To point: C↵
```

Related Commands

PLINE
TRACE
UNDO
3DPOLY

Related System Variable

LASTPOINT

LINETYPE

Screen **[SETTINGS] [LINETYP:]**

The LINETYPE command is used to load and list the linetypes available in the current drawing. You also can create new linetypes with this command and chose a new linetype for subsequent entities. The default linetype is BYLAYER, which new entities display in the linetype assigned to the layer on which they are created.

Linetype definitions supplied with AutoCAD are stored in the support file ACAD.LIN, and must be loaded into AutoCAD before they can be used in a drawing. Once a linetype is used in the current drawing, its definition is stored with the drawing file. You can define your own linetypes within the AutoCAD drawing editor and store them in ACAD.LIN, save them in a different file with the extension LIN, or modify the ACAD.LIN file directly.

Prompts and Options

- **?/Create/Load/Set:**

  Presents all the choices available with the Linetype command. An explanation of each option follows.

- **File to list <ACAD>:**

  When you choose the ? option, the Select Linetype File dialog box appears. By default, the ACAD.LIN file is highlighted. Pressing Enter lists all of the linetypes in the ACAD.LIN file. If you want, you can use the Directories and Files list boxes to select another file to list. By default, AutoCAD considers any file with an LIN extension to contain linetype definitions.

- **Name of linetype to create:**

285

Choosing the Create option enables you to create a linetype definition from within the AutoCAD drawing editor. Enter the name you want to give the linetype. The name can be up to 31 characters long but cannot contain any spaces.

After entering the name of the linetype you want to create, the Create or Append Linetype File dialog box appears. It enables you to add the linetype to the ACAD.LIN file or create a new file for storing the linetype.

- **Descriptive text:**

Enter up to 47 characters and spaces to describe the linetype you are about to create. Dashes, underscores, periods, and spaces are used semi-graphically to depict what the linetype actually looks like. This text is displayed next to the linetype name, when you list linetypes.

- **Enter pattern (on next line) A,**

The linetype pattern is a series of dashes or spaces of different lengths and dots that make up one complete linetype pattern, which is repeated between the line endpoints according to the current linetype scale. A positive number indicates the length of a line segment; a negative number indicates a space. If you want a dot in the linetype definition, use the value zero (0). For example, the definition 2,-.5,0,-.5 produces a line segment of 2 units, a space of one-half unit, a dot, and then another space of one-half unit before repeating.

- **Linetype(s) to load:**

This prompt appears when you choose the Load option. At this prompt, enter the name of the linetype you want added to the drawing. By default, the Select Linetype File dialog box selects the ACAD.LIN file from which to load linetypes.

- **Linetype** *linetype name* **is already loaded. Reload it? <Y>**

If the linetype name you specified is already loaded in the drawing, you receive this prompt. The only time you need to reload a linetype definition is if it has been changed and the drawing needs to be updated.

- **New entity linetype <default>:**

    If you choose the Set option, enter the name of a linetype currently loaded into the drawing. This linetype is used when you create any new entities with commands such as LINE, ARC, and CIRCLE. Setting the value to BYLAYER causes new entities to assume the linetype assigned to the layer on which they are created.

Example

This example shows the process for loading a new linetype from the ACAD.LIN file and making it the default linetype used for drawing new entities. The various linetypes are shown in figure LINETYPE.1.

```
Linetypes defined in file H:\ACAD12\SUPPORT\ACAD.lin:

        Name            Description
        _____     _____

BORDER              __ __ . __ __ . __ __ . __ __ . __ __ . __
BORDER2             _ _ . _ _ . _ _ . _ _ . _ _ . _ _ . _ _ .
BORDERX2            ___  ___  .  ___  ___  .  ___  ___  .  ___
CENTER             ____ _ ____ _ ____ _ ____ _ ____ _ ____ _
CENTER2            ___ _ ___ _ ___ _ ___ _ ___ _ ___ _ ___ _

CENTERX2           _____  __  _____  __  _____  __  _____
DASHDOT           __ . __ . __ . __ . __ . __ . __ . __ . __ .
DASHDOT2          _._._._._._._._._._._._._._._._._._._._._._
DASHDOTX2         ____ . ____ . ____ . ____ . ____ . ____ . _
DASHED            __ __ __ __ __ __ __ __ __ __ __ __ __ __ __

DASHED2           _ _ _ _ _ _ _ _ _ _ _ _ _ _ _ _ _ _ _ _ _ _
DASHEDX2          ____  ____  ____  ____  ____  ____  ____  __
DIVIDE            __ . . __ . . __ . . __ . . __ . . __ . . __
DIVIDE2           _ . . _ . . _ . . _ . . _ . . _ . . _ . . _
DIVIDEX2          ____ . . ____ . . ____ . . ____ . . ____ . .
— Press RETURN for more —
```

Figure LINETYPE.1:
Linetypes loaded from the ACAD.LIN file.

```
Command: LINETYPE↵
?/Create/Load/Set: L↵
Linetype(s) to load: DASHDOT ↵
```

Make sure that ACAD.LIN is highlighted in the dialog box and click on the OK button.

```
Linetype DASHDOT loaded.
?/Create/Load/Set: S↵
New entity linetype (or ?) <BYLAYER>:
DASHDOT↵
?/Create/Load/Set: ↵
```

Related Commands

CHANGE
CHPROP
DDCHPROP
DDEMODES
DDMODIFY

Related System Variables

LTSCALE
CELTYPE
FILEDIA
PSLTSCALE

LIST

?

Screen [INQUIRY] [LIST:]

Pull down [Utility] [List]

The LIST command displays information about entity properties stored in the drawing database. The properties include information such as line lengths, the layer in which an entity resides, or scaling factors of blocks. If the information is too lengthy and begins to scroll off the screen, type Ctrl-S to pause scrolling and then press any key to resume. Press Ctrl-C to cancel the command. You can turn on the printer echoing by typing Ctrl-Q, and all entities listed on-screen also are printed.

Prompts and Options

- **Select objects:**

  Choose the entities about which you want information displayed.

Example

This example invokes the LIST command to view the properties of a line.

```
Command: LIST↵
Select objects:

    LINE            Layer: 0
                    Space: Model space
    from point, X=  16.6089  Y=   4.4457  Z=   0.0000
      to point, X=  -7.9727  Y=  -8.1630  Z=   0.0000
Length =  27.6267,  Angle in XY Plane =    207
       Delta X = -24.5816, Delta Y = -12.6087, Delta Z = 0.0000
```

Related Commands

> **AREA**
> **DBLIST**
> **DIST**
> **ID**

Related System Variables

> **AREA**
> **PERIMETER**

LOAD

Screen **[DRAW] [next] [SHAPE:] [LOAD:]**

The LOAD command is used to load compiled shape definition files into the drawing editor from disk for use with the SHAPE command. Note that, unlike blocks, shape definitions are not stored in the drawing. The shape files must be accessible every time you load a drawing for editing.

Prompts and Options

When the FILEDIA variable is set to 1, this command presents no prompts. Instead, the Select Shape File dialog box appears. In the `Files:` list box are listed any files that have an SHX extension. Select one of these files and its shapes are then available from the SHAPE command. If the FIELDIA variable is set to 0, you receive the `Name of shape file to load (or ?):` prompt. Enter the name of the shape definition file containing shapes you want to use within the drawing.

Example

The following example demonstrates using the LOAD command to load a shape file, and then uses the SHAPE command to determine what shapes are available.

```
Command: LOAD ⏎
```

Choose the PC.SHP file that comes with the AutoCAD software.

```
Command: SHAPE⏎
Shape name (or ?): ? ⏎

Available shapes:
File: PC.SHX
  FEEDTHRU          DIP8
  DIP14             DIP16
  DIP18             DIP20
  DIP24             DIP40
```

Related Command

SHAPE

Related System Variables

FILEDIA
SHPNAME

LTSCALE

Screen **[SETTINGS] [next] [LTSCALE:]**

The LTSCALE command controls the display of noncontinuous linetypes. Each linetype is a pattern of dashes, dots, and spaces; and the pattern has a fixed size. By setting the LTSCALE value, you may adjust the scale of the pattern in order closely to match the scale at which you are plotting. Typically, you set the value of LTSCALE equal to the scale of your drawing.

In a large drawing, if the linetype scale is set to a low number, screen regeneration can be slow. You can improve screen regeneration speed by assigning a high value to the linetype scale until you are ready to plot the drawing.

Prompts and Options

- **New scale factor <1>:**

    The current linetype scale factor is shown in angle brackets. Enter any positive number at the prompt. Decimal fractions are enabled. After the next screen regeneration, the display reflects the new linetype scale.

Example

This example displays the difference in linetypes by using two different LTSCALE factors (see fig. LTSCALE.1).

```
Command: LTSCALE ↵
New scale factor <1>: ↵
Command: LTSCALE ↵
New scale factor <1>:5 ↵
```

Related Commands

LINETYPE
REGENAUTO

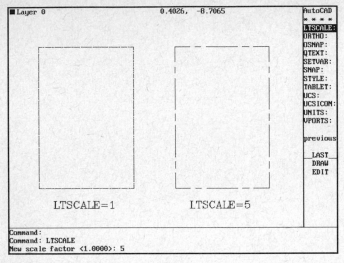

Figure LTSCALE.1:
The Center linetype at a LTSCALE factor of 1 and 5.

Related System Variables

LTSCALE
PSLTSCALE

MEASURE

Screen **[EDIT] [next] [MEASURE:]**

Pull down **[Construct] [Measure]**

The MEASURE command places equally spaced points along an entity at a specified distance. Blocks can be substituted for points if the blocks are already defined within the drawing with the BLOCK command. You can measure arcs, circles, lines, and 2D or 3D polylines.

The MEASURE command is useful for generating smooth camera and target points in two or three dimensions when making animations. Draw a 3D polyline, line, or arc to depict the camera path and use MEASURE or DIVIDE to place points along this path at even intervals for each frame of the animation.

Prompts and Options

- `Select object to measure:`

  Pick the entity to mark at equal distances. The MEASURE command works with only one entity at a time. The starting location for the placement of points or blocks is the end point closest to the point used to pick the entity. From the end point, measure points are calculated at equal intervals until no more will fit. You can use the Previous selection set option to select all the points or blocks that are placed along the entity. Use the PDMODE and PDSIZE variables to alter the visual appearance of the points.

- `<Segment length>/Block:`

  At this prompt, specify a distance or pick two points to show a distance for measuring the entity. If you enter **B** to invoke the Block option, you must enter a block name already defined within the drawing. If you enter a block name, the following prompt appears:

- `Align block with object? <Y>:`

  Answer **Y** to rotate the inserted blocks about their insertion points so that they are aligned with the entity being measured.

Example

This example shows how the MEASURE commands draws points at even spacings along a polyline. The entity shown in figure MEASURE.1 contains points placed at three-inch intervals.

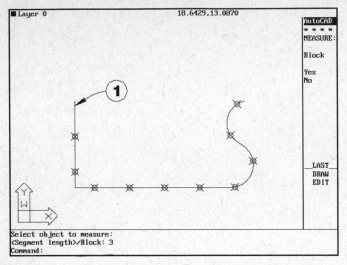

Figure MEASURE.1:
Points placed along a polyline with the MEASURE command.

```
Command: MEASURE ↵
Select object to measure: Pick point ①
<Segment length>/Block: 3 ↵
```

Related Commands

> **DIVIDE**
> **OSNAP**
> **POINT**

Related System Variables

> **PDMODE**
> **PDSIZE**

MENU

Screen [UTILITY] [MENU:]

The MENU command enables you to load alternative menu files into the AutoCAD drawing editor. AutoCAD is supplied with the menu ACAD.MNU, which includes menu selections for each command supplied with the software as well as additional selections for running packages such as the Advanced Modeling Extension, AutoSHADE, and Autodesk Renderman. Typically, add-on packages that increase the functionality of AutoCAD have a customized menu for accessing their functions.

Prompts and Options

By default, the MENU command displays a dialog box that allows you to select the menu file you want to use. If the FILEDIA variable is set to 0, you see instead the `Menu File name or . for none <ACAD>:` prompt, where you enter the name of a valid menu file. The Select Menu File dialog box initially displays the names of any files with either a MNU or MNX extension. If the file you want to load is in the list, you can highlight it and click on the OK button. You also can navigate the Directories: list box if the file is in a different drive or directory.

Related System Variables

MENUNAME
MENUECHO

MINSERT

Screen **[BLOCKS] [MINSERT:]**

Screen **[DRAW] [MINSERT:]**

The MINSERT (Multiple INSERT) command inserts a block multiple times in a regular pattern. This command combines the INSERT and ARRAY commands into a single command. After the MINSERT command has been used, the array of blocks become a single entity that cannot be exploded. As a single entity, these blocks take up less space in the drawing database. If you need to modify any of the individual blocks, use the INSERT and ARRAY commands instead.

Prompts and Options

- **Block name (or ?):**

  At this prompt, you enter the name of a block defined in the current drawing or in the AutoCAD library search path. You may not precede a block with an asterisk (*) to insert it as pre-exploded, as you can with the INSERT command. You can enter a question mark to display a list of defined blocks, or enter a tilde (~) to display the Select Block dialog box to insert a drawing from disk.

- **Insertion point:**

  You specify the insertion point for the multiple arrayed block. This point is the location where the first block will be inserted in the array.

- **X scale factor <1.000>:**

  At this prompt, you enter a scale factor for the block in the current X axis.

- **Y scale factor (default=X):**

  You enter a scale factor for the block in the current Y direction. By default, the Y scale factor is set to the same value as the X axis scale factor.

- **Rotation angle:**

  At this prompt, you enter a non-zero number to rotate the array. This has the same effect as using the ROTATE command on an array of blocks.

- **Number of rows (--):**

  At this prompt, you enter any positive, non-zero number for the number of rows of the array.

- **Number of columns (|||):**

  At this prompt, you enter any positive, non-zero number for the number of columns of the array.

- **Unit cell or distance between rows (--):**

You enter a number for the distance between rows of the block array. A positive number will create rows along the positive Y axis; a negative value will create rows along the negative Y axis. Specify a point to indicate that you want to show AutoCAD both the distance between rows and the distance between columns by defining a unit cell rectangle. The width of the rectangle becomes the column spacing; the height of the rectangle specifies the row spacing.

- **Other corner:**

  You specify a unit cell rectangle corner point opposite the point specified above.

- **Distance between columns (|||):**

  You enter a number for the distance between columns of the array.

Example

This example demonstrates how to create an arrayed insertion of a chair block, as shown in figure MINSERT.1.

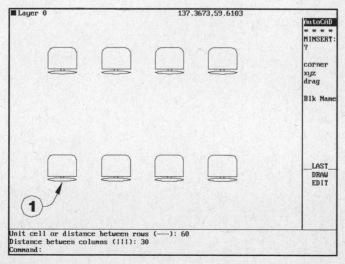

Figure MINSERT.1:
A 2 x 4 array of the chair block.

```
Command: MINSERT ↵
Block name (or ?) <ARROW>: CHAIR ↵
Insertion point: Pickpoint ①
X scale factor <1> / Corner / XYZ: ↵
Y scale factor (default=X): ↵
Rotation angle <0>: ↵
Number of rows (--) <1>: 2 ↵
Number of columns (||||) <1>: 4 ↵
Unit cell or distance between rows (--): 60 ↵
Distance between columns (||||): 30 ↵
```

Related Commands

ARRAY
BLOCK
INSERT
ROTATE

MIRROR

Screen **[EDIT] [next] [MIRROR:]**

Pull down **[Construct] [Mirror]**

The MIRROR command creates copies of selected entities symmetrically about a temporary mirror line. You can opt to remove the original entities from the drawing after the mirrored entities are created or leave the original entities intact.

Text, attribute, and attribute definition entities specified in a MIRROR selection set are literally mirrored to create new copies; they read backwards or upside-down depending on the angle of the mirror line. Associative dimension text is not affected. To mirror text, attributes, and attribute definitions so that the text reads correctly, set the MIRRTEXT system variable to 0. Text and constant attributes within a block will be inverted regardless of the value of MIRRTEXT. Note that you cannot explode a mirrored block.

Prompts and Options

- `Select objects:`

  You select the entities to be mirrored.

- `First point of mirror line:`

  You specify one endpoint of a rubber-band line, which can be of any length.

- `Second point:`

  You specify the second endpoint of the mirror line. The entities selected will be mirrored after you select this point.

- `Delete old objects? <N>`

  If you press Enter at this prompt, the original entities will remain in the drawing. If you answer **Y** to this prompt, the original entities will be erased after your mirrored entities are created.

For easier editing, use the Grip Edit Mirror mode. See the *AutoCAD Reference Manual* for details.

Example

This example demonstrates the effects of using the MIRROR command on both line and text entity types. The points used to create the mirror line, and the new entities created, are shown in figure MIRROR.1.

```
Command: MIRROR↵
Select objects: W↵
First corner: Pick point ①
Other corner: Pick point ②
7 found
Select objects: ↵
First point of mirror line: Pick point ③
Second point: Pick point ④
Delete old objects? <N> ↵
```

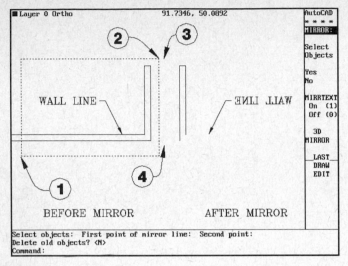

Figure MIRROR.1:
The mirrored entities.

Related System Variable

MIRRTEXT

MIRROR3D

Screen **[EDIT] [next] [MIRROR:] [3D MIRROR]**

Pull down **[Construct] [Mirror 3D]**

MIRROR3D enables you to mirror entities about any plane in three dimensions.

Prompts and Options

- **Select objects:**

  You select the object you want to mirror. You can use any of the AutoCAD entity selection modes.

- **Delete old objects <N>:**

  You can enter **Y** to delete the object in its current location; enter **N** to duplicate the entity in its mirrored location.

- **Plane by Entity/Last/Zaxis/View/XY/YZ/<3points>:**

  At this prompt, you choose a method for specifying the plane about which to mirror. You can use the following options with the MIRROR3D command.

- **Entity.** The Entity option specifies the construction plane of a 2D entity as the mirroring plane. Entity displays the following prompt:

  `Pick circle, arc or 2D-polyline segment:` You select the entity or segment to define the plane for mirroring.

- **Last.** The Last option specifies the last mirroring plane. If there is no last plane, you are warned and reprompted with the original prompt.

- **Zaxis.** The Zaxis option specifies the mirroring plane as a point on a plane and a point on the Z axis of the plane. Zaxis displays two prompts.

  `Point on plane:` You enter a point on the current plane.

  `Point on Z-axis (normal) of the plane:` You enter a point to define the Z axis of the plane.

- **View.** The View option aligns the mirroring plane with the current viewing plane through a selected point. View has one prompt:

  `Point on view plane <0,0,0>:` You enter a point for the mirroring plane to pass through.

- **XY.** The XY option aligns the mirroring plane with the XY plane that passes through a selected point. XY has one prompt:

  `Point on XY plane <0,0,0>:` You enter a point for the mirroring plane to pass through.

- **YZ.** The YZ option aligns the mirroring plane with the YZ plane that passes through a selected point. YZ has one prompt:

  `Point on YZ plane <0,0,0>:` You enter a point for the mirroring plane to pass through.

- **ZX.** The ZX option aligns the mirroring plane with the ZX plane that passes through a selected point. ZX has one prompt:

  `Point on ZX plane <0,0,0>:` You enter a point for the mirroring plane to pass through.

- **<3points>.** This option specifies a mirroring plane that passes through three selected points. The 3points option has three prompts:

  `1st point on plane:` You enter the first point of the mirroring plane.

  `2nd point on plane:` You enter the second point of the mirroring plane.

  `3rd point on plane:` You enter the third point of the mirroring plane.

Example

The following example mirrors a solid about a plane using the Z option.

```
Command: MIRROR3D↵
Select objects: Pick point ①
Select objects: ↵
Plane by Entity/Last/Zaxis/View/XY/YZ/ZX/<3points>: Z ↵
Point on plane: Pick point ②
Point on Z-axis (normal) of the plane: Pick point ③
Delete old objects? <N> ↵
```

Related Commands

MIRROR
ROTATE
ROTATE3D

MOVE

Screen **[EDIT] [next] [MOVE:]**

Pull down **[Modify] [Move]**

The MOVE command relocates entities to another position in a drawing. The MOVE command works both in 2D or 3D; nothing but the position of the entities changes.

Prompts and Options

- **Select objects:**

  You select the entities to be moved using AutoCAD's standard object selection methods.

- **Base point or displacement:**

  You specify a base point for the move in the current User Coordinate System (UCS). The base point need not be on any selected entity. Or, enter an XYZ distance to move the current selection set. You may specify a 2D or 3D point, and the point's XYZ values will be considered the displacement for the selected entities in each of those axes.

- **Second point of displacement:**

  After you have specified a base, enter a second point to move the entity or entities towards. You can enter a location by picking the point, entering a relative location, or giving an absolute XYZ location.

For easier editing, use the Grip Edit Move mode. See the *AutoCAD Reference Manual* for details.

Example

This example shows a typical application of the MOVE command. The selected entities shown in figure MOVE.1 are moved to a new location, as displayed in the figure.

```
Command: MOVE↵
Select objects: Pick point ①
1 found
Select objects: ↵
Base point or displacement: Pick point ②
Second point of displacement: Pick point ③
```

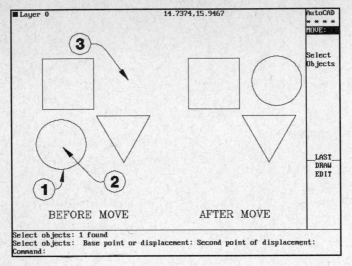

Figure MOVE.1:
An object being relocated with the MOVE command.

Related Command

COPY

MSLIDE

Screen   [UTILITY] [SLIDES] [next] [next] [MSLIDE:]

The MSLIDE command creates slide files. Slides are snapshot images of the current screen display. Although slides cannot be edited like normal drawing files, they have the advantages of taking up little space on your disk and loading quickly. You can use slide files for icon items in icon menus, for referencing other drawings, and for creating presentations of your work.

Prompts and Options

• Slide file <default>:

By default, the MSLIDE command displays a dialog box that allows you to enter the name of the slide file to create. If the FILEDIA variable is set to 0, you receive instead the `Slide file <default>:` prompt, where you should enter the name to give the slide file. The Create Slide File dialog box initially displays the names of any current slide files. You can navigate the Directories: list box if you want to save the slide in a different drive or directory.

The slide file is given the extension SLD. After you enter a valid file name, AutoCAD redraws the screen and creates the image file. Slides made in model space contain only the current viewport. Slides made in paper space include all visible viewport entities and their contents. To make a slide, adjust your screen display with the AutoCAD display commands ZOOM, PAN, VIEW, and so on to achieve the view you want. Then execute the MSLIDE command. The command line area, screen menu area, status line, crosshairs, and UCS icon are not included in the slide image.

You can create an automated slide show by using a script in AutoCAD. See the SCRIPT and DELAY commands for more information.

Related Commands

SCRIPT
DELAY
VSLIDE

MSPACE

Screen [MVIEW] [MSPACE]

Pull down [View] [Model Space]

The MSPACE command switches from paper space to model space and works only when paper space is active and at least one viewport has been created in paper space. Model space is active when the normal UCS icon is visible (if the UCSICON command is On) in each viewport and the crosshairs are constrained within the current viewport. The MSPACE command is not allowed if TILEMODE is set to 0.

Related Commands

> MVIEW
> PSPACE

Related System Variable

> TILEMODE

MULTIPLE

MULTIPLE is a command modifier for issuing another command many times in succession. Enter **MULTIPLE** at the Command: prompt, followed by the name of the command to be repeated. The command is repeated until you cancel it by pressing Ctrl-C. You can use MULTIPLE with any command except PLOT, QUIT, and END.

MULTIPLE does not remember any of the specified command's options. If you select MULTIPLE INSERT, for example, you must answer all the INSERT command's prompts each time the command is repeated.

Example

The following example places many points in the drawing using MULTIPLE to repeat the POINT command (see fig. MULTIPLE.1).

```
Command: MULTIPLE POINT↵
POINT Point:
POINT Point:
POINT Point:
```

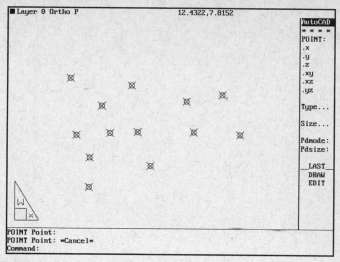

```
■ Layer 0 Ortho P                    12.4322,7.8152
```

POINT Point:
POINT Point: *Cancel*
Command:

Figure MULTIPLE.1:
Using MULTIPLE to execute the POINT command repeatedly.

Related Command

COPY

MVIEW

Screen   **[MVIEW]**

Screen   **[DISPLAY] [MVIEW:]**

Pull down **[View] [Mview >]**

The MVIEW command controls the creation and display of viewpoints in paper space. MVIEW controls the size, number, and location of viewports as they are created in paper space. If model space is active, AutoCAD automatically switches to paper space to perform the MVIEW command's options. As with any paper space commands, you must set the TILEMODE system variable to 0 (off) in order to use the

MVIEW command. The maximum number of active viewports cannot exceed 16 on MS-DOS systems.

Prompts and Options

- `ON`:

  The ON option enables the display of entities within a selected viewport. You must first select the viewports by picking the viewport boundary. The entities within the selected viewports are then displayed.

- `OFF`:

  The OFF option disables the display of all entities within a selected viewport.

- `Hideplot`:

  Hideplot controls whether hidden lines are removed or not removed in the selected viewport when paper space is plotted. After you specify this option, you see the `ON/OFF`: prompt, at which you can specify whether hidden lines are removed during plotting of the viewport (ON) or not.

- `Fit`:

  The Fit option fills the current display with a single viewport.

- `2`:

  This option creates two equal size paper space viewports either side by side or one directly over the other, as directed by the `Horizontal/<Vertical>`: prompt. Horizontal creates a horizontal division between the two viewports; Vertical (the default) creates a vertical division. After you choose either horizontal or vertical orientation, you will receive the `Fit/<First Point>`: prompt. This prompt directs you to define the area used to create the two viewports.

- `3`:

  This option creates three viewports, one large, two small, with the orientation defined by the `Horizontal/Vertical/Above/ Below/Left/<Right>`: prompt. After you choose an orientation, you will receive the `Fit/<First Point>:` prompt to specify the area used to create the three viewports.

- **4:**

  This option divides the screen into four equal size paper space viewports.

- **Restore:**

  This option creates a paper space viewport configuration equivalent to a model space viewport configuration saved with the VPORTS command. The Restore option is an effective way to transfer views created for modeling purposes to paper space for hard copy output. After choosing to restore a viewport configuration, you will receive the `Fit/<First Point>:` prompt, to specify the area used to restore the viewports within.

- **?/Name of window configuration to insert <default>:**

  Type **?** to list the saved viewport configurations within the current drawing or enter the name of the viewport configuration for retrieval into paper space.

- **<First point>:**

  You specify a point for one corner of a single paper space viewport.

- **Other corner:**

  You specify a point for the opposite corner of the viewport. After you enter a point, the current model space viewport is displayed in the newly created paper space viewport.

Example

The following example uses MVIEW to create three viewports within paper space (see fig. MVIEW.1).

```
Command: MVIEW↵
ON/OFF/Hideplot/Fit/2/3/4/Restore/<First Point>: 3↵
Horizontal/Vertical/Above/Below/Left/<Right>: B↵
Fit/<First Point>: Pick point ①
Second point: Pick point ②
Regenerating drawing.
```

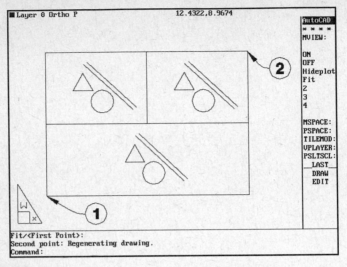

Figure MVIEW.1:
Three viewports created with the MVIEW command.

Related System Variables

MAXACTVP
PSLTSCALE
TILEMODE
VISRETAIN

Related Commands

MSPACE
PSPACE
VPLAYER
VPORTS

MVSETUP

Pull down [View] [Layout] [MV Setup]

The MVSETUP AutoLISP program provides automated drawing setup for AutoCAD. It supports both paper space and model space. If you want to use only model space, the MVSETUP routine performs the drawing setup as the SETUP command did in versions of AutoCAD prior to Release 11. If you want to use both paper space and model space, however, MVSETUP enables you to define, align, and scale viewports, as well as place a title block in paper space within which the model space viewports can be arranged.

The MVSETUP program has two options to the setup routine. The first option executes the setup routine that AutoCAD used in pre-Release 11 versions. This routine is limited to setting the proper units and scale and to inserting a border scaled to the paper size on which you will be plotting. The second option invokes the setup routine that places a drawing border in paper space and enables you to define viewports to display your model space entities. To use the pre-Release 11 setup option, answer No at the `Enable Paper/Modelspace? <Y>:` prompt.

Prompts and Options

- **`Enable Paper/Modelspace? <Y>:`**

  The type of setup performed depends on whether or not paper space is activated. If you answer **N**, the setup routine described following is used. If you activate paper space, the paper space setup routine is performed. AutoCAD displays this prompt only if TILEMODE is set to 1; the paper space setup routine is executed if TILEMODE is set to 0 when the MVSETUP command is issued.

The Model Space Setup Routine

- **`Select the Units from the screen menu:`**

  The screen menu displays a list of five different types of units available in AutoCAD. Select the unit system with which you will create your drawing. This sets the AutoCAD UNITS command to the proper value.

- **Select the Scale from the screen menu:**

  The screen menu displays a list of common drawing scales (1=1, 1/8"=1'0", 1"=20', and so on). Select the scale that you want to use when you plot your drawing. If that scale is not listed, select the OTHER option. When you enter a value for the scale, that value should be equal to the number of drawing units to plot within each one plotting unit. This value is used to set the LTSCALE system variable.

- **Select the Paper size from the screen menu:**

  The screen menu displays a list of common paper sizes ranging from A to E size. Select one that fits the size of paper on which you will plot your drawing. If the paper size you need does not appear in the list, use the OTHER option to specify the horizontal and vertical size of the paper.

The Paper Space Setup Routine

The paper space setup routine is executed if you answer yes to the `Enable Paper/Modelspace? <Y>:` prompt or if the TILEMODE system variable is set to 0 when the MVSETUP command is issued. When paper space is activated, the MVSETUP command automates the process of inserting a title block, creating paper space viewports, scaling paper space viewports, and aligning the views of paper space viewports.

- **Align viewports/Create/Scale viewports/Options/Titleblock/Undo:**

  This prompt is the first of many that appear when you use the paper space setup routine. Each of these options has its own set of prompts, which are discussed in the following paragraphs. The only prompt not discussed is the Undo option, which appears here and in each of the options prompts. The Undo option is similar to the AutoCAD Undo command; it reverses any steps that have been performed thus far by MVSETUP.

- **Align viewports.** You receive the following prompt after you specify the Align viewports option:

- `Angled/Horizontal/Vertical alignment/Rotate view/ Undo:`

  The Angled option enables you to pan a view in a paper space viewport to a specific distance and angle from a base point. If you specify Angled, you receive the following prompts:

- `Basepoint:`

  You specify a point in the viewport that will remain stationary and be used as a reference point for the pan.

- `Other point:`

  You enter a point in the viewport to be panned. This point will be moved so that it is the specified distance and angle away from the basepoint of the first viewport.

- `Distance from basepoint:`

  You enter the distance that the two points will be located apart from each other.

- `Angle from basepoint:`

  You enter the desired angle between the two points chosen. After you enter this value, the second viewport is panned by this angle and the distance.

The angled alignment of viewports is sometimes difficult to use. You might find it easier to exit the MVSETUP command and use the AutoCAD PAN command to move around the viewport.

If you specify the Horizontal or Vertical alignment options, you receive two prompts. Horizontal alignment pans one viewport up or down to align two points that you specify. Vertical alignment pans one viewport left or right to align two points that you specify.

- `Basepoint:`

  You enter a point in the viewport that will remain stationary and be used as a reference point.

- **Other point:**

  You enter a point in the viewport that you want to line up with the basepoint that was chosen. The viewport is then panned so that the two points line up with each other.

  If you specify the Rotate view option from the Align viewports prompt, you receive the following prompts:

- **Basepoint:**

  You enter a point around which the view within the viewport will be rotated by the value entered at the following prompt.

- **Angle from basepoint:**

  You enter a value to rotate the view. It is always measured from 0 degrees, so if you want to have the viewport rotated from a current value of 15 degrees to 60 degrees, you enter **60** at this prompt. If you enter 0 at this prompt, the view returns to its non-rotated state.

- **Create.** You receive the following prompt after you specify the Create option at the first MVSETUP paper space prompt:

- **Delete objects/Undo/<Create viewports>:**

  If you specify the Delete objects option, you receive the following prompt:

- **Select the objects to delete:**

  Pick any entities you want to delete.

  If you specify the default option, Create, you receive the following prompt:

- **Redisplay/<Number of entry to load>:**

  The Redisplay option redisplays the currently available viewport configurations. The four supplied viewport configurations·are the following:

- **None.** No viewports are created, and you return to the previous prompt.

- **Single.** A single viewport is created. You must define the area of the viewport by specifying two points.

- **Std. Engineering.** A group of four viewports is created in a rectangular area that you define. Each of the viewports is set with a different view into your model space drawing. These views are the top view (XY plane of the UCS); isometric view (Viewport rotated to -45 degrees in the XY plane and elevated 30 degrees in the Z axis); front view (XZ plane of the UCS); and right side view (YZ plane of the UCS).

- **Array of viewports.** A rectangular array of viewport entities is created. You can define the quantity by entering the number of viewports along the X and Y axes.

 Only 16 active viewports are permitted in the DOS versions of AutoCAD. If you need more than 16 viewports, you must turn off some viewports to allow others to be turned on. Use the MVIEW command to turn on and off viewports.

If you specify the Single, Std. Engineering, or Array of viewports options, you receive the following prompts:

- **Bounding area for viewports... First point:**

  You specify the first corner point of a rectangular area that will hold the viewports to be created.

- **Other point:**

  You specify the opposite corner of the area to hold the viewports.

  If you specify the Array of viewports option, you receive the following prompts.

- **Number of viewports in X. <1>:**

  You enter the number of viewports in the X direction (columns).

- **Number of viewports in Y. <1>:**

  You enter the number of viewports in the Y direction (rows).

  If you specify the Std. Engineering or Array of viewports options, you receive the following prompts.

- **Distance between viewports in X. <0.0>:**

  You enter a distance between adjacent viewport edges in the X direction.

- **Distance between viewports in Y. <0.0>:**

You enter a distance between adjacent viewport edges in the Y direction.

- **Scale viewports.** You receive the following prompts after you specify the Scale viewports option from the first MVSETUP paper space prompt:

- **Select the viewports to scale:**

Pick each of the viewports that you want to specify a scale for.

- **Set zoom scale factor for viewports. Interactively/<Uniform>:**

If you selected more than one viewport at the preceding prompt, you are presented with this prompt. You can scale all of the viewports at once (uniform) or specify separate scales (interactively) for each viewport.

- **Number of paper space units. <1.0>:**

For each viewport that you scale, you must define the ratio of paper space units to model space units. The default of one unit is adequate for most drawings.

- **Number of model space units. <1.0>:**

You enter the number of model space units to plot within the number of paper space units specified in the last prompt. To create a 1/4"=1'-0" scale viewport, for example, enter **1** at the previous prompt and **48** here.

- **Options.** You receive the following prompt after you select the Options option from the first paper space MVSETUP prompt.

- **Set Layer/LImits/Units/Xref:**

If you specify the Set Layer option, you receive the following prompt:

- **Layer name for title block or . for current layer:**

You enter the name of the layer on which the title block created by the Title block option of the first paper space MVSETUP prompt should be placed. You can enter a period to place the title block on the current layer.

If you specify the LImits option, you receive the following prompts.

- **Set drawing limits? <N>:**

  You can enter **Y** at this prompt to automatically set the paper space limits to the size of the title block.

  If you specify the Units option at the Options prompt, you receive the following prompt.

- **Paperspace units are in Feet/Inches/ MEters/Millimeters? <in>:**

  You enter the unit type for paper space units. The default is inches.

  If you specify the Xref option at the Options prompt, you receive the following prompt.

- **Xref Attach or Insert title block? <Insert>:**

  You enter the placement method for the title block. If you specify Insert, the title block will be inserted as a block in your drawing. If you specify Xref, the title block will be attached as an external reference.

- **Title block.** You receive the following prompt after you select the Title block option from the first MVSETUP paper space prompt:

- **Delete objects/Origin/Undo/<Insert title block>:**

  If you specify the Delete objects option, you receive the following prompt.

- **Select objects:**

  Pick any existing entities that you do not want in your drawing.

  If you select the Origin option from the Title block option prompt, you receive the following prompt:

- **New origin point for this sheet:**

  You specify a new insertion point for the title block.

  If you select the default option, Insert title block, from the Title block option prompt, you receive the following prompts:

- **Add/Delete/Redisplay/<Number of entry to load>:**

  A numbered list of the available title blocks is displayed on the screen. If you select one of these numbers, that title block is drawn in paper space. The Redisplay option displays the list of available title blocks on the screen again.

- **Title block description:**

  The Add option displays this prompt. You also can add your own title blocks to the list. When adding a new title block, you must provide a brief description to differentiate it from the other title blocks.

- **Drawing to insert:**

  After you have described the new title block to add, you need to specify its name and location to have it added to the MVSETUP information file. Type in the full path name and file name of the drawing. The drawing will be inserted into paper space and the description and location of the file are saved to a file named MVSETUP.DFS.

- **Number of entry to delete from list:**

  When you want to delete an entry from the title block list, enter its number at this prompt after specifying the Delete option at the previous prompt.

- **Create a drawing named** *drawing name*? **<Y>:**

  The default title blocks created by the MVSETUP command do not exist as drawing files. They are stored as a series of drawing instructions within the MVSETUP.DFS file. When you insert one of these title blocks (the ANSI-? title blocks in the title block list), AutoCAD then asks if you want the title block saved as a drawing file. If you plan to use any of the title blocks often, you can save it as a drawing file so that the title block is reloaded faster the next time it is needed. Also, in order for the title block to be inserted as a block or an external reference (XREF), you must create a drawing file.

Example

The following example uses the MVSETUP command to set up a title block in paper space, display the drawing in multiple scaled viewports, and then align the object between viewports.

Command: **MVSETUP** ↵
Paperspace/Modelspace is disabled.
The pre-R11 setup will be invoked unless it is enabled.
Enable Paper/Modelspace? <Y>: ↵
Entering Paper space.
Use MVIEW to insert Model space viewports.
Regenerating drawing.
MVSetup, Version 1.15, (c) 1990-1992 by Autodesk, Inc.
Align/Create/Scale viewports/Options/Title block/Undo: **O** ↵
Set Layer/LImits/Units/Xref: **LI** ↵
Set drawing limits? <N>: **Y** ↵
Set Layer/LImits/Units/Xref: **X** ↵
Xref Attach or Insert title block? <Insert>: **X** ↵
Set Layer/LImits/Units/Xref: ↵
Align/Create/Scale viewports/Options/Title block/Undo: **T** ↵
Delete objects/Origin/Undo/<Insert title block>: ↵
Available title block options:
0: None
1: ISO A4 Size(mm)
2: ISO A3 Size(mm)
3: ISO A2 Size(mm)
4: ISO A1 Size(mm)
5: ISO A0 Size(mm)
6: ANSI-V Size(in)
7: ANSI-A Size(in)
8: ANSI-B Size(in)
9: ANSI-C Size(in)
10: ANSI-D Size(in)
11: ANSI-E Size(in)
12: Arch/Engineering (24 x 36in)
13: Generic D size Sheet (24 x 36in)
Add/Delete/Redisplay/<Number of entry to load>: **9**
Create a drawing named ansi-c.dwg? <Y>: ↵
Align/Create/Scale viewports/Options/Title block/Undo: **C** ↵
Delete objects/Undo/<Create viewports>: ↵
Available Mview viewport layout options:
0: None
1: Single
2: Std. Engineering
3: Array of Viewports
Redisplay/<Number of entry to load>: **2** ↵
Bounding area for viewports. Default/<First point >: **2,2** ↵
Other point: **15,14** ↵

```
Distance between viewports in X. <0.0>: ↵
Distance between viewports in Y. <0.0>: ↵
Align/Create/Scale viewports/Options/Title block/Undo: S ↵
Select the viewports to scale:
Select objects: Pick point at ① (see fig. MVSETUP.1)
Other corner: Pick point at ②
4 found
```

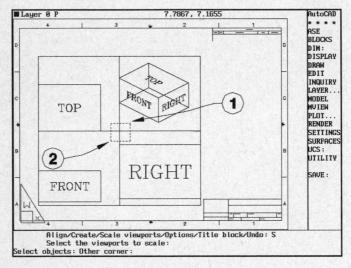

Figure MVSETUP.1:
The pick points for scaling the viewports.

```
Select objects: ↵
Set zoom scale factors for viewports.
Interactively/<Uniform>: ↵
Enter the ratio of paper space units to model space units...
Number of paper space units.  <1.0>: ↵
Number of model space units.  <1.0>: ↵
Align/Create/Scale viewports/Options/Title block/Undo: A ↵
Angled/Horizontal/Vertical alignment/Rotate view/Undo? H ↵
Basepoint: INT ↵
of Pick point ③
Other point: INT ↵
of Pick point ④
Angled/Horizontal/Vertical alignment/Rotate view/Undo? V ↵
Basepoint: INT↵
```

of *Pick point* ④
Other point: **INT**↵
of *Pick point* ⑤

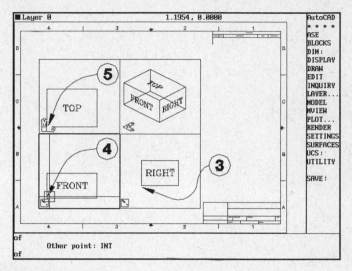

Figure MVSETUP.2:
The pick points for aligning the viewports.

Angled/Horizontal/Vertical alignment/Rotate view/Undo? ↵
Align/Create/Scale viewports/Options/Title block/Undo: ↵
The completed setup appears in figure MVSETUP.3.

Related System Variables

LTSCALE
TILEMODE

NEW

Pull down **[File] [New...]**

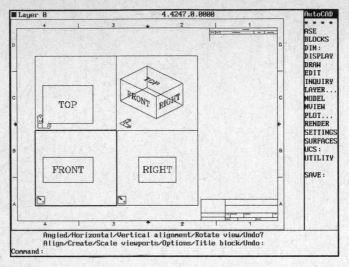

Figure MVSETUP.3:
The results of the MVSETUP example.

The NEW command begins and initializes a new drawing in the drawing editor. If you have made any modifications to the current drawing, you can save them, discard them, or cancel the NEW command. The Create New Drawing dialog box displays for you to specify a new file name and prototype drawing (see fig. NEW.1).

Figure NEW.1:
The Create New Drawing dialog box.

Prompts and Options

NEW displays no command-line prompts. Instead, you make selections from the following dialog boxes and options.

The Create New Drawing dialog box offers the following options:

- **Prototype.** This button is enabled if the No Prototype button below it is not checked. Clicking on the Prototype button displays the Prototype Drawing File dialog box, where you can select a prototype for the new drawing (see fig. NEW.2). Alternatively, you can enter the name of a known file in the text box to the right of the button. The new drawing inherits all of the entities and settings of the prototype. When a prototype drawing has been selected, its name appears in the text box. If no prototype file is selected, AutoCAD uses defaults from the configured default prototype drawing file.

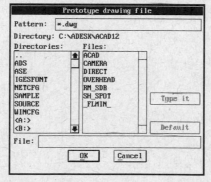

Figure NEW.2:
The Prototype Drawing File dialog box.

- **No Prototype.** If this box is checked, the new drawing uses no prototype file, and AutoCAD's default settings, as shipped, are used.
- **Retain as Default.** Checking this box causes AutoCAD to store the name of the prototype drawing file selected above as the default for subsequent new drawings.
- **New Drawing Name.** Clicking this button displays the Create Drawing File dialog box (see fig NEW.3). You can use this dialog box to select a destination directory and specify a file name for the new drawing. After you have selected a directory and file name, they appear in the text box to the right of the button. Alternatively,

you can simply enter a new file name in the text box and the
drawing is placed in the default directory. By entering a new file
name followed by the equal sign (=) and the name of an existing
file, you can specify both the new name and the prototype
AutoCAD should use. For example, entering WIDGET=GADGET
would create a new drawing named WIDGET with all of the
objects and settings from a drawing named GADGET. You can
also omit the prototype name in this method to specify no prototype.

Figure NEW.3:
The Create Drawing File dialog box.

Related Commands

END
OPEN
QUIT
SAVE
SAVEAS

Related System Variable

ACADPREFIX

OFFSET

Screen **[DRAW] [OFFSET:]**

Screen **[EDIT] [next] [OFFSET:]**

Pull down **[Construct] [Offset]**

The OFFSET command creates a copy of an entity parallel to the original entity. You can offset arcs, circles, lines, and two-dimensional polylines. When used on circles and arcs, the new entity has the same center point as the original. If the OFFSET command is used to copy a polyline, the new polyline has the same width(s) as the original, and the vertices of the polyline is offset in the direction selected.

The OFFSET command works only on one entity at a time. To offset a single entity many times, use the Array command. When you offset entities that have an extrusion distance, the results are unpredictable if the current UCS is not the same as the UCS in which the entity was created.

Prompts and Options

- **Offset distance or Through: <Through>**

  You enter a distance to offset the entity that you select at the next prompt. You can pick two points that define the distance you want to use, or select the Through (default) option, which instructs AutoCAD to offset the entity through a chosen point.

- **Select object to offset:**

  You pick the entity to be offset.

- **Through point:**

  This prompt appears if you specified the Through option at the first prompt. The point supplied at this prompt provides AutoCAD with the direction and offset distance for the new entity.

- **Side to offset?**

  If a distance is supplied for the OFFSET command, AutoCAD asks on which side of the original to place the new entity.

Example

The following example offsets polyline and circle entities shown in figure OFFSET.1.

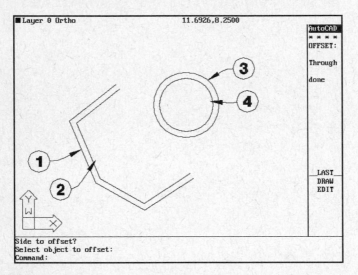

Figure OFFSET.1:
Duplicate entities created by the OFFSET command.

```
Command: OFFSET↵
Offset distance of Through <Through>: .25↵
Select object to offset: Pick point ①
Side to offset? Pick point ②
Select object to offset: Pick point ③
Side to offset? Pick point ④
```

Related Commands

> ARRAY
> COPY

Related System Variable

> OFFSETDIST

OOPS

Screen [BLOCKS] [BLOCK:] [OOPS]

Screen [EDIT] [ERASE:] [OOPS:]

Pull down [Modify] [Erase] [Oops!]

The OOPS command restores entities that have been removed from the drawing by the ERASE, BLOCK, or WBLOCK commands. The OOPS command only restores the last set of entities removed.

 The OOPS command provides a function not available with the UNDO command. If you have problems selecting the correct entities for an edit command, erase the troublesome entities and then perform the edit on the remaining entities. You can then use the OOPS command to restore the erased entities back to their original condition.

 The OOPS command does not restore entities deleted before you use the PLOT command. Instead, you must use the UNDO command in order to restore deleted entities.

Related Commands

UNDO
U

OPEN

Pull down [File] [Open...]

The OPEN command loads a drawing into the drawing editor. If you have made any modifications to the current drawing, you can save them, discard them, or cancel the OPEN command. The Open Drawing dialog box displays to enable you to specify a file name (see fig. OPEN.1).

Figure OPEN.1:
The Open Drawing dialog box.

Prompts and Options

The OPEN command does not display command-line prompts. Instead, you can make selections from the following options available in the Open Drawing dialog box.

- **Pattern.** This edit box contains the pattern specification for files to appear in the Files list box below. The wild cards ? and * can be used to refine the list to desired file names.

- **Directories.** This list box contains a listing of the subdirectories available from the current directory, displayed following Directory above. Use the scroll bar to display more file names and drive letters. Double-click on a directory name or drive letter to change the current directory.

- **Files.** This list box contains a listing of the files available in the current directory. Use the scroll bar to display more file names. Double-click on a file name, or click on it once and click on the **O**K button to proceed.

- **Select Initial View.** Checking this box permits you to select a view defined in the selected drawing to be displayed when the drawing loads. A simple dialog box appears when you enter the drawing editor for you to make your selection.

- **Read Only Mode.** When this box is checked, AutoCAD does not allow any modifications to the selected drawing to be saved in the drawing file.
- **File.** Displays the name of the file selected above in an edit box. You may type the name of a desired file here or edit an existing name.

 Use Read Only mode to open drawings for viewing that may need to be edited concurrently by others on a network. When drawings are opened in Read Only mode, AutoCAD does not create a lock, and the drawing may be opened by other users.

Related Commands

NEW
QUIT
SAVE
SAVEAS

Related System Variables

DWGWRITE
ACADPREFIX

ORTHO

Screen **[SETTINGS] [ORTHO]**

The ORTHO command is a drawing aid that constrains points to right angles from each other. You can press Ctrl-O or F8 to turn Ortho on or off. When Ortho mode is on, the word Ortho is displayed on the left end of the status bar. Ortho is affected by the current UCS and Snap style. Any coordinate entry from the keyboard overrides Ortho mode. You can turn Ortho mode on or off through a radio button in the DDRMODES dialog box.

You can execute the ORTHO command transparently by preceding the command name with an apostrophe ('ORTHO).

Prompts and Options

- **ON/OFF<Off>:**

  Turns orthogonal mode on or off.

Example

The following example demonstrates how to set the Ortho mode to ON, and Ortho mode's effects on a command such as the LINE command.

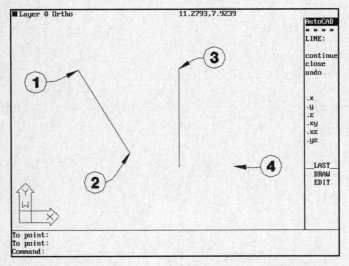

Figure ORTHO.1:
Lines drawn with Ortho mode turned on.

```
Command: LINE ⏎
From point: Pick point ①
To point: Pick point ②
```

```
To point: Pick point ⑩
Command: ORTHO↵
ON/OFF <Off>: ON↵
Command: LINE↵
From point: Pick point ③
To point: Pick point ④
To point: ↵
```

Related Command

DDRMODES

Related System Variable

ORTHOMODE

OSNAP

Screen **[* * * *]**

Screen **[SETTINGS] [next] [OSNAP:]**

Pull down **[Assist [Object Snap]**

The OSNAP (Object SNAP) command causes AutoCAD to use a specific geometric point on an existing entity when a command requests point entry. Twelve different geometric modes are available, and are described in the following section. The OSNAP command can be set to one or more running object snap settings. You can also temporarily activate any of the object snap modes within a command by entering the first three letters of the snap mode before you pick a point. This is known as *Object Snap Override*, and is active only for the single point selection.

R12	You can execute the OSNAP command transparently by preceding the command name with an apostrophe ('OSNAP).

331

Prompts and Options

- **Object snap modes:**

  You can specify one or more object snap modes by typing the first three letters of the mode. More than one mode can be requested by separating each mode with a comma. The following mode options are available:

- **CENter.** Snaps to the center point of the picked arc or circle.

- **ENDpoint.** Snaps to the nearest endpoint of an arc, line, polyline, mesh, or 3dface vertex. Endpoint object snap also snaps to the end points of extruded edges.

- **INSertion.** Snaps to the insertion point of text, attributes, blocks, or shapes.

- **INTersection.** Snaps to the nearest intersection of any combination of lines, polylines, arcs, or circles. The intersection point is only found if the objects intersect in three-dimensional space. Intersection also snaps to the corners of solid entities, lines, and extruded polyline segments, or the intersecting edge of two wide entities.

- **MIDpoint.** Snaps to the middle point of a line or arc. Midpoint also snaps to the midpoint of all four edges of an extruded line or polyline segments and the midpoint of an arc's extruded edge.

- **NEArest.** Snaps to the point on an entity that is nearest to the crosshairs.

- **NODe.** Snaps to a point entity.

- **PERpendicular.** Snaps to a point that is perpendicular from the previous point to the selected entity. The resulting point does not have to be located on the selected entity.

- **TANgent.** Snaps to a point that forms a tangent between the arc or circle and the previous point.

- **QUAdrant.** Snaps to the nearest point on an arc or circle that is located at 0, 90, 180, or 270 degrees.

- **QUIck,<osnap>.** Forces all object snap modes to accept the first point that satisfies the current mode(s), not necessarily the most accurate. Quick generally finds the snap point on the most recently drawn entities within the aperture box. Intersection object snap ignores the Quick object snap modifier.

- **NONe.** Nullifies any running object snap.

Example

The following example uses object snap overrides to choose specific points on the entities shown in figure OSNAP.1.

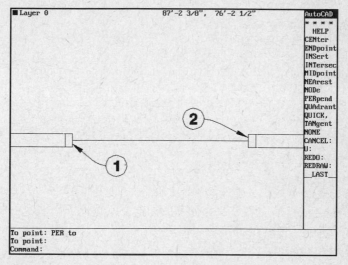

Figure OSNAP.1
A line drawn with the help of object snap overrides.

```
Command: LINE ⏎
From point: MID of Pick point ①
To point: PER of Pick point ②
To point: ⏎
```

Related Commands

APERTURE
DDOSNAP

333

Related System Variables

APERTURE
OSMODE

PAN

Screen **[DISPLAY] [PAN:]**

Pull down **[View] [Pan]**

The PAN command shifts the view of your drawing that is currently on-screen to another location. The PAN command is typically used to view adjacent areas of your drawing without changing the zoom scale. You can use the PAN command transparently (preceded by an apostrophe) if the requested view does not require a screen regeneration.

Prompts and Options

- **Displacement:**

  At this prompt, you select a starting point that serves as a reference to shift the view of the current drawing.

- **Second point:**

  At this prompt, you enter the second point for moving the display. If you press Enter at this prompt, a relative displacement is used based on the point you enter at the Displacement: prompt.

Example

Figure PAN.1 shows the result of using the PAN command in two viewports, one before the command and one after.

Command: **PAN**↵
Displacement: *Pick point* ①
Second point: *Pick point* ②

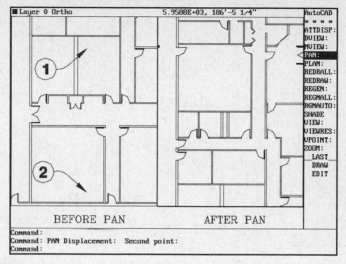

```
■ Layer 0 Ortho              5.9588E+03, 186'-5 1/4"       AutoCAD
                                                          * * * *
                                                          ATTDISP:
                                                          DVIEW:
                                                          MVIEW:
                                                         ◄PAN:
                                                          PLAN:
                                                          REDRALL:
                                                          REDRAW:
                                                          REGEN:
                                                          REGNALL:
                                                          RGNAUTO:
                                                          SHADE
                                                          VIEW:
                                                          VIEWRES:
                                                          VPOINT:
                                                          ZOOM:
                                                           LAST
                                                           DRAW
                                                           EDIT
        BEFORE PAN              AFTER PAN
Command:
Command: PAN Displacement:  Second point:
Command:
```

Figure PAN.1:
Using the PAN command to view other portions of a drawing.

Related Command

ZOOM

PCXIN

PCXIN imports a Zsoft PCX raster file into AutoCAD. AutoCAD scans the raster image and creates a block consisting of a solid for each rectangular colored pixel in the PCX file. After you have imported a raster image into AutoCAD, you can trace over the raster image with AutoCAD geometry to create an AutoCAD drawing of the raster image. When you are through, you can erase the raster image. Raster images can be scaled, mirrored, and rotated like regular entities.

 Do not explode the block representation of a raster file—the resulting entities use large quantities of disk space and memory.

The system variable GRIPBLOCK should be set to 0 to avoid
highlighting all of the solid entities in the block.

TIP

Prompts and Options

- `PCX file name:`

  You enter the name of the PCX file you want to import. You do not
  need to include the extension.

- `Insertion point <0,0,0>:`

  You enter the X, Y, and Z coordinates or pick the insertion point
  for the raster file.

- `Scale Factor:`

  You enter a number or drag the crosshairs to scale the raster file
  from the insertion point.

- `New length:`

  If you press Enter at the Scale Factor prompt, you are prompted to
  pick a point to specify the scale factor.

See the listing in the GIFIN command summary for the description of a
series of options that control how a raster file is imported (RIASPECT,
RIBACKG, RIEDGE, RIGAMUT, RIGREY, and RITHRESH).

Example

The following example imports a PCX file called TEST.PCX into
AutoCAD at 3,3,0.

```
Command: PCXIN↵
PCX file name: TEST↵
Insertion point <0,0,0>: 3,3,0↵
Scale factor: 2 ↵
```

Related Commands

GIFIN
TIFIN

Related System Variable

GRIPBLOCK

PEDIT

Screen **[EDIT] [next] [PEDIT:]**

Pull down **[Modify] [PolyEdit]**

The PEDIT command edits 2D and 3D polylines and polygon meshes. Each of these entities is a variation of the basic polyline entity; thus, the PEDIT command performs a variety of manipulations of these entities. Each type of polyline produces a different response from the PEDIT command. The next section explains how each form of editing works.

Prompts and Options

- **Select polyline:**

  At this prompt, select a polyline for editing by using any of the standard AutoCAD object selection methods. If the selected entity is not a polyline or mesh, the following message appears:

      Entity selected is not a polyline

  If the selected entity is a line or an arc, it will be highlighted and you will receive the following prompt:

- **Do you want to turn it into one? <Y>**

  The PEDIT command can change a "normal" line into a 2D polyline. If you decide not to transform the entity, the PEDIT command terminates.

2D Polylines

The following prompts and options appear when you use the PEDIT command to edit 2D polyline entities:

- **Close/Join/Width/Edit vertex/Fit/Spline/Decurve/ Ltype gen/Undo/eXit <X>:**

  After a 2D polyline has been selected or created, you see these options.

- **Close.** The Close option creates a closing polyline segment from the end of the polyline back to its beginning. If the ending segment is an arc, the Close option creates a closing arc segment. After the polyline is closed, this option changes to Open. The Open option removes closing polyline segments.

- **Join.** When you specify the Join option, you see the `Select objects:` prompt. You can select line, arc, and polyline segments to add to the current polyline, each segment chosen must meet the adjacent segment at its endpoint, forming a continuous chain. After performing the join operation, the Pedit command reports how many segments were added.

- **Width.** The Width option enables you to set a constant width for all segments of the polyline. If individual segments have tapered widths, this value will override the previous width information. When you choose the Width option, you receive the following prompt:

  `Enter new width for all segments:`

- **Edit vertex.** The Edit vertex option presents this new prompt line of options. These options are used to edit a polyline on a vertex-by-vertex basis. When you edit vertices, the PEDIT command marks the current vertex with an X. Each of the options that has additional prompts are described with their prompts. The options without additional prompts are described in the following paragraphs.

- **Next/Previous/Break/Insert/Move/Regen/Straighten/ Tangent/Width/eXit <X>:**

- **Next.** The Next option enables you to move the vertex marker (the X) to the next polyline vertex. The Previous option moves the vertex marker to the preceding vertex.

- **Regen.** When you make vertex edits, you can easily obscure the current shape of the polyline. The Regen option forces a regeneration of only the polyline so that you can view it in its current form.

- **Break** and **Straighten.** If you select either the Break or Straighten options, you are presented with the prompt `Next/ Previous/Go/eXit <N>:`. The Break option removes the section of the polyline between the specified vertices. The Straighten option removes all of the vertices between the two specified vertex points and replaces them with one polyline segment. With either option, the current position of the vertex marker is considered the starting point for breaking or straightening.

- **Next, Previous, Go,** and **eXit.** The Next or Previous options locate the ending vertex for your edit. After that vertex is located, use the Go option to execute the break or straighten actions. The eXit option returns to the previous prompt without performing any editing.

- **Insert.** The Insert option allows you to specify the coordinates of a new polyline vertex to be created. The Insert option issues this prompt: `Enter location of new vertex:`.

- **Move.** The Move option enables you to alter the location of the current polyline vertex by supplying a new location for the current vertex. The Move option issues the following prompt: `Enter new location:`.

- **Tangent.** The Tangent option enables you to determine the tangent direction used by fitted curves at the current vertex. The Tangent option issues the prompt: `Direction of tangent:`. The tangent direction is indicated by an arrow through the Edit vertex mode's X's.

- **Fit.** The Fit option creates a continuous smooth curve composed of arcs among all of the polyline's vertices. If you specify any tangent directions for vertices (under the Edit vertex option), the directions are used to compute the curve direction at the vertices. If you explode a curve-fit polyline or use the BREAK or TRIM commands on the polyline, a pair of arcs will appear between each vertex.

- **Spline.** The Spline option uses the existing polyline vertices to form the frame for fitting either a quadratic B-spline or a cubic B-spline curve (based on the value of the SPLINETYPE variable) along the polyline. The resolution (number of lines or arcs between each pair of vertices) is set by the value of the SPLINESEGS system variable. If SPLINESEGS is positive, the spline uses lines; if negative, the spline uses arcs to create the B-spline.

- **Decurve.** The Decurve option removes any curve-fitting or spline-fitting arc segments from the polyline.

- **Ltype gen.** By default, when AutoCAD displays polylines with noncontinuous linetypes, the pattern begins and ends at each vertex. Setting Ltype gen ON forces linetypes to be rendered between endpoints, ignoring intermediate vertices.

- **Undo.** The Undo option reverses the last action performed on the polyline. If you make many changes in the Edit vertex option, all the changes can be reversed by a single undo.

- **eXit.** The eXit option terminates the polyline editing and returns you to the `Command:` prompt.

- **Width.** The Width option enables you to vary the width of the polyline segment between the current vertex and next vertex. The Width option displays the following prompt: `Enter starting width <default>:`. Enter a value to be used for the starting width and the ending width. If the polyline has a width currently assigned, that width appears as the default. The polyline does not show the effects of the change in width until you use the Regen option, or if you exit to the main PEDIT prompt line.

3D Polylines

The following prompt and options appear when you use the PEDIT command to edit 3D polyline entities:

- `Close/Edit vertex/Spline curve/Decurve/Undo/eXit <X>:`

- **Close.** The Close option creates a closing polyline segment from the end of the polyline back to its beginning. When the polyline is closed, this option changes to Open in the prompt line. The Open option removes a closing polyline segment.

- **Spline curve.** The Spline curve option works the same as for 2D polylines except that the curve is generated in 3D space and consists of straight line segments only, regardless of the value of SPLINESEGS.

- **Decurve.** The Decurve option removes any spline-fitting and restores the polyline to its original state.

- **Undo** and **Regen.** The Undo and Regen options function the same as for 2D polylines.

- **Edit vertex.** The Edit vertex option displays the following prompt. Each option edits vertices in the same manner as in 2D polyline editing, except that now you can supply a 3D location for the polyline's vertices.

  ```
  Next/Previous/Break/Insert/Move/Regen/Straighten/
  eXit <X>:
  ```

Polygon Meshes

The following prompt appears when you use the PEDIT command to edit polygon meshes:

- **Edit vertex/Smooth surface/Desmooth/Mclose/Nclose/ Undo/eXit <X>:**

- **Edit vertex.** The Edit vertex option displays the following prompt, which enables you to relocate the position of each of the vertices of the polygon mesh. The prompt displays the current position of the vertex you are editing in both the M and N directions.

- **Vertex (m,n). Next/Previous/Left/RIght/Up/Down/ Move/REgen/eXit <X>:**

  For meshes generated by commands affected by the SURFTAB1 and SURFTAB2 system variables, the M direction corresponds to the SURFTAB1 setting, and the N direction corresponds to the SURFTAB2 setting. The options Next, Previous, Left, Right, Up, and Down all move the current vertex X marker through the mesh.

341

- **Move.** The Move option of Edit vertex enables you to relocate the current polyline vertex by specifying a new coordinate anywhere within 3D space. The Move option displays the prompt: Enter new location:.

- **Smooth surface.** The Smooth Surface option fits a smooth surface to the framework of the mesh by using one of three smoothing options based on the value of the SURFTYPE variable. If the variable is equal to 5, quadratic B-spline surface smoothing occurs. If its value is 6, a cubic B-spline smoothing routine is used. If the variable value is 8, the surface is smoothed with a Bezier curve equation. The density of the smoothed surface is controlled by the SURFU system variable in the M direction and by the SURFV system variable in the N direction. The surface does not pass through the vertex (control) points of the mesh, but is controlled by them—as in spline-fitting a 2D or 3D polyline.

- **Desmooth.** The Desmooth option reverses any smoothing and restores the original polygon mesh.

- **Mclose** and **Nclose.** The Mclose and Nclose options close the polygon mesh in the M or N directions. If the polygon mesh is currently closed in either the M or N direction, the close option for that direction is replaced with Mopen or Nopen.

- **Undo.** The Undo option reverses the previous action performed on the mesh. If you make many changes in the Edit vertex option, all the changes can be reversed by a single undo.

- **Exit.** The Exit option terminates editing and returns to the Command: prompt.

Example

The following example uses the PEDIT command to edit a 2D polyline, shown in figure PEDIT.1, by inserting a vertex, relocating another vertex, and then creating a spline-fit polyline. In order to see the original polyline, set the SPLFRAME variable to 1 before beginning the command sequence.

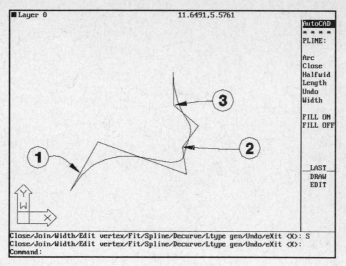

Figure PEDIT.1:
The polyline and the new splined shape.

```
Command: PEDIT↵
Select polyline: Pick point ①
Close/Join/Width/Edit vertex/Fit/Spline/Decurve/Ltype gen/Undo/
eXit <X>: E↵
Next/Previous/Break/Insert/Move/Regen/Straighten/Tangent/Width/
eXit <N>: ↵
Move to the next vertex
Next/Previous/Break/Insert/Move/Regen/Straighten/Tangent/Width/
eXit <N>: ↵
Move to the next vertex
Next/Previous/Break/Insert/Move/Regen/Straighten/Tangent/Width/
eXit <N>: I↵
Enter location of new vertex: Pick point ②
Next/Previous/Break/Insert/Move/Regen/Straighten/Tangent/Width/
eXit <N>: ↵
Move to the next vertex
Next/Previous/Break/Insert/Move/Regen/Straighten/Tangent/Width/
eXit <N>: ↵
Next/Previous/Break/Insert/Move/Regen/Straighten/Tangent/Width/
eXit <N>: ↵
Next/Previous/Break/Insert/Move/Regen/Straighten/Tangent/Width/
eXit <N>: M↵
Enter new location: Pick point ③
```

343

```
Next/Previous/Break/Insert/Move/Regen/Straighten/Tangent/Width/
eXit <N>: X↵
Close/Join/Width/Edit vertex/Fit/Spline/Decurve/Ltype gen/Undo/
eXit <X>: S↵
Close/Join/Width/Edit vertex/Fit/Spline/Decurve/Ltype gen/Undo/
eXit <X>: ↵
```

Related Commands

> EDGESURF
> LASTPOINT
> PFACE
> PLINE
> REVSURF
> RULESURF
> TABSURF
> 3DFACE
> 3DMESH
> 3DPOLY

Related System Variables

> SPLFRAME
> SPLINESEGS
> SPLINETYPE
> SURFTAB1
> SURFTAB2
> SURFTYPE
> SURFU
> SURFV

PFACE

Screen **[DRAW] [next] [3D Surfs] [PFACE:]**

The PFACE command creates a polygon mesh by first locating points in 3D space and then connecting these points to form a face. Virtually any number of points (called vertices) can be defined. Many different faces can be created from these vertices. The polyface entity that is created can be modified in the same manner as any other polygon mesh. This command was designed for use with AutoLISP programs and ADS applications, so input for this command can be quite complicated.

No matter how many faces are created, they are linked together as one entity. Each face can be given a separate color or can be placed on a different layer as it is created. The edges of a face can be made invisible. If a frozen layer contains one of the polyfaces, the entire polyface is invisible until the layer is thawed.

Prompts and Options

- **Vertex x:**

  At this prompt, you enter a point, either 2D or 3D. The prompt continues until you press Enter, signifying the end of the vertex definition.

- **Face x, Vertex x:**

  This prompt defines the edges of each face. As you define the first face, enter each vertex (by the number defined) as they connect to form the face. After all vertices for the face are identified, press Enter to define the next face. Pressing Enter at the first vertex prompt of any face instructs AutoCAD to complete the command and create the polyfaces. If you want an edge of the face to be invisible, precede the vertex number with a minus sign, such as -3.

  You also can enter **Color** and **Layer** at this prompt. These two options enable you to create a polyface that has individual faces of different colors and are located on different layers.

Example

This example creates a simple polyface entity, shown in figure PFACE.1, using the PFACE command.

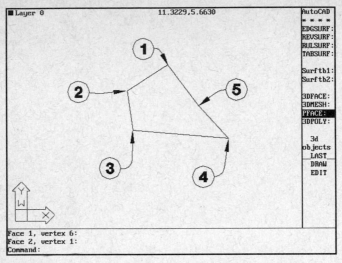

Figure PFACE.1:
A simple polygon mesh created with the PFACE command.

```
Command: PFACE⏎
Vertex 1: Pick point ①
Vertex 2: Pick point ②
Vertex 3: Pick point ③
Vertex 4: Pick point ④
Vertex 5: Pick point ⑤
Vertex 6: ⏎
Face 1, vertex 1: 1⏎
Face 1, vertex 2: 2⏎
Face 1, vertex 3: 3⏎
Face 1, vertex 4: 4⏎
Face 1, vertex 5: 5⏎
Face 1, vertex 6: ⏎
```

Related Commands

PEDIT
REVSURF
RULESURF
TABSURF
3DFACE
3DMESH

PLAN

Screen **[DISPLAY] PLAN:]**

Pull down **[View] [Set View >] [Plan View >]**

The PLAN command sets the view to the plan view of one of three possible coordinate systems. When you are working in model space, the plan view is parallel to the X-Y plane of the coordinate system. The PLAN command provides a quick method of setting your viewport to 0,0,1.

Prompts and Options

- **<Current UCS>/UCS/World:**

    The default option, <Current UCS>, changes the view to the plan of the current UCS. The UCS option changes the view to the plan of a previously saved UCS. If you select the World option, the drawing regenerates and you can view your drawing from the WCS.

- **?/Name of UCS:**

    At this prompt, you enter the name of a saved User Coordinate System. You can use the **?** option to display a list of currently saved User Coordinate Systems.

- **UCS name(s) to list <*>:**

    At this prompt, you enter the name of a UCS to list, or press Enter to view a list of all defined User Coordinate Systems.

Example

This example shows how to restore the plan view of a named UCS. Figure PLAN.1 shows, in two viewports, the difference in the display.

```
Command: PLAN↵
?/Name of UCS: FACE1 ↵
<Current UCS>/UCS/World: U ↵
```

347

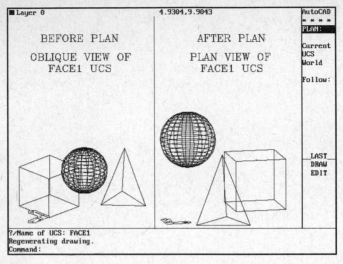

Figure PLAN.1:
The initial SITE-3D drawing before setting the plan view.

Related Commands

DDUCSP
DDVPOINT
DDVIEW
VPOINT
UCS

Related System Variables

UCSFOLLOW
UCSNAME

PLINE

Screen [DRAW] [next] [PLINE:]

Pull down [Draw] [Polyline >] [2D]

The PLINE command draws polyline entities. Polylines are complex entities that are a combination of line and arc segments, but are treated by AutoCAD as a single entity. As a complex entity, 2D polylines have great flexibility to meet special needs in an AutoCAD drawing—from custom leader lines to hatch boundaries.

Prompts and Options

- `From point:`

  At this prompt, you enter the starting point of the polyline.

- `Arc/Close/Halfwidth/Length/Undo/Width/<Endpoint of line>:`

  This prompt contains all of the major options of the PLINE command.

- `Arc`. This option presents this additional prompt:

- `Angle/CEnter/CLose/Direction/Halfwidth/Line/ Radius/Second pt/Undo/Width/<Endpoint of arc>:`

  Each of the possible polyline arc options is discussed in the following paragraphs.

- `Angle`. This option asks you to enter the included angle of the arc. The Angle option issues the `Included angle:` prompt. After you have entered the value for the included angle, you receive this prompt: `Center/Radius/<Endpoint>:`. Enter the center point for the arc, the arc's radius, or use the default option to specify an endpoint for the arc.

- `CEnter`. This option displays the prompt `Center point:`, at which you enter the arc's center point. By default, the PLINE command draws arcs tangent from the last segment and automatically locates the arc's center point. This option enables you to override the default action of the PLINE command.

- `Angle/Length/<End point>:`

  If you used the Center option displayed previously, enter the additional information needed to create the arc. You can enter the included angle, a value for the chord length, or simply specify the arc's endpoint (the default option).

- **Close**. This option draws a polyline arc segment back to the beginning of the polyline.
- **Direction**. This option enables you to specify the direction that the arc will be drawn from the arc's starting point. The Direction option issues the `Direction from starting point:` prompt. The PLINE command draws the arc tangent to the starting point by default. If you want to override this default, pick a point in the drawing editor to indicate the arc's new direction.
- **End point:**

  After the polyline arc direction has been entered, locate the end point of the arc by specifying a point.
- **Halfwidth**. This option enables you to enter a value for the width of a polyline segment based on the width from the center of the polyline to its edge. The actual width of the polyline segment will be double the value you enter at the prompt below.

  `Starting half-width <0.000>:`
- **Ending half-width <0.000>:**

  The ending polyline half-width is the same as its starting half-width by default. This gives the polyline segment a uniform width. If you want the width tapered from the beginning to the end, enter an ending half-width that differs in value from the starting half-width.
- **Line**. This option returns you to the Line mode prompt.
- **Radius**. This option accepts a value for the radius of an arc.
- **Angle/<End point>:**

  After you enter the radius, locate an ending point at the prompt above to create the arc or enter a value for the arc's included angle.
- **Second point**. Polyline arc segments can be created similar to a standard three-point arc with this option. Enter the second of three points that will describe the arc.
- **End point:**

  After the second point of the polyline arc is located, specify the end point at this prompt to properly create the polyline arc.

- **Undo.** This option undoes individual segments one at a time.

- **Width.** The Width option works in the same manner as the half-width option. It enables you to assign a width at the Starting with <0.000> prompt for the current polyline segment. The difference is that the width is measured from the edges of the polyline, not from the center to the edge.

- **Ending width <0.000>:**

  The ending polyline width is the same as its starting width by default. This gives the polyline segment a uniform width. If you want the width to taper from beginning to end, enter an ending width at the above prompt that differs from the starting width.

- **Endpoint of arc.** The default option, enables you to select the endpoint for an arc that is drawn tangent to the last segment.

Following are the remaining PLINE Line mode options:

- **Close.** This option works in the same manner as the Close option of Arc mode, except that it draws a straight segment back to the beginning of the polyline.

- **Halfwidth, Undo,** and **Width.** These options work the same as when you draw polyline arc segments.

- **Length.** You enter a value for the length of the next segment. The segment will be drawn at the same angle as the previous segment. If no segment exists, an angle of 0 degrees is used to draw the next segment.

- **Endpoint of line.** This option, which is the default, enables you to specify the location for another segment endpoint.

Example

This example demonstrates using some of the PLINE command's options to create the polyline shown in figure PLINE.1.

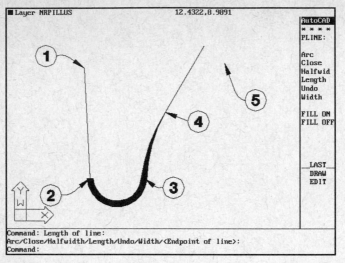

Figure PLINE.1:
A polyline created with various PLINE options.

```
Command: PLINE↵
From point: Pick point ①
Arc/Close/Halfwidth/Length/Undo/Width/<Endpoint of line>: Pick point ②
Arc/Close/Halfwidth/Length/Undo/Width/<Endpoint of line>: W↵
Starting width <0.0000>: .25↵
Ending width <0.2500>: ↵
Arc/Close/Halfwidth/Length/Undo/Width/<Endpoint of line>: A↵
Angle/CEnter/CLose/Direction/Halfwidth/Line/Radius/Second pt/Undo/
Width/<Endpoint of arc>: Pick point ③
Angle/CEnter/CLose/Direction/Halfwidth/Line/Radius/Second pt/Undo/
Width/<Endpoint of arc>: W↵
Starting width <0.2500>: ↵
Ending width <0.2500>: 0↵
Angle/CEnter/CLose/Direction/Halfwidth/Line/Radius/Second pt/Undo/
Width/<Endpoint of arc>: ④
Angle/CEnter/CLose/Direction/Halfwidth/Line/Radius/Second pt/Undo/
Width/<Endpoint of arc>: L↵
Arc/Close/Halfwidth/Length/Undo/Width/<Endpoint of line>: L↵
Length of line: ⑤
Arc/Close/Halfwidth/Length/Undo/Width/<Endpoint of line>: ↵
```

Related Commands

FILL
PEDIT
TRACE

Related System Variables

PLINEGEN
PLINEWID

PLOT

R12

Screen **[PLOT...]**

Pull down **[File] [Plot...]**

The PLOT command produces a hard copy of your drawing on an installed and configured plotting device. The PLOT command outputs only the current drawing. You can specify one of several different drawing areas to plot, including the most recent display view, the extents of the drawing, the limits as established by the LIMITS command, a named view, or a user-specified window. Each plot may be directed either to the configured plotter or to a file on disk.

Prompts and Options

In AutoCAD Release 12, the plotting facility has been completely renovated to work from a comprehensive dialog box. The Plot Configuration dialog box, shown in figure PLOT.1, displays each of the plotting options in a series of radio buttons, check boxes, and option buttons, divided into logical groups. The functions of each of these groups are described in the following paragraphs.

```
┌─────────────────────────────────────────────────────────────┐
│                      Plot Configuration              °        │
│ ┌Device and Default Information─┐ ┌Paper Size and Orientation┐│
│ │Epson printers ADI 4.2 - by Autodesk│ ■ Inches  ┌─────┐      ││
│ │  ┌Device and Default Selection...┐ │ │        │Size...│ MAX  ││
│ │  └───────────────────────────────┘ │ □ MM     └─────┘      ││
│ ┌Pen Parameters────────────────┐   Plot Area 8.00 by 11.00  ││
│ │ ┌Pen Assignments...┐ ┌Optimization...┐│┌Scale, Rotation, and Origin┐│
│ │ └──────────────────┘ └──────────────┘││ ┌Rotation and Origin...┐   ││
│ ┌Additional Parameters──────────┐     │ └──────────────────────┘   ││
│ │ ■ Display    □ Hide Lines       │ Plotted Inches = Drawing Units ││
│ │ □ Extents                       │ ┌────────┐   ┌────────┐       ││
│ │ □ Limits     □ Adjust Area Fill │ │   8    │ = │12.4431 │       ││
│ │ □ View                          │ └────────┘   └────────┘       ││
│ │ □ Window     □ Plot To File     │ ⊠ Scaled to Fit              ││
│ │ ┌View...┐ ┌Window...┐ ┌File Name...┐│┌Plot Preview─────────────┐││
│ │ └───────┘ └─────────┘ └───────────┘││┌Preview...┐ ■ Partial □ Full│││
│ │              ┌───OK───┐ ┌Cancel┐    │└──────────┘              │││
│ └──────────────┴────────┴─┴──────┴────┴────────────────────────┘│
└─────────────────────────────────────────────────────────────┘
```

Figure PLOT.1:
The Plot Configuration dialog box.

> **TIP** The Plot Configuration dialog box is controlled by the CMDDIA system variable. If CMDDIA is set to 0, then no dialog box will be shown and the prompts used in previous versions of AutoCAD will be displayed. This setting is most useful if you need to perform plotting from a script file.

The Device and Default Information group has a single button that performs the following function:

• **Device and Default Selection.** This button allows you to choose from up to 29 predefined plotter configurations that you can use to plot your drawing. Because the PRPLOT command has been removed in Release 12, both printer plotter and pen plotter configurations can be placed in this list to use as your output device.

This button displays the Device and Default Selection dialog box. This dialog box contains a list box of the defined plotter configurations. You must use the CONFIG command to create plotter configurations. To make one of the configurations active, highlight it and click on the OK button. If you click on the Cancel button, any modifications you have made in the dialog box will be removed. This dialog box also contains the following buttons:

- **Save Default To File.** This button allows you to save all the plotting parameters you have chosen from the Configuration Plot dialog box, to a plot configuration file. This file can be used at a later time to restore all the defaults you have chosen. Plot configuration files have an extension of PCP.

- **Get Default From File.** This button retrieves any previously saved plotter configuration file and updates the current plot parameters.

- **Show Device Requirements.** This option displays additional configuration information about the plotter. If this button is greyed, there are no additional requirements for this particular plotting device.

- **Change Device Requirements.** This option enables you to change plotter configuration values if the selected plotter has any additional possible values. If this button is greyed, no other values are possible.

The Pen Parameters group is used to specify information that is specific to the type of plotter you have selected. This group has two buttons:

- **Pen Assignments.** This button is used to assign AutoCAD color numbers to plotter pens. This button displays the Pen Assignments dialog box, which is used to define which AutoCAD color is assigned to each plotter pen number, and also assign such attributes as hardware linetype, pen speed, and pen width. Click on the Feature Legend. button to display which of these attributes may be assigned using the current plotter.

- **Optimization.** At plot time, AutoCAD optimizes the plot information so that your plotter does not waste time.

> **TIP** You can configure the types of optimization you want by selecting one of the radio buttons provided in the Optimizing Pen Motion dialog box. Some plotters perform optimization, and if you modify any of these options, you may instead increase your plot time.

355

The Additional Parameters group determines what information in your drawing gets sent to the plotter. The group of radio buttons allows you to plot out the current display, the drawing's extents, the drawing's limits, a named view, or a windowed area of your drawing. You can also choose to hide lines that may be obscured in a 3D drawing, adjust the fill area based on the width of the pen in use, or send all the plot information to a file. The buttons in this group perform the following functions:

- **View.** If you choose to plot a view, this button displays the View Name dialog box. This box contains a list of all the named views within the current drawing. To plot one of the views, highlight the name in the list box, and click on the OK button.

- **Window.** If you choose to plot a windowed area of your drawing, this button displays the Window Selection dialog box. This box allows you to enter the absolute X and Y locations for the window's corners, or you pick the window by clicking on the Pick button.

- **File Name.** You can choose to plot the drawing to a file, instead of the plotter. Typically, the default plot file name is set with the CONFIG command, but you can use this button to select a different file name for the plot file.

The Paper Size and Orientation buttons are used to tell AutoCAD the size of the output for your plot. The radio buttons in this group determine which type of units, Inches or Millimeters, are used for displaying the size of the plot. The final button, **S**ize, performs the following action:

- **Size.** The Size button allows you to choose the size of plotted output for the current plot. The Paper Size and Orientation dialog box displays a list of possible paper sizes based on the current plotter configuration. You can also specify custom plot sizes by filling in the User edit boxes. You may also choose to have the plot oriented normally in landscape mode, or rotated 90 degrees and placed in portrait mode.

The Scale, Rotation, and Origin group is used to determine the final plot parameters before output. You can directly enter the scale for the plot in the supplied edit boxes, or you may choose to fit the plot within the boundaries of the paper you have chosen by checking the Scaled to Fit check box. The only button in this group performs the following actions:

- **Rotation and Origin.** This button allows you to rotate the plotted output and locate the starting point on the paper where the plot will begin.

The final group of plot options is the Plot Preview group. It allows you to perform an on-screen preview before any information gets sent to the plotter. This has the advantage of displaying any possible problem with the plot before actually putting any information down on paper. The two options, Partial or Full, determine the amount of detail shown when you click on the Preview button.

When you perform a partial preview, you will see an accurate rendering of the paper size you are plotting to, along with an indicator of the amount of space needed to plot the drawing. This preview shows no drawing geometry and is quick. A full preview, on the other hand, shows exactly what will plot in the area that is assigned. This method takes longer to preview due to the greater amount of detail required.

Example

This example of the PLOT command shows you how to set plot parameters and perform a full plot preview. When shown in preview mode, the drawing looks similar to figure PLOT.2.

Command: **PLOT**↵
Click on the Extents *radio button*
Click on the Size *button*
Select "C" size from the list box, then press the OK button
Set the scale to 1=1
Click on the Full *button, then click on the* Preview *button*
Click on the End Preview *button*
Click on the Cancel *button*

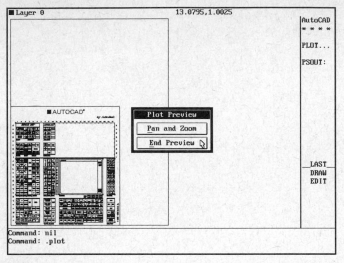

Figure PLOT.2:
The Plot Configuration dialog box.

Related Commands

CONFIG
FILL
QTEXT

Related System Variables

CMDDIA
PLOTID
PLOTTER

POINT

Screen **[DRAW] [next] [POINT:]**

Pull down **[Draw] [Point]**

The POINT command creates a point entity in your drawing. You can enter a point coordinate from the keyboard, or you can pick a point on the screen. If you enter 2D coordinates, the Z elevation defaults to the current construction plane. Point entities can be used for object snap points when you use the NODe object snap mode.

You can alter the style and size of point display by using the PDMODE and PDSIZE system variables. After you change these variables, all subsequently created points reflect the new settings. Existing points do not display in the new style and size until the drawing is regenerated.

AutoCAD also creates points when you create associative dimensions. These points are placed on a layer named DEFPOINTS. If you move these points, AutoCAD automatically updates the associated dimension. These dimension points are not affected by the settings of the PDMODE and PDSIZE variables.

Prompts and Options

- `Point:`

  At this prompt, you specify the new point entity's location.

Related Commands

DIVIDE
MEASURE

Related System Variables

PDMODE
PDSIZE

POLYGON

Screen **[DRAW] [next] [POLYGON:]**

Pull down **[Draw] [Polygon]**

The POLYGON command creates a multisided regular polygon as a polyline entity. Each entity has sides of equal length and spacing around the center. Polygons are closed polyline entities made up of at least three segments (up to 1,024 segments).

Prompts and Options

- **Number of sides <4>:**

  At this prompt, you specify the number of sides for the polygon. Enter any number from 3 to 1,024. The default creates a square.

- **Edge/<Center of polygon>:**

  When you specify an edge, you draw one side of the polygon. The other edges are drawn using the same length. If you want to draw the polygon by using a circle as a guide, specify the circle's center point.

- **First endpoint of edge:**

  This Edge option's first prompt requests the starting point for the polygon face.

- **Second endpoint of edge:**

  At this prompt, you specify a point to define the end point of the polygon's first edge.

- **Inscribed in circle/Circumscribed about circle (I/C) <I>:**

  This prompt appears after you specify the polygon's center point.

  You enter **I** if you want to specify the polygon using a circle to inscribe it. When the polygon is inscribed in the circle, the circle's radius defines the distance from the center to the corners of the sides.

You enter **C** if you want to specify the polygon by using a circle to circumscribe it. If the entity is circumscribed by the circle, the radius measures the distance from the center perpendicular to one of the edges. This distance is often referred to as the distance across the flats, as you measure the head of a bolt.

- `Radius of circle:`

  At this prompt, you enter a distance for the radius, and the polygon is created with the first side aligned with the X axis. Pick a point to indicate the radius and the polygon is created using that point to set its size and orientation.

Example

This example creates a polygon with eight sides. The results are shown in figure POLYGON.1.

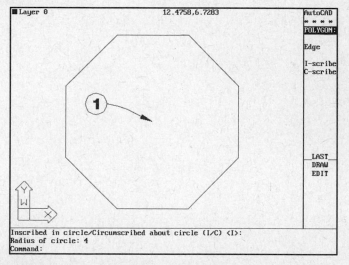

Figure POLYGON.1:
An octagon drawn with the POLYGON command's Circumscribed option.

```
Command: POLYGON↵
Number of Sides <4>: 8↵
Edge/<Center of polygon>: Pick point ①
Inscribed in circle/Circumscribed about circle (I/C) <I>: C↵
Radius of circle: 4 ↵
```

PSDRAG

PSDRAG controls the display of PostScript images while they are
placed and scaled by the PSIN command.

Prompts and Options

- **PSIN drag mode <0>:**

  You can enter **0** (the default) or 1. Enter **0** to display just the boundary of PostScript images while dragging. Enter **1** to display the
  rendered PostScript image.

   The PSIN drag mode has no effect if the PSQUALITY system
  variable is set to 0; only boundaries are displayed.

Related Commands

PSIN
PSFILL

Related System Variable

PSQUALITY

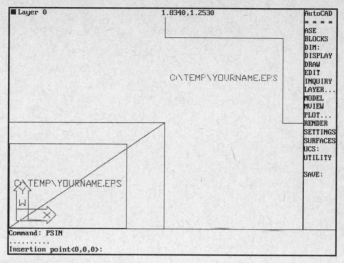

Figure PSDRAG.1:
A PostScript font with PSDRAG set to 1.

PSFILL

The PSFILL command fills areas that are enclosed by 2D polylines. PSFILL uses a pattern defined in the AutoCAD PostScript support file ACAD.PSF. The fill pattern is visible only on hard-copy output and is not drawn on-screen in the drawing editor.

Prompts and Options

- `Select polyline:`

  You pick the polyline for which you want to specify a PostScript fill pattern. The new pattern is assigned to the area within the polyline.

- `PostScript fill pattern (. = none) <.>/?:`

  You enter the name of a fill pattern to assign to the selected area. The default for this prompt is none. You can enter a question mark to list the names of available fills. You can precede the pattern name with an asterisk to prevent printing of the solid polyline outline on hard copy; only the fill pattern is plotted. Fill patterns included with Release 12 include Grayscale, RGBcolor, AIlogo, Lineargray, Radialgray, Square, Waffle, Zigzag, Stars, Brick, and Specks.

Related Commands

FILL
PEDIT
PLINE

Related System Variables

FILLMODE
PLINEWID
PLINEGEN

PSIN

Pull down **[Draw] [Import/Export] [PostScript In]**

The PSIN command imports an existing Encapsulated PostScript (EPS) file into the current drawing. You can drag the image on screen and place it by picking. Before the image is placed, it appears as a box outlining the size and shape of the image. The file name of the image appears within the box. After the EPS image has been imported, it becomes an anonymous (unnamed) AutoCAD block. The original PostScript data is appended to the block as extended entity data in case the image is output back to an EPS file with the PSOUT command.

Prompts and Options

- `File:`

At this prompt, you enter the name of an existing EPS file without
the extension or select a file with the Select PostScript File dialog
box.

- **Insertion point <0,00>:**

  You enter an insertion point for the lower left corner of the image
  or accept the default.

- **Scale factor:**

  You enter a scale factor for the imported image.

Example

This example uses PSIN to import an EPS file into the current drawing (see
fig. PSIN.1).

```
Command: PSIN↵
Insertion point <0,00>: ↵
Scale factor: 1 ↵
```

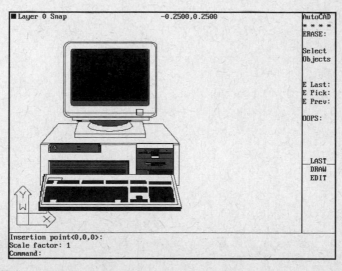

Figure PSIN.1:
Encapsulated PostScript image imported into AutoCAD with PSIN.

Related Commands

DXBIN
DXFIN
IGESIN
PSOUT
PSQUALITY

PSOUT

Screen **[UTILITY] [PSOUT:]**

Pull down **[File] [Import/Export] [PostScript Out]**

The PSOUT command exports the current drawing as an Encapsulated PostScript (EPS) file. The file is given the same name as the current drawing, with the extension EPS. The EPS file can then be imported into another graphics or desktop publishing program. A user-selectable resolution screen image may be included for previewing the file within other programs. If any blocks exist in the drawing with PostScript information in extended entity data, such as created by PSIN, that information is output to the EPS file as well.

Prompts and Options

- **File:**

  Use the Create PostScript File dialog box to enter the output file name or specify an existing file to overwrite.

- **What to export — Display, Extents, Limits, View or Window <D>:**

  At this prompt, you enter an option for the area of the current drawing to export. The initial default is Display.

- **Display.** This option exports an area equivalent to the visible drawing area.

- **Extents.** This option exports an area containing all the entities in the current space.
- **Limits.** This option exports an area equivalent to the current drawing's limits as set by the LIMITS command.
- **View.** This option exports an area defined by an existing view created by the VIEW command.
- **Window.** This option exports an area bounded by a window you draw on screen.
- **Include a screen preview image in the file? (None/EPSI/TIFF) <None>:**

  You enter the type of screen preview to include within the EPS file or accept the default, None. EPSI-type preview images are predominantly used by the Macintosh platform TIFF previews are usually necessary for DOS. If you specify a preview image type, the following prompt appears.

- **Screen preview image size (128x128 is standard)? (128/256/512) <128>:**

  You enter a number for the resolution of the screen preview image. Smaller sizes display faster than larger ones. Higher-resolution images display with more detail.

Example

The following example creates an EPS file of the current display and includes a TIFF-format screen preview image.

```
Command: PSOUT↵
File:  Enter the file name in the edit box
What to export — Display, Extents, Limits, View or Window <D>: ↵
Include a screen preview image in the file? (None/EPSI/TIFF)
<None>: T↵
Screen preview image size (128x128 is standard)? (128/256/512)
<128>: ↵
Effective plotting area: 7.50 wide by 5.43 high
```

Related Commands

DXFOUT
DXBOUT
IGESOUT
PSIN
PSQUALITY

PSPACE

Screen   **[MVIEW] [PSPACE:]**

Pull down   **[View] [Paper Space]**

The PSPACE command switches the active drawing space from model space to paper space. This command works only when the TILEMODE system variable is set to 0 (off). The MVIEW command pull-down menu item sets TILEMODE to 0, which activates paper space. You must make paper space active to create or edit paper-space entities.

When paper space is active, the UCS icon appears only in paper space (as a triangle), a P appears on the status line, and the crosshairs are active over the entire drawing screen (see fig. PSPACE.1). Model space must be active if you want to work on model-space entities or to pan, zoom, or modify the viewport contents. When model space is active, a normal UCS icon appears in each mview viewport, and the crosshairs are active only in the current mview viewport. You use the MSPACE command to make model space active.

Prompts and Options

Although the PSPACE command does not have any options, it issues two informational prompts:

- **** Command not allowed unless TILEMODE is set to 0 ****

  If TILEMODE is not 0 (off), this message reminds you that it must be set to 0 before you can use paper space.

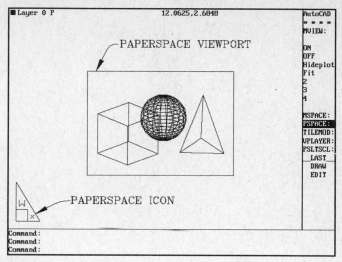

Figure PSPACE.1:
The drawing editor in paper space.

- **Already in paper space.**

  If paper space is the active drawing space, this prompt appears.

Related Commands

MSPACE
MVIEW

Related System Variable

TILEMODE

PSQUALITY

The PSQUALITY command sets the image quality for PostScript images imported by the PSIN command. Images may be rendered at varying levels of equivalent dots-per-inch resolution, as either outlines or filled regions, or not at all.

Prompts and Options

- **New value for PSQUALITY<75>:**

  At this prompt, you enter the number of pixels in PostScript files to render for each AutoCAD drawing unit. Higher numbers generate greater detail, and lower numbers reduce drawing file size. A negative number causes AutoCAD to render images to the absolute value of the number, but outlines are not filled, speeding up display. A value of 0 renders the image as a box representing the image's size, shape, and file name. The default is 1 initially.

Related Commands

FILL
PSIN

Related System Variable

FILLMODE

PURGE

Screen **[UTILITY] [PURGE:]**

The PURGE command selectively removes from the drawing unreferenced definitions of blocks, dimension styles, layers, linetypes, shapes, and text styles. By using the PURGE command to remove unused definitions, you can reduce the size of the drawing and speed up the loading of drawings.

The PURGE command must be used before you use any drawing or editing command or any command that creates named definitions, such as blocks, layers, and so on. If you need to use the PURGE command to remove unused entities, you should do this immediately after you enter the drawing editor.

Named definitions that are nested, such as blocks, are purged only one level per session. Therefore, you must purge the highest level first, end the drawing, and then re-enter the drawing to purge the nested items. You may have to do this procedure several times to purge all unused items if they are deeply nested.

Prompts and Options

- **Purge unused Blocks/Dimstyles/LAyers/LTypes/ SHapes/STyles/All:**

  At this prompt, you enter the capital letter(s) of the definition type to purge. Enter an **A** to purge unreferenced definitions of all types.

- **Purge *item NAME?* <N>**

  If any unreferenced definitions of the specified type exist (listed in the prompt), the PURGE command displays each unreferenced definition's name (in the prompt) and asks if you want to remove it. PURGE continues to prompt for all unreferenced items of that type. If you specify the All option, PURGE prompts for all unreferenced definitions of each of the types.

Example

This example uses the PURGE command to remove a block definition from the drawing.

```
Command: PURGE↵
Purge unused Blocks/Dimstyles/LAyers/LTypes/SHapes/STyles/All: B↵
Purge block CHAIR? <N> Y ↵
```

QSAVE

R12

Pull down **[File] [Save]**

The QSAVE command works the same way as the SAVE command, saving any changes to the current drawing to disk without exiting the drawing editor. The difference between QSAVE and SAVE is that QSAVE does not prompt for a file name; the current drawing is saved to the default file name without hesitation. If the current drawing has not yet been named, the Save Drawing As dialog box appears so that you can specify a file name.

 Use the QSAVE command to save your work periodically. It saves changes to the default drawing quickly.

Related Commands

END
QUIT
SAVE
SAVEAS

Related System Variables

DBMOD
DWGNAME
DWGPREFIX

QTEXT

Screen [SETTINGS] [next] [QTEXT:]

The QTEXT command turns quick text mode on and off. When quick text mode is on, any text entity is regenerated as boxes that indicate the approximate size of the text entity, instead of text characters. The screen regenerates and redraws much faster with quick text mode on, especially if the drawing contains much text or uses a complex font. New text displays as text characters until the next screen regeneration. Quick text mode does not affect the text editing commands CHANGE, DDATTE, and DDEDIT.

Prompts and Options

- **ON/OFF:**

  You enter **ON** to turn quick text mode on. After the next regeneration, the display shows all existing text as boxes.

  You enter **OFF** to disable quick text mode. After the next regeneration, all text displays normally.

Example

The following example shows the effect of quick text mode on existing text in a drawing (see fig. QTEXT.1).

```
Command: QTEXT ↵
On/Off <Off>: ON ↵
Command: REGEN ↵
```

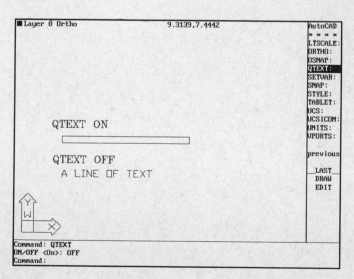

Figure QTEXT.1:
Text as it appears normally, and with QTEXT on.

373

Related Command

REGEN

Related System Variable

QTEXTMODE

QUIT

Screen   **[UTILITY] [next] [QUIT:]**

Pull down   **[File] [Exit AutoCAD]**

The QUIT command terminates AutoCAD without saving the current drawing.

Prompts and Options

R12 In Release 12, the QUIT command uses a comprehensive dialog box that prevents you from mistakenly exiting an editing session before you have saved your drawing. The new QUIT dialog box has the following buttons:

- **Save Changes**. This button is automatically highlighted, and enables you to save your work before exiting the AutoCAD program.

- **Discard Changes.** This button immediately exits to the operating system without saving any changes you have made to your drawing.

- **Cancel Command.** This button cancels the QUIT command and places you back in the drawing editor to continue drawing.

Example

The following example describes how to quit the drawing without saving
your changes.

```
Command: QUIT↵
```
Press Tab
Press Enter

Related Commands

> END
> SAVE
> SAVEAS

RCONFIG

Pull down **[Render] [Preferences] [Reconfigure]**

The RCONFIG (ReCONFIGure) command enables you to change the
configured display and hard-copy rendering devices used by the
RENDER command. All other AutoCAD display and output are
through devices configured by the CONFIG command. After the
RCONFIG command is issued, AutoCAD switches focus to the text
display and then displays the current rendering device configuration.
The configuration menu has four options.

Prompts and Options

- **Enter selection <0>:**

  You enter one of the four configuration menu options at this
  prompt.

- **0. Exit to drawing editor**

  This option prompts you to save your configuration changes and
  then returns you to the drawing editor.

- **1. Show current configuration**

  This option redisplays the opening screen of the RCONFIG command, showing the current configuration.

- **2. Configure rendering device**

  This option displays the currently available rendering and combined rendering/display devices and enables you to configure them. The prompts and options vary depending on the device. Consult the *Interface, Installation, and Performance Guide* and your rendering driver's documentation for more information.

- **3. Configure hard copy rendering device**

  This option displays the currently available hard-copy rendering devices and enables you to configure them. The prompts and options vary depending on the device. Consult the *Interface, Installation, and Performance Guide* and your rendering driver's documentation for more information.

Related Commands

CONFIG
RENDER
RPREF

RECTANG

Pull down **[Draw] [Rectangle]**

RECTANG allows you to draw orthogonal rectangles by picking any two opposing corners. The rectangle is a closed polyline, and as such, can be edited with the PEDIT command, solidified, or extruded.

Prompts and Options

- **First corner:**

  You specify the first corner of the rectangle. You can enter coordinates, pick a point, or use the object snap modes.

- **Other corner:**

    You specify the second corner of the rectangle. You can enter coordinates, pick a point, or use the object snap modes.

Example

The following example draws a rectangle (see fig. RECTANG.1).

```
Command: RECTANG ↵
First corner: 4,3↵
Second corner: 8.5,6 ↵
```

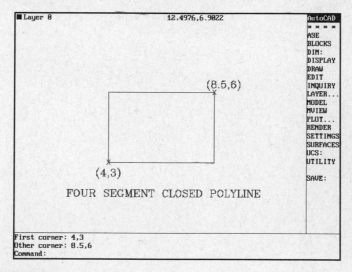

Figure RECTANG.1:
A rectangle created with the RECTANG command.

Related Commands

PEDIT
POLYGON
POLYLINE

REDEFINE

The REDEFINE command reverses the UNDEFINE command by restoring an AutoCAD command to its original action. The UNDEFINE command disables AutoCAD commands so that they cannot be used. You also can use AutoLISP or ADS to define a custom command to replace an undefined command. For example, you can change the END command so that it asks you to confirm that you really want to exit the drawing editor before you exit.

If you do not want to redefine the command, but you still need to use it with its original actions, you can enter the command name preceded by a period at the Command: prompt. For example, if END is undefined, you can still use it by typing .END at the Command: prompt.

Prompts and Options

- **Command name:**

  You enter the name of the AutoCAD command to restore.

Example

The following example uses the UNDEFINE command to disable the ELEV command. The REDEFINE command is then used to restore the ELEV command back to its original action.

```
Command: UNDEFINE↵
Command name: ELEV↵
Command: ELEV↵
Unknown command
Type ? for list of Commands.
Command: ELEV↵
New current elevation <0.0000>: *Cancel* Press Ctrl-C
Command: REDEFINE↵
Command name: ELEV↵
Command: ELEV↵
New current elevation <0.09000>: Press Ctrl-C
*Cancel*
```

Related Commands

UNDEFINE

REDO

Screen **[* * * *] [REDO:]**

Pull down **[Assist] [Redo]**

The REDO command reverses the effects of a single UNDO command. REDO only works if the immediately preceding command was UNDO (or U).

Example

The following example creates a line and uses the UNDO command to remove the line. The REDO command reverses the UNDO command, which restores the line.

```
Command: LINE↵
From point: 1,1↵
To point: 5,5↵
To point: ↵
Command: U↵
Command: REDO ↵
```

Related Commands

PLOT
PRPLOT
UNDO

REDRAW

Screen **[DISPLAY] [REDRAW:]**

Screen **[* * * *]** **[REDRAW:]**

Pull down **[View]** **[Redraw]**

The REDRAW command redisplays the image in the current viewport. You can use this command as a transparent command within another command by entering **'REDRAW**. Blips are removed from the display.

Use this command to refresh the display after you erase entities that overlap, or to return to the current drawing after viewing a slide with the VSLIDE command.

REDRAW is substantially faster than the REGEN command, which also refreshes the displayed image. The REGEN command, however, regenerates the current view in addition to redrawing it.

The current viewport automatically redraws when a layer is turned on or off, or the grid is turned off. Note that the grid's density affects the speed of the redraw. Entities on layers that are turned off add to the time that REDRAW takes. However, entities on frozen layers do not take additional time to redraw. You can stop a redraw operation by pressing Ctrl-C. In this case, you can select only displayed entities until a complete redraw takes place.

Related Commands

> REDRAWALL
> REGEN
> REGENALL

REDRAWALL

Screen **[DISPLAY]** **[REDRALL:]**

Pull down **[View]** **[Redraw All]**

The REDRAWALL command is similar to the REDRAW command, except that it redisplays the images in all active viewports on the screen, not just the current viewport. You can use this command transparently by entering 'REDRAWALL.

Related Commands

REDRAW
REGEN
REGENALL

REGEN

Screen [DISPLAY] [REGEN:]

The REGEN command regenerates the geometry of all entities within the drawing and redisplay the image in the current viewport. You cannot use this command transparently. If you make modifications to a drawing, you may need to issue the REGEN command to ensure that the modifications are displayed correctly.

A regeneration occurs automatically when the drawing is loaded into memory with the OPEN command. Certain command options, such as ZOOM All and LAYER Freeze/Thaw, always regenerate the drawing automatically. Other actions, such as redefining a block or text style, or resetting linetype scale, automatically regenerate the drawing unless automatic regenerations have been turned off. Automatic regeneration by such commands is controlled by the REGENAUTO command. The REGEN command also smooths out arcs and circles that look segmented due to the current zoom factor.

To speed up the regeneration process, you should freeze out layers that are not in use. You can stop the screen regeneration by pressing Ctrl-C. In this case, any entities not displayed may not be selected or redrawn until a completed regeneration takes place.

Related Commands

REDRAW
REDRAWALL
REGENALL
REGENAUTO

REGENALL

Screen **[DISPLAY] [REGNALL:]**

The REGENALL command regenerates the entire drawing and redisplays the current views in all active viewports. The REGENALL command differs from the REGEN command in that REGENALL regenerates every active viewport. If you have only one active viewport, the REGENALL command works exactly the same as the REGEN command.

Related Commands

REDRAW
REGEN
REDRAWALL
REGENAUTO

REGENAUTO

Screen **[DISPLAY] [RGNAUTO:]**

The REGENAUTO command controls automatic screen regenerations caused by commands such as BLOCK, STYLE, LTSCALE, LAYER, and ZOOM, which automatically cause a screen regeneration.

You can execute the REGENAUTO command transparently by preceding the command name with an apostrophe ('REGENAUTO).

Prompts and Options

*   ON/OFF <On>:

    When REGENAUTO is on, AutoCAD executes a screen regeneration when certain commands require it.

    If REGENAUTO is off, AutoCAD disables automatic regeneration caused by certain actions. With some commands, this forces AutoCAD to prompt you to verify that you want a screen regeneration. If you execute such a command, the following prompt appears:

        About to regen, proceed? <Y>

    Note that you can suppress this prompt by setting the EXPERT system variable to a value of 1 or more.

Related Commands

REGEN
REGENALL

Related System Variables

EXPERT
REGENMODE

REINIT

 R12

Screen [UTILITY] [next] [REINIT:]

The REINIT command reinitializes the peripherals that AutoCAD communicates with. Use REINIT when operation of your display, digitizer, or plotter has been lost or interrupted by another program, or by disconnecting and reconnecting the peripheral. You also can use REINIT to reload the ACAD.PGP file after changes have been made in the current editing session.

Prompts and Options

This command issues no prompts. All options are selected from the Re-initialization dialog box (see fig. REINIT.1).

I/O Port Initialization

The following options re-initialize communications with your system's input and output ports. Selecting an option may not necessarily re-establish communications with the peripheral attached to the specified port. See the Device and File Initialization options below.

- **Digitizer.** Checking this box initializes the port specified for the digitizer during AutoCAD configuration.
- **Plotter.** Checking this box initializes the port specified for the plotter during AutoCAD configuration.

Device and File Initialization

The following options attempt to re-initialize communications directly with peripherals attached to your system.

- **Digitizer.** Checking this box initializes the configured digitizer. If the I/O port itself, to which the digitizer is connected, has been reset by other software, I/O port initialization may need to be performed. See the I/O Port Initialization options above.
- **Display.** Checking this box initializes the configured display. Both the AutoCAD graphics screen and text screen are completely redrawn. Use this option if another program executed from within AutoCAD does not restore the screen contents upon exiting.

- **PGP File.** Checking this box reloads the ACAD.PGP file. Any changes made to ACAD.PGP will not take effect until the file is loaded by the REINIT command or when AutoCAD is started.

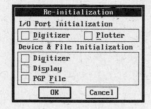

Figure REINIT.1:
The REINIT command dialog box.

Related Command

CONFIG

Related System Variable

RE-INIT

RENAME

Screen [UTILITY] [RENAME:]

The RENAME command changes the names of named items such as dimension styles, layers, views, and text styles. You cannot rename an item, however, to an existing name used by the same type of item, nor can you rename colors. In addition, the linetypes BYLAYER, BYBLOCK, or CONTINUOUS, the layer 0, or anonymous blocks such as those created by the HATCH command cannot be renamed.

  The new DDRENAME dialog box is much easier to use than the RENAME command when you are renaming defined items.

Prompts and Options

- **Block/Dimstyle/LAyer/LType/Style/Ucs/VIew/VPort:**

  This prompt contains a list of the named items that you can rename. Type the uppercase letter(s) for the item type you want to rename.

- **Old item name:**

  At this prompt, you enter the current name of the item that you want to rename. If the name you enter does not belong to a current item, the command exits and the prompt Old item *NAME* not found appears.

- **New item name:**

  At this prompt, you enter a new name for the item. The new name is subject to the standard limitations on name length and valid characters used by AutoCAD for all other item names. When you rename a linetype, the new name applies only to the current drawing. The linetype name in the ACAD.LIN file remains the same. When a block that was inserted from an external drawing file is renamed, the external file remains unaffected.

Example

The following example renames a layer named DOOR-2 to UNUSED_DOORS.

```
Command: RENAME↵
Block/Dimstyle/LAyer/LType/Style/Ucs/VIew/VPort: LA↵
Old layer name: DOOR-2↵
New layer name: UNUSED_DOORS ↵
```

Related Command

DDRENAME

RENDER

Screen   [RENDER] [RENDER:]

Pull down **[Render] [Render]**

The RENDER command creates a realistically shaded image of three-dimensional surface or solid objects within AutoCAD. Finish, lighting, scene, and rendering preference information is used to produce the shaded image. The rendered image can be output to the full AutoCAD screen, a viewport, a hardcopy device, or a file.

Make sure AME is loaded before rendering any solids created with AME. The AME entities are translated into meshes before rendering and thus produce a better rendering.

Related Commands

FINISH
HIDE
LIGHT
RPREF
SCENE
SHADE

RENDSCR

The RENDSCR (RENDering SCRreen) command redisplays the last rendered image on single-monitor systems. After an image is displayed on the full screen, you can press any key to return to the current drawing. The F1 key continues to work normally, flipping between the drawing editor and text display.

Related Commands

RCONFIG
RENDER
VSLIDE

Related System Variable

SCREENMODE

REPLAY

Pull down **[Render] [Files] [Replay Image]**

Screen **[RENDER] [REPLAY]**

The REPLAY command enables you to display raster image files on the configured rendering display. You can display GIF, TGA, TIFF, and RND files.

Any rectangular area of a GIF, TGA, or TIFF file can be displayed by specifying an XY image offset (in pixels) and an image size (in pixels). The area can then be placed anywhere on the rendering screen by specifying an XY screen offset (in pixels). This process is useful if the image file was created by a system with a different rendering display resolution. The REPLAY command can only display entire RND files on rendering displays for which they were created.

The REPLAY command displays the REPLAY file dialog box, which displays the Image Specifications dialog box when you specify a valid file name. The REPLAY dialog box operates like any other file dialog box. However, the Image Specifications dialog box appears only with files with GIF, RND, TGA, or TIF file extensions.

The REPLAY command can be used for crude bitmap tracing. Just scan your line drawing into a TIFF, TGA, or GIF file and use the REPLAY command to display it in an AutoCAD viewport. Then trace over the image with lines, circles, and other elements. The image remains on screen until the screen is redrawn. You must use a rendering display driver capable of rendering to a viewport to use this technique.

Prompts and Options

- **Image Name.** The Image Name edit box shows the path and name of the image file to be loaded.

- **IMAGE Size.** The IMAGE icon enables you to specify visually the area of the image file to display. To specify the image area, pick two points on the icon for the opposite corners of the image area rectangle. The size of the image file is displayed next to the icon title.

- **SCREEN Size.** The SCREEN icon enables you to specify visually the position of the specified image area on the rendering screen. Pick a point on the icon for the center of the image area rectangle, to position it on the rendering screen. The size of the screen is displayed next to the icon title.

- **Image Offset.** In the X and Y Image Offset edit boxes, you specify the size of the specified image area rectangle in pixels. Values for the X and Y image offset must be positive and cannot exceed the entire image size.

- **Image Size.** In the X and Y Image Size edit boxes, you specify the number of pixels the upper left corner of the image area rectangle is located from the X and Y image offset. Values for the X and Y image size must be positive and cannot exceed the entire image size.

- **Screen Size.** The X and Y values displayed show the actual size of the image area that will be displayed. The values will be equal to the Image Size up to a maximum of the value displayed in SCREEN.

- **Screen Offset.** The X and Y Screen Offset edit boxes specify the number of pixels the lower left corner of the image area rectangle is from 0,0 of the AutoCAD rendering screen. Values for the X and Y screen offset must be positive and cannot exceed the size of the rendering screen.

- **Reset.** The Reset button sets all parameters back to the defaults.

Related Commands

RCONFIG
RENDER
RENDSCR
VSLIDE

RESUME

The RESUME command continues a script file that has been halted. If you stop a script file by pressing Backspace, enter **RESUME** at the Command: prompt to restart it at the next line of the script. If you stop the script with Ctrl-C as it executes a command, you can use the RESUME command transparently by entering **'RESUME**.

Related Commands

DELAY
RSCRIPT

REVSURF

Screen [DRAW] [next] [3D Surfs] [REVSURF:]

Pull down [Draw] [3D Surfaces >] [Surface of Revolution]

The REVSURF command is one of six commands that create 3D polygon meshes. This command creates a mesh defined by rotating a profile entity (path curve) around an axis of rotation. The REVSURF command is useful for creating objects that are radially symmetrical about one axis, such as a wine goblet. This command can create surfaces that are open like a vase, closed like a spindle, or hollow like a tire. The SURFTAB1 and SURFTAB2 system variables are used to control the M and N densities of the mesh.

Prompts and Options

- **Select path curve:**

  The path curve may be an arc, circle, line, 2D polyline, or 3D polyline. You can pick only one entity as the path curve. The path curve defines the N direction of the mesh. If the path curve is a circle or closed polyline, the 3D polygon mesh produced by the REVSURF command will be closed in the N direction. If you select an invalid entity for the path curve, the error message `Entity not usable to define surface of revolution` appears.

- **Select axis of revolution:**

  The axis of revolution may be a line, 2D polyline, or 3D polyline. When a curved or multisegmented polyline is selected as the axis of revolution, the vector from the first vertex to the last vertex defines the actual axis of revolution. The axis of revolution defines the M direction of the 3D polygon mesh. The pick point used to select the axis of rotation influences the rotation angle. See the following discussion about the direction of revolution.

  If you choose an entity other than a line or an open polyline, the error message `Entity not usable as rotation axis` appears. The same entity cannot be both the curve path and the axis of revolution. If you attempt to connect the two entities, the error message `Entity has already been selected` displays.

- **Start angle <0>:**

  The default of 0 degrees for the start angle begins creating the mesh at the location of the path curve. If you specify an angle other than 0 degrees, the mesh is offset from the path curve by that angle.

- **Included angle (+=ccw, -=cw)<Full circle>:**

  The included angle specification determines the extent to which the path curve sweeps around the axis of revolution. If the default Full circle option is used, the resulting mesh is closed in the M direction. A positive included angle causes the mesh to be generated in a counterclockwise direction. The mesh generates with respect to the pick point that you used to select the axis of revolution.

Direction of Revolution

The direction of revolution is determined by the pick point used for selecting the axis of revolution and included angle specification. The end point of the axis of revolution closest to the pick point becomes the base of the vector that defines the axis of revolution. The opposite end becomes the top. If you look from the top of the vector to the base, a positive included angle constructs the polygon mesh in the counter-clockwise direction, offset by the start angle.

The method in which meshes generate can be visualized easily by using the right-hand rule. Imagine placing your thumb along the axis of revolution with the top of your thumb pointing to the top of the axis of revolution vector. Next, curl your fingers around the axis of revolution vector. The curl of your fingers indicates the direction of revolution for a positive included angle. The start angle direction can be visualized in the same manner.

Example

The following example uses the REVSURF command to construct a polygon mesh, as shown in figure REVSURF.1. The left viewport shows the original path curve and axis of revolution, while the right viewport displays the completed mesh.

```
Command: REVSURF↵
Select path curve: Pick point ①
Select axis of revolution: Pick point ②
Start angle <0> Pick point ↵
Included angle (+=ccw, -=cw) <Full circle>: ↵
```

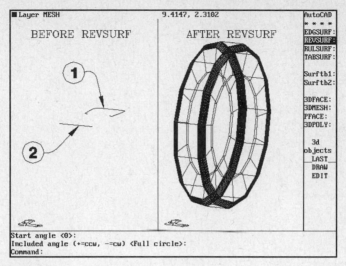

Figure REVSURF.1:
The surface of revolution.

Related Commands

    EDGESURF
    PFACE
    RULESURF
    TABSURF
    3DFACE
    3DMESH

Related System Variables

    SURFTAB1
    SURFTAB2

ROTATE

Screen **[EDIT] [next] [ROTATE:]**

Pull down **[Modify] [Rotate]**

The ROTATE command rotates selected entities about a fixed point in the current construction plane. After you choose the fixed point, AutoCAD asks you for the amount, in degrees, that you want to rotate the entities. The new orientation of the entities is based on the rotation value entered.

Prompts and Options

- **Select objects:**

  You can use any object selection method to choose all the entities you want to rotate.

- **Base point:**

  The base point is the location about which the entities are rotated. After you enter the rotation value, the chosen entities are rotated about the Z-axis of the base point.

- **<Rotation angle>/Reference:**

  At this prompt, you enter a value with which to rotate the entities. A positive number changes the entities' orientation in a counter-clockwise direction. A negative number rotates the entities in a clockwise direction. A rubber-band line appears between the base point and the crosshairs. The entities that are being rotated are highlighted and dragged as you move the crosshairs.

- **Reference angle <0>:**

  The Reference option enables you to define the angle of rotation by specifying a reference angle and a new angle.

- **New angle:**

  The selected entities are rotated by the difference between the reference angle and the new angle that you specify at this prompt.

Example

This example demonstrates how to use the ROTATE command to change the orientation of a group of entities shown in figure ROTATE.1.

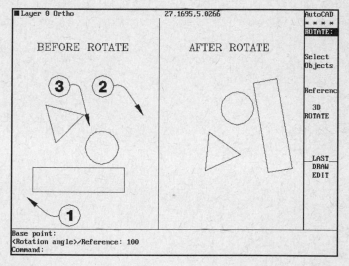

Figure ROTATE.1:
Rotating a group of entities.

```
Command: ROTATE↵
Select objects: W↵
First corner: Pick point ①
Other corner: Pick point ②
Base point: Pick point ②
<Rotation angle>/Reference: 100 ↵
```

Related Command

DDMODIFY

Related System Variables

DRAGMODE
HIGHLIGHT

ROTATE3D

Screen **[EDIT] [next] [ROTATE:] [3D ROTATE]**

Pull down **[Modify] [Rotate 3D]**

ROTATE3D enables you to rotate an object about a 3D axis. The axis of rotation is defined by selecting one of the options below.

Prompts and Options

- **Select objects:**

  You select the objects you want to rotate about a 3D axis.

- **<Rotation angle>/Reference:**

  You enter the degree of rotation about the 3D axis or specify the Reference option to enter the current angle and a new angle. Reference displays the prompts below:

- **Reference angle <0>:**

  Enter the current degree of rotation of the selected entities.

- **New angle:**

  Enter the new angle of the selected entities.

- **Axis by Entity/Last/View/Xaxis/Yaxis/Zaxis/ <2point>:**

  You specify the desired method of defining the 3D axis of rotation. The prompt's options are described below.

  You can use the following options with the ROTATE3D command.

- **Entity.** This option aligns the axis of rotation with an existing entity. The Entity option displays the following prompt:

- **Pick a line, circle, arc, or 2D-polyline segment**

  Select the entity to define the 3D axis of rotation. The circle and arc options use the 3D axis of the circle or arc.

- **Last.** This option uses the last axis of rotation. If there is no last axis, you are warned and reprompted with the Axis prompt.

- **View.** This option aligns the axis of rotation with the current view passing through a selected point. The View option displays the following prompt:

- **Point on view direction axis <0,0,0>:**

  Enter a point that the axis of rotation passes through.

- **Xaxis.** Aligns the axis of rotation with the X axis, passing through a selected point. the Xaxis option displays one prompt:

- **Point on X axis <0,0,0>:**

  Enter the point on the X axis that the axis of rotation passes through.

- **Yaxis.** Aligns the axis of rotation with the Y axis, passing through a selected point. the Yaxis option displays one prompt:

- **Point on Y axis <0,0,0>:**

  Enter a point on the Y axis that the axis of rotation passes through.

- **Zaxis.** Zaxis aligns the axis of rotation with the Z axis, passing through a selected point. The Zaxis option displays one prompt:

- **Point on Z axis <0,0,0>:**

  Enter a point on the Z axis that the axis of rotation passes through.

- **<2points>.** Zpoints pecifies two points that define the axis of rotation. 2points displays 2 prompts.

- **1st point on axis:**

  Enter the first point of the axis of rotation.

- **2nd point on axis:**

  Enter the first point of the axis of rotation.

Example

The following example uses ROTATE3D to rotate a solid around a line in 3 dimensions. See figure ROTATE3D.1.

```
Command: ROTATE3D↵
Select objects: Pick point ①
Select objects: ↵
Axis by Entity/Last/View/Xaxis/Yaxis/Zaxis/<2points>: 2↵
1st point on axis: Pick point ②
2nd point on axis: Pick point ③
<Rotation angle>/Reference: 90 ↵
```

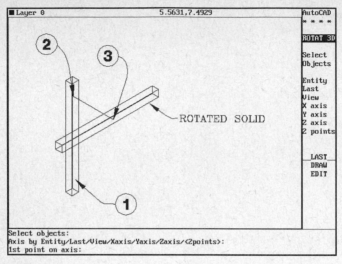

Select objects:
Axis by Entity/Last/View/Xaxis/Yaxis/Zaxis/<2points>:
1st point on axis:

Figure ROTATE3D.1:
A solid rotated in three dimensions about a line.

Related Commands

MIRROR3D
ROTATE

RPREF

Screen **[RENDER] [RPREF]**

Pull down **[Render] [Preferences]**

The characteristics of the image that the RENDER command produces
are controlled by options of the RPREF command. The RPREF command displays the Rendering Preferences dialog box, enabling you to
modify the rendering characteristics. The characteristics that can be
modified include type of rendering, type of shading, finish use, output
destination, black and white or color output, and color separation.

Prompts and Options

Rendering Preferences is the main dialog box for the RPREF command. All other preferences-related dialog boxes and options are accessed through this dialog box.

The Rendering Preferences Dialog Box

- **Full Render.** This option of the Rendering Type group produces the most accurate rendered image. Full Render causes the rendered image to be created using 3D polygons. Full Render also causes edge artifacts and overlapping faces to be considered by the RENDER command.

- **Quick Render.** This option of the Rendering Type group produces the fastest rendered image. Quick Render causes the rendered image to be created in scanlines. A *scanline* is a horizontal row of pixels. Quick Render does not consider edge artifacts or overlapping faces.

  The difference in speed between Full Render and Quick Render increases as the complexity of your model and the amount of memory you have increase. Quick Render slows down for high-resolution output devices.

- **ACAD RenderMan.** This option is not yet available.

- **Smooth Shading.** This option of the Rendering Options group causes the transition between adjacent polygon mesh surfaces to appear smooth when rendered. AutoCAD uses the Gouraud algorithm for smooth shading.

  The *Gouraud algorithm* calculates the color at all vertices of a mesh face and then blends the color across the face. The angle between two face normals must be 45 degrees or less for the Gouraud algorithm to be applied to the faces. A *normal* is an imaginary line that is perpendicular to the center of a polygon mesh face.

- **Merge.** With 24-bit frame buffers, this option of the Rendering Options group enables multiple images to be merged in the frame buffer. This is a time-saving option. If a complex drawing is changed in one area, that area can be rendered and then merged with the original image. Merge only works with full render.

- **Apply Finishes.** This option of the Rendering Options group enables you to control the application of defined finishes. If Apply Finishes is off, all entities are rendered with the default *GLOBAL* finish.

- **More Options.** This button in the Render Options group accesses the Full or Quick Render Options dialog box depending on the current rendering type. The Full/Quick render Options dialog box enables you to control output mode (color or black and white), color separations, and several face parameters.

- **Select Query.** This drop-down list enables you to choose between rendering all objects in the drawing or selecting specific objects. The two options are listed as Select All and Make Selection.

- **Framebuffer.** This option of the Destination group sends rendering output to your rendering video display. Images rendered to the screen can be saved in various raster file formats for input into other programs or recall at a later time. See the SAVEIMG and REPLAY commands for more information.

- **Hardcopy.** This option of the Destination group sends rendering output to your rendering hardcopy device. Images can be saved as encapsulated PostScript (EPS) files for use with other third-party programs such as desktop publishing or vector-based drawing applications. To create an EPS file, configure the hardcopy rendering device for the RHEXPORT.EXP driver.

- **Best Map/No Fold.** This option in the Color Map Usage group maintains a separate color map for each rendering viewport and does not change the AutoCAD colors 9-255 to the closest color in the 1-8 color range. Entity colors in inactive nonrendering viewports are altered according to the color map of the rendering viewport.

- **Best Map/Fold.** This option in the Color Map Usage group maintains a separate color map for each rendering viewport and changes the AutoCAD colors 9-255 to the closest color in the 1-8 AutoCAD color range. This means that all entities with AutoCAD color values above 8 in nonrendering viewports are changed to the closest color in the 1-8 AutoCAD color range. This prevents entity colors changing after rendering in another viewport.
- **Fixed ACAD Map.** This option in the Color Map Usage group uses the standard AutoCAD color map for both nonrendering and rendering viewports. Results from this option are usually poor renderings and inconsistent results.

 The color map options are only available for 256-color display devices.

- **RMan Prompting.** This option of the Settings group in conjunction with Autodesk AutoShade Version 2 enables you to place and render spotlights, add and render colored lights to your drawing, and render with shadows.
- **Icon Scale.** This edit box in the Settings group specifies the scale factor to apply to rendering blocks (lights and finishes). Set the icon scale to the same scale as other symbols in your drawing.
- **Information.** This button displays the AVE Render copyright notice and the current AVE Render display and hardcopy configuration.
- **Reconfigure.** This button executes the RCONFIG command, enabling you to change the AVE Render configuration.

Related Commands

RCONFIG
STATS

RSCRIPT

The RSCRIPT command causes a script to repeat itself from the beginning. You can execute the RSCRIPT command only from a script file. The script continues to repeat until you press Ctrl-C or Backspace.

Related Commands

DELAY
RESUME
SCRIPT

RULESURF

Screen **[DRAW] [next] [3D Surfs] [RULESURF:]**

Pull down **[Draw] [3D Surfaces >] [Ruled Surface]**

The RULESURF command is one of six commands that create a 3D polygon mesh. This command creates a 2×N mesh defined by a ruled surface between two boundary entities. These boundaries may be arcs, lines, points, and open or closed polylines (either 2D or 3D). If one of the boundaries is a closed entity (a circle or closed polyline), the other boundary must be open. Note that you can use a point for one boundary.

The end of the entity that is closest to the point used to pick the entity becomes the starting point for that end of the mesh. The mesh is then created along the entity, defined by ruling lines spanning the space between each boundary. The SURFTAB1 variable determines the density of the mesh in the N direction.

Prompts and Options

• **Select first defining curve:**

Pick a point to select the first boundary edge for the polygon mesh. The end point of the entity, closest to the point picked, determines the beginning of the mesh's first end.

- **Select second defining curve:**

  Pick a point to select the second boundary for the mesh. The end point of the entity closest to the point picked determines the beginning of the mesh's second end.

Example

This example creates a ruled surface between two polylines (see figure RULESURF.1).

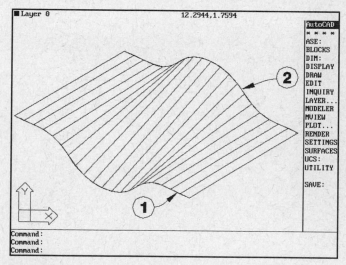

Figure RULESURF.1:
Polygon mesh created with the RULESURF command.

```
Command: RULESURF ⏎
Select first defining curve: Pick point ①
Select second defining curve: Pick point ②
```

Related Commands

3DFACE
3DMESH
EDGESURF
PFACE
REVSURF
TABSURF

Related System Variable

SURFTAB1

SAVE

Screen **[SAVE:]**

Pull down **[File] [Save]**

The SAVE command displays the Save Drawing As dialog box, requests a file name, and saves the current drawing as a file with the extension DWG. Entering a tilde (~) at the `Save current changes as:` prompt displays the Save Drawing As dialog box, if the system variable FILEDIA is set to 0. You can enter the drawing name in the File edit box or select a name from the Files list box. Do not include the DWG extension; it is assumed. If the drawing has already been named, SAVE uses that name as a default in the File edit box. Each time you use SAVE, the previous saved drawing is renamed as the backup (BAK) drawing.

Save your drawing regularly during a drawing session to avoid data loss due to system failure or power loss. Use the SAVETIME system variable to set the number of minutes between automatic saves. Setting SAVETIME to 0 disables the autosave feature.

Prompts and Options

- **Save current changes as:**

  If FILEDIA is set to 0, SAVE displays this prompt. Enter the name of the drawing file to save changes, or accept the default file name.

- **Pattern:**

  Enter a pattern to filter files in the Files list box. The pattern can use the * and ? wild-card characters. The pattern defaults to *.DWG.

- **Directories:**

  Pick a drive or directory to list its contents in the Files list box. Double-click on any item in the list to select it. Select the double dot (..) to move back one directory and the backslash (\) to display the root directory. Available drive letters are shown in angle brackets (<>). If the directory list is longer than the Directories list box, a slider bar is displayed on the right side of the list box. The current directory is listed above the Directories list box.

- **Files:**

  Pick a drawing file name in which to save the current changes. Click on any file name to select it. If the list of files is longer than the Files list box, a slider bar is displayed on the right side of the list box. If you pick a file name from the list, an AutoCAD message dialog box displays the warning The specified file already exists. Do you want to replace it?

 The MAXSORT system variable determines how many files or directories are to be sorted. MAXSORT defaults to 200 sorted entries. If the number is fewer than the number of entries in the list box, none are sorted.

- **Type it**

  Click on the **T**ype it button to enter the drawing file's name at the Command: prompt instead of the dialog box.

- **Default:**

  Click on the **D**efault button to reset the dialog box to its original state. This resets the Pattern edit box, Directories list box, Files list box, and File edit box to their values when the dialog box was displayed. The default is not available until a file name has been entered.

- **File:**

  Enter the name of the file to save or accept the default name. If the current drawing has already been named, the name is displayed in the Files edit box. You can accept the name by clicking on OK or pressing Enter.

Related Commands

END
NEW
OPEN
QSAVE
QUIT
SAVEAS

Related System Variables

DWGNAME
DWGPREFIX
DWGTITLED
DWGWRITE
FILEDIA
MAXSORT
SAVEFILE
SAVETIME
TDUPDATE

SAVEAS

Pull down **[File] [Save as...]**

The SAVEAS command works like the SAVE command—saving any changes to the current drawing to disk without exiting the drawing editor—except that this command asks for a new file name. The Save Drawing As dialog box appears (see fig. SAVEAS.1), and the current drawing name is the default. Clicking on OK accepts your file name choice.

Use the QSAVE command to periodically save your work. QSAVE automatically saves changes to the default drawing name and bypasses the dialog box.

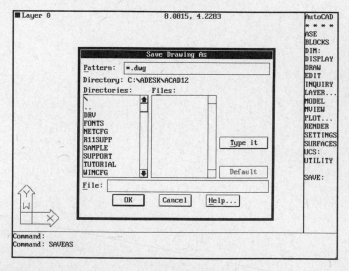

Figure SAVEAS.1:
The Save Drawing As dialog box.

Prompts and Options

SAVEAS displays no command-line prompts unless FILEDIA is set to a value of 0. Instead, you make selections from the following dialog box options:

- **Pattern.** This edit box contains the pattern specification for files to appear in the Files list box. You can use the wild cards ? and * to refine the list to desired file names.

- **Directories.** This list box contains a list of the subdirectories that are available from the current directory. Use the scroll bar to display more names and drive letters. Double-click on a directory name or drive letter to change the current directory.

- **Files.** This list box contains a list of the files available in the current directory. Use the scroll bar to display more file names. Double-click on a file name, or then click on it once and click on the OK button to proceed.

- **File.** Displays the name of the default drawing (if it has been named) or of a selected file. You either can type the name of a desired file in the edit box or edit an existing name.

- **Type it.** Click on this button to enter the drawing file's name at the command line instead of in the dialog box.

Related Commands

END
QSAVE
QUIT
SAVE

Related System Variables

DBMOD
DWGNAME
DWGPREFIX
FILEDIA
MAXSORT

SAVEIMG

Screen **[RENDER] [SAVEIMG]**

Pull down **[Render] [Files] [Save Image]**

The SAVEIMG command displays the Save Image dialog box, which enables you to save the current viewport, drawing area, or full-screen image to a TGA, TIFF, GIF, or RND file. You can view saved images by using the REPLAY command and many other programs.

One of two Save Image dialog boxes displays when the SAVEIMG command is executed, depending on the rendering display driver configuration. If you have the rendering display driver configured for rendering in a viewport, the Portion group shows three options for specifying the area of the screen to save. If you have the rendering display driver configured for full-screen rendering, the Portion group displays an icon, enabling you to interactively specify the area of the screen to save. The Save Image dialog box for viewport rendering is shown in figure SAVEIMG.1.

Prompts and Options

- **Image Name.** You can use the Image Name edit box to specify the file name for the rendered image. Do not include a file extension. The default file name is the file name of the current drawing. If the drawing does not have a name, the file name is UNNAMED.

- **Directory.** The Directory edit box shows the directory of the image file. The default directory is the directory that was current when you started your AutoCAD session.

- **TGA.** The TGA option of the Format group causes the image file to be saved in 32-bit RGBA Truevision V2.0 format. TGA files have the TGA extension. The TGA file can be either compressed or uncompressed, depending on the settings of the TGA Options dialog box. The TGA Options dialog box is accessed through the Options button.

409

- **TIFF.** The TIFF option of the Format group causes the image file to be saved in 32-bit Tagged Image File Format. The TIFF file extension is TIF. The TIFF file can be compressed (using one of two methods), or it can be uncompressed, depending on the settings of the TIFF Options dialog box. The TIFF Options dialog box is accessed through the Options button.

- **GIF.** The GIF option of the Format group causes the image file to be saved in Graphics Interchange Format, which is developed by CompuServe Information Service. The saved GIF file has the GIF extension.

- **RND.** The RND option of the Format group causes the image file to be saved in the RND file format. RND is an Autodesk-defined format. Offset and Size settings are not available for RND files.

- **Portion.** If the rendering driver is configured for full-screen rendering, the Portion group displays an icon, enabling you to interactively choose the area of the rendered image to save. Pick two opposite corner points to define the area to be saved.

- **Active viewport.** The Active viewport option of the Portion group saves only the area of the active viewport.

- **Drawing area.** The Drawing area option of the Portion group saves the drawing area. The drawing area does not include the command area, screen menu, or pull-down menu bar.

- **Full screen.** The Full screen option of the Portion group saves the entire screen including command area, screen menu, and pull-down menu bar.

- **Options.** The Options button either displays the TGA Options or the TIFF Options dialog box, depending on the image file format selection. The TGA Options dialog box enables you to choose between no compression and RLE (run length encoded) compression for TGA files. The TIFF Options dialog box enables you to choose from no compression or PACK (packbits) and LZW (Lempel-Ziv and Welch) compression.

- **Reset.** The Reset button sets the saved area offset and size to the defaults.

- **Offset.** The Offset X and Y edit boxes show the distance in pixels from the lower left corner of the screen to the lower left corner of the save area. Values must be positive and cannot be greater than the Size X and Y values. You can change the value by using this edit box.

- **Size.** The Size X and Y edit boxes show the distance in pixels from the lower left corner of the save area to the upper right corner. Values must be positive and cannot be greater than the screen size. You can change the value by using this edit box.

- **Default.** Default displays the maximum save area size in pixels.

Related Commands

HIDE
MSLIDE
RENDER
REPLAY
SHADE

SCALE

Screen **[EDIT] [next] [SCALE:]**

Pull down **[Modify] [SCALE]**

The SCALE command enlarges or reduces selected entities by a specified value. You can specify the new size by entering a numeric scale factor or by specifying an existing object, typically using a new length relative to a reference length.

Use the SCALE Grip edit mode to scale an entity without issuing the SCALE command. The SCALE Grip edit mode allows for multiple copies of scaled items.

You can scale a viewport in paper space to increase or decrease the amount of model space visible in the viewport.

Prompts and Options

• `Select objects:`

Choose all the entities you want to enlarge or reduce by means of any of the object selection methods.

Use the CHANGE command to change the scale, blocks, and size of text.

• `Base point:`

Enter a base point in the current coordinate system around which to scale entities. When the scaling occurs, all points on selected entities move closer to the base point or farther away from the base point as their scale is reduced and enlarged.

Choose a base point that relates to the entity or entities being scaled and positions them correctly after scaling. You generally pick a corner or the center of the object being scaled.

• `<SCALE factor>/Reference:`

Specify a scale factor by which to scale entities. A number greater than one enlarges the entities; a number between 0 and one reduces the entities. You can enter a number or pick a point to show a distance. If you pick a point, a rubber-band line appears between the base point and the crosshairs. The entities to be scaled are highlighted and dragged as you move the crosshairs.

Enter an **R** for the Reference option if you want to define the scale factor in reference to a length, such as the size of an existing entity.

You cannot scale the X, Y, or Z values independently.

- **Reference length <1>:**

    If you specify the Reference option, the scale factor is defined by the ratio of the two lengths that you specify. You also can pick two points, usually on an existing object, to show the reference length.

- **New length:**

    Enter the new length to scale the reference length to. The selected entities are then scaled by the ratio between the reference length and the new length. You also can pick one point to show the new length as a distance from the base point. As you move the cursor to pick the new length, AutoCAD shows a rubber-band line from the base point.

Example

This example uses the SCALE command to enlarge and reduce entities, using both a set scale factor and a reference length. The results are shown in figure SCALE.1.

```
Command: SCALE
Base point: Pick a point near the center of the text
<SCALE factor>/Reference: 2↵
Command: SCALE
Select objects: Select the text
Select objects: ↵
Base point: Pick a point in the center of the text
<SCALE factor>/Reference: R
Reference length <1>: .5 Specifies the starting height of the text
New length: .625 Specifies the final text height
```

Related command

CHANGE

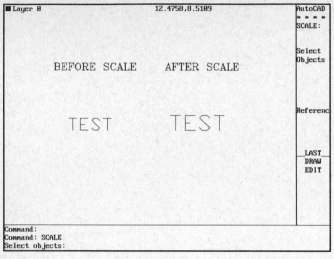

Figure SCALE.1:
The text before and after the SCALE command.

SCENE

Screen **[RENDER] [SCENE]**

Pull down **[Render] [Scenes]**

The SCENE command enables you create, name, restore, modify, and delete combinations of multiple views and related lighting that produce a specific image. One or more lights assigned to a single view define a scene. Lights not associated with a scene are not considered when the scene is rendered.

Prompts and Options

The SCENE command has three dialog boxes. The first Scenes dialog box accesses the New Scene and Modify Scene dialog boxes. Figure SCENE.1 shows the Scenes dialog box.

Figure SCENE.1:
The Scenes dialog box.

The Scenes Dialog Box

- **Scenes.** The Scenes list box displays the currently defined scenes and specifies the scene to be modified, deleted, or rendered. If the *NONE* scene is selected, the current view and all lights are used for rendering. You can highlight a scene and exit the dialog box with OK to specify the scene to be rendered by the RENDER command.

- **New.** The New button accesses the New Scene dialog box, enabling you to add a new scene to your drawing

- **Modify.** The Modify button accesses the Modify Scene dialog box (see fig. SCENE.2), enabling you to change scene parameters including scene name, view for scene, and associated lights. To modify a scene, highlight a scene name in the Scenes list box and then click on Modify.

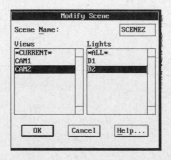

Figure SCENE.2:
The Modify Scene dialog box.

- **Delete.** The <u>D</u>elete button removes a scene from the drawing. To delete a scene, highlight a scene name in the Scenes list box and then click on the <u>D</u>elete button.

The New Scene and Modify Scene Dialog Boxes

Because the New Scene and Modify Scene dialog boxes have identical features, they are discussed together.

- **Scene Name.** The Scene Name edit box enables you to specify or change the name of the scene. The scene name must be eight characters or fewer; long names are truncated to eight characters.
- **Views.** The Views list box displays all the saved views in the drawing. The highlighted view is the scene view. To change the view for a scene, highlight a different view. The *CURRENT* view is the view in the current active viewport.
- **Lights.** The Lights list box displays all the defined lights in your drawing and enables you to select the lights for the scene. The highlighted lights are selected for the current scene. You can click on an unhighlighted light name to highlight it and add it to the scene. You can click on an highlighted light name to remove that light from the scene. The *ALL* light name uses all the defined lights in the scene.

Example

This example demonstrates how to add a scene to a drawing. Use the PINS2 drawing in the \ACAD\TUTORIAL subdirectory. After the drawing is loaded, change the view with the VPOINT or DVIEW command, and then use the VIEW command to save the new view as CAM2.

Choose Render, *then* Scenes
In the Scene Name *edit box, enter* **SCENE2** ↵
Click on CAM2 *in the* Views *list box*
Click on D2 *in the* Lights *list box*
Click on OK *in the two subsequent dialog boxes*
Restore the CAM1 view
Choose Render, *then* Render
The SCENE2 scene is rendered with the CAM2 view and the D2 light.

Related Commands

LIGHT
RENDER
VIEW

SCRIPT

Screen **[UTILITY] [SCRIPT:]**

R12 The SCRIPT command displays the Select Script File dialog box and invokes the selected script file. If the FILEDIA system variable is set to 0, you are prompted with `Script file <drawing name>:` at the command prompt. You can execute the SCRIPT command transparently by preceding the command name with an apostrophe ('SCRIPT).

A *script file* is a set of steps to execute AutoCAD commands and options. You must create this file in ASCII format with the SCR extension. AutoCAD interprets and executes the contents of a script file exactly as if you were entering the characters at the keyboard. Therefore, any extra spaces, returns, blank lines, or typographical errors cause problems. You can undo the effects of the SCRIPT command by issuing a single Undo. You can stop scripts by pressing Ctrl-C. You can use the EXPERT system variable to eliminate conditional prompts in scripts.

You also can execute script files automatically when you load AutoCAD by putting the script's file name after the drawing's file name. For example, you can type the following:

```
C:\> ACAD DRAWING1 SCRIPT1
```

 If a script file contains a SCRIPT command, the current script is stopped, and the specified script becomes current.

417

Scripts are often used to display slide shows, plot drawings, and reset system variables. If you change drawing standards and need to update existing drawings, use script files to do the work.

Prompts and Options

- **Script file<drawing name>:**

  If the system variable FILEDIA is set to 0, SCRIPT displays this prompt. Enter the name of the script file you want to run; do not enter the SCR extension. Preface the file name with a drive and a path specification if needed. The default script file name is the same as the drawing name. Enter a tilde (~) to display the dialog box.

- **Pattern:**

  Enter a pattern to filter files in the Files list box. The pattern can use the * and ? wild-card characters. The pattern defaults to *.SCR.

- **Directories:**

  Pick a drive or directory to list its contents in the Files list box. Double-click on any item in the list to select it. Select double dot (..) to move back one directory or backslash (\) to display the root directory. Available drive letters are listed in angle brackets (<>). If the directory list is longer that the Directories list box, a slider bar is displayed on the right side of the list box. The current directory is listed above the Directories list box.

- **Files:**

  Pick a script file to execute. Double-click on any file name to select it. If the list of files is longer than the Files list box, a slider bar is displayed on the right side of the list box.

 The MAXSORT system variable determines how many files or directories are sorted. MAXSORT defaults to 200 sorted entries. The value of MAXSORT must exceed the number of entries in the list box in order to have an effect.

- **Type it**

  Click on the **T**ype it button to enter the script file's name at the `Command prompt:` instead of the dialog box.

- **File:**

  Enter the name of the script to execute or accept the default name. If the current drawing has already been named, the drawing name is displayed in the Files edit box as the default script name. You can accept the name by clicking on OK or pressing Enter.

Related Commands

DELAY
GRAPHSCR
RESUME
RSCRIPT
TEXTSCR

Related System Variables

EXPERT
FILEDIA
MAXSORT

SELECT

Screen **[EDIT] [next] [SELECT:]**

R12 The SELECT command enables you to create a selection set to use with another command. At the other command's `SELECT objects:` prompt, you can enter **P** to specify the selection set established with the SELECT command.

If the PICKFIRST system variable is on, you can select objects with the cursor and then issue the SELECT command to add the objects to the selection set. If PICKFIRST is off, you cannot preselect entities, you must issue SELECT, and then select the entities using the options described below. PICKFIRST is new to Release 12.

 You cannot select entities from paper space that were created in model space, and vice versa.

Prompts and Options

- **SELECT objects:**

  Select all the entities that you want in your selection set. You can use any of the selection methods described below.

  You can use the following options with the SELECT command:

- **A point.** Picks the entity passing through the specified point.
- **ALL.** Selects all of the entities in the drawing.
- **Add (A).** Adds entities to the selection set.
- **Auto (AU).** If a pick fails to select an object, the selection method becomes the BOX option.
- **BOX.** If you move the crosshairs to the right it becomes a window— to the left it becomes a crossing window.
- **CPolygon (CP).** Selects all entities crossing or enclosed in a user-defined irregular polygon.
- **Crossing.** Selects entities crossing or enclosed in a window area.
- **Ctrl-C.** Cancels the selection process without creating the selection set.
- **Fence.** Selects entities that cross the fence line.
- **Last (L).** Selects the most recently created entity that is currently visible.
- **Multiple (M).** Enables you to pick multiple points on-screen before SELECT searches for entities. Press Enter to proceed.
- **Previous (P).** Selects the previous select set.
- **Remove (R).** Removes specified entities from the selection set.

R12

R12

R12

- **SIngle (SI).** Selects the first object found and completes the selection set.
- **Undo (U).** Removes the last group of selected entities.
- **Window (W).** Selects entities enclosed within a window area.

- **WPolygon (WP).** Selects all entities enclosed in a user-defined irregular polygon.

Example

The following example uses SELECT to create a selection set. See figure SELECT.1

```
Command: SELECT
SELECT objects: W
First corner: Pick point ① of a window
Other corner: Pick point ②
SELECT objects: Include x found message ↵
Command: SELECT
SELECT objects: F
First fence point: Pick point ③
Undo/<Endpoint of line>: Pick point ④
Undo/<Endpoint of line>: Include x found message ↵
```

Related System Variables

HIGHLIGHT
PICKADD
PICKAUTO
PICKFIRST
PICKDRAG

SETVAR

Screen [* * * *] [SETVAR:]

Screen [SETTINGS] [next] [SETVAR:]

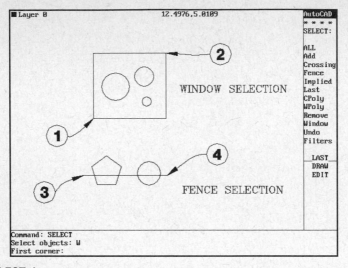

Figure SELECT.1:
Window and fence selection sets.

The SETVAR (SET VARiable) command modifies and lists the settings of AutoCAD system variables. System variables store values used to control the behavior of AutoCAD commands. These values may be text strings, integers, real numbers, or coordinates. Variables that cannot be modified are called *read-only* variables. Almost all string variables are read-only.

You can directly access most system variables by entering the name of the variable at the `Command:` prompt. You can use SETVAR transparently to modify a variable setting while using another command, by prefacing SETVAR with an apostrophe ('SETVAR). You also can transparently access most system variables while using another command by prefacing the variable name with an apostrophe.

Prompts and Options

- **`Variable name or ? <variable name>:`**

  Enter the name of the variable you want to modify or enter a question mark (?) to list variables.

- **`Variable(s) to list <*>:`**

  Enter the name(s) of the variables you want to list. If you press Enter, AutoCAD displays a list of all the variables, one page at a time. You can specify more than one variable by separating each with a comma or by using wild-card characters such as a question mark (?) or an asterisk (*).

- **`New value for`** *`VARIABLE`* **`<current value >:`**

  Enter a new value for the variable or press Enter to leave the current value unchanged. If the specified variable is read-only, the variable is displayed with the current value and the `New value for:` prompt does not display.

Example

The following example demonstrates setting an AutoCAD variable:

```
Command: SETVAR
Variable name or ?: EXPERT
New value for EXPERT <0>: 2
```

Related Commands

SOLVAR
DDSOLVAR

Related System Variables

A complete list of AutoCAD system variables and dimension variables are listed in *Inside AutoCAD Release 12*.

SHADE

Screen [DISPLAY] [SHADE] [SHADE:]

Pull down [Render] [Shade]

The SHADE command generates a shaded rendering of a 3D model by filling every face in the current viewport with a color. The color displayed is based on the entity's color, the distance of the face from the current viewpoint, the setting of the SHADEDGE and SHADEDIF system variables, and your display hardware's capabilities. You cannot select or plot the image, but you can make a slide of it with MSLIDE.

The SHADEDGE system variable controls the color in which edges are drawn. AutoCAD calculates the shading as if the objects were illuminated by a single light source directly behind you as you face the screen. The ratio of diffuse reflection from the light source to ambient (background) light is controlled by the SHADEDIF system variable. Regenerate the drawing to remove shading.

 You can reduce the time required for the SHADE command by freezing unnecessary layers, excluding irrelevant objects from the view, and by minimizing the size of the viewport in which the shading is performed.

Example

The following example shades the 3D entities shown in the viewport of figure SHADE.1.

```
Command: SHADE
Regenerating Drawing.
Shading XX% done.
Shading complete
```

Related Commands

HIDE
RENDER
MSLIDE
VSLIDE

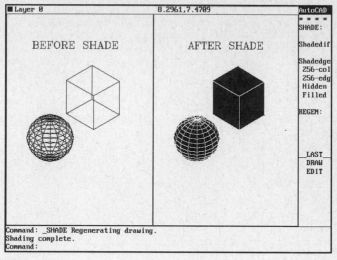

Figure SHADE.1:
The right viewport displays the shaded entities of the left viewport.

Related System Variables

SHADEDGE
SHADEDIF
SOLRENDER

SHAPE

Screen **[DRAW] [next] [SHAPE:]**

The SHAPE command inserts a shape entity into a drawing at a specified location. Shapes are entities that you can define in an actual file (*.SHP) using lines, arcs, and subshapes. Shape entities can be inserted into the drawing similar to blocks. Shape definitions, however, do not become part of the drawing. The actual shape entities that become a part of the drawing contain only the entity's location, size, and a reference to the shape definition file.

425

Shape definitions must be compiled with the COMPILE command and loaded with the LOAD command before they can be inserted. You can use the Insert object snap mode to snap to a shape's insertion point. When you load a drawing file, AutoCAD loads the compiled definition file corresponding to any inserted shapes.

 If you modify a shape definition file, you must recompile it or AutoCAD continues to use the old shape definition.

 In Release 11 and 12, you can use Xrefs instead of shapes if you need the efficiency and automatic updating provided by external definitions. Xrefs are easy to create and modify.

 Shapes that are in an externally referenced drawing (xref) are not available in the drawing that the xref is attached to.

Prompts and Options

- **Shape name (or ?) <default>:**

  Enter the name of a shape to insert. It must be already loaded into the drawing. Enter a question mark (?) to see a list of all currently loaded shapes.

- **Shape(s) to list <*>:**

  Press Enter to list all the shapes currently loaded in the drawing. You also can enter more than one name to list by separating each name with a comma or use a wild-card search string to list only shapes that match the wild-card pattern.

- **Starting point:**

  Enter a point in the drawing to locate the origin of the shape.

- **Height <1.0>:**

Enter a value to use as a multiplier for the shape's height. The shape's height initially is based on its definition in the shape file. You also can point to define the height.

- **Rotation angle <0.0>:**

  Enter the angle you want to rotate the shape around its starting point. The shape's initial orientation is defined in the shape file. You also can point to define the rotation angle.

Example

This example first loads a shape file from one of AutoCAD's sample shape files. After the shape file is loaded, its shape names are listed and then a shape is inserted into the drawing.

```
Command: LOAD
File: PC
Specify the PC.SHX file in the AutoCAD SAMPLE directory
Command: SHAPE
Shape name (or ?): ?
Shape(s) to list <*>: ↵
Available Shapes:
File: C:\ACAD\SAMPLE\PC.shx
FEEDTHRU        DIP8
DIP14           DIP16
DIP18           DIP20
DIP24           DIP40
Command: ↵
SHAPE Shape name (or ?): DIP24
Starting point: Pick any point
Height <1.0>: 2
Rotation angle <0>: 90
```

Related Commands

BLOCK
COMPILE
LOAD
PURGE
XREF

427

Related System Variable

SHPNAME

SHELL/SH

Screen **[UTILITY] [External Commands] [SHELL:]**

The SHELL command and the less-powerful SH command enable you to run other programs or temporarily exit to the operating system prompt without ending the current drawing session. When you execute either command, AutoCAD suspends the drawing editor, switches focus to the text display, and presents a prompt. After issuing one operating system command, you are returned to the drawing editor and AutoCAD resumes.

You may encounter memory problems with the SHELL command and larger programs. If so, you are prompted with `Shell error: insufficient memory for command`.

The SH command uses less memory but can only execute operating system commands.

Do not use the SH or SHELL command to perform any of the following tasks:

- Delete any files having extensions of ??K, ac, ac, or $a
- Run the CHKDSK command with a /F option on DOS or OS/2 systems
- Execute programs that reset serial ports (avoid Microsoft BASIC and programs compiled with it) on DOS or OS/2 systems
- Run programs that write to the same graphics memory as AutoCAD
- Swap drawing disks
- Execute TSR (Terminate and Stay Resident) programs on DOS systems unless the programs are loaded before you load AutoCAD

Remember to save your drawing file before you temporarily exit the drawing editor.

Prompts and Options

- **OS Command:**

    Enter the name of the single command or program you want to run, or press Enter and an operating system prompt appears.

    If you press Enter to get an operating system prompt, you can then execute any number of programs or operating system commands. Issue the EXIT command to return to the drawing editor.

Make sure that you exit the SHELL or SH command from the same directory as you entered.

Example

The following example uses the SHELL command to list the drawing files in the SAMPLE directory, using the DOS DIR command.

```
Command: SHELL
OS Command: DIR C:\ACAD\SAMPLE\*.DWG
```

The list varies depending on the files in your directory and the version of DOS you are running.

SKETCH

Screen **[DRAW] [next] [SKETCH:]**

The SKETCH command creates a contiguous series of lines as you move the cursor. This feature enables you to draw freehand or to trace curves on a paper drawing in tablet mode. If you set the AutoCAD system variable SKPOLY to 1, each group of individual lines converts to a single polyline when the command is completed. A common application of this command is to trace contour lines from a site plan.

If the current thickness is set to a non-zero value, the sketched lines or polylines are not extruded until they are placed in the drawing with the Record or eXit option. The SKETCH command is affected by the current snap, ortho, and tablet settings.

 You cannot turn tablet mode on and off while sketching.

The length on the individual SKETCH lines is controlled by the record increment. If the record increment is set to 0.2 units, a new line is generated each time the cursor moves to more than 0.2 units. The length of the SKETCH lines is also affected by the speed at which the cursor is moved across the screen. If the you move the cursor, the segments created may be longer than the length specified by the record increment.

The SKETCH command creates temporary lines that can be edited before they are placed on the drawing. If you create more temporary entities than can be stored in memory, AutoCAD prompts you to stop sketching entities and writes them to the disk. If you do not pause while AutoCAD writes to disk, input is lost and accuracy suffers.

 You must use the continuous linetype when sketching.

Prompts and Options

- **Record increment** < *value*>:

  Enter the length for each line segment. After the pointing device is moved this distance, the temporary segment is created on-screen. Use the largest value that produces sufficient detail.

- **Sketch. Pen eXit Quit Record Erase Connect .**

  Select one of the options described below. These options control how and when the SKETCH lines are drawn.

  You can use the following options with the SKETCH command:

- **. (period):**

  Draws a single line segment from the last point to the current pointing device location. Record increment does not affect the line length.

- **Pen:**

  This option turns the sketching on and off by placing the pen "up" and "down" on the drawing. When the pen is down, you can record lines.

- **eXit:**

  Records temporary line segments and exits the SKETCH command.

- **Quit:**

  Discards temporary line segments and returns to the `Command:` prompt.

- **Record:**

  Records temporary line segments and remains in the SKETCH command.

- **Erase:**

  Erases temporary line segments in the opposite order from which they were entered as you move your pointing device back over the line segments.

- **Connect:**

  By moving your pointing device close to the endpoint of the last temporary line segment, you can connect to that endpoint and continue sketching. If you enter **Connect** while the pen is down, you get the prompt `Connect command meaningless when pen down`. You can abort the connect by pressing Ctrl-C or entering any other option.

Example

The following example shows you how to draw curved polylines using the SKETCH command:

```
Command: SKPOLY
New value for SKPOLY <0>: 1
Command: SKETCH
Record increment <0.1000>:↵
Sketch. Pen eXit Quit Record Erase Connect . P<Pen down>
```
Begin creating entities at ① *by dragging the pointing device to* ② *(see fig. SKETCH.1)*
```
P <Pen up>
Sketch. Pen eXit Quit Record Erase Connect . X
1 polyline with XX edges recorded.
```

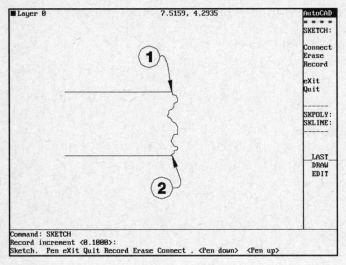

Figure SKETCH.1:
Using SKETCH to draw connecting lines.

Related Commands

> LINE
> PLINE
> PEDIT

Related System Variables

SKETCHINC
SKPOLY

SNAP

Press **^B** *or* **F9**

Screen **[SETTINGS] [next] [SNAP:]**

Pull down **[Settings] [Drawing Aids]**

SNAP restricts the movement of the crosshairs to specified increments enabling you to accurately enter points in the drawing area. You can alter the snap spacing in the X and Y directions, reset the base point of the snap and grid, and rotate the snap and grid about a point in the drawing. You also can use SNAP in Isometric mode to create drawings that appear to be three-dimensional but are actually two-dimensional. Each viewport may have individual snap settings. You can override any snap settings with keyboard input or object snap modes.

 You can execute the SNAP command transparently by preceding the command name with an apostrophe ('SNAP).

Prompts and Options

- **Snap spacing or ON/OFF/Aspect/Rotate/Style <1.000>:**

  Enter a new snap increment or enter one of the options described as follows to configure the SNAP command. Enter a number or pick two points to specify the snap increment.

- **ON:**
  This option turns on SNAP. You also can turn it on with the F9 key or Ctrl-B.

- **OFF:**

  This option turns off SNAP. You also can turn it off with the F9 key or Ctrl-B.

- **Aspect:**

  This option enables you to set different X and Y axis values for the snap spacing. The following prompts appear:

- **Horizontal spacing <1.0000>:**

  You can enter a number or pick two points to specify a distance.

- **Vertical spacing <1.0000>:**

  You can enter a number or pick two points to specify a distance.

- **Rotate:**

  This option enables you to rotate the snap and the crosshairs in the drawing. This rotation also affects the grid and Ortho mode. After you specify the Rotation option, the following prompts appear:

- **Base point <0.0000,0.0000>:**

  You can enter coordinates or pick a point.

- **Rotation angle <0>:**

  You can enter an angle of rotation or pick a point to define the angle of rotation.

Resetting the rotation of the snap and grid does not affect the origin or orientation of the current UCS. It is generally better to use the UCS command than to rotate or offset snap.

If you want to create an ARRAY at an angle, rotate the snap angle.

- **Style:**

  This option enables you to set the snap style to either Standard (the default) or Isometric. Style displays the following prompt:

- **Standard/Isometric <current>:**

  Standard resets the snap style to the default setting. Isometric enables isometric drafting, based on snap angles of 30, 90, 150, 210, 270, and 330. After you specify Isometric, AutoCAD displays the prompt:

- **Vertical spacing <1.0000>:**

  Specify the distance between the snap points.

 You can check current SNAP settings by using the STATUS and DDRMODES commands.

Example

Follow this example to adjust the horizontal and vertical spacing of the SNAP command and to specify a rotation angle:

```
Command: SNAP
Snap spacing or ON/OFF/Aspect/Rotate/Style <1.000>: A
Horizontal spacing <1.0000>: .5
Vertical spacing: <1.0000> 1
Command: SNAP
Snap spacing or ON/OFF/Aspect/Rotate/Style <A>: R
Base point: <0.0000,0.0000>: Press Enter
Rotation angle <0>: 25
Command: GRID
Grid spacing(X) or ON/OFF/Snap <0.0000>: S
```

Figure SNAP.1 illustrates what your screen should now look like.

Related Commands

DDRMODES
GRID
ISOPLANE
OSNAP
STATUS

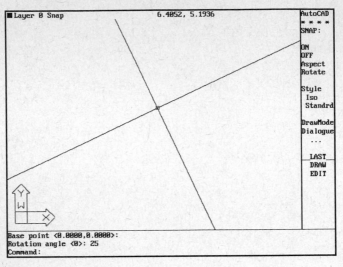

Figure SNAP.1:
The grid and crosshairs after adjusting snap spacing and rotation.

Related System Variables

SNAPANG
SNAPBASE
SNAPISOPAIR
SNAPMODE
SNAPSTYL
SNAPUNIT

SOLAREA

Screen **[MODEL] [INQUIRY] [SOLAREA:]**

Pull down **[Model] [INQUIRY >] [Area Calc.]**

The SOLAREA command calculates the surface area of solid entities. If you select more than one solid entity, SOLAREA reports the total area.

The area is calculated by totaling the area enclosed by the boundaries of the selected regions, minus any holes in the regions. Because the calculations are based on region boundaries, the wire mesh density does not affect accuracy. The SOLAREAU system variable determines the unit of measure for the area, the default is square centimeters.

 If you select a region that does not have a surface mesh, SOLAREA adds the mesh based on the SOLSOLIDIFY system variable.

Prompts and Options

- `Select objects:`

  Select the objects you want to include in the calculation. After you finish selecting objects, AutoCAD responds with the following message: `Surface area of solids is` *value* `sq cm` .

Example

The following example shows SOLAREA calculating the surface area of a region one drawing unit by one drawing unit:

```
Command: SOLAREA
Select objects: Select a region
Surface area of solids is 1 sq cm.
```

Related Commands

SOLMASSP
SOLLIST
SOLVAR

Related System Variables

SOLAREAU
SOLSOLIDIFY

SOLCHP

Screen **[MODEL] [MODIFY] [SOLCHP:]**

Pull down **[Model] [Modify] [Change Prim.]**

SOLCHP stands for *SOLid CHange Properties*. SOLCHP edits a solid primitive's properties, even if the primitive is part of a composite.

 Any change to a primitive that is part of a composite causes a partial re-evaluation of the composite. This can be time-consuming for complex composite regions.

 When creating or editing a composite model, you may accidentally create a region with no area (called a *null region*). If this occurs, AutoCAD identifies the null region with a THETA symbol (ø).

Prompts and Options

- **Select a solid or region:**

  Select the solid or region. You cannot use the AutoCAD window, crossing, previous, or last selection modes. If you select a composite region, you receive the following prompt:

- **Select primitive:**

  Pick a feature on the selected solid. If you cannot pick the primitive you want, use the Next option in the following prompt to cycle through the primitives.

- **Color/Delete/Evaluate/Instance/Move/Next/Pick/ Replace/Size/eXit <N>:**

  Select the type of change you want to make or primitive to edit. These options are described next.

- **Color.** The Color option changes the selected primitive's color. Enter a color number or name.

- **Delete.** The Delete option erases the specified primitive. If the solid was part of a composite solid, AutoCAD displays the `Retain detached primitive? <N>:` prompt, giving you the opportunity to keep it as a separate primitive. Answer **N** to erase the primitive completely; answer **Y** to create a separate solid.

- **Evaluate.** The Evaluate option causes a reevaluation of the composite region and stays in the SOLCHP command. Use Evaluate after performing many edits on an existing composite solid to see your changes.

- **Instance.** The Instance option copies the selected primitive as a separate region at the same coordinates in space as the original primitive. Instance is useful for making copies of a primitive that is part of a composite solid without breaking the composite apart. The copy is drawn on the current layer with the selected primitive's color.

- **Move.** The Move option moves the selected primitive, in the same manner as AutoCAD's MOVE command. You are prompted with `Base point or displacement` and `Second point of displacement`.

- **Next.** The Next option cycles through the solid primitives that make up the selected composite solid. When the desired primitive is highlighted, select one of the other SOLCHP options.

- **Pick.** The Pick option enables you to directly select a solid primitive for editing.

- **Replace.** The Replace option substitutes a specified composite or primitive solid for the currently selected primitive. At the `Select solid to replace primitive...` prompt, pick a new solid to replace the selected primitive. Note that the new solid is not moved to the location of the replaced primitive. If you replace a primitive that is part of a composite, you are prompted with `Retain detached primitive?<N>:`. If you answer yes, a copy of the primitive is placed on the layer on which it was originally created.

439

NOTE The location of the replacement is not altered during the replacement. The replacement is made in the CSG tree structure only.

- **Size.** The Size option resizes any user-specified dimensions of the primitive. The MCS icon is displayed, which represents the primitive's X, Y, and Z axes. The current dimensions of each axis are displayed one at a time in the following prompts: `Length along X axis <value>:`, `Length along Y axis < value>:`, and `Length along the Z axis < value>:`.

- **Exit.** The Exit option completes the SOLCHP by re-evaluating the region's CSG tree and exiting to the `Command:` prompt.

Example

The following example demonstrates SOLCHP's options, using the solids shown in figure SOLCHP.1.

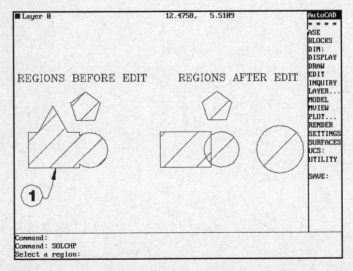

Figure SOLCHP.1:
Composite and primitive solids before and after editing.

```
Command: SOLCHP
Select a region: Pick the composite solid
Select primitive: Pick the box at ①
Color/Delete/Evaluate/Instance/Move/Next/Pick/
Replace/Size/eXit <N>: C
New color <7 (white)>: 1
Color/Delete/Evaluate/Instance/Move/Next/Pick/
Replace/Size/eXit <N>: ↵
```

AutoCAD highlights the circle primitive.

```
Color/Delete/Evaluate/Instance/Move/Next/Pick/
Replace/Size/eXit <N>: I
```

AutoCAD creates a copy of the circle in the same location; the copy is not yet visible.

```
Color/Delete/Evaluate/Instance/Move/Next/Pick/
Replace/Size/eXit <N>: M
Base point of displacement: Pick the circle's center
Second point of displacement: Pick at point @25<0
Color/Delete/Evaluate/Instance/Move/Next/Pick/
Replace/Size/eXit <N>: S
Radius of circle <0.75>: 1
Color/Delete/Evaluate/Instance/Move/Next/Pick/
Replace/Size/eXit <N>: E
Color/Delete/Evaluate/Instance/Move/Next/Pick/
Replace/Size/eXit <N>: ↵
Color/Delete/Evaluate/Instance/Move/Next/Pick/
Replace/Size/eXit <N>: ↵
Color/Delete/Evaluate/Instance/Move/Next/Pick/
Replace/Size/eXit <N>: R
Select region to replace primitive: Pick the region primitive
Retain detached primitive <N>: ↵
Color/Delete/Evaluate/Instance/Move/Next/Pick/
Replace/Size/eXit <N>: X
```

Note that although the replacement box did not move to the cylinder's position, it is part of the composite solid.

Related Commands

CHANGE
CHPROP
SOLPURGE

Related System Variable

SOLRENDER

SOLDISP

The SOLDISP command changes a solid or region display to a mesh or wireframe representation. Regions and solids are drawn as wireframes by default. If you are rendering your regions or solids, use SOLDISP to create a mesh representation before rendering to get the best results from RENDER. If AME is loaded, it automatically transforms its entities into meshes before rendering.

You can set the SOLDISPLAY system variable to mesh or wireframe. SOLDISPLAY affects all new entities. Use SOLDISP to modify existing entities.

Prompts and Options

- `Mesh/<Wire>:`

  Specify Mesh to display the selected entities as mesh representations. Specify Wire (the default) to display selected entities as wireframe representations.

- `Select objects:`

  Select the objects to represent as meshes or wireframes. You can use all of AutoCAD's selection modes.

Example

The following example uses the SOLDISP command to change a wireframe region to a mesh representation (see fig. SOLDISP.1).

```
Command: SOLDISP
Mesh/<Wire>: M
Select objects: Pick the region
Select objects: ↵
1 region selected
```

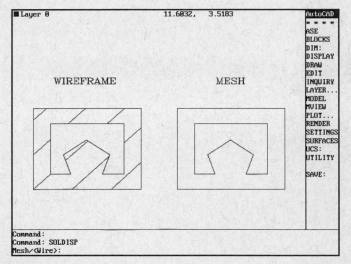

Figure SOLDISP.1
A wireframe region before and a mesh region after using SOLDISP.

Related System Variable

SOLDISPLAY

443

SOLFEAT

Screen **[MODEL] [DISPLAY] [SOLFEAT:]**

Pull down **[Model] [Display] [Copy Feature]**

The SOLFEAT (SOLid FEATure) command makes a 2D copy of a 3D edge or face of a solid object. The SOLFEAT command creates an anonymous block containing the lines, arcs, polylines, and circles that represent the selected edge or face. This block is inserted at the same location as the current edge or face, on the current layer. You use this command primarily to create 2D elevations from 3D solid models.

To select the block created by SOLFEAT, use the Last object-selection option available with most AutoCAD editing commands.

Prompts and Options

Depending on your initial selection, you receive different prompts requesting further information. These prompts provide the following options:

- **Edge/<Face>:**

  The Edge option enables you to create a block by copying the geometry of the selected edge of a solid. After you select Edge, the following prompt appears:

- **All/<Select>:**

- **All.** This option creates a new block for every edge in the selected solid.

- **Select.** This option creates a block for each edge you select. You are prompted with `Select an edge:`. You must pick the edges individually; you cannot use the AutoCAD entity selection options.

  You can pick an entity only if it is a wireframe representation. If you pick a mesh, AutoCAD displays the following prompt:

- **PMESH region. Change it to WIREFRAME for feature selection? <Y>:**

  If you answer yes, the entity is converted to a wireframe representation and you are reprompted to select an edge. If you answer no, the entity is ignored, and you are prompted to select a new entity.

- **Face.** The default option, Face, creates a block by copying the geometry of the selected face of a solid. After you specify Face, the following prompt appears:

- **All/<Select>:**

- **All.** This option creates a new block for every face in the selected region.

- **Select.** This option creates a block for each face you select. You are prompted with `Select a face:`, and you must pick the faces individually. You cannot use the AutoCAD entity selection options.

  You can pick an entity, only if it is a wireframe representation. If you pick a mesh, AutoCAD displays the following prompt:

- **PMESH region. Change it to WIREFRAME for feature selection? <Y>:**

  If you answer yes, the entity is converted to a wireframe representation and you are reprompted to select an edge. If you answer no, the entity is ignored, and you are prompted to select a new entity.

 Use the SOLDISP command and the SOLDISPLAY system variable to create wireframe representations of entities, before using SOLFEAT.

Example

The following example demonstrates use of the SOLFEAT command to copy a solid edge and face.

```
Command: SOLFEAT
Edge/<Face> : E
All/<Select>: ↵
```

```
Pick an edge: Pick ① (see fig. SOLFEAT.1)
Pick an edge: ↵
Command: SOLFEAT
Edge/<Face> : ↵
All/<Select>: ↵
Pick a face... Pick ①
```

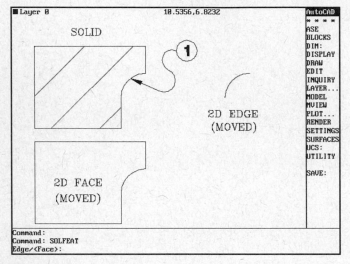

Figure SOLFEAT.1:
Solid selected by the SOLFEAT command, and 2D edge and face blocks moved away from the Solid.

Related Command

SOLDISP

Related System Variable

SOLDISPLAY

SOLID

Screen **[DRAW] [next] [SOLID:]**

SOLID draws solid-filled areas. These areas can be defined by three or four points. The points are entered in an edge-to-edge order. The first two points are the endpoints of a starting edge. The next point defines the third point of a triangle, or you can enter a fourth point to define an ending edge. If FILL or the system variable FILLMODE is on, the areas are filled.

To save time during regenerations and redraws, turn FILL off. To see the results of turning FILL on or off, regenerate the drawing.

Prompts and Options

- **First point:**

  Specify the first point of the solid entity.

- **Second point:**

  Specify the next point of the entity.

- **Third point:**

  The direction in which you select the third point determines the appearance of the solid. If points are selected in a clockwise or counterclockwise direction, the solid appears as a bow tie. See figure SOLID.1 for an example.

- **Fourth point:**

  You do not have to specify a point at this prompt. If you pick a point, AutoCAD draws a four-sided solid. If you press Enter at this prompt, AutoCAD creates a three-sided solid. In either case, the command continues with a prompt for the next solid. The next solid uses the last two points that you picked as the first and second points of the new solid. The new prompt asks you for the new solid's third point.

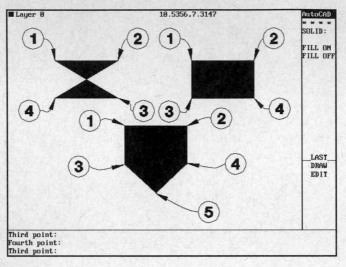

Figure SOLID.1:
Creating solids with FILL on.

Example

The following example illustrates the method for creating solid entities.

```
Command: SOLID
First point: Pick point ① (see fig. SOLID.1)
Second point: Pick point ②
Third point: Pick point ③
Fourth point: Pick point ④
Third point: Pick point ⑤
Fourth point: ↵
Third point: ↵
```

Related Command

FILL

Related System Variable

FILLMODE

SOLIDIFY

Screen **[MODEL] [SOLIDIFY]**

Pull down **[Model] [Solidify]**

The SOLIDIFY command converts 2D entities into solid regions. Valid
2D entities include polylines, polygons, circles, ellipses, traces, donuts,
and AutoCAD 2D solid entities. Open polylines must have at least two
segments and are solidified as though they had a closing segment
connecting their end points. They cannot have any crossing segments.
Entities with a negative thickness value cannot be solidified without the
optional AME software. Polylines with width information are solidified
from their center line.

 The SOLDELENT system variable determines whether or not
the selections are deleted from the drawing file after they are
extruded.

The SOLSOLIDIFY system variable controls whether or not other solid
commands solidify 2D entities when encountered.

 You can assign a thickness before entity creation, change an
entity's thickness with CHANGE or CHPROP before using
SOLIDIFY, or use the SOLEXT command—all with the same
results.

Prompts and Options

- **Select objects:**

  Select the objects you want to solidify. You can use any of
  AutoCAD's entity selection options.

Example

The following example uses the SOLIDIFY command to create solid regions from different 2D AutoCAD entities. Figure SOLIDIFY.1 illustrates the entities before and after conversion.

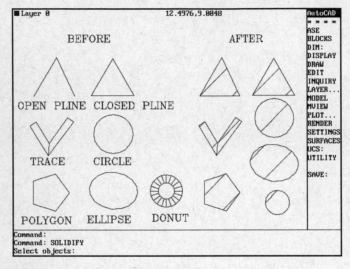

Figure SOLIDIFY.1:
2D objects before and after conversion by the SOLIDIFY command.

```
Command: SOLIDIFY
Select objects: ALL
```

Related Commands

SOLEXT
SOLMESH
ELEV

Related System Variables

SOLDELENT
SOLSOLIDIFY
THICKNESS

SOLINT

Screen **[MODEL] [SOLINT:]**

Pull down **[Model] [Intersect]**

The SOLINT command creates a composite region from the intersection of two or more regions. If you select an object that is not a region, it is solidified according to the current setting of the SOLSOLIDIFY system variable. Selected objects that are not regions and cannot be solidified are rejected, and the command proceeds. If an intersection would result in a region with no area (null region), the entities are rejected, and the command is terminated.

Prompts and Options

- **Select objects:**

  Select the objects you want to use to create the new composite solid. To end the selection process, press Enter. The program then creates the new composite solid. If the regions are not solid and cannot be solidified, you are prompted with **n non-region objects ignored.**

  If the selected regions or solids result in a null region, you are prompted with **Null intersection encountered.**

Be careful to avoid creating a null solid by using SOLINT on nonintersecting solids. You cannot see the null solid, but you can purge it using the SOLPURGE command.

Example

The following example shows you how to create an intersection region from two overlapping regions. (see fig. SOLINT.1)

```
Command: SOLINT
Select objects: Select the cylinder and box
Select objects: ↵
```

451

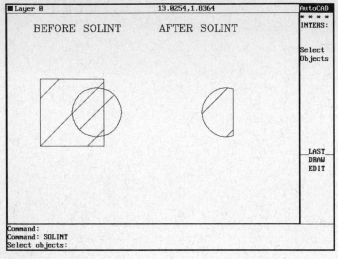

Figure SOLINT.1:
The circle and box, before and after using the SOLINT command.

Related Commands

SOLPURGE
SOLSUB
SOLUNION

Related System Variable

SOLSOLIDIFY

SOLLIST

Screen **[MODEL] [INQUIRY] [SOLLIST:]**

Pull down **[Model] [Inquiry >] [List Objects]**

SOLLIST displays information about a region, an edge, a face, or a region's CSG (Constructive Solid Geometry) tree. Set the SOLPAGELEN system variable to control the number of lines per page of the list.

Prompts and Options

- `Edge/Face/Tree/<Object>:`

  Select an option. Each of the options are described below.

- **Edge.** Enter **E** to receive information about the edge of a solid object. If you select a mesh region, you are prompted with the following:

  `PMESH region. Change it to WIREFRAME for feature selection? <Y>:`

- **Face.** Enter **F** to receive information about the face of a solid object.

- **Tree.** Enter **T** to receive information on components at all levels of a solid model's CSG tree.

- `Object.` Press Enter or enter **O** to receive information on only the primitive or composite at the first level of a solid's CSG tree.

- `Pick an edge:`

  You receive this prompt if you specify the Edge option. Carefully select an edge of the solid model. The information displayed varies depending on the type of edge you select.

- `Select a face:`

  You receive this prompt if you specify the Face option. Select a visible edge of the face you want to list.

- `Select objects:`

  This prompt appears after you specify the Tree or Object options. You can select multiple solid objects at this prompt. The prompt is repeated until you press Enter. The Tree option then displays information for the entire CSG tree for the selected solids. With Object, you receive the information about the composite solid at the top of the selected solid's CSG tree only.

- **Select objects:**

  If you specify the Object option, you receive this prompt, which enables you to select multiple solid objects. The prompt is repeated until you press Enter.

Example

The following example shows the list for an edge and for the entire tree of the region shown in figure SOLLIST.1.

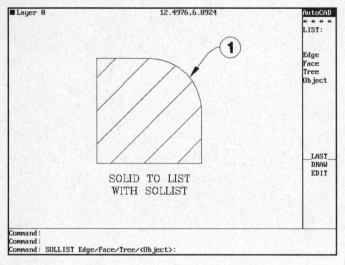

Figure SOLLIST.1:
The composite solid to list.

```
Command: SOLLIST
Edge/Face/Tree/<Object>: E
Pick an edge: Pick point ①
Circular edge, length = 1.570596,
radius = 1, center: (4, 4, 0)
```

```
Command: SOLLIST
Edge/Face/Tree/<Object>: T
Select objects: Pickpoint ①
Select objects: ↵
Object type = REGION (6)   HANDLE =E9
     Area not computed   Material = MILD_STEEL
     Representation= WIREFRAME   Render type CSG
```

Related System Variable

SOLPAGELEN

SOLMASSP/DDSOLMASSP

Screen **[MODEL] [INQUIRY] [SOLMASP:]**

Screen **[MODEL] [INQUIRY] [DDSOLMSP:]**

Pull down **[Model] [Inquiry >] [Mass Property]**

SOLMASSP is an inquiry command that reports the mass properties of selected regions. These properties include the area, perimeter, bounding box, and centroid (center of area). If the X,Y plane of the selected regions is coplaner with the current UCS, SOLMASSP also calculates moment of inertia, product of inertia, radius of gyration, and principal moments and directions about the centroid. You can save the information to a file. Use the SOLMASS system variable to control the unit of measure.

 Use the File button from the DDSOLMASSP dialog box or the File name <current drawing name> prompt from the SOLMASSP command, to save the calculations to a file.

DDSOLMASSP delivers the same information in a dialog box. You can enter DDSOLMASSP at the Command: prompt or select Mass Property from the Inquiry option of the Model pull-down menu.

Prompts and Options

- `Select objects:`

  Select the objects you want to use. The prompt is repeated for you to select multiple objects; press Enter to end the selection process. Any solids or regions that are not coplaner with the first selection are ignored. If you select an object that is not a region, it is solidified according to the current SOLSOLIDIFY settings.

- `Write to a file? <N>:`

  Enter **Y** to save the calculations to a file for later use. Enter **N** or accept the default to terminate the command.

- `File name < default>:`

  Enter a valid file name to save calculations. If the system variable FILEDIA is set to 0, this prompt appears. Otherwise, a file dialog box appears. The default extension is MPR.

If you want to list several objects at once, make sure that they are all coplaner with the first object selected.

Example

The following example uses the DDSOLMASSP dialog to display the properties of a square region inserted at 4,4,0 with the other corner at 6,6,0 (see fig. DDSOLMASSP.1).

```
Command: DDSOLMASSP
Select objects: Select the box
Select objects: ⏎
```

Related System Variables

PDMODE
PDSIZE
SOLAREAU
SOLDECOMP

SOLLENGTH
SOLSOLIDIFY
SOLSUBDIV
SOLMASS
SOLVOLUME

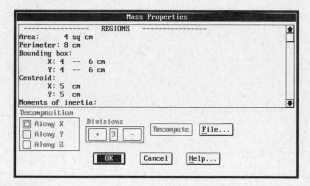

Figure DDSOLMASSP.1:
The Mass Properties calculations displayed by DDSOLMASSP.

SOLMESH

Screen **[MODEL] [DISPLAY] [SOLMESH:]**

Pull down **[Model] [Display] [Mesh]**

The SOLMESH command converts solids from a wireframe representation to a surface-mesh representation. A mesh represents solids as a series of faces that approximate the curves and surfaces. Meshed solids explode into polyface mesh (polyline) entities. A mesh representation is required for hidden-line removal or shaded images. Although the mesh and wireframe blocks may exist for a region, only one can be displayed at a time; the other is hidden on the AME_FRZ layer.

You can convert a mesh to a wireframe using the SOLWIRE command.

You cannot use the tangent, quadrant, or center object snap modes on a meshed arc or circle.

Prompts and Options

- `Select objects:`

  Select the objects you want to convert to a mesh representation. After you complete your selection set, press Enter to mesh the solids and complete the command. If you select an object that is not a region, it is converted according to the current setting of the SOLSOLIDIFY system variable.

Example

The following example shows you how to convert a solid from a wireframe representation to a mesh representation. See figure SOLMESH.1

```
Command: SOLMESH
Select objects: Select the region
Select objects: ↵
```

Using xref is an easy way to build complex models, but be careful when using external files that include solids. After you use xref, you cannot edit the solids while they are part of an xref, and the solids can be shaded only if they already are converted to a mesh representation.

Because a mesh approximates solid surfaces, complex surfaces might be distorted with too small a SOLWDENS setting. Thin shells (two parallel, curved surfaces a small distance apart) also might be represented improperly. If this situation occurs, increase the dimension between the surfaces, or set SOLWDENS to a higher value.

Related Commands

SOLDISP
SOLWIRE

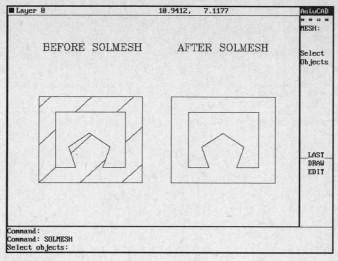

Figure SOLMESH.1
A region before and after SOLMESH

Related Commands

SOLDISP
SOLWIRE

Related Variables

SOLWDENS
SOLDISPLAY

SOLMOVE

Screen **[MODEL] [MODIFY] [SOLMOVE:]**

Pull down **[Model] [Modify] [Move Object]**

The SOLMOVE command combines into one command the functions of AutoCAD's MOVE and ROTATE commands. SOLMOVE creates a temporary Motion Coordinate System (MCS) in which you move and rotate your selected objects (see fig. SOLMOVE.1); all movement is relative to the MCS. The MCS origin is the intersection of the X, Y, and Z axes. The MCS icon is placed oriented to the current UCS by default. The MCS also can be oriented to the WCS, any face, or any edge. If the MCS is set to an edge of the solid being moved, the MCS moves with the solid. The X axis of the MCS has one arrow, the Y axis has two arrows, and the Z axis has three arrows.

Prompts and Options

- **Select objects:**

  Select the solids you want to move or rotate. If the object selected is not a region, it is converted to the current settings of the SOLSOLIDIFY system variable.

- **?/<Motion description>:**

  Enter the desired motion description code for the selected objects. (Note that you can combine motion description codes.) The ? option lists the motion description codes. Press Enter at this prompt to exit SOLMOVE.

  You can choose from among the following motion-description codes.

- **A[efuw].** Aligns objects with the selected coordinate system; to use this code, enter **A**, followed by one of the letters in brackets: **e** = edge, **f** = face, **u** = UCS, or **w** = WCS.

- **R[xyz]** *degrees.* Rotates objects about the selected axis; to use this code, enter **R** followed by the axis letter and the number of degrees.

- **T[xyz]** *degrees.* Translates objects along the selected axis; enter **T** followed by the axis letter and the distance to move.

- **E.** Sets MCS to an edge coordinate system.

- **F.** Sets MCS to a face coordinate system.

- **U.** Sets MCS to the UCS (User Coordinate System).
- **W.** Sets MCS to the WCS (World Coordinate System).
- **O.** Restores objects to their original orientations and positions.

The following example, you flip and move a region with the SOLMOVE command (see fig. SOLMOVE.1). This maneuver requires both a rotation of the region and a translation of the region.

```
Command: SOLMOVE
Select objects: Pick the region
1 found
Select objects: ↵
1 solid selected.
<Motion description>/?: RX180
<Motion description>/?: TY3
<Motion description>/?: ↵
```

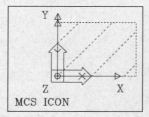

Figure SOLMOVE.1
The MCS icon during the SOLMOVE command.

 You can combine several SOLMOVE motion description codes on one line, separated by commas. This procedure enables you to move and rotate a solid in one step. You can combine all the steps from the preceding command sequence into one command, for example, by typing **RXI180,TY3** at the `<Motion de-scription>/?:` prompt.

Related Commands

MOVE
ROTATE
UCS

461

Related System Variables

SOLAXCOL
SOLSOLIDIFY

SOLPURGE

Screen [MODELS] [UTILITY] [SOLPURG:]

Pull down [Model] [UTILITY >] [Purge Objects]

The SOLPURGE command erases information stored with solid objects and releases that memory. More memory and less information to hold can improve performance and reduce the size of drawing files. If purged information is needed later, it is recalculated which causes some commands to take longer to perform. Use the SOLPURGE command on solids that are not likely to change.

Prompts and Options

- Memory/2dtree/Bfile/Pmesh/<Erased>:

  Enter an option, or accept the default which purges secondary solid entities which remain after a solid has been erased. Memory associated with erased solids also is released. This option is the default because it is the safest and most commonly used option. The following are the other options for the SOLPURGE command:

- Memory. This option releases memory associated with solids and regions. You specify which solids to release from memory at the All/<Select>: prompt.

- All/<Select>:

  The All option releases memory used by all the solid entities in your drawing.

  The Select option releases memory for specified solid entities. Nonsolid entities are ignored.

• **2dfile.** Organizes a region's structure to reduce its size and complexity.

• **Bfile.** Removes boundary files from solids. This can significantly reduce the size of a drawing.

 Purging Bfile entities can slow AME operations requiring those entities because AME must re-create them on the fly.

• **Pmesh.** The Pmesh option removes selected Pmesh entities. If the selected solids are currently viewed as a mesh, AutoCAD switches them back to wireframe representations before purging the mesh.

 Use the Erased option frequently to keep memory free and minimize paging to disk.

Related Command

PURGE

SOLSEP

Screen **[MODEL] [MODIFY] [SOLSEP:]**

Pull down **[Model] [Modify] [Separate]**

The SOLSEP command separates solids used in a composite solid. SOLSEP breaks down solids into their components until the solid primitive level is reached. The SOLSEP command reverses any SOLINT, SOLUNION, and SOLSUB commands that have been performed. The resulting solids are placed on the layers on which they were originally created.

 You cannot separate solid primitives. They already are at the lowest possible level on the CSG tree.

463

SOLSEP sometimes returns unexpected results, depending on how the composite solids were created originally. If you mistakenly separate the wrong solids, use the UNDO command to return them to their original composite form.

Prompts and Options

- `Select objects:`

  Select one or more composite solids for separating.

- `Only booleaned regions can be separated. Primitives ignored.` This warning message appears when one or more of the solids selected is a solid primitive.

Example

The following example applies the SOLSEP command to the composite solid shown in figure SOLSEP.1. This solid was generated by applying the SOLUNION command to a box and a cylinder.

```
Command: SOLSEP
Select objects: Pick the region
Select objects: ↵
1 solid selected.
```

Related Commands

SOLUNION
SOLINT
SOLSUB

SOLSUB

Screen **[MODEL] [SOLSUB:]**

Pull down **[Model] [Subtract]**

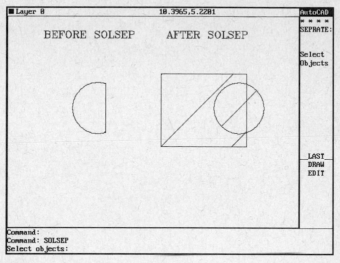

Figure SOLSEP.1:
The composite region before and after separating.

The SOLSUB command performs a Boolean subtraction operation. SOLSUB uses two selection sets. The first selection set defines the source object(s). If more than one solid object is selected, they are all combined with a union operation. The second selection set defines the object(s) that are to be subtracted from the first selection set. If you select more than one solid for this set, they are combined with a union operation. Any solids contained in both selection sets are ignored in the second selection set. Any intersecting area is subtracted and a new composite solid results.

Prompts and Options

- **Source objects...**
  Select objects:

  Pick the solids you want to subtract from at this prompt. If you select an object that is not a region, it is solidified according to the current setting of the SOLSOLIDIFY system variable.

- **Objects to subtract from them...**
  Select objects:

  Pick the solids you want to subtract from the first selection set. A *null solid* (a solid without volume) can result by subtracting too much of a solid. The following message is displayed as the command is reversed:

  `Null solid encountered. Automatically separating.`

   If there are no regions in the select set to subtract that are coplaner with a source selection set, the source selection set is rejected.

Example

The following example uses the SOLSUB command to subtract a circle from a box (see fig. SOLSUB.1).

```
Command: SOLSUB
Source objects...
Select objects: Pick the box
Objects to subtract from them...
Select objects: Pick the circle
```

Related Commands

  SOLINT
  SOLUNION

Related System Variable

  SOLSOLIDIFY

SOLUCS

Screen **[MODEL] [UTILITY] [SOLUCS:]**

Pull down **[Model] [UTILITY >] [SolUCS]**

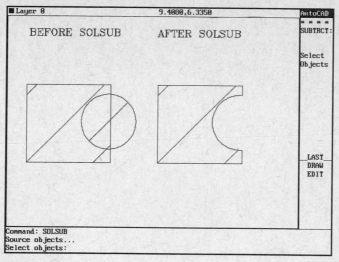

Figure SOLSUB.1:
The regions before and after the SOLSUB command.

The SOLUCS command aligns the UCS with either an edge or a face of a solid entity. This cannot be done with solids using the UCS command.

Prompts and Options

- **Edge/<Face>:**

  Specify the option corresponding to the solid feature you want to align the UCS with. Press Enter to accept the default option, Face.

- **Pick an edge...**

  Pick an edge with which to align the UCS.

- **Pick a face...**

  Pick a face to align the UCS with by picking an edge. Edges are created by the boundaries of two faces, so you must indicate which face you want to align the UCS with at the next prompt.

- **<OK>/Next:**

  If the highlighted face is the one you want to align with, press Enter. Otherwise, enter **N** to select the adjacent face.

Example

The following example demonstrates aligning the UCS with the face of a
solid using the SOLUCS command (see fig. SOLUCS.1.

```
Command: SOLUCS
Edge/<Face>: ↵
Select a face... Pick the region
Next/<OK>: N
Next/<OK>: ↵
```

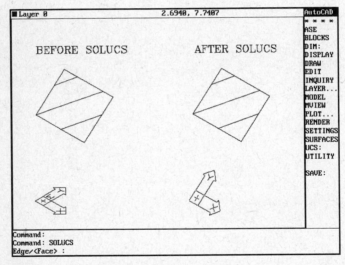

Figure SOLUCS.1:
UCS icon before and after aligning with a region.

Related Command

UCS

SOLUNION

Screen   **[MODEL] [SOLUNON:]**

Pull down   **[Model] [Union]**

The SOLUNION command combines two or more solid objects with a Boolean union operation to create a single composite solid. The selected objects need not intersect.

Prompts and Options

- **Select objects:**

  Pick the solids you want to unite using AutoCAD's general object selection methods. If a selected object is not a region, it is solidified according to the current settings of the SOLSOLIDIFY system variable

Example

The following example uses the SOLUNION command to combine a solid box and a solid cylinder.

Command: **SOLUNION**
Select objects: *Pick the box and circle*

Figure SOLUNION.1 shows the regions before and after the SOLUNION command.

Related Commands

SOLINT
SOLSUB

Related System Variable

SOLSOLIDIFY

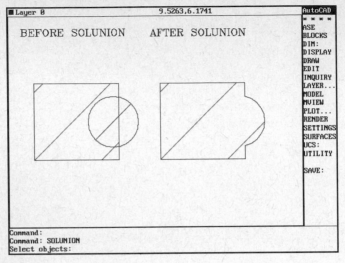

Figure SOLUNION.1:
Solids before and after the SOLUNION command.

SOLVAR/DDSOLVAR

Screen **[MODEL] [UTILITY] [SETUP] [SOLVAR:]**

Pull down **[Model] [Setup] [Variables]**

The DDSOLVAR command provides access to the solid modeling
system variables, much like the SETVAR command does for AutoCAD
system variables. You also can type the name of the solid system variables at the Command: prompt and bypass the DDSOLVAR command.
The DDSOLVAR command displays the AME System Variables dialog
box, which enables you to graphically set the solid system variables.

Prompts and Options

- Variable name or ?:

Enter the name of a valid solid variable you want to change. Type
? to list all of the solid variables with a brief description of their
purpose. You can omit the SOL prefix from the variable name, and
most variables can be further abbreviated.

You can enter the variable name directly at the Command:
prompt

Example

The following example changes the value of the solid variables that control
units.

Command: **DDSOLVAR**
Click on Units
Enter **INCH** *in the Length edit box (see Fig. DDSOLVAR.1)*
Turn Consistent Units *on by clicking on the check box*
Click on OK twice

Figure DDSOLVAR.1:
The Region System Variables dialog box.

Related Command

SETVAR

Related System Variable

For a list of solid system variables, see *Inside AutoCAD Release 12.*

SOLWIRE

Screen **[MODEL] [DISPLAY] [SOLWIRE:]**

Pull down **[Model] [Display] [Wireframe]**

The SOLWIRE command changes the display of selected solids from mesh to wireframes. A wireframe display enables you to use object snaps, which are not possible with mesh displays. Both the wireframe and mesh blocks of a solid can exist in a drawing at the same time but only one can be displayed. The other block is hidden on the frozen AME_FRZ layer.

You can switch between wireframes and meshes as often as you want using the SOLWIRE and SOLMESH commands.

A solid must have a mesh representation to be properly shaded or rendered.

Prompts and Options

- **Select objects:**

   Pick solid objects to display as wireframe blocks. If the selected object is not a region, it is converted according to the current settings of the SOLSOLIDIFY command.

Example

The following example shows you how to use the SOLWIRE command to wire a cylinder (see fig. SOLWIRE.1).

```
Command: SOLWIRE
Select objects: Pick the region
Select objects: ↵
```

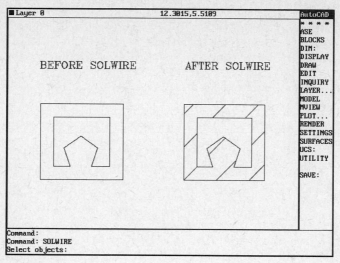

Figure SOLWIRE.1:
A region before and after SOLWIRE.

Related Command

SOLMESH

Related System Variables

SOLDISPLAY
SOLSOLIDIFY
SOLWDENS

STATS

Screen **[RENDER] [STATS]**

Pull down **[Render] [Statistics]**

The STATS command displays statistical information about the last rendering and enables you to save the statistics as a file.

Prompts and Options

- **Scene name.** Scene name displays the name of the last scene rendered. If no scene was current at the time, (none) is displayed.
- **Last rendering type.** Last rendering type shows what rendering type was used to create the rendered image. The possible values are Full Render or Quick Render.
- **Rendering time.** Rendering time displays how much time the last rendering took to complete.
- **Total faces.** Total faces displays the number of faces rendered in the last rendering.
- **Total triangles.** Total triangles displays the number of triangles rendered in the last rendering.
- **Cyclic overlaps corrected.** If the last rendering was a full render, this value is the number of cyclic overlaps corrected. A cyclic overlap occurs when face A overlaps face B, which overlaps face C, which overlaps face D, which in turn overlaps face A. Cyclically overlapping faces increase rendering time.
- **Triangles chopped.** Triangles chopped displays the number of triangles that intersect after face intersection correction has been applied to the intersecting faces.

- **Original extents.** Original extents displays the minimum and maximum X, Y, and Z coordinates of the drawing extents.

- **Projected extents.** Projected extents displays the minimum and maximum X, Y, and Z coordinates of the drawing after it appears on screen.

- **Save statistics to file.** The Save statistics to file check box and edit box enable you to write the statistical information to a file. First, place a check in the check box, then enter a file name, including the extension, in the edit box. The resulting file is an ASCII file, which you can display by using any text editor or the DOS TYPE command. If the file name you enter already exists, the information is appended to that file.

STATUS

? ,

Screen **[INQUIRY] [STATUS:]**

The STATUS command provides detailed information about the current drawing and AutoCAD's memory usage. (See fig. STATUS.1.) In Release 12 STATUS can be issued transparently if you preface the command name with an apostrophe ('STATUS). Information that STATUS provides includes the number of entities in the drawing; the drawing's limits and whether or not they are being exceeded; the current color, layer, and linetype; and the status of drawing aids, such as Snap and Ortho modes. STATUS also displays information on disk and memory usage. The number format is controlled by the UNITS command.

Use the STATUS command to monitor your free disk space. If the disk fills up, AutoCAD cannot continue.

```
0 entities in UNNAMED
Model space limits are X:     0.0000   Y:     0.0000   (Off)
                        X:    12.0000   Y:     9.0000
Model space uses        *Nothing*
Display shows           X:     0.0000   Y:     0.0000
                        X:    12.4867   Y:     9.0000
Insertion base is       X:     0.0000   Y:     0.0000   Z:     0.0000
Snap resolution is      X:     1.0000   Y:     1.0000
Grid spacing is         X:     0.0000   Y:     0.0000

Current space:          Model space
Current layer:          0
Current color:          BYLAYER -- 7 (white)
Current linetype:       BYLAYER -- CONTINUOUS
Current elevation:      0.0000   thickness:     0.0000
Fill on  Grid off  Ortho off  Qtext off  Snap off  Tablet off
Object snap modes:      None
Free disk: 3203072 bytes
Virtual memory allocated to program: 6008 KB
Amount of program in physical memory/Total (virtual) program size: 49%
Total conventional memory: 392 KB        Total extended memory: 2800 KB
-- Press RETURN for more --
Swap file size: 3300 KB
Command:
```

Figure STATUS.1:
Status information regarding the current drawing and system.

Related Command

UNITS

STRETCH

Screen **[EDIT] [next] [STRETCH:]**

Pull down **[Modify] [Stretch]**

The STRETCH command moves and stretches entities by relocating the points that define the entities. To select objects for STRETCH, you drag a crossing window. Entities in the window are moved; entities that cross the edge of the window are stretched. You cannot stretch some entities, such as circles, shapes, text, blocks, and points. You can move these entities, however, if their primary definition point is located within the crossing window.

You can stretch two-dimensional entities only in their construction plane. Before you issue the STRETCH command, set the UCS so that it aligns with the entities.

Use the Grip Edit Stretch mode for quicker stretching and as a copy option. You can also stretch a circle's radius with the Grip Edit Stretch mode.

Prompts and Options

- `Select object to stretch by window or polygon...`
  `Select objects:`

  At this prompt, you must use a crossing window to select entities. The prompt repeats until your selection set is complete.

- `First corner:`

  Select the first point of a crossing window.

- `Other corner:`

  Select the second point to define a crossing window. If you specify more than one crossing window, only the entities selected with the last crossing window are affected by STRETCH.

- `Base point or displacement:`

  Enter the base point of displacement or a coordinate amount of displacement.

- `Second point of displacement:`

  Enter the new endpoint for the stretched entities.

Example

The following example uses STRETCH on the entities shown in figure STRETCH.1.

```
Command: STRETCH
Select object to stretch by window or polygon...
Select objects: Pick point ①
Other corner: Pick point ②
1 found
Select objects: ↵
Base point or displacement: Pick point ③
Second point of displacement: Pick point ④
```

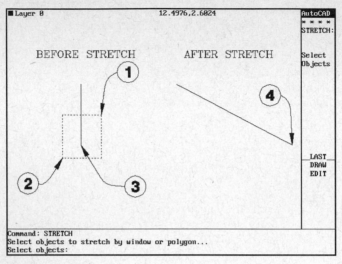

Figure STRETCH.1:
A line before and after STRETCH.

Related Commands

CHANGE
EXTEND
MOVE
TRIM

STYLE

Screen **[SETTINGS] [next] [STYLE:]**

R12 The STYLE command loads fonts that you can use with the TEXT, DTEXT, ATTDEF, and dimensioning commands to create text. In addition, STYLE enables you to define the look of a text font in the drawing. In Release 12 you can issue the STYLE command transparently if you preface it with an apostrophe ('STYLE).

If you change a style, all text created with that style is changed.

Prompts and Options

- **Text style name (or ?) < *current style* >:**

  Enter the desired name for the text style. Each unique text style must have its own name. The default name for the text style is the name of the file that contains the font. Use the question mark option (?) to obtain a list of the currently defined fonts in the drawing.

   The LIST command displays the STYLE settings of a text object.

- **Text style(s) to list <*>:**

  If you choose the question mark option (?), you can specify which style(s) you want to view. If you press Enter, all loaded text styles are listed. You also can enter a wild-card search string to list only styles that match the wild-card pattern.

- **File:**

  The Select Font File dialog box is displayed (see fig. STYLE.1). Enter the name of the file that contains the font definition. This file has an SHX extension. (You do not enter the extension.) If you press Enter, the style is based on the font file of the current style.

- **Height <0.0>:**

  Specify a height of 0 if you want the TEXT and DTEXT commands to prompt for a text height each time you use them. Enter the default height for the style if you want all text created with this style to have a uniform height.

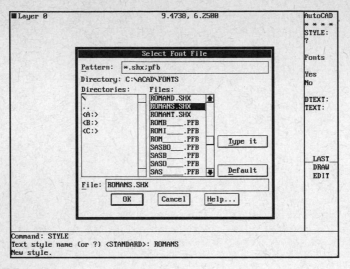

Figure STYLE.1:
The Select Font File dialog box.

- **Width factor <1.0>:**

  The width factor expands or compresses the amount of space taken up by each letter. A default value of 1.0 uses the text as defined in the font file. A value smaller than 1 compresses the text; a value greater than 1 expands the text.

- **Obliquing angle <0>**

  Enter an angle that forces the font to be slanted. A positive value slants the text forward by the specified degree; a negative value slants the text backward.

- **Backwards? <N>**

  A backward font is a horizontal mirror image of normal text.

- **Upside-down? <N>**

  An upside-down font is a vertical mirror image of normal text.

- **Vertical? <N>**

  This prompt appears only if the vertical option is enabled in the font file definition. A font entered vertically is drawn with each letter below the previous one.

Unlike blocks, font files are stored externally. Unique font files must accompany the drawing file in drawing exchanges.

Example

The following example defines a text style using the ROMANS font file.

```
Command: STYLE
New Style. Text style name (or ?) <STANDARD>:ROMANS
File: ROMANS
Height <0.000>:↵
Width factor <1.00>:↵
Obliquing angle <0>↵
Backwards? <N>↵
Upside-down? <N>↵
Vertical? <N>↵
ROMANS is now the current text style.
```

Related Commands

> **CHANGE**
> **DIM**
> **DTEXT**
> **PURGE**
> **RENAME**
> **TEXT**

Related System Variables

> **TEXTSTYLE**
> **TEXTSIZE**
> **FILEDIA**

TABLET

Screen **[SETTINGS] [next] [TABLET:]**

481

The TABLET command prepares AutoCAD to receive input from a digitizer tablet. It also prepares a tablet menu to supply command input. The TABLET command enables you to synchronize the drawing editor's coordinate tracking with a paper (or other media) drawing that you want to digitize (trace) accurately into AutoCAD.

Prompts and Options

- **Option (ON/OFF/CAL/CFG)**

  Enter the full two- or three-character option desired. The CAL and CFG options are discussed in the following prompts. The ON and OFF options turn tablet mode on and off. When tablet mode is on (and the tablet has been calibrated), the tablet is used for digitizing a paper drawing. When tablet mode is off, the tablet is used for screen pointing and tablet menu selection. A shortcut is to press F10, which turns tablet mode on or off.

 AutoCAD enables you to use up to four points when calibrating AutoCAD's coordinate space with a paper drawing. The location of these points determines the type of coordinate transformation used by AutoCAD when interpreting digitized information.

If only two points are used for the calibration, AutoCAD performs an *Orthogonal* transformation of the information you are digitizing. This is a uniform interpretation of the coordinates entered, and is most useful for drawings that are considered accurate.

For drawings that may have uneven scaling in the two axes, AutoCAD enables you to digitize three points to assign an *Affine* transformation to the coordinates. This type of transformation corrects for the uneven scaling in both axes.

Drawings that are actually two-dimensional perspective images should use four digitizing points. AutoCAD performs a *Projective* transformation of the information entered, and tries to correct for the uneven scaling and lack of parallel lines in any axis.

- **Digitize point #** *number*:

  The CAL option (short for CALibrate) enables you to synchronize a paper drawing—that is attached to a digitizer tablet—with points in the drawing editor. The number of coordinates you use determines the accuracy of the coordinates in the drawing editor. First you pick the point on the paper drawing, and then you are prompted for its coordinates.

- **Enter coordinates point #** *number*:

  Enter the known coordinate for the point you digitized. When you have chosen all the points that you want to digitize, press Enter. AutoCAD reports on the success or failure of establishing a successful coordinate transformation.

- **Select transformation type...**
  Orthogonal/Affine/Projective/<Repeat table>:

  Enter the type of coordinate transformation you want to use when digitizing the current drawing. Press Enter to display the table showing the success or failure of establishing a proper coordinate transformation.

- **Configuration Prompts and Options:**

  If you choose the CFG option (short for ConFiGure), you can define the screen pointing area and the areas used by a tablet menu for entering commands.

- **Enter number of tablet menus desired (0-4) <4>:**

  The default AutoCAD tablet menu uses four separate areas that define executable commands. If the tablet you are using has a different number of areas, enter that number here. The maximum number of tablet menu areas is four.

- **Do you want to realign tablet menu areas? <N>**

  This prompt appears if you currently are using a tablet menu, and you accepted the default number of menu areas at the previous prompt. This prompt enables you to change the location of the areas. If you do not want to change the location, press Enter at this prompt. The following prompts appears for specifying the screen pointing area:

- **Digitize upper left corner of menu area menu #number:**

  For each of the menu areas, you must pick three points that define the pointing area for the menu's commands. The *number* shown in the prompt is a digit from 1 to 4, specifying which tablet menu area you are configuring. This prompt asks for the first point of that area.

- **Digitize lower left corner of menu area #number:**

  Pick the second point to define the tablet menu area.

- **Digitize lower right corner of menu area #number:**

  Pick the final point to define the tablet menu area.

- **Enter number of columns for menu area #number:**

  Each tablet menu is divided into a series of rows and columns. Each box in this array can correspond to a menu item to execute. Enter the number of columns in the tablet menu area (*#number*). AutoCAD's default template has menu areas defined with the following numbers of rows and columns: area 1 is 25×9, area 2 is 11×9, area 3 is 9×13, and area 4 is 25×7.

- **Enter number of rows for menu area #number:**

  Enter the number of rows in the tablet menu area shown on the prompt line.

- **Do you want to respecify the screen pointing area?:**

  This option enables you to define an area on the digitizer tablet that corresponds to the drawing area in the drawing editor. This area should not overlap any of the defined menu areas, but otherwise it can be as large or as small as you want.

- **Digitize lower left corner of screen pointing area:**

  Pick the first point of the rectangular area that you want to use for picking points in the drawing editor.

- **Digitize upper right corner of screen pointing area:**

Pick the second point of the rectangular area that you want to use
to pick objects in the drawing editor. After you enter this point, the
tablet menu becomes active.

Example

The following example shows you how to configure the supplied AutoCAD
tablet menu ACAD.MNU. Use figure TABLET.1 as a guide.

```
Command: TABLET ↵
Option (ON/OFF/CAL/CFG): CFG↵
Enter the number of tablet menus desired (0-4) <0>: 4↵
Digitize the upper left corner of menu area 1: Pick point ①
Digitize the lower left corner of menu area 1: Pick point ②
Digitize the lower right corner of menu area 1: Pick point ③
Enter the number of columns for menu area 1: 25↵
Enter the number of rows for menu area 1: 9↵
Digitize the upper left corner of menu area 2: Pick point ②
Digitize the lower left corner of menu area 2: Pick point ④
Digitize the lower right corner of menu area 2: Pick point ⑤
Enter the number of rows for menu area 2: 11↵
Digitize the upper left corner of menu area 3: Pick point ⑥
Digitize the lower left corner of menu area 3: Pick point ⑦
Digitize the lower right corner of menu area 3: Pick point ⑧
Enter the number of columns for menu area 3: 9↵
Enter the number of rows for menu area 3: 13↵
Digitize the upper left corner of menu area 4: Pick point ④
Digitize the lower left corner of menu area 4: Pick point ⑨
Digitize the lower right corner of menu area 4: Pick point ⑩
Enter the number of columns for menu area 4: 25↵
Enter the number of rows for menu area 4: 7
Do you want to respecify the screen pointing area (Y) ↵
Digitize lower left corner of screen pointing area: Pick point S-LL
Digitize upper right corner of screen pointing area: Pick point S-UR
```

TABSURF

Screen **[DRAW] [next] [3D Surfs] [TABSURF:]**

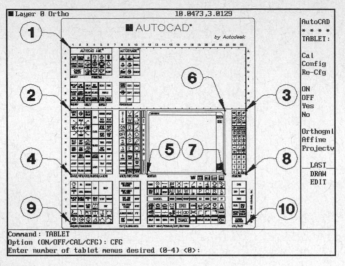

Figure TABLET.1:
Pick points for configuring the standard tablet menu.

Screen   **[SURFACES] [TABSURF:]**

Pull down   **[Draw] [3D Surfaces] [Tabulated Cylinder]**

The TABSURF command is one of six AutoCAD commands that create 3D polygon meshes. This command creates a tabulated surface (TABulated SURFace). The surface is a $2 \times N$ mesh, defined by a path curve and direction vector. The mesh projects, in the M direction, to the length and in the direction of the direction vector, from the starting point to the other endpoint.

The path curve may be an arc, circle, line, or an open or closed polyline (either 2D or 3D). The endpoint nearest your pick point becomes the start of the point mesh. The direction vector is defined by the first and the last endpoints of a selected line or open polyline. The endpoint nearest your pick point is the starting point of the direction vector.

The SURFTAB1 variable determines the density of the mesh in the N direction. The mesh projects the distance in the M direction, from the starting point to the other endpoint. The original entities used to define the path curve and direction vector are unchanged by TABSURF. If you use the EXPLODE command on the mesh, the mesh breaks into individual 3D faces.

Prompts and Options

- `Select path curve:`

  At this prompt, select the entity to be projected.

- `Select direction vector:`

  Select the line or open polyline to define the distance and direction of the desired projection. The endpoint that is closest to the pick point of the entity determines the beginning of the mesh. If you select a polyline, AutoCAD uses the first and last vertices to calculate the distance and direction.

Example

The following example creates a TABSURF mesh from a different line and an open polyline. Figure TABSURF.1 shows the entities before and after the command.

```
Command: TABSURF ↵
Select path curve: Pick point ① (see fig. TABSURF.1)
Select direction vector: Pick point ②
```

Related Commands

EDGESURF
PFACE
REFSURF
RULESURF
3DFACE
3DMESH

Related System Variable

SURFTAB1

487

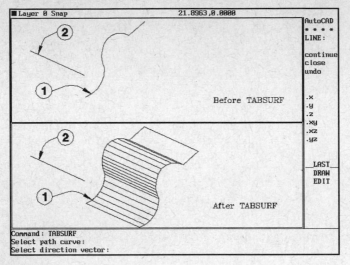

Figure TABSURF.1:
A tabulated surface mesh.

TEXT

Screen **[DRAW] [next] [TEXT:]**

The TEXT command adds a single text string to the drawing. Characters display on the screen after you type the string and press Enter at the Text: prompt. This command is similar to the DTEXT command except that the DTEXT command displays the text string on the drawing as you type it and accepts multiple lines of text. You can justify the text string with one of 15 options. You also can enhance the text by underlining it, or include such special characters as degree symbols, plus or minus symbols, or diameter symbols.

The effect of MIRROR on a text string is dependent on the MIRRTEXT system variable. If this variable is set to 1 (on), the text string is mirrored. If set to 0, the text is adjusted for the mirror angle so that it is readable.

Prompts and Options

- **Start Point.** The default option asks you to pick the starting point for left-justified text. Press Enter to place new text directly beneath the last text drawn.

- **Height.** Enter the height of the text, adjusted for the intended plot scale. Note that this prompt appears only if the current text style has a height setting of 0. If the defined style has a fixed height, you cannot alter its value.

- **Rotation angle.** Enter the angle at which the text is to be placed. A rotation angle of 180 (degrees) places the text upside down. Common angles are 0 and 90 degrees.

- **Text.** Enter the text string to add to the drawing. You may use spaces in the string. When you press Enter, the string appears in the drawing and the `Command:` prompt appears.

- **Style.** The second option of the main prompt enables you to specify a text style to become the current style. Note that any text style must first be defined in the drawing with the STYLE command. After you select the Style option, the following prompt appears:

- **Style Name (or ?) < *current*>:**
  Enter the name of an existing text style. The current style is shown in the angle brackets.

- **?.** If you enter a question mark (**?**), AutoCAD displays the styles defined in the drawing and the following prompt appears:

- **Text style(s) to list <*>:**
  You can use wild-card characters at this prompt to specify text styles. If you press Enter, all the defined styles are listed.

- **Justify.** This first option at the main prompt for the TEXT command enables you to specify the justification for the text string. One of the following two prompts displays after you select this option:

- **Align/Fit/Center/Middle/Right/TL/TC/TR/ML/MC/MR/ BL/BC/BR:**
- **Align/Center/Middle/Right:**
  If the style you are using is vertically oriented, the latter prompt, Align/Center/Middle/Right: , displays. In all other cases, the former prompt displays. If you are familiar with the justification abbreviations, you can skip the Justify option and enter any of these options at the TEXT command's main prompt. The justification options are discussed next.
- **Align.** The Align option specifies the height and rotation of the text by picking two points. The size of text is adjusted by the align option to make the entire text string fit between the picked points. After you select this option, you are prompted to select the following points:
  First text line point:
  Second text line point:
- **Fit.** Similar to Align, the Fit option asks you to specify two points for the location and orientation of the text string. You are prompted for the text height. The width factor for the text string is adjusted so that the text fits between the picked points. This option is not available for vertically-oriented text. If you choose this option, the following prompts appear:
  First text line point:
  Second text line point:
  Height <default>:
- **Center.** The Center option requests a point that is used to center justify the text. The baseline of the text string is centered at the picked point. The prompts for this option are similar to those of the Start point option (for left-justified text).
- **Middle.** The Middle option centers the text horizontally, similar to the Center option, but it also centers the text string vertically. This option center justifies subsequent lines of text at the specified middle point below the previous line of text. The Middle option and the MC option do not work in exactly the same way. If the string has characters with descending elements (for example, the letters "y," "g," and "p") or ascending elements ("b," "h," and "t"),

the Middle option calculates the middle point of an imaginary box that represents the extents of these characters. The MC option does not calculate the middle point in the same way. Therefore, the results may differ based on the text string's characters.

- **Right.** The Right option places right-justified text at a point you specify. The prompts for this option resemble those of the Start point option (for left-justified text).

- **TL:**

  (Top Left) AutoCAD prompts you for the top left point. The subsequent prompts for this option are similar to those of the Start point option (for left-justified text).

- **TC:**

  (Top Center) AutoCAD prompts you for the top center point. The subsequent prompts for this option are similar to those of the Center option (for center-justified text).

- **TR:**

  (Top Right) AutoCAD prompts you for the top right point. The subsequent prompts for this option are similar to those of the Right option (for right-justified text).

- **ML:**

  (Middle Left) AutoCAD prompts you for the middle left point. The subsequent prompts for this option are similar to those of the Start point (for left-justified text).

- **MC:**

  (Middle Center) AutoCAD prompts you for the middle center point. The subsequent prompts for this option are similar to those of the Center option (for center-justified text).

- **MR:**

  (Middle Right) AutoCAD prompts you for the middle right point. The subsequent prompts for this option are similar to those of the Right option (for right-justified text).

- **BL:**

  (Bottom Left) AutoCAD prompts you for the bottom left point. The subsequent prompts for this option are similar to those of the Start point option (for left-justified text).

491

- **BC:**

  (Bottom Center) AutoCAD prompts you for the bottom center point. The subsequent prompts for this option are similar to those of the Center option (for center-justified text).

- **BR:**

  (Bottom Right) AutoCAD prompts you for the bottom right point. The subsequent prompts for this option are similar to those of the Right option (for right-justified text).

For a sample of these options, see figure TEXT.1.

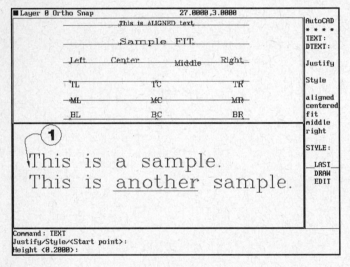

Figure TEXT.1:
Left-justified text strings entered with the Start point option.

You may place any of the following special codes in the text string to create the symbols described in the following list. These codes affect all fonts provided with AutoCAD. Fonts obtained from third-party sources may contain these and more characters:

Code	Character
%%c	The diameter symbol
%%d	The degrees symbol
%%p	The plus/minus symbol
%%o	Overscore (On or Off)
%%u	Underscore (On or Off)
%%%	The percent symbol

Example

The example below demonstrates the procedure for entering multiple lines of text that are left-justified:

```
Command: TEXT ↵
Justify/Style/<Start point>: Pick point ① (see fig. TEXT.1)
Height <0.2000>: .5 ↵
Rotation angle <0>: ↵
Text: This is a sample. ↵
Command: TEXT ↵
Justify/Style/<Start Point>: ↵
Text: This is %%uanother%%u sample. ↵
```

Related Commands

DDEDIT
DTEXT
QTEXT
STYLE

Related System Variables

MIRRTEXT
TEXTEVAL
TEXTSIZE
TEXTSTYLE

TEXTSCR

Enter **TEXTSCR**

Enter **F1 (key)**

The TEXTSCR command causes the text screen or windows to display on a single monitor. The purpose of the TEXTSCR command is to provide a method for macros and scripts to flip to the text screen. The TEXTSCR command has the opposite effect of the GRAPHSCR command. You can use the TEXTSCR command transparently by preceding the command with an apostrophe. Neither command has any effect on a system with dual monitors. Pressing the F1 key also flips between the text and graphics screens.

Related Command

GRAPHSCR

TIFIN

TIFIN imports a Tagged Image File Format raster file into AutoCAD. AutoCAD scans the raster image and creates a block consisting of a rectangular colored solid for each pixel in the TIF file. Once a raster image is imported into AutoCAD, you can trace over the raster image with AutoCAD geometry to create an AutoCAD drawing of the raster image. When you are through, you can erase the raster image. Raster images can be scaled, mirrored, and rotated like regular entities.

Do not explode the block representation of a raster file—the resulting entities will use large quantities of disk space and memory.

The system variable GRIPBLOCK should be set to 0 to avoid highlighting all of the solid entities in the block.

Prompts and Options

- **`TIF file name:`**

  You enter the name of the TIF file you want to import (you do not need to include the extension).

- **`Insertion point <0,0,0>:`**

  You enter the X, Y, and Z coordinates or pick the insertion point for the raster file.

- **`Scale Factor:`**

  You enter a number or drag the crosshairs to scale the raster file from the insertion point.

- **`New length:`**

  If you press Enter at the Scale Factor prompt, you will be prompted to pick a point to specify the scale factor.

See the listing in the TIFIN command summary for the description of a series of options that control how a raster file will be imported (RIASPECT, RIBACKG, RIEDGE, RIGAMUT, RIGREY, and RITHRESH).

Example

The following example imports a TIF file called TEST.TIF into AutoCAD at 3,3,0.

```
Command: TIFIN↵
TIF file name: TEST ↵
Insertion point <0,0,0>: 3,3,0↵
Scale factor: 2 ↵
```

Related Command

PCXIN

495

Related System Variable

GRIPBLOCK

TIME

Screen **[INQUIRY] [TIME:]**

R12 The TIME command displays information regarding the current time and date, date and time of the last modification to the drawing, total time spent in the drawing editor, elapsed time, and the time until the next automatic save. (The interval between automatic saves is controlled by the system variable SAVETIME).

The time and date of the last modification to the drawing are updated when the End command or the Save command is used. The total time spent in the drawing editor is continuously updated. The current editing session's time, however, is lost if the drawing is quit. The elapsed timer is similar to a stopwatch.

Only the elapsed timer can be turned on, off, or reset to zero. The computer's clock provides the current time and date. All AutoCAD time values display in military, 24-hour format, which is accurate to the nearest millisecond.

R12 You can execute the TIME command transparently by preceding the command name with an apostrophe ('TIME).

Prompts and Options

• **Display:**

  Displays all the current time information.

- **ON:**

  Turns on the elapsed timer. The timer is on by default.

- **OFF:**

  Turns off the elapsed timer.

- **Reset:**

  Resets the elapsed timer.

Example

The following example displays the current time information, resets the elapsed timer to zero, and displays the new time information. (The variable SAVETIME has been set to 15 minutes.)

```
Command: TIME ↵
Current time: 15 Jun 1992 at 11:12:00.352
Times for this drawing:
  Created: 23 Jan 1992 at 09:15:34.453
  Last updated: 14 Jun 1992 at 14:00:34.732
  Total editing time: 0 days 01:42:45.253
  Elapsed timer (on): 0 days 00:10:34.182
  Next automatic time save in: 0 days 00:14:10.190
Display/ON/OFF/Reset: R ↵
Timer reset.
Display/ON/OFF/Reset: D ↵
Current time:  15 Jun 1992 at 11:12:05.352
Times for this drawing:
  Created: 23 Jan 1992 at 09:15:34.453
  Last updated: 14 Jun 1992 at 14:00:34.732
  Total editing time: 0 days 01:42:50.253
  Elapsed timer (on): 0 days 00:00:00.832
  Next automatic time save in: 0 days 00:13:41.040
Display/ON/OFF/Reset: ↵
```

Related System Variables

> CDATE
> DATE
> SAVETIME

TDCREATE
TDINDWG
TDUPDATE
TDUSRTIMER

TRACE

Screen **[DRAW] [next] [TRACE:]**

The TRACE command creates solid filled entities similar to polyline segments with width. TRACE segments are similar to polyline segments in that the end points are mitered to meet each other. They are much more limited than polylines, however. The miter angles are calculated for both ends of each segment before it is drawn. Thus, a segment is drawn after the angle of the following segment is known. You cannot use the following editing commands on a trace entity: CHANGE, EXPLODE, EXTEND, OFFSET, and TRIM.

You cannot execute UNDO when you are drawing the trace segments, nor does the TRACE command have a close option. The appearance of the completed trace entity is solid if the FILL mode is on; otherwise, only the outline of the entity displays.

Prompts and Options

- **Trace width:**

  You can alter the default width of .05 units by entering any value you choose. The value becomes the default for the next use of TRACE.

- **From point:**

  This point is the starting location of the trace entity.

- **To point:**

  Enter the second point of the trace. This prompt repeats until you press Enter or Ctrl-C.

Example

The following example illustrates the method for creating a simple TRACE
entity. Notice how the resulting corners are mitered as shown in figure
TRACE.1. (Fill has been turned off in this example.)

```
Command: TRACE ↵
Trace width <0.0500>: .5↵
From point: Pick point ①
To point: Pick point ②
To point: Pick point ③
To point: Pick point ④
To point: ↵
```

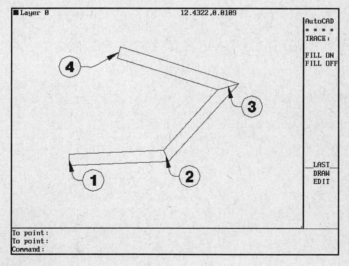

Figure TRACE.1:
A simple application of the TRACE command.

Related Commands

> FILL
> LINE
> POLYLINE

499

Related System Variables

FILLMODE
TRACEWID

TREESTAT

TREESTAT displays the status of the current drawing's spatial index. The information displayed by TREESTAT can be used to improve system performance. AutoCAD indexes all drawing entities spatially using a tree structure. TREESTAT uses two main branches, a 2D branch for paper space (quad-tree), and a 2D or 3D branch (oct-tree) for model space. The TREESTAT command displays two particularly important pieces of information, the number of nodes and the average entities per node.

Use the TREEDEPTH system variable to increase or decrease the length of the tree to attain the best possible performance. The oct-tree structure is more effective if there are fewer entities per node. Therefore, a deep tree with many nodes is preferable. Each node takes about 80 bytes of memory, so too many nodes will consume memory and force disk swapping. Usually, you do not need to tune AutoCAD's performance unless you are working with an extremely large drawing. The ideal setting depends on your system's configuration and the size of the drawing.

 A negative tree depth makes AutoCAD ignore the Z coordinates of entities and use a quad-tree for model space indexes.

TREESTAT has no prompts or options.

Example

The following example displays and resets the tree depth using the TREESTAT command and the TREEDEPTH system variable. See figure TREESTAT.1.

Command: **TREESTAT** ↵

The resulting display varies depending on your system and drawing. Notice the tree depth. The default in a new drawing is 30 for model space and 20 for paper space.

Command: **TREEDEPTH** ↵
New value for TREEDEPTH <3020>: **4030** ↵
Command: **TREESTAT** ↵

The tree depth is now 40 for model space and 30 for paper space.

```
Model-space branch
------------------
Oct-tree, depth limit = 40
Subtree containing entities with defined extents:
     Nodes: 1   Entities: 0
     Average entities per node: 0.00
     Average node depth: 5.00
     Nodes with population 0: 1
Total nodes: 4   Total entities: 0

Paper-space branch
------------------
Quad-tree, depth limit = 30
Subtree containing entities with defined extents:
     Nodes: 1   Entities: 0
     Average entities per node: 0.00
     Average node depth: 5.00
     Nodes with population 0: 1
Total nodes: 4   Total entities: 0


Command:
```

Figure TREESTAT.1:
The spatial tree with reset tree depths.

Related System Variable

TREEDEPTH

TRIM

Screen   **[EDIT] [next] [TRIM:]**

Pull down   **[Modify] [Trim]**

The TRIM command edits the length of lines, open or closed 2D polylines, circles, and arcs to match a cutting edge(s). The cutting edge(s) can be lines, circles, arcs, open or closed 2D polylines, or paper space viewport entities. You cannot trim or use as a cutting edge the following entities: blocks, shapes, meshes, 3D faces, text, traces, shapes, or points. To trim a circle, you must intersect cutting edges in at least two places.

You can select multiple cutting edges. Entities to be trimmed must be picked one at a time. The same entity can be both a cutting edge and an object to trim. You can perform trims only on entities that lie parallel to the current UCS. The TRIM command cuts polylines to the center of the polyline, with the ends remaining squared. If you select an associative dimension to trim, AutoCAD trims and updates the dimension. Note that you may not split a dimension entity in two.

Prompts and Options

- **Select cutting edge(s)...**
  Select objects:

  Select the entities that you want to use as the cutting edges for the command. These may be lines, arcs, circles, open or closed 2D polylines, or paper space viewports.

- **Select object to trim>/Undo:**

  Pick the object to trim. Only one object can be picked at one time. If you specify the Undo option, Undo restores the last trimmed entity to its former appearance. This prompt repeats until you press Enter.

  The following error message is related to this command:

  The entity is not parallel to the UCS.

Example

The following example demonstrates the command by trimming existing entities, as shown in figure TRIM.1.

```
Command: TRIM ↵
Select cutting edge(s)...
Select objects: Select all lines
Select object(s): ↵
<Select object to trim>/Undo: Pick points ① or ② (prompt repeats)
<Select object to trim>/Undo: ↵
```

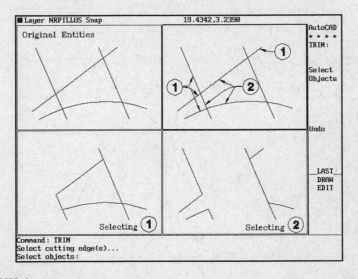

Figure TRIM.1:
Before and after images of entities to be trimmed.

Related Commands

BREAK
EXTEND
FILLET
CHANGE
STRETCH

U

Screen **[* * * *] [U:]**

Pull down **[Assist] [UNDO]**

The U command is an abridged version of the UNDO command. This command reverses the effects of the previous command. The U command has no effect if the drawing has just been loaded, or if the previous command was PLOT, SH, or SHELL. You can disable the U command with the UNDO command's Control option. Undo options are available in the entity selection mode; and with the DIM, DIM1, EXTEND, LINE, PLINE, and TRIM commands. You can reverse all of the effects of running a script by executing a single U command. Any transparent commands executed during the previous command are also reversed by executing the U command.

AutoCAD presents the following prompt if the U command cannot be executed:

    Everything has been undone.

Related Commands

>   REDO
>   UNDO

Related System Variable

>   UNDOCTL

UCS

Screen **[UCS:]**

Pull down **[Settings] [UCS>]**

The UCS command enables you to define an arbitrary coordinate system. This system can make drafting 3D entities much easier. UCS stands for *User Coordinate System* and is relative to the World Coordinate System (called WCS). AutoCAD uses the current coordinate system when you enter any coordinate locations. You also can set and modify the UCS with a dialog box. See the DDUCS command for more information.

Prompts and Options

- **Origin.** Define a new UCS by specifying a different origin point relative to the current UCS. You can specify a point relative to the WCS by preceding the coordinates with an asterisk (*). The current UCS is moved, but the direction of the existing X, Y, and Z axes are maintained.

- **ZAxis.** The ZAxis option prompts you to select an origin point and then a point along the positive Z axis. If you press Enter at the second prompt, this option has the same effect as the Origin option. The ZAxis option is useful for rotating the UCS to work on a different side of a model.

- **3point.** The 3point option defines the UCS based on three points you select. The first point determines the origin point, the second defines the positive direction along the X axis, and the third point defines the positive direction of the axis.

- **Entity.** If an entity exists that was created in a specific UCS, you can return immediately to the UCS by selecting the entity. The type of entity picked determines the origin and X-Y plane. You cannot use certain entities, such as 3D polylines, polygon meshes, and paper space viewports.

- **View.** The View option defines the UCS so that it is parallel to the current view. This option does not modify the origin point.

- **X/Y/Z.** The X, Y, and Z options rotate the UCS around the specified axis. The right rule is used to determine rotation direction. This option is handy for creating a UCS from the existing UCS, such as making a side UCS from the plan view.

- **Previous.** The Previous option restores the previously defined UCS. You can step back up to ten User Coordinate Systems with this option. If the variable TILEMODE is set to 0, the 10 previous UCS's in both paper space and model space are saved. The UCS restored with the Previous option depends on the current space.

- **Restore.** The Restore option works in conjunction with the Save option. Restore retrieves a saved UCS.

- **Save.** The Save option saves the current UCS in the drawing. After you save a UCS, you can retrieve it with the Restore option.

- **Delete.** Use the Delete option to remove saved User Coordinate Systems from the drawing.

- **?.** This option lists the User Coordinate Systems that have been saved in the drawing.

- **World.** If you accept the default option of World, AutoCAD restores the World Coordinate System (WCS).

Example

The following example uses the UCS command options to define three User Coordinate Systems and save them (see fig. UCS.1).

```
Command: UCS↵
Origin/ZAxis/3point/Entity/View/X/Y/Z/Prev/
Restore/Save/Del/?/<World>: O↵
Origin point <0,0,0>: *3,3,0↵
Command: ↵
Origin/ZAxis/3point/Entity/View/X/Y/Z/Prev/
Restore/Save/Del/?/ <World>: S↵
?/Desired UCS name: TOP↵
Command: ↵
Origin/ZAxis/3point/Entity/View/X/Y/Z/Prev/
Restore/Save/Del/?/<World>: ZA↵
Origin point <0,0,0>: ↵
Point on positive portion of Z-axis
<0.0000,0.0000,1.0000>: 0,-1,0↵
Command: ↵
Origin/ZAxis/3point/Entity/View/X/Y/Z/Prev/
Restore/Save/Del/?/<World>: S↵
```

```
?/Desired UCS name: FRONT↵
Command: ↵
Origin/ZAxis/3point/Entity/View/X/Y/Z/Prev/
Restore/Save/Del/?/<World>: Y↵
Rotation angle about Y-axis <0>: 90↵
Command: ↵
Origin/ZAxis/3point/Entity/View/X/Y/Z/Prev/
Restore/Save/Del/?/<World>: O↵
Origin point <0,0,0>: 0,0,5↵
Command: ↵
Origin/ZAxis/3point/Entity/View/X/Y/Z/Prev/
Restore/Save/Del/?/<World>: S↵
?/Desired UCS name: SIDE ↵
```

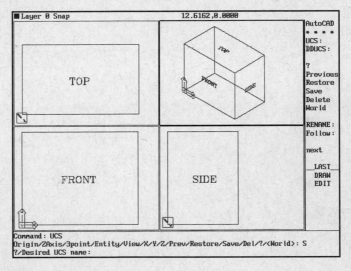

Figure UCS.1:
Viewports with the three different UCSs saved in the example.

Related Commands

DDUCS
PLAN
UCSICON

Related System Variables

UCSFOLLOW
UCSICON
UCSNAME
UCSORG
UCSXDIR
UCSYDIR
WORLDUCS

UCSICON

Screen [SETTINGS] [next] [UCSICON:]

Pull down [Settings] [UCS] Icon>

The UCSICON command controls the display of the graphical icon for the current coordinate system. The UCS icon indicates the orientation of the current coordinate system and whether the current coordinate system is the World Coordinate System (WCS) or a User Coordinate System (UCS). This icon also indicates whether you are viewing the drawing from above (positive Z) or from below (negative Z) and indicates the current space, model, or paper. Figure UCSICON.1 shows these four icons.

You can turn the UCS icon on or off and set it to display at the origin (when it fits on the screen) or at the lower left corner of the viewport. You can set the icon separately in each viewport.

Prompts and Options

- **ON.** Turns on the display of the UCS icon in the current viewport.
- **OFF.** Disables the display of the icon in the current viewport.
- **All.** Applies the settings made by the current UCSICON command to all active viewports. The prompt repeats.

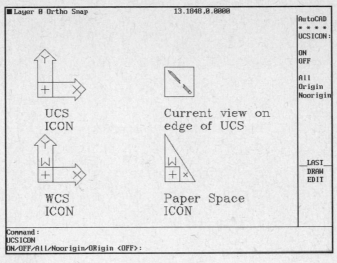

Figure UCSICON.1:
Coordinate system icons.

- **Noorigin.** Sets the current viewport to display the UCS icon in the lower left corner, regardless of the origin of the current coordinate system.
- **ORigin.** Sets the current viewport to display the UCS icon at the current coordinate system's origin point. If this point is located off the screen or if the location of the origin would force part of the icon off the screen, the icon is displayed instead in the lower left corner of the viewport.

Example

This example disables the UCSICON.

```
Command: UCSICON↵
ON/OFF/All/Noorigin/ORigin <ON>: OFF ↵
```

Related Commands

> **DDUCS**
> **UCS**

509

Related System Variable

UCSICON

UNDEFINE

Enter **UNDEFINE**

The UNDEFINE command disables specified AutoCAD commands so that they cannot be executed in the normal manner. You can replace a disabled (undefined) command with an AutoLISP or ADS defined command, which then executes in place of the original command. An undefined command still can be executed by prefacing its name with a period as in **.QUIT**. You can use the REDEFINE command to restore undefined commands.

Prompt and Option

- **Command name:**

   At this prompt, enter the name of the AutoCAD command that you want to disable.

Example

This example disables the QUIT command so that it is unusable in the drawing editor. Afterward, this example uses a leading period to execute the command in spite of its being undefined. For this example, the system variable FILEDIA is set to 0.

```
Command: UNDEFINE↵
Command name: END↵
Command: END↵
Unknown command. Type ? for list of commands.
Command: .END↵
End AutoCAD.
```

Related Command

REDEFINE

UNDO

Screen **[EDIT] [next] [UNDO:]**

The UNDO command reverses the effects of previous commands or groups of commands. You can set markers during the editing session and later automatically undo all the commands back to these markers. The effects of an UNDO can be reversed with the REDO command. The U command is a simpler version of the UNDO command that only reverses the previous single command.

The following commands and system variables are not affected by the UNDO command:

ABOUT	AREA	ATTEXT	COMPILE	CONFIG
CONFIG	CVPORT	DELAY	DIST	DXFOUT
END	FILES	FILMROLL	GRAPHSCR	HELP
HIDE	ID	IGESOUT	LIST	MSLIDE
NEW	OPEN	PLOT	PSOUT	QSAVE
QUIT	RECOVER	REDRAW	REGEN	REGENALL
REINIT	RESUME	SAVE	SAVEAS	SHADE
SHELL	STATUS	TEXTSCR		

Prompts and Options

- **Auto.** Causes UNDO to interpret menu picks as one command. After you select this option, the following prompt appears:

- **ON/OFF <*default*>:**

  When set to ON, UNDO reverses the effects of a menu selection, no matter how many steps it includes. For example, if a menu selection changes layers, inserts a block, and rotates it as needed, one execution of UNDO treats all these steps as one. If the Auto option is set to OFF, each step is removed individually. The *default* displays the current setting.

- **Back.** Instructs AutoCAD to undo all commands until a mark is found. You can use the Mark option (explained later) to place multiple marks throughout the drawing. If no mark is in the drawing, AutoCAD displays the following prompt:

  `This will undo everything. OK? <Y>`

- **Control.** Enables the normal UNDO, disables it, or limits it to one step or command. If you select this option, the following options appear:

- **All.** The All option enables the UNDO command fully to operate.

- **None.** The None option disables completely the UNDO and U commands. If you select this option and then later enter the UNDO command, the `Control:` prompt immediately displays.

- **One.** This option restricts U and UNDO to a single step. You cannot perform multiple UNDO commands if you select this option. When this mode is active, UNDO displays the following prompt instead of the standard UNDO prompt:

- **Control /<1>:**

  Press Enter to UNDO a single action, or enter **C** to modify the settings.

  AutoCAD may present the following prompt if the U command cannot be executed:

  `Everything has been undone.`

- **End.** This option turns off the Group option.

- **Group.** This option treats a sequence of commands as one command. These commands are usually entered at the keyboard. Preceed the commands with **Group**, finish the set with **End** (as discussed earlier), and then you can use a single U command to undo all the commands.

- **Mark.** This option works in conjunction with the Back option. You can place marks periodically as you enter commands. Then you can use Undo Back to undo all the commands that have been executed since the last mark.

- **Number.** You can enter a number to tell AutoCAD to undo the last *number* of commands issued.

Example

The following example demonstrates several features of the UNDO command.

```
Command: UNDO↵
Auto/Back/Control/End/Group/Mark/<number>: M↵
Command: LINE↵
From point: Pick a point
To point: Pick a point
To point: ↵
Command: MOVE↵
Select objects: L↵
1 found
Select objects: ↵
Base point or displacement: 0,0↵
Second point of displacement: 2,2↵
Command: COPY↵
Select objects: P↵
Select objects: ↵
<Base point or displacement>/Multiple: 2,2↵
Second point of displacement: 4,4↵
Command: UNDO↵
Auto/Back/Control/End/Group/Mark/<number>: 2↵
COPY MOVE
Command: REDO↵
Command: UNDO↵
Auto/Back/Control/End/Group/Mark/<number>: B↵
COPY MOVE LINE
Mark encountered
```

513

Related Commands

OOPS
REDO
U

UNITS

Screen **[SETTINGS] [next] [UNITS:]**

The UNITS command specifies the units that AutoCAD uses when it reports and accepts numeric information. You use the UNITS command to tell AutoCAD what type of distance and angle formats to use. If you are drawing a building floor plan, for example, you can use architectural units; if you are designing a printed circuit board, you may want to specify decimal units. The DDUNITS command enables easier operation by means of a dialog box.

R12 You can execute the UNITS command transparently by preceding the command name with an apostrophe ('UNITS).

Prompts and Options

- **Report Formats:**   (Examples)
  1. Scientific   1.55E+01
  2. Decimal   15.50
  3. Engineering   1'-3.50"
  4. Architectural   1'-3 1/2"
  5. Fractional   15 1/2
  Enter choice, 1 to 5 < *default***>:**

Enter the desired units format number. The type of units you choose also is expected when you enter distances. No matter what type of units you decide to use, you can always enter measurements in decimal units. When you choose engineering units, you can enter distances either in feet and decimal inches or in decimal inches; however, AutoCAD always reports measurements in feet and decimal inches. When you use architectural units, separate the fractional inches from the inches with a hyphen, such as 1'6-3/4".

- **Number of digits to right of decimal point (0 to 8) <** *default***>:**

  Enter the number of decimal places to display after the decimal point. AutoCAD rounds distances to the specified accuracy for display, but maintains full precision in the drawing.

- **Denominator of smallest fraction to display (1, 2, 4, 8, 16, 32, or 64) <** *default***>:**

  If you work with fractional inches, specify at this prompt the smallest denominator that you intend to use. When you work in architectural units, this value is typically 8 or 16.

- **System of angle measure:**

1.	Decimal Degrees	45.5
2.	Degrees/minutes/seconds	45d00'0.00"
3.	Grads	50.0000g
4.	Radians	0.7854r
5.	Surveyor's units	N 45d00'0" E

  Enter choice, 1 to 5 < *default***>:**

  Requests the units for displaying angles. Enter the desired system number.

- **Number of fractional places for display of angles (0 to 8)<** *default***>:**

  Determines the degree of accuracy that AutoCAD uses when it reports angles. If you specify 0 decimal places, AutoCAD reports only the number of degrees. If you previously specified Degrees/minutes/seconds or Surveyor's units and you specify 1 to 2 decimal places, AutoCAD reports degrees and minutes. For 3 to 4 decimal places, AutoCAD reports degrees, minutes, and seconds. For more decimal places, AutoCAD also reports decimal seconds.

- **Direction for angle 0:**

East	3 o'clock	=	0
North	12 o'clock	=	90
West	9 o'clock	=	180
South	6 o'clock	=	270

- **Enter direction for angle 0 <** *default***>:**

  AutoCAD usually measures angles using the three o'clock position as the 0 degree direction. You can use this option to specify a different starting direction for 0 degrees.

- **Do you want angles measured clockwise? <N> :**

  AutoCAD typically measures angles counterclockwise. Enter **Y** to change this, so that angles are measured in a clockwise direction.

Example

This example changes the default units system to architectural measurements.

```
Command: UNITS↵
Report Formats:        (Examples)
  1. Scientific        1.55E+01
  2. Decimal           15.50
  3. Engineering       1'-3.50"
  4. Architectural     1'-3 1/2"
  5. Fractional        15 1/2
With the exception of Engineering and Architectural formats, these
formats can be used with any basic unit of measurement. For ex-
ample, decimal mode is perfect for metric units as well as decimal
English units.
Enter choice, 1 to 5 <2>: 4↵
Denominator of smallest fraction to display
(1, 2, 4, 8, 16, 32, or 64) <16>: ↵
Systems of angle measure:      (Examples)
  1. Decimal Degrees           45.0000
  2. Degrees/minutes/seconds   45d0'0"
  3. Grads                     50.0000g
  4. Radians                   0.7854r
  5. Surveyor's units          N 45d0'0" E
```

```
Enter choice, 1 to 5 <2>: ↵
Number of fractional places for display of angles
(0 to 8) <4>: ↵
Direction for angle 0d0'0":
  East       3 o'clock   =   0d0'0"
  North     12 o'clock   =   90d0'0"
  West       9 o'clock   =   180d0'0"
  South      6 o'clock   =   270d0'0"
Enter direction for angle 0d0'0" <0d0'0">: ↵
Do you want angles measured clockwise? <N> ↵
```

Related Command

DDUNITS

Related System Variables

LUNITS
LUPREC
AUNITS
AUPREC
ANGBASE
ANGDIR

VIEW

Screen **[DISPLAY] [VIEW:]**

Pull down **[View] [Set View] [Named View...]**

The VIEW command enables you to save displays of the current drawing under a name that you can later display. This is different from saving the screen's display as accomplished with the MSLIDE command. When AutoCAD saves a view, it stores information about the current view, not the entities in the view. This includes all information needed to restore the view, including 3D viewpoint and perspective (if perspective viewing is on). When you restore the view, AutoCAD uses the information to display that portion of your drawing quickly.

517

Views can greatly speed the process of moving between different areas of your drawing. Defining a view also can aid in plotting—should the same area of a drawing be plotted often—as the view is retained in the drawing file for future use.

Prompts and Options

- **?:**

  Enter **?** to list the defined views. You then see the following prompt:

- **View(s) to list <*>:**

  If you press Enter, all the view names are listed. You also can enter a wild-card search string to list only view names that match the wild-card pattern.

- **View name(s) to delete:**

  If you no longer need one of the defined views, you can delete it from the list of views. Enter the name of the view you want to delete. If the name you have entered does not match a current view, the VIEW command reports: `No matching view names found.`

- **View name to restore:**

  Enter the name of a saved view, and AutoCAD displays it in the current viewport. The view is enlarged or shrunk to fit in the current viewport. If you use the VIEW command transparently (by prefixing it with an apostrophe), the named view cannot be one that requires a drawing regeneration. If a view created for paper space is restored while the drawing editor is in model space (and vice versa), AutoCAD switches to the correct space.

- **View name to save:**

  Both the Save and Window options of the VIEW command present this prompt, which asks you to enter a name to assign the current

R12

view. After you enter a valid name, the Save option stores the view information for the current viewport. The Window option enables you to define a rectangular area that is stored with the view name. If you specify an existing view name, it is overwritten without warning. The following prompts appear:

- **First corner:**

  When you use the Window option of the VIEW command, you must define a rectangular area that is saved with the view name. Enter a point for the first corner of the rectangular area.

- **Other corner:**

  Enter a point for the opposite corner of the window.

Example

This example defines a view of the current drawing with the Windows option in one viewport and restores it in another. (See figure VIEW.1.)

```
Command: VIEW↵
?/Delete/Restore/Save/Window: W↵
View name to save: DETAIL↵
First corner: Pick①
Other corner: Pick②
Click in another viewport
Command: VIEW↵
?/Delete/Restore/Save/Window: R↵
View name to restore: SCHEDULE↵
```

Related Command

DDVIEW

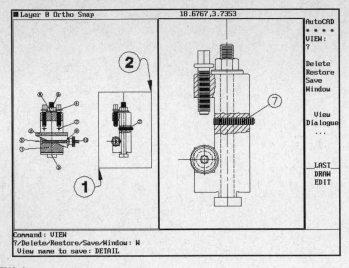

Figure VIEW.1:
The defined view on the left, and the restored view on the right.

VIEWRES

Screen **[DISPLAY] [VIEWRES:]**

The VIEWRES command controls the display resolution of circles and arcs. AutoCAD calculates and displays arcs and circles as series of short, straight line segments. It also controls whether most zooms can be performed at redraw speed instead of requiring a regeneration. If VIEWRES is set for *fast zooms*, most pans and zooms execute at redraw speed. The VIEWRES Circle zoom percent setting controls the resolution of arcs and circles. A setting of 100 always regenerates with sufficient line segments to approximate smooth circles and arcs. As you zoom into the drawing, the line segments become apparent unless you have the fast zoom feature turned off. A higher circle zoom percent enables you to zoom farther in before the line segments become apparent; a lower setting makes them apparent at lower levels of zoom magnification, or even at each regeneration.

The circle zoom percent affects only the displayed image. Any printed or plotted output is created at the highest resolution possible by the printer or plotter.

Prompts and Options

- **Do you want fast zooms? <Y>:**

  If you answer no at this prompt, AutoCAD forces a screen regeneration after any PAN, ZOOM, or VIEW Restore; thus, any attempt at a transparent zoom is useless. If you answer yes, AutoCAD zooms at redraw speed whenever possible. Zooms outside the currently generated area or significantly small zoomed views still require a screen regeneration.

- **Enter circle zoom percent (1-20000) <100>:**

  Your response to this prompt determines the accuracy for the display of circles and arcs, including any arcs in font styles. The higher the number, the more segments are displayed for an arc or circle, and the smoother the arc or circle appears. The disadvantage to a higher number is an increase in screen display time. The default of 100 is sufficient for most purposes. On faster systems with less complicated drawings, you can set the circle zoom percent higher with little loss of performance.

Example

The following example uses the VIEWRES command to initiate fast zooms and to set the circle zoom percent to 16 in one viewport and to 200 in another. The example assumes that two viewports are active, with a circle visible in each, as shown in figure VIEWRES.1.

```
Command: VIEWRES↵
Do you want fast zooms? <Y>: ↵
Enter circle zoom percent (1-20000) <100>: 16↵
Regenerating drawing Click on the right viewport to make it current.
Command: VIEWRES↵
Do you want fast zooms? <Y>: ↵
```

Enter circle zoom percent (1-20000) <16>: **200**↵
Regenerating drawing

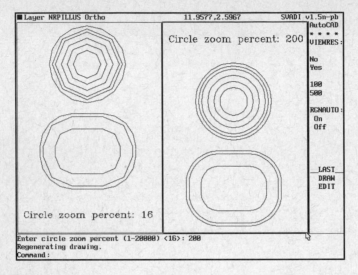

Figure VIEWRES.1:
The effect of different VIEWRES settings on entity appearance.

Related Command

REGEN

VPLAYER

Screen **[MVIEW] [VPLAYER:]**

Pull down **[View] [Mview] [Vplayer]**

The VPLAYER (ViewPort LAYER) command controls the freeze or
thaw status of layers within individual viewports. The VPLAYER
command works in both paper space and model space, but the
TILEMODE system variable must be set to 0. If layers are frozen or

turned off with the LAYER command, they are invisible in every viewport, regardless of the settings made in this command.

You may adjust the visibility of layers for all the current viewports. It is more beneficial quickly to freeze a layer in all the viewports, than it is to thaw the same layer in a single viewport.

Prompts and Options

- **?:**

  Lists the status of layers for a given viewport. If you are working within model space, AutoCAD temporarily switches to paper space. You then receive the `Select a viewport:` prompt. Picking a viewport at this prompt lists the layers that are frozen within the selected viewport.

- **Freeze:**

  Freezes one or more layers within a selected viewport. You receive the `Layer(s) to Freeze:` prompt. You can enter more than one layer at the prompt by separating each layer name with a comma. You also can use wild-card characters, after which you are asked to select the viewports within which to freeze the layers by the `All/Select/<Current>:` prompt.

  If you select All, the layer status is modified in all the current viewports, including paper space viewports that are not displayed. The Select option prompts you to select which viewports are to be modified. The default affects the display only in the current viewport.

- **Thaw:**

  Reverses the effect of the Freeze option. Note that if a specific layer is frozen globally with the Layer command, this command has no effect. You receive the `Layer(s) to Thaw:` prompt. After selecting the layer or layers to thaw, you are prompted to choose which viewports are to be affected. (See the Freeze option for a description.)

- **Reset:**

  Restores the default visibility of a layer as defined by the Vpvisdflt option, discussed in the following paragraphs. You receive the `Layer(s) to Reset:` prompt, and then you are asked to select the viewports to be reset. (See the Freeze option for a description of this prompt.)

- **Newfrz:**

  Creates new layers that are to be frozen in all viewports. This option is most useful for making layers that are intended to be displayed in only one viewport. Thaw the viewport of choice. You receive the `New viewport frozen layer name(s):` prompt. You can enter multiple layer names by separating each one with a comma. The default value for each of the new layers also is set to frozen. This ensures that the layer is frozen in new viewports.

- **Vpvisdflt:**

  Enter **V** to specify the default visibility for a specific layer, or group of layers. This feature affects any viewports created after the command is completed, as well as those currently displayed.

  This feature is useful for modifying layers that contain text or dimensions that should not be displayed in other viewports. You receive the `Layer name(s) to change default viewport visibility:` prompt. More than one layer can be specified by separating each layer name with a comma, or by using wild-card characters. After specifying the layer names, the default visibility is set with the response to the prompt `Change default viewport visibility to Frozen/<Thawed>:`

Example

The following example shows the effects of adjusting the viewport's layer visibility.

```
Command: VPLAYER↵
?/Freeze/Thaw/Reset/Newfrz/Vpvisdflt: F↵
Layer(s) to Freeze: TEXT,DIMENSION↵
All/Select/<Current>: S↵
```

```
Select Objects: Select the bottom viewport
?/Freeze/Thaw/Reset/Newfrz/Vpvisdflt: ↵
Regenerating drawing.
```

The results are shown in figure VPLAYER.1.

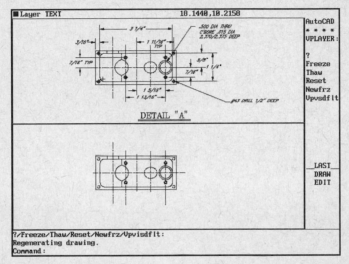

Figure VPLAYER.1:
Layers frozen in one viewport by VPLAYER.

Related Commands

LAYER
DDLMODES

Related System Variables

TILEMODE
VISRETAIN

VPOINT

Screen **[DISPLAY] [VPOINT:]**

Pull down **[View] [Set View] [Viewpoint]**

The VPOINT command enables you to look at your drawing from any location in 3D space. You may specify a 3D coordinate for the viewpoint, rotate the current view by specifying two perpendicular angles, or interactively specify a viewpoint by using two graphical aids. After a viewpoint coordinate is supplied, the resulting view is constructed by displaying the extents of the drawing within the current viewport, as seen from the viewpoint looking through the origin point (typically 0,0,0). VPOINT displays images in parallel projection. For the dynamic selection of a 3D view, or for perspective projection, use the DVIEW command.

Prompts and Options

- **Rotate:**

  Enter **R** to rotate the current viewpoint by specifying two rotation angles. The first angle rotates in the X-Y plane of the WCS. The second angle rotates the viewpoint up in the Z direction. All angles are calculated from the 0,0,0 coordinate. The prompts for these two angles are as follows:

  ```
  Enter angle in XY plane from X axis<current>:
  Enter angle from XY plane<current>:
  ```

- **View point:**

  Press Enter to select a new viewpoint interactively with the compass and axes tripod icons (see fig. VPOINT.1). The icon located in the upper right corner symbolizes a flattened globe that represents all possible 3D viewpoints around your model, which is located at the center. The center point of the icon is the north pole (looking down), the middle ring shows the equator, and the outer circle represents the south pole. As the cursor is moved around this globe, the axes move to show the X, Y, and Z axes for this view-point.

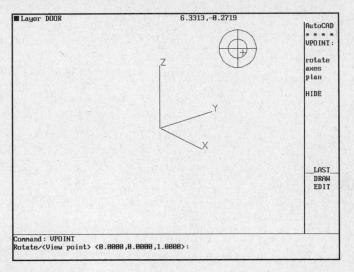

Figure VPOINT.1:
The graphical method of specifying a VPOINT coordinate.

The model can be viewed from below, if the cursor is placed between the "equator" and the "south pole." Pressing Enter while at this screen aborts the option and accepts the previous viewpoint coordinate.

- **<0.0000,0.0000,1.0000>:**

The default setting shows the current viewpoint coordinates are seen in brackets. Enter a new 3D coordinate to view the model from that location.

Example

The following example creates four views: top, front, right side, and isometric by using VPOINT options. Each view is displayed in a viewport, as seen in figure VPOINT.2.

527

Command: *Click in the lower right viewport*
Command: **VPOINT**↵
Rotate/<View point> <0.0000,0.0000,1.0000>: ↵ *(See fig. VPOINT.1)*
Command: *Click in the lower left viewport*
Command: **VPOINT**↵
Rotate/<View point> <0.0000,0.0000,1.0000>: **0,-1,0** ↵
Command: *Click in the upper right viewport*
Command: **VPOINT**↵
Rotate/<View point> <0.0000,0.0000,1.0000>: **R** ↵
Enter angle in XY plane from X axis <270>: **0** ↵
Enter angle from XY plane <90>: **0** ↵
Regenerating drawing.

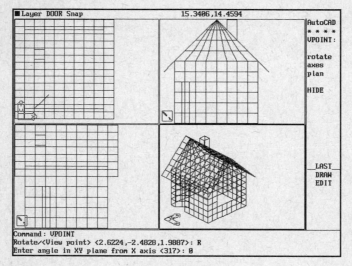

Figure VPOINT.2:
Four views of the sample drawing DHOUSE.DWG obtained with the VPOINT command.

Related Command

DVIEW

Related System Variables

    WORLDVIEW
    TARGET
    VIEWDIR

VPORTS

Screen **[SETTINGS] [next] [VPORTS:]**

The VPORTS (or Viewports) command enables multiple concurrent views within the AutoCAD drawing editor. This command can create up to either four or 16 viewports, depending on your display. The viewports that you create and control with the VPORTS command are specifically for use within model space. Viewports are tiled; that is, they cannot overlap.

The TILEMODE system variable must be set to 1 (on) to use VPORTS. You cannot use VPORTS within paper space (see the MVIEW command). When using viewports, only the contents of the current viewport can be plotted.

Each viewport presents a view of your drawing. These views are updated automatically as changes to the drawing are made. Only the current viewport is affected by a screen display command such as HIDE, PAN, REDRAW, REGEN, SHADE, and ZOOM. The current viewport is identified by a heavy outline around its border. Only one of the viewports can be current. It is easy, however, to switch between viewports, or even select entities visible in different viewports, while within one command. To change the current viewport, click on the desired viewport.

You can begin almost any command in the current viewport, and alternate between viewports as needed while still within the command. The commands that do not accept a change to another viewport are DVIEW, GRID, PAN, SNAP, VPLAYER, VPORTS, VPOINT, and ZOOM.

The crosshairs are displayed only in the current viewport. When the cursor is moved to any other viewport, the crosshairs become an arrow.

Initially, entities are highlighted and dragged only in the viewport in which they were selected. However, if you click in another viewport to make it current while dragging, entities being dragged are highlighted in the new current viewport as well as each previous current viewport.

Prompts and Options

The prompts and options for this command control the size and location of the viewports, and enable you to save and retrieve their arrangement:

- **Save:**

  The current viewport configuration can be saved with this option. Each viewport configuration stores the number of viewports, size, location, and the views displayed within each viewport. Additional information saved for each viewport is listed as follows:

  2D display information (viewpoint)

  3D display information (viewpoint or dynamic view information)

  Front and back clipping planes (set with the command)

  Grid mode and settings

  Perspective mode (set with the DVIEW command)

  Snap mode and settings

  UCSICON setting

  VIEWRES mode and settings

  A saved viewport configuration can be retrieved with the Restore option (described later in this section) or can be retrieved into paper space with the MVIEW Restore command. After selecting this option, you receive the following prompt:

- **?/Name for new viewport configuration:**

  Enter the name of the viewport configuration to save. You also can obtain a list of defined viewports by entering a question mark (?) at this prompt, or at the prompts issued by the Restore or Delete options (see the following paragraphs). You then are prompted for the named viewports to list, and you can use wild-card characters.

You can use up to 31 characters for the name when saving viewports.

- **Restore:**

  You can redisplay viewports that have been saved previously with the VPORTS command with this option.

  ?/Name of viewport configuration to restore: Enter the name of the viewport configuration to restore.

- **Delete:**

  You can remove a defined viewport with this option. You are prompted for the name of the viewport to delete. Deleting saved viewports reduces drawing size slightly.

  ?/Name of viewport configuration to delete: Enter the name of the viewport configuration to delete.

- **Join:**

  You can merge two displayed viewports into one with this option. The boundaries of the two define the new viewport's boundary. The resulting viewport must be rectangular for the join to take effect. Join displays the following prompts:

  Select dominant viewport < *current*>:
  Click in the viewport that you want to provide the settings (see the list under the Save option) for the combined viewport.

  Select viewport to join:
  Pick the second viewport, to combine it with the dominant viewport.

- **Single:**

  This option returns the display to a single viewport. The screen is filled with the contents of the current viewport, and the drawing settings assume the settings of the current viewport.

- **?:**

  This option lists the saved viewport configurations. You receive the following prompt:

  Viewport configuration(s) to list <*>:
  Wild-card characters are accepted. Pressing Enter displays all the

saved viewport configurations. The data displayed represent the 2D screen coordinates for the lower left corner and upper right corner of each viewport. The screen coordinate values range from 0,0 (lower left) to 1,1 (upper right). When listing the viewports, the current configuration always is displayed first, with the current viewport shown at top. The viewport(s) specified at the prompt follow.

- **2:**

  This option creates two viewports. The following prompt appears:

  `Horizontal/<Vertical>:`

  Type **V** (or press Enter) or **H** to specify a vertical or horizontal configuration.

- **3:**

  This option creates three viewports. You receive the following prompt:

- `Horizontal/Vertical/Above/Below/Left/<Right>:`

  Enter the first letter of one of these options to specify the arrangement of viewports. The options operate as follows:

- `Horizontal:`

  This option divides the current display into three equal-sized viewports, divided horizontally across the screen.

- `Vertical:`

  This option creates equal-sized viewports that divide the display vertically.

- `Above, Below, Left or Right:`

  These options determine the location of one larger-sized viewport in relation to two smaller (and equally sized) viewports.

Example

The following example uses the VPORTS command to create three tiled viewports within model space in a left-biased arrangement. (Refer to figure VPORTS.1).

```
Command: VPORTS ↵
Save/Restore/Delete/Join/Single/?/2/<3>/4: 3↵
Horizontal/Vertical/Above/Below/Left/<Right>: L ↵
```

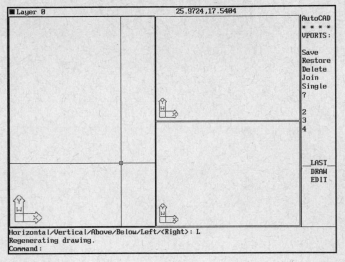

Figure VPORTS.1:
Three tiled (non-overlapping) model space viewports.

Related Command

MVIEW

Related System Variables

CVPORT
MAXACTVP
TILEMODE

VSLIDE

Screen [UTILITY] [SLIDES] [VSLIDE]

The VSLIDE command displays previously created slide files. Slide files (extension SLD) can be used to create presentations of your work. Slides are only snap shots; they contain no entity information, so they load much more quickly than drawings. They cannot be edited, however. Slides take up very little space and are therefore excellent for showing highlights of your work.

Multiple slides files can be compiled into a slide library (extension SLB) by using the SLIDELIB.EXE program that accompanies AutoCAD. The ACAD.SLB file contains slides used by icon items in icon menus. When a slide is displayed, the current drawing is concealed but still active.

 You can create an automated slide show by using a script within AutoCAD. See the SCRIPT and DELAY commands for more information.

Prompts and Options

The options for viewing slide images are outlined as follows:

- **Slide file <default>:**

  Enter the name of the slide file (without the extension) you want to display on the screen. If the FILEDIA system variable is set to 1 (on), a file dialog box displays instead of this prompt. If so, use the dialog box to specify the file name.

  The default name for the slide file is the same name as the current drawing. After you enter the appropriate file name, AutoCAD displays the image saved in the slide file in the current viewport. To redisplay your drawing, invoke the REDRAW command.

  The VSLIDE command also can display slides stored in slide file libraries. To view slides stored within slide file libraries, you must put the slide file name in parentheses after the name of the library. To view the file showing the Romans text style out of the ACAD.SLB file, for example, you would enter **ACAD(ROMANS)** as the slide name.

Example

The following example uses VSLIDE to view both an individual slide file and a slide stored within a slide file library. The example assumes that the

COLORWH.SLD and ACAD.SLB files are in the AutoCAD program directory or another directory in AutoCAD's search path (see fig. VSLIDE.1).

```
Command: VSLIDE↵
Slide file <default>: COLORWH ↵
Command: VSLIDE↵
Slide file <default>: ACAD(CONE) ↵
```

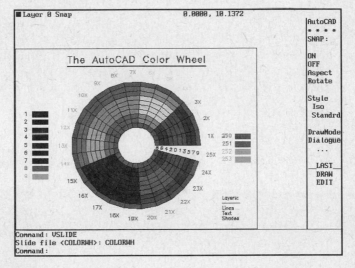

Figure VSLIDE.1:
The COLORWH slide displayed by VSLIDE.

Related Commands

> MSLIDE
> SCRIPT
> DELAY

Related System Variables

> FILEDIA
> SORTENTS

WBLOCK

Screen **[BLOCKS] [WBLOCK:]**

The WBLOCK command copies a block definition or selection set to an external file. This file can be edited like any other drawing file. The file then can be inserted in another drawing with the INSERT command. The file created by the WBLOCK command inherits all the drawing settings and definitions that are used by the selected block or entities in the current drawing. Named views, UCS's, and viewport configurations are not copied. The current UCS in the current drawing becomes the WCS of the new drawing.

Prompts and Options

- **File name:**

  Enter a name for the new file (without the extension). The extension DWG is added for you. If the file already exists, AutoCAD asks whether you want to overwrite the existing file.

- **Block name:**

  Enter the name of the block to copy as a drawing file. If you enter an equal sign (=), AutoCAD looks for, and uses if found, a block name that is the same as the file name given above. If you enter an asterisk (*) here, AutoCAD copies all the entities of the current drawing. If you press Enter at this prompt, you can select the entities that you want copied to a separate file.

If you issue an asterisk (*) for the block name, AutoCAD copies all the entities in the drawing. Unused information such as unreferenced block names, layers, linetypes, text styles, and dimension styles are not included in the new drawing file. This is an excellent means of reducing file size should the drawing contain additional, unused data. This is especially applicable when you archive completed drawings.

- **Insertion point:**

  This prompt appears if you press Enter at the `Block name:` prompt. Specify the insertion base point for the new drawing file, relative to the entities you select. This is similar to choosing an insertion point for a block.

- **Select objects:**

  This prompt appears if you press Enter at the `Block name:` prompt. Select each of the entities you want copied to the new file. You can use any appropriate selection method. The selected entities are erased from the current drawing. Use the OOPS or U command to restore them, if desired.

Example

The following example demonstrates how to create a new drawing that contains specific entities.

```
Command: WBLOCK↵
File name: DETAIL↵
Block name: Press Enter to select specific entities
Insertion base point: Pick a point for the new drawing's origin (0,0,0) point
Select objects: Select the entities to be placed in the drawing file
```

The entities are copied to the DETAIL drawing file and removed from the current drawing. To restore the entities back to the drawing, use the OOPS or UNDO command.

Related Commands

BLOCK
INSERT
OOPS

XBIND

Screen **[BLOCKS] [XBIND:]**

The XBIND (eXternal BIND) command permanently attaches dependent symbols of an external reference drawing to the current drawing database. Normally, none of the information stored within external references is made a permanent part of the drawing database. If you need to use some of the external reference's dependent symbols, such as dimension styles or blocks, you must add them to the database with XBIND. Otherwise, the external reference might be deleted, and those objects no longer would be available for your use.

Prompts and Options

- **Block/Dimstyle/LAyer/LType/Style:**

  This is the list of dependent symbol types that can be permanently bound into the drawing database from the external reference. Type the capitalized letters of the dependent symbol type you want to bind into the current drawing database.

- **Dependent *symbol* name(s):**

  After you have determined the dependent symbol you want to bind into the drawing database, enter its name at this prompt. The XBIND command scans the external reference for the named symbol. If it is found, that symbol is added to the drawing database. If it is not found, you are so informed. External-reference-named dependent symbols are easy to locate—they have the external reference file name, plus a vertical bar (|), and the named object's name. Once bound, the vertical bar is replaced with $*number*$. For the first occurrence of the bound entity, *number* is set to 0. Each time a symbol with the same name is bound, this number is increased.

Example

In the following example, two layers belonging to an external reference file are bound into the TABLET drawing file.

```
Command: LAYER⏎
?/Make/Set/New/ON/OFF/Color/Ltype/Freeze/Thaw/
LOck/Unlock: ?⏎
Layer(s) to LIST <*>: ⏎
Command: XBIND⏎
Block/Dimstyle/LAyer/LType/Style: LA⏎
Dependent layer name(s): TABLET-B|OUTLINES,TABLET-B|PLINES⏎
Scanning...
2 Layer(s) bound.
Command: LAYER⏎
?/Make/Set/New/ON/OFF/Color/Ltype/Freeze/Thaw/
LOck/Unlock: ?⏎
Layer(s) to LIST <*>: ⏎
```

Related Command

XREF

XREF

Screen **[BLOCKS] [XREF:]**

The Xref (eXternal REFerence) command enables you to insert references to external drawings. An external reference is similar to a block, except that no part of the external reference resides within the drawing database. After an external reference is attached to a drawing, only a reference to the external file is placed in the drawing database.

An external reference has two advantages over a block: It takes up less space within a drawing file, and it cannot be edited from within the drawing into which it was inserted. The external reference is similar to any other drawing file. The next time the file containing the external reference is loaded into the drawing editor, or plotted with the PLOT

539

command, the current version of the external reference is loaded. In contrast, the only way to edit a block is to explode it, modify the entities, and then redefine the block by using the modified entities.

Prompts and Options

The XREF command contains a number of options and suboptions, many of which provide information about current drawing files that are referenced.

- **?.** If you specify the ? option, the external references that are a part of the drawing file are listed.

- `Xref(s) to list <*>:`

  If you press Enter at this prompt, all current external references are listed. You also can enter a wild-card search string to list only external reference names that match the wild-card pattern.

- `Bind.` Binding makes an external reference a permanent part of the current drawing database.

- `Xref(s) to bind:`

  Enter the name or names of external references that you want placed in the drawing database. If you are binding multiple external references, separate each name with a comma. The external reference is stored as a block, and all related dependent symbols (blocks, dimension styles, layers, linetypes, and text styles) are given names that combine the name of the original external reference file, a dollar sign, a number, another dollar sign, and then the name of the original dependent symbol. This procedure ensures that the names used in the external reference are not confused with any similarly-named objects within the current drawing.

If you only want to bind some of the external references' dependent symbols, use the XBIND command.

- **Detach.** Detaching an external reference completely severs it from the current drawing.

- **Xref(s) to detach:**

  Enter the name of an external reference that you want removed from the drawing. If you are removing multiple external references, separate each name with a comma.

- **Path.** If you selected the Path option, you can respecify the path used to find external reference files.

- **Edit path for which Xref(s):**

  Enter the name of the external reference at this prompt. You can change the path for several external reference files with this option.

- **Old path: <current path and filename for XREF >**
  New path:

  The current path for the external reference is displayed, followed by a prompt asking you to enter a new file path. After you enter a valid path and file name, you are returned to the `Command:` prompt.

 You get an error message if you attempt to edit an existing drawing that has had of one of its referenced files renamed at DOS or with the FILES command. The Path option of the XREF command is most helpful for telling AutoCAD what the new name is. Otherwise, you must use XREF Delete, and then use the Attach option with the new file name.

- **Reload.** The Reload option updates the external reference without having to exit the drawing editor. This option is especially convenient in a network environment in which other users might be making modifications to an external reference that you have inserted into your drawing. After they have completed their changes, you can use the Reload option to update your copy of the external reference.

- **Xref(s) to reload:**

  Enter the name of a referenced file to be reloaded.

- **<Attach>.** The default option of the first external reference prompt inserts an external reference into the drawing file.

- **Xref to attach <*current XREF name* >:**

   Enter the name of the file you want placed within the drawing. The following prompts are then used to locate and size the external reference in the drawing editor.

- **Insertion point:**

   The base point of an external reference is used to place it within the drawing editor. This point (0,0,0, by default, set by the BASE command) is the insertion point for the external reference when it is placed, scaled, and rotated. This insertion point is similar to the insertion point for blocks.

   Until you specify a point in the drawing editor for the external reference you are inserting, the external reference is shown highlighted. This gives you an idea of the way the external reference appears when placed. If you already know the various insertion parameters (X, Y, and Z scales, and rotation), they can be preset so that the highlighted image is more accurate before you insert it. These preset options are entered at this prompt before specifying the insertion point. Each option is described in the following table.

Parameter	Function
SCALE	Presets the scale in each of the three axes (X, Y, and Z) to the same value. The highlighted external reference is scaled, and then you can specify its insertion point. After the external reference is located in the drawing, you are not asked to enter values for scale factors.
XSCALE	Presets the scale only in the X axis. Insertion then proceeds, and you are not prompted for the remaining scale values.
YSCALE	Presets the scale only in the Y axis. Insertion then proceeds, and you are not prompted for the remaining scale values.
ZSCALE	Presets the scale only in the Z axis. Insertion then proceeds, and you are not prompted for the remaining scale values.

ROTATE   Presets the external reference rotation value. The highlighted entity is rotated, and then insertion can proceed as before. This angle is used after the external reference is located; you are not asked to supply this value, as seen when this command is typically executed.

The following five options enable you to preset the highlighted external reference values, and also to display the normal prompts for scale factors and rotation after insertion. They are primarily used by AutoCAD applications initially to scale and rotate external references for on-screen dragging before permitting user scaling and rotation.

Parameter	Function
PSCALE	Presets all three axis scales. After the external reference is located, you still are asked to enter an external reference scaling factor.
PXSCALE	Presets the scale factor of the external reference's X axis. After the external reference is located, you are asked for the scale along this axis.
PYSCALE	Presets the scale factor of the external reference's Y axis.
PZSCALE	Presets the scale factor of the external reference's Z axis.
PROTATE	Presets the highlighted external reference's rotation.

- **`X scale factor <1>/Corner/XYZ:`**

    This prompt is displayed if none of the scale factors are preset. Its default value sets the X-axis scale factor for the inserted external reference. A negative value mirrors the external reference that appears about the X axis.

    You also can pick a point within the drawing editor or specify the Corner option. In either case, the distance between this first point and a second point that you select is used to set the scale factors for both the X and Y axes.

- **Y scale factor (*default=X*):**

  Enter a Y-axis scale factor. The default is the same value used in the previous prompt.

- **Rotation angle <0>:**

  Enter a rotation value for the external reference. It is then rotated about its insertion point by this value.

- **X scale factor <1>/Corner:**

  If your external reference needs to be scaled in the Z direction, use the XYZ option. By default, you only enter values for the X- and Y-axis scale when you insert an external reference. The Z axis is then given the same scale factor as the X axis.

- **Y scale factor (*default=X*):**

  Specify a scale factor for the Y axis. By default, this is set to the same scale as used for the X axis.

- **Z scale factor (*default=X*):**

  Specify a scale factor for the Z axis. By default, this is set to the same scale as used for the X axis.

Example

The following example uses the Attach option of XREF to add an external reference. (Note the change from fig. XREF.1 to fig. XREF.2.)

```
Command: XREF↵
?/Bind/Detach/Path/Reload/<Attach>: A↵
Xref(s) to Attach: ADESK_B↵
Attach Xref ADESK_B: ADESK_B
ADESK_B loaded.
Insertion point: 0,0↵
 X scale factor <1>/corner/XYZ: ↵
 Y scale factor (default=X): ↵
 Rotation angle (0): ↵
Command: XREF↵
?/Bind/Detach/Path/Reload/<Attach>: ?↵
Xref(s) to list <*>: ↵
Xref Name                                Path
------------------------------------     --------------------
ADESK_B                                  adesk_b
Total Xref(s): 1
```

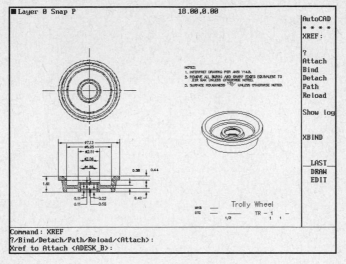

```
Command : XREF
?/Bind/Detach/Path/Reload/<Attach>:
Xref to Attach <ADESK_B>:
```

Figure XREF.1:
The trolley wheel, drawing TROL1.DWG with no border.

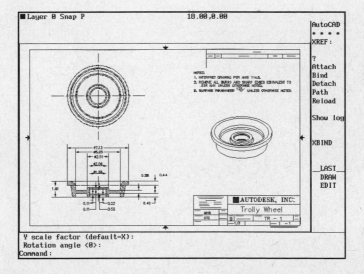

```
Y scale factor (default=X):
Rotation angle <0>:
Command :
```

Figure XREF.2:
The same drawing after attaching the external reference for the border.

Related Command

XBIND

ZOOM

```
Screen  [DISPLAY] [ZOOM:]

Pull down  [View] [ZOOM] [Window]
Pull down  [View] [ZOOM] [Dynamic]
Pull down  [View] [ZOOM] [Previous]
Pull down  [View] [ZOOM] [All]
Pull down  [View] [ZOOM] [Extents]
Pull down  [View] [ZOOM] [Vmax]
```

The ZOOM command enlarges or reduces the display of the drawing to aid in drafting and editing. If more than one viewport is active, the display seen in each viewport can be zoomed independently.

R12 You can execute the ZOOM command transparently by preceding the command name with an apostrophe ('ZOOM), so you can use it while other commands are pending. To optimize the ZOOM command, use the VIEWRES command to enable fast zooms and turn automatic screen regenerations off with the REGENAUTO command.

If used in model space with paper space enabled, the ZOOM Scale XP option enables a paper space viewport to be scaled relative to paper space. The Vmax option makes the view as large as possible without causing a screen regeneration.

Prompts and Options

- **All/Center/Dynamic/Extents/Left/Previous/Vmax/ Windows/<Scale (X/XP)>:**

  This is the main ZOOM prompt, at which you enter an option or scale factor.

- **All.** If the current display is the plan view of the World Coordinate System (WCS), this option zooms to the greater of the drawing's extents or limits. If the display shows a view of a 3D model, this option displays the model's extents. The All option always causes a screen regeneration.

- **Center.** Specify the center and magnification of the zoomed view. You receive the Center point: prompt, at which you specify the center of the view to be zoomed. AutoCAD then presents the Magnification or Height <default>: prompt, at which you enter the height of the view in drawing units. The default value shows the current magnification. Selecting a smaller value increases the screen's magnification. If the number is followed by an X, the new view is based relative to the current display. Type **4** at this prompt, for example, to create a view four units high; type **4X** to create a view four times as large as the current display. You also can type **XP** after a number to scale the current display relative to paper space.

- **Dynamic.** This option enables you graphically to indicate the desired view. The ZOOM Dynamic screen appears after you select the Dynamic option, as shown in figure ZOOM.1. On color displays, the outermost box indicates the drawing limits, the box indicated by the red corner brackets shows the currently generated information, the green dashed box indicates the current view, and the gray box with an X indicates the view to be zoomed.

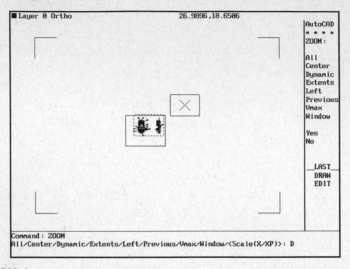

Figure ZOOM.1:
The ZOOM Dynamic screen.

You can resize the X box by pressing the pick button. The X turns into an arrow, indicating that the window can be resized. Press the pick button again to return to the X. Press Enter to accept the new view. If the X box is moved outside the currently generated area, an hourglass appears in the lower left corner of the screen to indicate that a regeneration is taking place.

- **Extents.** ZOOM Extents creates a view that fills the display with the drawing's entities. This is unlike ZOOM Limits (described in following paragraphs) because the limits of a drawing can be far greater than the area used by the entities.

- **Left.** This option is similar to the Center option, which was discussed earlier. Specify a point that is to be the lower left corner of the new view at the Lower left corner point: prompt. AutoCAD then prompts for the size of the zoomed view with the Magnification or Height <default>: prompt. Enter the number of drawing units for zoom height at this prompt.

- **Previous.** This option zooms to the previous view that was on the display within that specific viewport. This command displays the previous view, whether it was created with the PAN, VIEW, or ZOOM commands. The last ten views are saved for each viewport. The view created with this command may differ from the time it was last seen if the drawing has been modified, but the display shows the same area.

- **Vmax.** This option creates the largest available view that does not require a regeneration. This command usually provides the view needed at a redraw speed. As such, ZOOM All, which forces a regeneration, should be used only after finding that the view created by ZOOM Vmax is undesirable.

- **Window.** If a point is selected or coordinates given, the ZOOM command then defaults to the Window option. Window may also be selected by entering the Window option. The ZOOM Window option is the most common way to create the desired view. You are asked to drag a window around the area to zoom in on with the following prompts:

  First corner:
  Other corner:

- **Scale.** This option creates a view when you enter a scale factor number. The drawing is then displayed relative to the drawing's limits. The number given can be any positive number. If the number is less than one, the entities within the display are smaller in the new view. If the number is followed by an X, as in 4X, the created view is scaled relative to the current display. If you want to create a scaled view relative to paper space units, type **XP** after the number, as in **5XP**. If the paper space is to be plotted at 1=1 scale, the view shown in this case is scaled to .2 (five times the scale of the paper space units).

Example

The following example demonstrates the ZOOM command's Window option.

```
Command: ZOOM↵
All/Center/Dynamic/Extents/Left/
Previous/Vmax/Window/<Scale (X/XP)>Pick①
```
(see figure ZOOM.2)
```
Other corner: Pick②
```

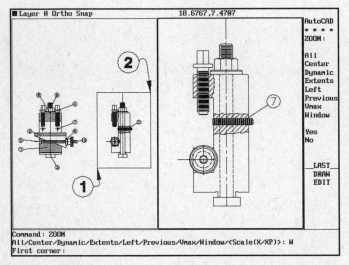

Figure ZOOM.2:
The ZOOM Window in progress.

Related Commands

PAN
VIEW
REGENAUTO
VIEWRES

Related System Variables

ENTMAX
EXTMIN
LIMMAX
LIMMIN
VIEWCTR
VIEWSIZE
VSMAX
VSMIN

3D

Screen **[DRAW] [next] [3D Surfs] [3D Objects]**

Pull down **[Draw] [3D Surfaces]**

The 3D command is an AutoLISP program that enables you to create three-dimensional objects, including boxes, spheres, domes, dishes, meshes, pyramids, and wedges. Each object is constructed as a 3Dmesh.

The AutoLISP file that defines this command is loaded the first time you make the screen or pull-down menu selections. You also can load the file by entering **3D** at the Command: prompt. After you enter **3D** at the Command: prompt, the command prompts you to specify which type of object you want to draw. The 3D.LSP file also defines individual commands that you can execute at the Command: prompt to draw specific objects.

The individual object commands are AI_BOX, AI_CONE, AI_DOME, AI_DISH, AI_MESH, AI_PYRAMID, AI_SPHERE, AI_TORUS, and AI_WEDGE. As with all entities within the AutoCAD drawing editor, the points that you enter for the 3D objects are relative to the current UCS. Generally, you can enter values or pick points to show distances and angles at the prompts.

Prompts and Options

- **Box/Cone/DIsh/DOme/Mesh/Pyramid/Sphere/Torus/ Wedge:**

  This is the initial prompt for the 3D command. You specify which three-dimensional object to draw by entering the capital letter(s) shown in the prompt for that type of object. The sections that follow list the prompts and options for each object type.

Box

- **Corner of box:**

  You specify the first corner of the box by entering a coordinate or by picking a point in the drawing editor.

- **Length:**

  You enter the length of the box along the X axis.

- **Cube/<Width>:**

  If you specify the cube option by entering **C**, the distance that you entered for the length is also used for both the width and the height of the box. If you pick a point or enter a different value for the width (Y axis), the box will be rectangular.

- **Height:**

  You specify the height of the box in the Z axis.

- **Rotation angle about Z axis:**

  You specify an angle to rotate the box around its starting corner.

Cone

- **Base center point:**

  You specify the center point of the base of the cone.

- **Diameter/<radius> of base:**

  You specify a value or pick a point to show a distance for the radius of the cone, or enter **D** if you prefer to specify a value for the cone's diameter.

- `Diameter of base:`

  You supply a value or pick a point for the diameter of the cone's base.

- `Diameter/<radius> of top <0>:`

  You can accept the default of 0 for the radius at the top, specify a different radius, or enter **D** to specify the diameter at the top of the cone. To create a cylinder or tube, set the top and bottom radius values to the same number.

- `Diameter of top <0>:`

  You can enter a value or pick a point to specify the diameter of the cone top. A value of zero for the diameter causes the cone to form a point.

- `Height:`

  You specify the height from the base point that you entered to the top of the cone.

- `Number of segments <16>:`

  The cone is created from a series of 3D mesh faces. This prompt enables you to specify the number of faces that should be used. The more segments that you use to create the cone, the smoother the cone looks.

Dish, Dome, and Sphere

Both the dome and dish are hemispheres. The dome is the top half of the sphere, and the dish is the bottom half.

- `Center of dish`, `Center of dome`, or `Center of sphere:`

  You can enter coordinates or pick a point to locate the center of the dish, dome, or sphere.

- `Diameter/<Radius>:`

  You can enter a value or pick a point to show a distance for the dish, dome, or sphere's radius; or enter **D** for the Diameter option.

- **`Diameter:`**

  If you selected the Diameter option at the previous prompt, specify the value here.

- **`Number of longitudinal segments <16>:`**

  You enter the number of "wedges" that will be used to approximate the shape of the dish, dome, or sphere. As with the cone, the object is created from a series of 3D mesh faces. The greater the number of faces you use, the smoother is the surface.

- **`Number of latitudinal segments <8>:`**

  You enter the number of faces that each longitudinal section will be divided into to approximate the shape of the dish, dome, or sphere. As with the longitudinal segments, the greater the number of faces that you use, the smoother is the surface of the object. The default number of latitudinal segments for a sphere is twice that of the dish and dome.

Mesh

- **`First corner:`**

  You specify the first corner point of the mesh. A *mesh* is a four-sided surface, defined by four arbitrary 3D points at the corners, and divided by vertices in two directions, M and N. After you locate each corner of the mesh area, the surface is created within those points.

- **`Second corner:`**

  You specify the second corner point of the mesh.

- **`Third corner:`**

  You specify the third corner point of the mesh.

- **`Fourth corner:`**

  You specify the fourth and final corner point of the mesh.

- **`Mesh M size:`**

  You specify the number of vertices in the M direction (from the first to the fourth corner points). When requesting this number, AutoCAD highlights the side representing the M direction.

- **`Mesh N size:`**

  You specify the number of vertices in the N direction (from the first to the second corner points). When requesting this number, AutoCAD highlights the side representing the N direction.

Pyramid

The Pyramid option creates three- or four-sided pyramids that can meet at a top point or be truncated with a three- or four-sided top. A four-sided pyramid also can terminate in a top ridge, specified by two points.

- **`First base point:`**

  You specify a point for the first corner of the pyramid base.

- **`Second base point:`**

  You specify a point for the second corner of the pyramid base.

- **`Third base point:`**

  You specify a point for the third corner of the pyramid base.

- **`Tetrahedron/<Fourth base point>:`**

  A pyramid's base can be three- or four-sided. Specify a point to create a four-sided base pyramid or enter a **T** for the Tetrahedron option, which draws a three-sided pyramid.

- **`Top/<Apex point>:`**

  This prompt appears after you specify the T option at the previous prompt. Specify the shape for the top of the tetrahedron at this prompt. If you specify an apex point, the sides of your pyramid will meet at a single point. If you enter a **T** for the Top option, you are prompted for three points to define the plane of the top.

- **First corner:**, **Second corner:**, and **Third Corner:**

  At these prompts, you specify the corner points of the top of the pyramid. To locate each corner, you must specify the Z coordinate. If you do not, the top of the pyramid probably will lie within the same plane as the base.

- **Ridge/Top/<Apex point>:**

  This prompt appears after you specify a fourth point for the base of the pyramid. Specify an Apex point to create a pyramid in which the sides meet at a single point. The Top option enables you to specify the four corner points that will be used to create a flattened top for the pyramid. The Ridge option enables you to specify the end points of an edge line along which the pyramid's four sides will meet.

- **First corner:**, **Second corner:**, **Third Corner:**, and **Fourth point:**

  You specify the corner points of the top of the pyramid at these prompts. To locate the end corner, you must enter a value for the Z coordinate. If you do not, the top of the pyramid probably will lie within the same plane as the base.

- **First ridge point:**

  You specify the first end point of the ridge edge. The side defined by the first and fourth base points will meet at this point. The sides defined by the first and second base points, and by the third and fourth base points, will meet along the ridge edge.

- **Second ridge point:**

  You specify the second end point to the ridge edge. The side defined by the second and third base points will meet at this point.

 When you specify the points used to create the pyramid's ridge or top, always locate the points in the same order and direction as the first two base points. Locating these points out of order results in a twisted pyramid.

Torus

- **`Center of torus:`**

  You specify the center point of the torus.

- **`Diameter/<radius> of torus:`**

  You can size the torus by entering a value or picking a point to show a distance for the radius. You also can enter a **D** for the Diameter option.

- **`Diameter:`**

  If you specified the Diameter option at the previous prompt, enter the diameter value here or pick a point to show a distance for the diameter.

- **`Diameter/<Radius> of tube:`**

  You can size the tube by entering a value or picking a point to show a distance for the radius. You also can enter a **D** for the Diameter option.

- **`Diameter:`**

  If you specified the Diameter option at the previous prompt, specify the diameter value here.

- **`Segments around tube circumference <16>:`**

  You enter the number of segments to use to approximate the cross section of the torus tube. The more segments you use, the smoother the torus appears.

- **`Segments around torus circumference <16>:`**

  You enter the number of segments used to create the torus. The more wedges you use, the smoother the torus appears.

Wedge

- **`Corner of wedge:`**

  You can enter a value or pick a point for the first corner of the wedge. A wedge is created in a manner similar to the 3D box.

The only difference is that the top of the wedge slopes down to meet its base.

- **Length:**

  You specify the length along the X axis of the wedge's base.

- **Width:**

  You specify the width along the Y axis of the wedge's base.

- **Height:**

  You specify the height of the wedge in the Z axis.

- **Rotation angle about Z axis:**

  You specify a rotation angle by which to rotate the wedge about its first corner point in the current UCS.

Examples

The following examples show you how to create the 3D objects discussed previously. The examples assume that the 3D.LSP file is automatically loaded by AutoCAD. The examples show the creation of objects in three viewports, one with a plan view, one with a front view, and one with a 3D view.

```
Command: 3D↵
Box/Cone/DIsh/DOme/Mesh/Pyramid/Sphere/Torus/
Wedge: B↵ (See fig. 3D.1)
Corner of box: 2,2↵
Length: 15↵
Cube/<Width>: 8↵
Height: 10↵
Rotation angle about z axis: 0↵

Command: AI_CONE↵
Box/Cone/DIsh/DOme/Mesh/Pyramid/Sphere/Torus/
Wedge: C↵ (See fig. 3D.2)
Base center point: 10, 6.5↵
Diameter/<radius> of base: 4↵
Diameter/<radius> of top <0>: ↵
Height: 15↵
Number of segments<16>: 25↵
```

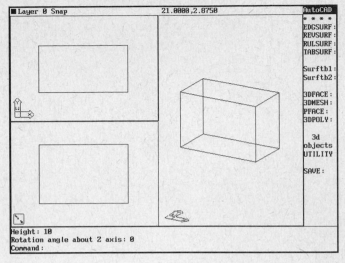

Figure 3D.1:
The 3D box.

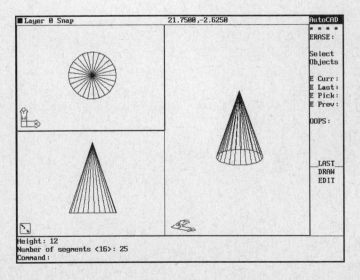

Figure 3D.2:
The 3D cone.

Command: **3D** ⏎
Box/Cone/DIsh/DOme/Mesh/Pyramid/Sphere/Torus/
Wedge: **DO** ⏎ *(See fig. 3D.3)*
Center of dome: **10,6.5,5** ⏎
Diameter/<Radius>: **6** ⏎
Number of longitudinal segments<16>: **25** ⏎
Number of latitudinal segments <8>: **30** ⏎

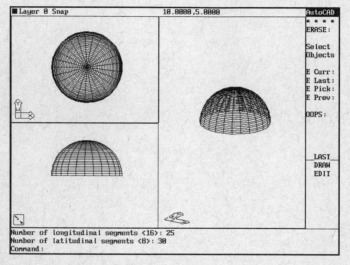

Figure 3D.3:
The 3D dome.

Command: **3D** ⏎
Box/Cone/DIsh/DOme/Mesh/Pyramid/Sphere/Torus/
Wedge: **M** ⏎ *(See fig. 3D.4)*
First corner: **4,4** ⏎
Second corner: **16,10,2** ⏎
Third corner: **19.5,4.25,8** ⏎
Fourth corner: **4,0,10** ⏎
Mesh M size: **25** ⏎
Mesh N size: **20** ⏎

Command: **3D** ⏎
Box/Cone/DIsh/DOme/Mesh/Pyramid/Sphere/Torus/
Wedge: **P** ⏎ *(See fig. 3D.5)*

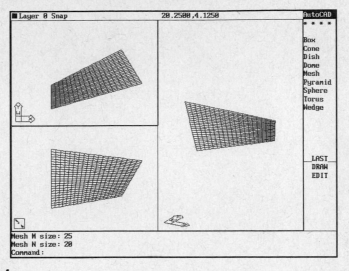

Figure 3D.4:
The 3D mesh with 25 M vertices and 20 N vertices.

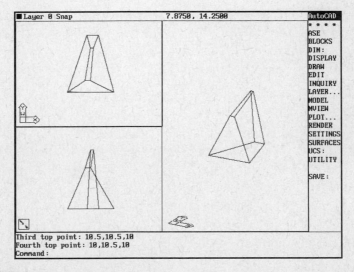

Figure 3D.5:
The 3D four-sided pyramid.

```
First base point: 6,3↵
Second base point: @8<0↵
Third base point: @10<105↵
Tetrahedron/<Fourth base point>: @2<180↵
Top/<Apex point>: T↵
First top point: 9,5,7↵
Second top point: 10,5,7↵
Third top point: 10.5,10.5,10↵
Fourth top point: 10,10.5,10 ↵
```

The following steps create a sphere:

```
Command: 3D↵
Box/Cone/DISh/DOme/Mesh/Pyramid/Sphere/Torus/
Wedge: S ↵ (See fig. 3D.6)
Center of sphere: 10,7,4↵
Diameter/<radius>: 7↵
Number of longitudinal segments <16>: 20↵
Number of latitudinal segments <16>: 20 ↵
```

The following steps create a torus:

```
Command: 3D↵
Box/Cone/DISh/DOme/Mesh/Pyramid/Sphere/Torus/
Wedge: T ↵ (See fig. 3D.7)
```

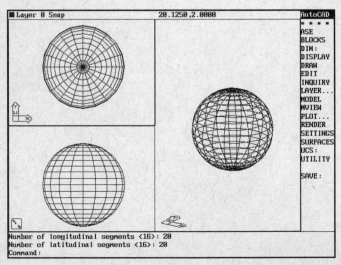

Figure 3D.6:
The 3D sphere.

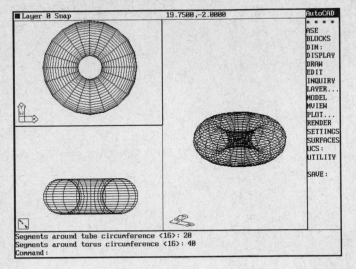

Figure 3D.7:
The 3D torus.

```
Center of torus: 10,7,2↵
Diameter/<radius> of torus: 8↵
Diameter/<Radius> of tube: 3↵
Segments around tube circumference <16>: 20↵
Segments around torus circumference <16>:40 ↵
Command: 3D↵
Box/Cone/DIsh/DOme/Mesh/Pyramid/Sphere/Torus/
Wedge: W↵(See fig. 3D.8)
Corner of wedge: 4,4↵
Length: 8↵
Width: 5↵
Height: 10↵
Rotation angle about Z axis : 0 ↵
```

3DARRAY

Pull down **[Construct] [Array 3D]**

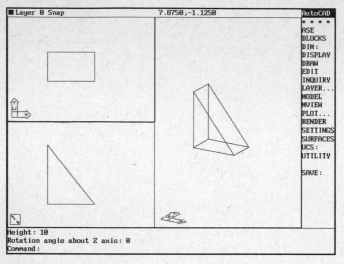

Figure 3D.8:
The 3D wedge.

The 3DARRAY command is an AutoLISP program that enables you to create 3D rectangular and polar arrays in AutoCAD's model space. An array repeats the selected objects in a regularly spaced circular (polar) or rectangular pattern. Rectangular arrays created with this command have rows, columns, and levels in the X, Y, and Z axes, respectively, of the current UCS. Polar arrays created by 3DARRAY are similar to polar arrays created by the ARRAY command. The difference is that the axis of rotation can be at any orientation in space, rather than being restricted to rotating about a point in the current construction plane, perpendicular to the current Z axis.

Prompts and Options

- **Select objects:**

  You can use any of the normal AutoCAD selection methods to select all of the entities that you want arrayed.

- **Rectangular or Polar Array (R/P)?**

  At this prompt, you specify whether you are creating a polar or rectangular array.

- **Number of rows (--)<1>:**

  If you specify a rectangular array, this prompt appears next. As with the ARRAY command, you must enter the number of rows you want to create. The default value of 1 means that you do not want to copy the selected items in the Y direction.

- **Number of columns (||||)<1>:**

  You enter the number of columns in the X direction. The default value of 1 indicates that you want no copies of selected items in the X direction.

- **Number of levels (...)<1>:**

  You enter the number of levels you want made in the Z direction. The default value of 1 indicates that you want no copies of the selected items in the Z direction.

- **Distance between rows (--):**

  This prompt appears if you entered a number other than 1 at the `Number of rows (--)<1>:` prompt. Enter the distance (in the Y direction) that each of the copies will be spaced between each of the succeeding rows.

- **Distance between columns (||||):**

  This prompt appears if you entered a number other than 1 at the `Number of columns (||||)<1>:` prompt. Enter the distance (in the X direction) that each copy will be spaced between each of the succeeding columns.

- **Distance between levels (...):**

  This prompt appears if you entered a number other than 1 at the `Number of levels (...)<1>:` prompt. Enter the distance (in the Z direction) that each of the copies will be spaced between each of the succeeding levels.

- **Number of items:**

  This prompt appears if you create a polar array. Enter the number of copies that you want to create with the polar array.

- **Angle to fill <360>:**

  You enter the portion of a circle, in degrees, in which you want to place the entities. The default value of 360 degrees causes the items that you are copying to be distributed within a full circle.

- **Rotate objects as they are copied? <Y>:**

  When creating polar arrays, you can rotate each copy or maintain their original orientation.

- **Center point of array:**

  You specify the first point of the axis about which the entities will be arrayed.

- **Second point on axis of rotation:**

  You specify the second point of the axis around which the entities are arrayed. They will be copied in a manner similar to a 2D polar array.

Example

The following example shows you how to use the 3DARRAY routine to create a rectangular array in model space. First create a 3D box, using the Box option in the 3D command.

```
Command: 3DARRAY↵
Select objects: Pick the box
Rectangular or Polar Array (R/P)? R↵
Number of rows (--)<1>: 4↵
Number of columns (||||) <1>: 4↵
Number of levels (...)<1>: 3↵
Distance between rows (--)
Distance between columns (||||): 4↵
Distance between levels (...): 4↵
```

After the final prompt, the array of entities is created. Your drawing should resemble figure 3DARRAY.2.

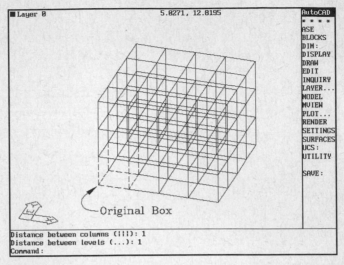

Figure 3DARRAY.1:
The arrayed 3D box.

Related Command

ARRAY

3DFACE

Screen **[DRAW] [next] [3DFACE:]**

Screen **[SURFACES] [3DFACE:]**

Pull down **[Draw] [3D Surfaces] [3D Face]**

The 3DFACE command creates entities that are made of three or four sides. The corners for these faces are entered in either clockwise or counterclockwise direction. 3Dfaces are not filled with color; their vertices can be in different planes. Three-dimensional faces do not have to be flat; the selected points can have different Z coordinates. Three-dimensional faces are colored with the SHADE command and treated as opaque by the HIDE command. The faces cannot be given a thickness. The edges of the face can be made invisible during the entity creation.

Prompts and Options

- **First/Second/Third/Fourth point:**

  Points are entered in a circular direction; either clockwise or counterclockwise around the face. Three-dimensional faces can be triangular; response to the fourth point is optional. Until you press Enter or Ctrl-C, 3DFACE repeats the third point and fourth point prompts to create adjacent 3D faces.

You may use the following options with the 3DFACE command:

- **Invisible.** If the edge you are defining should be invisible, type **I** or select the Invisible option from the screen menu before specifying the point that begins that edge.
- **ShowEdge.** This screen menu option displays all invisible edges of the face after the next screen regeneration.
- **HideEdge.** This screen menu option makes any hidden edges invisible after the next screen regeneration.

Example

The following example creates two 3Dfaces (see fig. 3DFACE.1). The edge that runs between coordinates 0,3,3 and 6,3,3 is invisible.

```
Command: 3DFACE ↵
First point: 6,0,0 ↵
Second point: 0,0,0 ↵
Third point: I ↵
0,3,3 ↵
Fourth point: 6,3,3 ↵
Third point: 6,6,0 ↵
Fourth point: 0,6,0 ↵
Third point: ↵
```

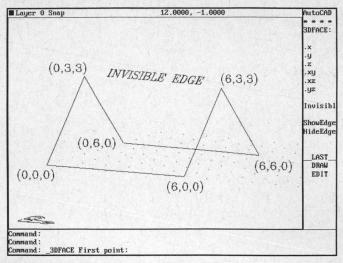

Figure 3DFACE.1:
Three 3Dfaces.

Related Commands

EDGESURF
PFACE
REVSURF
RULESURF
TABSURF
3DMESH

Related System Variable

SPLFRAME

3DMESH

Screen   [DRAW] [next] [3D Surfs] [3DMESH:]

```
Vertex (2, 2): 4,2,0↵
Vertex (3, 0): 6,0,0↵
Vertex (3, 1): 6,1,0↵
Vertex (3, 2): 6,2,2↵ (see fig. 3DMESH.1)
```

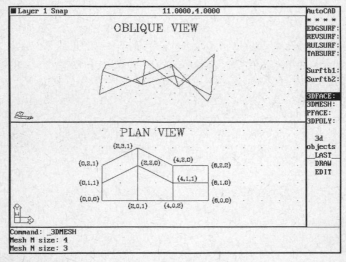

Figure 3DMESH.1:
A 4x3 mesh created with the 3DMESH command.

Related Commands

EDGESURF
MESH
PEDIT
PFACE
REVSURF
RULESURF
TABSURF
3DFACE

3DPOLY

Screen **[DRAW] [next] [3D Surfs] [3DPOLY:]**

Screen **[SURFACES] [3DPOLY:]**

Pull down **[Draw] [3D Poly]**

The 3DPOLY command creates special polylines that can have vertices located anywhere within 3D space. These polylines differ from 2D polylines, in that they cannot contain arcs, tangent information, or widths. The PEDIT command can be used to alter the entities after they are created. Curves can be approximated by spline fitting with multiple short, straight segments. Three-dimensional polylines can only have a continuous linetype.

Prompts and Options

- **From point:**

  You specify the starting point of the 3D polyline.

- **Close:**

  Closes the polyline from the end point of the current segment to the first point of the beginning segment.

- **Undo:**

  Removes the previous segment and redraws the entity.

- **Endpoint of line:**

  You specify an end point for the current segment. This prompt repeats until you press Enter or Ctrl-C to end the command.

Example

The following example demonstrates how to construct a simple three-dimensional polyline.

```
Command: 3DPOLY ↵
From point: 0,0,0 ↵
```

```
Close/Undo/<Endpoint of line>: 2,1,3↵
Close/Undo/<Endpoint of line>: 4,0,-1↵
Close/Undo/<Endpoint of line>: 5,4,3↵
Close/Undo/<Endpoint of line>: 2,5,1↵
Close/Undo/<Endpoint of line>: C↵
```

The finished 3D polyline is shown in figure 3DPOLY.1. The view also shows the same polyline after it has been edited with the PEDIT Spline Curve command sequence.

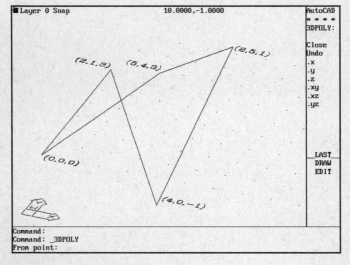

Figure 3DPOLY.1:
A 3D polyline created with the 3Dpoly command.

Related Commands

PEDIT
POLYLINE

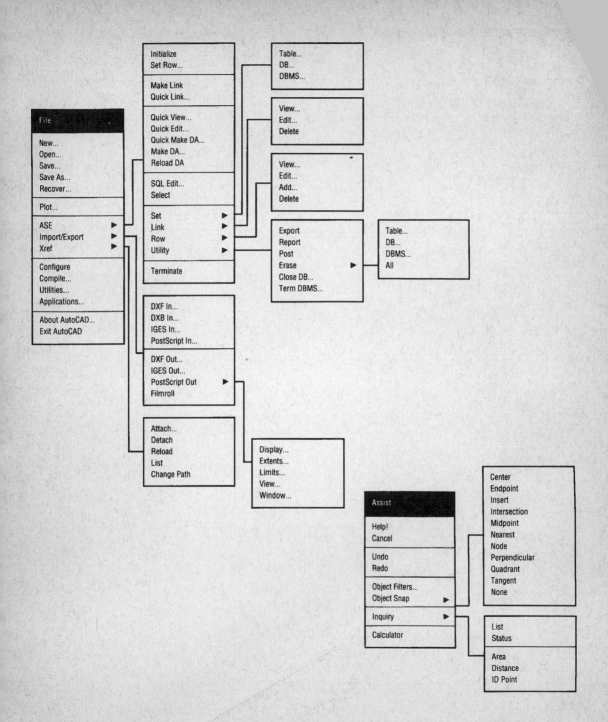

File
New...
Open...
Save...
Save As...
Recover...

Plot...

ASE ▶
Import/Export ▶
Xref ▶

Configure
Compile...
Utilities...
Applications...

About AutoCAD...
Exit AutoCAD

Initialize
Set Row...

Make Link
Quick Link...

Quick View...
Quick Edit...
Quick Make DA...
Make DA...
Reload DA

SQL Edit...
Select

Set ▶
Link ▶
Row ▶
Utility ▶

Terminate

DXF In...
DXB In...
IGES In...
PostScript In...

DXF Out...
IGES Out...
PostScript Out ▶
Filmroll

Attach...
Detach
Reload
List
Change Path

Table...
DB...
DBMS...

View...
Edit...
Delete

View...
Edit...
Add...
Delete

Export
Report
Post
Erase ▶
Close DB...
Term DBMS...

Table...
DB...
DBMS...
All

Display...
Extents...
Limits...
View...
Window...

Assist
Help!
Cancel

Undo
Redo

Object Filters...
Object Snap ▶

Inquiry ▶

Calculator

Center
Endpoint
Insert
Intersection
Midpoint
Nearest
Node
Perpendicular
Quadrant
Tangent
None

List
Status

Area
Distance
ID Point

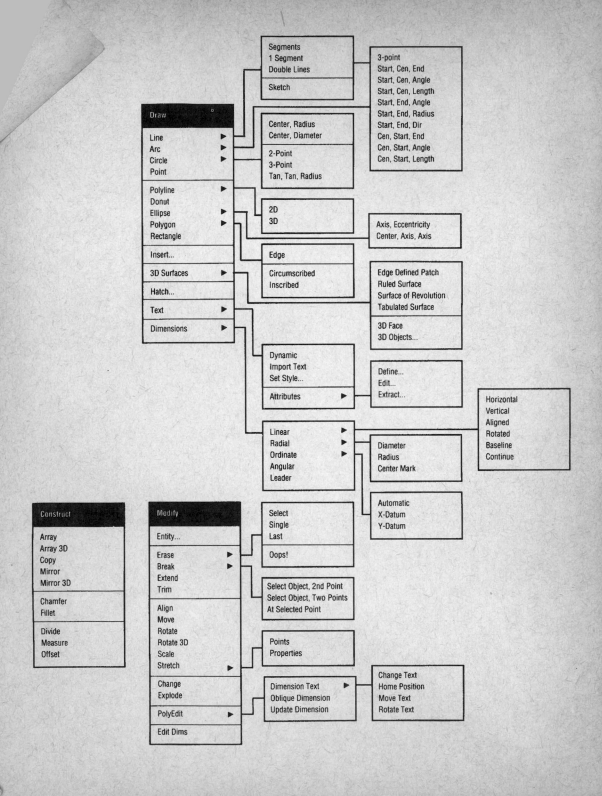

Draw

- Line ▶
  - Segments
  - 1 Segment
  - Double Lines
  - Sketch
- Arc ▶
  - 3-point
  - Start, Cen, End
  - Start, Cen, Angle
  - Start, Cen, Length
  - Start, End, Angle
  - Start, End, Radius
  - Start, End, Dir
  - Cen, Start, End
  - Cen, Start, Angle
  - Cen, Start, Length
- Circle ▶
  - Center, Radius
  - Center, Diameter
  - 2-Point
  - 3-Point
  - Tan, Tan, Radius
- Point
- Polyline ▶
  - 2D
  - 3D
- Donut
- Ellipse ▶
  - Axis, Eccentricity
  - Center, Axis, Axis
- Polygon ▶
  - Edge
  - Circumscribed
  - Inscribed
- Rectangle
- Insert...
- 3D Surfaces ▶
  - Edge Defined Patch
  - Ruled Surface
  - Surface of Revolution
  - Tabulated Surface
  - 3D Face
  - 3D Objects...
- Hatch...
- Text ▶
  - Dynamic
  - Import Text
  - Set Style...
  - Attributes ▶
    - Define...
    - Edit...
    - Extract...
- Dimensions ▶
  - Linear ▶
    - Horizontal
    - Vertical
    - Aligned
    - Rotated
    - Baseline
    - Continue
  - Radial ▶
    - Diameter
    - Radius
    - Center Mark
  - Ordinate ▶
    - Automatic
    - X-Datum
    - Y-Datum
  - Angular
  - Leader

Construct

- Array
- Array 3D
- Copy
- Mirror
- Mirror 3D
- Chamfer
- Fillet
- Divide
- Measure
- Offset

Modify

- Entity...
- Erase ▶
  - Select
  - Single
  - Last
  - Oops!
- Break ▶
  - Select Object, 2nd Point
  - Select Object, Two Points
  - At Selected Point
- Extend
- Trim
- Align
- Move
- Rotate
- Rotate 3D
- Scale
- Stretch ▶
  - Points
  - Properties
- Change
- Explode
- PolyEdit ▶
  - Dimension Text ▶
    - Change Text
    - Home Position
    - Move Text
    - Rotate Text
  - Oblique Dimension
  - Update Dimension
- Edit Dims

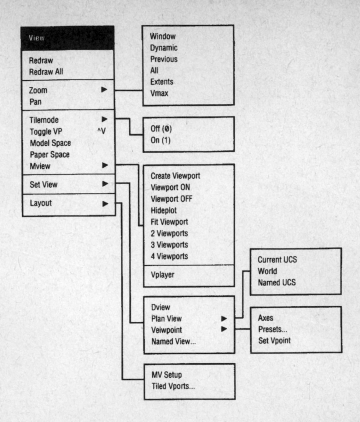

View

Redraw
Redraw All

Zoom ▶
Pan

Tilemode ▶
Toggle VP ^V
Model Space
Paper Space
Mview ▶

Set View ▶

Layout ▶

Window
Dynamic
Previous
All
Extents
Vmax

Off (0)
On (1)

Create Viewport
Viewport ON
Viewport OFF
Hideplot
Fit Viewport
2 Viewports
3 Viewports
4 Viewports

Vplayer

Current UCS
World
Named UCS

Dview
Plan View ▶
Veiwpoint ▶
Named View...

Axes
Presets...
Set Vpoint

MV Setup
Tiled Vports...

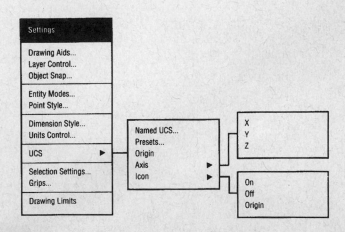

Settings

Drawing Aids...
Layer Control...
Object Snap...

Entity Modes...
Point Style...

Dimension Style...
Units Control...

UCS ▶

Selection Settings...
Grips...

Drawing Limits

Named UCS...
Presets...
Origin
Axis ▶
Icon ▶

X
Y
Z

On
Off
Origin

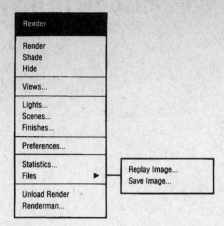

Render

Render
Shade
Hide

Views...

Lights...
Scenes...
Finishes...

Preferences...

Statistics...
Files ▶

Unload Render
Renderman...

Replay Image...
Save Image...

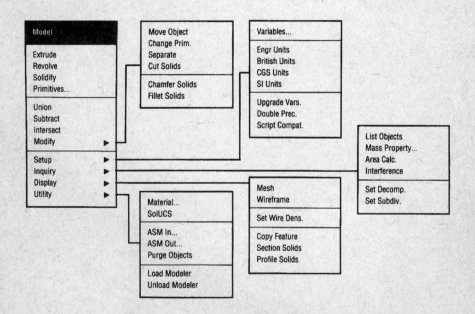

Model

Extrude
Revolve
Solidify
Primitives...

Union
Subtract
Intersect
Modify ▶

Setup ▶
Inquiry ▶
Display ▶
Utility ▶

Move Object
Change Prim.
Separate
Cut Solids

Chamfer Solids
Fillet Solids

Variables...

Engr Units
British Units
CGS Units
SI Units

Upgrade Vars.
Double Prec.
Script Compat.

List Objects
Mass Property...
Area Calc.
Interference

Set Decomp.
Set Subdiv.

Mesh
Wireframe

Set Wire Dens.

Copy Feature
Section Solids
Profile Solids

Material...
SolUCS

ASM In...
ASM Out...
Purge Objects

Load Modeler
Unload Modeler